THE POLITICS OF CONSCIENCE

T. H. GREEN AND HIS AGE

THE NATURE OF HUMAN SOCIETY SERIES
Editors: JULIAN PITT-RIVERS *and* ERNEST GELLNER

THE POLITICS OF CONSCIENCE

T. H. GREEN AND HIS AGE

Melvin Richter

*Associate Professor of Political Science, Hunter College,
of the City of New York*

HARVARD UNIVERSITY PRESS

Cambridge, Massachusetts

1964

© 1964 by Melvin Richter

PRINTED AND MADE IN GREAT BRITAIN

CONTENTS

PREFACE   9

1 IDEALISM AND THE CRISIS OF THE
   EVANGELICAL CONSCIENCE   13

2 THREE FAMILIES AND THEIR FAITHS   33

3 BALLIOL AND JOWETT   52

4 TOWARDS A THEOLOGY   97

5 PHILOSOPHY AS A PROFESSION   136

6 METAPHYSICAL FOUNDATIONS   165

7 ETHICS   191

8 THE PRINCIPLES OF POLITICAL OBLIGATION   222

9 FROM THE OLD LIBERALISM TO THE NEW:
   PRIVATE PROPERTY, CAPITALISM AND
   STATE INTERVENTION   267

10 A MID-VICTORIAN STYLE OF POLITICS:
   THE REFORMER, MUTUAL AID AND THE
   VOLUNTARY SOCIETY   292

11 THE LIFE OF CITIZENSHIP   344

   REFERENCES   377

   INDEX   407

ILLUSTRATIONS

Between pages 176 and 177

1   T. H. GREEN

2   COLONEL THOMAS SANDERS

3   CROMWELL MORTIMER

4   VALENTINE GREEN

5   THE REVEREND VALENTINE GREEN

6   BIRKIN RECTORY

7   THE OLD MORTALITY SOCIETY

8   T. H. GREEN AT THE TIME OF HIS MARRIAGE

9   MRS GREEN AT THE TIME OF HER MARRIAGE

10 MRS GREEN, AGED 84

11 ARNOLD TOYNBEE

12 THE BALLIOL EIGHT, 1869

13 MR AND MRS SYMONDS, THEIR DAUGHTER CATHERINE, AND CIÒ

14 BENJAMIN JOWETT

ACKNOWLEDGEMENTS

The author wishes to thank the following for permission to reproduce illustrations: Brigadier V. C. Green, C.B.E., for Plates 1, 2, 4, 5, and 6; Captain L. H. Green, O.B.E., for Plates 8, 9 and 10; Dame Janet Vaughan for Plate 13; Balliol College for Plates 11, 12 and 14; The Bodleian Library for Plate 7; The British Museum for Plate 3.

*To my mother
and the memory of my father*

PREFACE

THIS BOOK IS INTENDED neither to revive Green's philosophical reputation, nor to confirm the present low assessment of his worth. Rather it is a study of the man, his thought, his milieu and his influence. Because he wrote in the technical terms of Idealism and a prose which even his admirers hesitated to call felicitous, Green has been left by historians of the Victorian age to be treated by philosophers. These, however, for reasons connected with their subject's development in this century, have manifested little curiosity about the man who for the first time established philosophy as an independent discipline at Oxford and gave to Idealism a liberal aspect not always present in its German originals. Green's teaching exerted an unusually powerful effect. Why was he able to do so? Who comprised his audience? What was the political significance of his teaching?

To investigate these questions is to do more than to call attention to an obscure episode in Victorian intellectual history. For such an inquiry raises significant issues about the religious situation, the social character and the political style of the society in which Green lived. Thus the emphasis of this book falls, not upon what was personal, striking or eccentric about its subject, but upon those patterns of piety, of family and social life, of politics, education and voluntary association which formed Green and others like him. Together with Benjamin Jowett, Green dominated the great age of Balliol when the College held a position in the political life of Great Britain and its Empire that has been unequalled before or since. To understand Green's teaching is to learn something about what made this élite and the causes they served what they were, for better and for worse.

It may be not out of place to say something about the method applied here. When first I approached Green's work, it was his political philosophy which interested me. But I had begun to read such sociologists as Max Weber, Ernst Troeltsch and Karl

9

Mannheim, all of whom were concerned to explain ideas by the social position of their creators. This sociology of knowledge, as it is usually and misleadingly translated from the German, itself derives from reactions to the Marxist theory of ideology. Like that body of thought, the sociology of knowledge is highly suggestive, but contains many discrepant hypotheses not always supported by convincing evidence. Much is said in this literature about the styles of thought said to be characteristic of social classes; rather less about the actual texts of individual thinkers. The logic, internal consistency and adequacy of explanations found in the work of philosophers seemed to matter little to a theorist like Mannheim who, with one exception, passed over detailed studies and chose piquant examples to illustrate his soaring generalisations.

This procedure was quite different from that of another subject which attracted me. The history of ideas tends in practice to be meticulous in detail, but insignificant and mechanical in general theory. The questions investigated are usually less than fascinating: the influence of Jack on Jill, the relation of one or another thinker to his climate of opinion or *Zeitgeist*. All too often it is assumed that imitation is the only possible origin of thought, that prior models determine everything which may be said by a man of genius. To this dubious premiss is usually added another, deriving from that philosophy of history and culture, which the Germans call *Historismus*: the notion that history must be regarded as falling into discrete ages, each of which has a distinctive spirit animating every aspect of human activity, particularly ideas. When a thinker has been placed in relation to his age and the network of motifs which dominate it, the historian of ideas regards his task as done. He will seldom attempt to explain intellectual patterns in terms of the functions they may serve in a particular form of social and political organisation; he will not inquire about their relation to certain recurring situations, so familiar in one type of milieu, and quite unknown in another. Yet it seems plausible to argue that the history of ideas is most fruitful when connected to the sociology of knowledge. At the very least, it ought to be asked what and whose purposes are served by ideas, models and styles of thought.

Such were my concerns when I began my own work. I felt strongly that what I needed was first-hand acquaintance with at least one case, considered in detail and in relation to the hypotheses drawn from these two modes of analysis. Green was my choice because he had once possessed a considerable reputation, which now seemed mysterious; because his political philosophy was said to have affected actual policy; because the advent of Idealism to

England seemed to be thus far unexplained. Yet it seemed clear, before considering any of these questions, that there was a prior obligation: to read with care all of Green's texts; to accept provisionally the meaningfulness of his problems and the validity of his method. Surely there ought to be a presumption that a philosopher arrives at his conclusions by the most rigorous means at his disposal. The possibility of explaining his ideas by reference to any non-intellectual considerations—sociological, economic or psychological—arises only in certain instances. These include cases of internal inconsistency, of selective choices from known sources, of a striking incompatibility between a thinker's explanations and the evidence available to him. There is always the possibility that a philosopher may have committed an error in logic, that he took at random some elements of an admired model, that he just happened to ignore facts, which, on their face, were obvious to anyone. But if it turns out that such a mistake of omission or commission serves a vital function within the economy of his beliefs, justifies his position or fills a need essentially emotional, then it is proper for the investigator to inquire into the evidence for any of these hypotheses.

If this method is accepted, the next issue is what sort of evidence ought to be counted as relevant to the matter at hand. On this much might be said, for the application of sociological theories to historical materials is only now in its beginning. But discussions of methodology too often are substituted for practice. I have chosen to let my work speak for itself in this case. The reader will find no general propositions about the relation of ideas to their social base; he will find an analysis put in ordinary English rather than the specialised terms of sociology. The standard of evidence is meant to approximate to that used by historians.

Anyone who writes on Green must borrow heavily from the admirable memoir of him written by R. L. Nettleship. This is true, in part because of Nettleship's gifts; in part because he had access to correspondence and personal information that have not been preserved. On the other hand, many of his sources have been kept, together with Green's manuscripts, in the collection Mrs Green left to the Balliol College Library. It is rather more important a consideration that Nettleship could not treat Green with objectivity. Not only Nettleship's admiration, but his perspective, philosophical and religious, put limits on what his work can say to us today. This realisation, together with the lapses of the two writers from whom most is to be learned about Victorian England, encouraged me to think that there might be room for this book. G. M. Young referred only once to Green and this in telling a story; Elie Halévy, for once misled by a French bias, believed that Green owed his impact to a general admiration for everything German after the victory of 1871. Green was a greater force than Young's neglect would indicate; the reasons for this were not at all what Halévy stated. In fact the fortunes of Idealism were determined by the intellectual situation which challenged the grounds for belief of a generation brought up under the discipline of evangelical piety. Green adapted Idealism to the needs of those who wanted justification for the moral code and values of their parents; he gave conscience a political and social meaning, and gave an outlet to the strong sense of duty and obligation to serve, so characteristic of his generation. The crisis of conscience, its redirection towards political objectives by Green—these account for the title of this book.

Of the many debts I wish to acknowledge, the greatest is to my wife, Marcelle Thiébaux, for her encouragement and editorial assistance. Many friends patiently read drafts of my work; I must express particular thanks to Professor Harry Eckstein of Princeton, Dr Bernard Crick of the London School of Economics, and Professor Samuel Beer of Harvard, along with the members of his Social Sciences 2 Seminar. Captain L. H. Green, OBE, generously aided me in my research. Mr Noël Annan, Provost of King's College, Cambridge, made extensive and helpful suggestions on the basis of an early version. Professor Ernest Gellner, Editor of the series in which this volume is published, assisted me by his comments. My thanks are due to the Master and Fellows of Balliol College for making it possible for me to spend two years there; to Mr Vincent Quinn, Assistant Librarian of the College for his aid in using the Green Papers and other materials; to the Social Science Research Council of New York, for financial support; to the George N. Shuster Fund of Hunter College, for assistance in preparing the manuscript for publication.

Balliol College this year celebrates its seven hundredth anniversary. I should like to present this book in tribute to that occasion.

MELVIN RICHTER

Paris, January, 1963

CHAPTER ONE

IDEALISM AND THE CRISIS OF THE
EVANGELICAL CONSCIENCE

I

BETWEEN 1880 and 1914, few, if any, other philosophers exerted a greater influence upon British thought and public policy than did T. H. Green.[1] Bryce and Asquith have testified that Green's Liberal version of Idealism superseded Utilitarianism as the most prominent philosophical school in the universities.[2] And what was more startling, he and his followers proceeded to bring to life the heavy abstractions of the *Principles of Political Obligation*.[3] For Green converted Philosophical Idealism, which in Germany had so often served as a rationale of conservatism, into something close to a practical programme for the left wing of the Liberal Party. From aristocratic Oxford which Matthew Arnold could still describe as 'whispering from her towers the last enchantments of the Middle Age', there came a stream of serious young men dedicated to reform in politics, social work and the civil service. Many of them were to spend their lives in improving the school system, establishing settlement houses, reorganising charity and the Poor Law, and working in adult education. A rich literature of memoir and autobiography attests to the great mark Green left on the minds and lives of his generation.[4] The literary criticism of A. C. Bradley, the economic history of Arnold Toynbee, the view of the history of political thought taken by C. E. Vaughan, Sir Ernest Barker, and Lord Lindsay owe as much to Green as did the London Ethical Society, an agnostic organisation outside the Church of England, and the Christian Social Union and *Lux Mundi* movements within it.

And yet when a reader in the 1960's turns to Green's printed works, he is struck by the disparity between what they now communicate and the effects they produced upon Green's contemporary audience. The prose seems unrelentingly abstract; the involved Germanic sentences are laden with references to 'self-realisation', the 'common good' and the 'possible self'. It is not

13

merely Green's philosophical vocabulary that is unknown to us, but his moral universe as well. Much of his work now seems to be what G. K. Chesterton called the Crystal Palace, 'the temple of a forgotten faith'.[5] But we have the testimony of Alfred Marshall, the eminent economist, that in Green's lecture-room 'a hundred men—half of them BAs—ignoring examinations, were wont to hang on the lips of the man who was sincerely anxious to teach them the truth about the universe and human life'.[6] One of these students recalled that, 'For many terms previous I had followed his remarkable lectures with enthusiasm and tense strain. . . . I can remember that I did not understand a single word as I wrote down the perplexing tangle of phrases furiously and at lightning-speed: then in the quiet of my rooms I brooded over them till light seemed to gleam from the written word.'[7] And the philosopher, J. H. Muirhead, tells in his memoirs how a passage read from the work later printed as the *Prolegomena to Ethics* produced upon him an effect 'nearer to what in the language of the time was called "conversion" than anything else I have ever experienced'.[8] A. C. Bradley told a friend, fifty years after, that Green had saved his soul.

Green's philosophy did not find this type of reception because it was a conventional or familiar doctrine. When he began to develop his own ideas, the works of J. S. Mill, particularly his *Logic*, constituted the last word in philosophy at Oxford. Some of Green's first converts to Idealism, students as gifted as F. H. Bradley and R. L. Nettleship, were denied First Class Honours by examiners who were genuinely shocked by these young men so presumptuous as to discard the language of Mill for that of Kant, Hegel and Green.[9] And yet despite this entrenched opposition, Philosophical Idealism was to conquer Oxford and most other British universities through the efforts of Green and his students.[10]

This Idealist victory has often been described but never satisfactorily explained. For both before and after this interspace of Idealist dominance, British thought has been marked by a strong mistrust of metaphysics and by the preference for the language of common sense, by empiricism, hedonism, and the occasional tendency to exalt scientific method as the proper model for ethics and political philosophy. Yet Green in his Idealism deliberately rejected this tradition article by article. How, then, could he attract disciples and found his movement? And why did Idealism in Green's hands become a reforming creed even in conservative Oxford?

These questions are best answered by examining the religious position of Green and his audience, for he owed his success to a message that met the needs of men who shared both his inheritance and his dilemma. The inheritance was Evangelical; the dilemma, the great crisis of faith precipitated by science and scholarship. In mid-Victorian Oxford as in all of Great Britain, there existed an acute crisis of conscience which troubled those Christian believers who at the same time regarded themselves as thinking men. The root of the difficulty lay in the Evangelicals' success in identifying Christianity with the belief that the Scriptures are the unmediated and literal revelation of God's word. Evangelicalism, in the sense that it is here used, applies to no specific denomination but rather to that revival of fundamentalist and ascetic Protestantism begun by the Wesleys. The Church of England developed an Evangelical branch; the Nonconformists, almost moribund in the previous century, were revived in the nineteenth by the impulse originating in Methodism, which, contrary to the wishes of its founders, had become a new dissenting denomination. This movement which began as an attempt to rehabilitate Christianity among the lower orders of society succeeded so well that a century after the Wesleys began their work, the manners and morals of the ruling class showed a striking transformation. In Elie Halévy's classic phrase, we 'witness Methodism bring under its influence, first the Dissenting sects, then the Establishment, finally secular opinion'.[11]

2

Great religious movements which base their claim on divine revelation must first take hold among those classes largely unknown and uncared for by the authorities established in Church and State. Only the poor and uneducated unite simplicity and the capacity to believe with primitive energy and an urgent sense of religious need. Their total surrender is unqualified by intellectual training and questioning habits of mind. Members of more reflective and educated classes put complicated queries, opposing human wisdom to divine revelation. Those who demand that belief remain within the bounds of reason tend to regard in relative terms what is absolute and unconditional to true believers of classes below them. But however intense may be the convictions of submerged classes they seldom can determine the fate of their new religion. For neither do they hold political power, nor can their belief in its original form convince those in the upper classes who control opinion. Thus a crisis develops: either the new religion receives a compelling restatement in the style of abstract thought respected by the educated, or else it remains confined to the lower classes, a belief tolerated or persecuted as advantage may dictate, but never exerting the full force upon the whole society that comes from uniting faith with a creed formulated by first-rate minds on the highest intellectual level. The history of Christianity from the second generation onwards demonstrates that when a simple set of beliefs originating with the naïve and uneducated enlists men capable of a philosophical restatement, it can go on to gain a position of pre-eminence. There is, of course, the danger that rationalisation may go too far in the direction of sacrificing the essentials of the faith. But the contrary is no less true. If for some reason, credal or social, such a translation cannot be effected, then sooner or later unquestioning faith must be shattered by sophisticated criticisms to which believers can make no effective reply.

This hypothesis, first applied by Ernst Troeltsch to the development of primitive Christianity, is highly suggestive when applied to the history of Evangelicalism in Great Britain.[12] It helps to connect the origin of Evangelical theology with certain of its enduring characteristics; it points up the nature of the dilemma confronting those who, like Jowett and Green at a much later stage of this religious evolution, thought of themselves as purging Christianity of its mythical elements, as re-establishing its beliefs at an intellectual level that could attract and hold reasonable men. It was this Jowett had in mind when he wrote to Florence Nightingale 'that . . . something needs to be done for the educated, similar to what J. Wesley did for the poor'.[13]

The Methodist Revival of the eighteenth century had taken place among the lower middle and lower classes. Using methods that seemed to the Anglican orthodoxy of the day blatantly vulgar and even dangerously revolutionary, the early Methodist preachers displayed an extraordinary power to capture converts. Scarcely less striking was their ingenuity in devising a form of organisation, neither sect nor church, that held adherents once gained. In his *Journal*, John Wesley described how, excluded from the church at Epworth where his father had been vicar, he preached from his father's tomb to a great throng:

> I preached on the righteousness of the law and the righteousness of faith. While I was speaking, several dropped down as dead; and among the rest, such a cry was heard, of sinners groaning for the righteousness of faith, as almost drowned my voice. But many of these soon lifted up their heads with joy, and broke out into thanksgiving; being assured they now had the desire of their soul—the forgiveness of their sins.
>
> I observed a gentleman there, who was remarkable for not pretending to be of any religion at all. I was informed he had not been at

public worship of any kind for upwards of thirty years. Seeing him stand as motionless as a statue, I asked him abruptly, 'Sir, are you a sinner?' He replied, with a deep and broken voice, 'Sinner enough', and continued staring upwards till his wife and a servant or two, who were all in tears, put him into his chaise and carried him home.[14]

By such preaching did Wesley and his band spread their gospel. He himself rose every day at four in the morning and preached several times, often to great multitudes. Almost until his death at eighty-eight, he travelled, mostly on horseback, never less than 4,500 miles in a year.

The direct and intended consequence of the Wesleyan revival was to revitalise the Protestant religion. This it did in the Church of England and in the dissenting sects which had become a mere shadow of what they had been in the Great Rebellion. Although Wesley never ceased to regard himself as a clergyman of the Church of England, it became clear that the Church would not accept the Methodists into its communion. Thus a new Church was established and served as a link between the Establishment and the Nonconformists. This revival of religion was intended to have social consequences, to regenerate the society by causing its members to act on Christian principles. To those who conceived of holiness as the relation between a solitary individual and his God, John Wesley said, 'Holy solitaries is a phrase no more consistent with the gospel than holy adulterers'.[15] A famous sermon, delivered many t mes, made his meaning even clearer, 'I shall endeavour to show, first, that Christianity is essentially a social religion; and that to turn it into a solitary one is to destroy it'.[16]

What did this mean in practice? Wesley recorded in his journal what had been done for the colliers of Kingswood by the ministry of his co-worker, George Whitefield.

> Few persons have lived long in the west of England who have not heard of the colliers of Kingswood; a people famous . . . for neither fearing God nor regarding man. . . . Many last winter used tauntingly to say of Mr Whitefield, 'If he will convert heathens, why does not he go to the colliers of Kingswood?' In spring he did so. And as there were thousands who resorted to no place of public worship, he went after them into their own wilderness. . . . The scene is already changed. Kingswood does not now, as a year ago, resound with cursing and blasphemy. It is no more filled with drunkenness and uncleanness, and the idle diversions that naturally lead thereto. It is no longer full of wars and fightings, of clamour and bitterness, of wrath and envyings. Peace and love are there. Great numbers of the people are mild, gentle, and easy to be entreated.[17]

Thus did Evangelicalism soften the frank paganism of eighteenth-century Britain with its cruelty to man and beast, its callousness to suffering, its drunkenness. John Wesley and his followers were concerned with saving souls. Religion involved a profound experience of conversion and regeneration, a 'new birth'. But Wesley knew that emotion without organisation has little effect.[18] Hence, the emotional experience was kept alive in individuals by a relentless, methodical self-scrutiny of motives and actions; collectively, this was done through the mutual scrutiny of a small band or class which met regularly in addition to the public service. Indeed it was membership in the class that conferred membership in the Methodist Society. Membership tickets were issued quarterly, contingent on good behaviour. Dues were paid regularly. In the weekly meetings, each member took some part in the devotions: reading the lesson, offering a prayer, or telling of his religious experience. The leader of the class was a layman, selected because of his enthusiasm. Often such a person was asked to form a class with only his own name on the roll book. Thereafter it was his responsibility to win converts and to watch over their spiritual state.[19] The lay preacher, although a common man among common men, learned how to lead and organise. And the believers he led themselves developed, by their participation in the class, not only loyalty but the same sense that this religion was part of themselves. Thus in the class, Wesley had devised an extraordinarily effective form of organisation, yet one far removed from the Puritan Congregation.

What of the constitution of the Methodists? The classes in any locality were formed into a society. But the society was not an independent church. Methodism was constituted not on the principle of congregationalism but on 'connectionalism'. All the local societies formed one unified connection and this was strongly centralised. The effective unit was not the local society but the circuit made up of a number of societies. A superintendent was put at the head of the circuit, and under him served several itinerant preachers who went from society to society, preaching, supervising the work of the lay preachers and the class leaders. Each Society had a layman treasurer called the steward. What marked out the Methodists from the older Non-conformist sects was the absence of local autonomy, although not of local participation. For the stewards, lay preachers, and class leaders were chosen not by the society but by the superintendent of the circuit. Several circuits constituted a district; and the sum of the districts was the connection. While Wesley was alive, he ruled the connection. He was succeeded by a Conference made up from the body of preachers. The laity had no part either in choosing the members of the Conference or in its deliberations.[20]

Such an organisation could counter the individualism which otherwise might have been expected from a religion which stressed conversion and salvation. When every man was taught to look to saving his soul, it was well that he should work together with the members of his class. At the same time that he acquired a sense of his own worth, he learned the discipline of working in a collective enterprise. To Nonconformity, the Methodists brought a new emphasis on the importance of organisation, new techniques useful in mutual aid and collective action. The laity was utilised most effectively. At the same time that it developed a sense of participation, its conduct was subjected to rigorous scrutiny. To candidates for membership in a class Wesley would say:

> Do you desire to be told of all your faults and that plain and home? . . . Consider! Do you desire we should tell you whatsoever we fear, concerning you? Do you desire that, in doing this, we should come as close as possible, that we should cut to the quick, and search your heart to the bottom?[21]

Such unrelenting examination of motive by self and group characterised all Evangelicals, whether Methodist or not. And combined with the fervour produced by conversion and assurance, such methods helped to create a forceful, if limited, type of character. Evangelical homes had a way of instilling, even in those of its sons who went over to the Church of Rome, as did J. H. Newman, or to the Church of Science, as did T. H. Huxley, an emotional dynamic, a dedication to cause and a calling to self-sacrifice. These traits and values often survived the loss of faith in their parental creed. They constituted the common heritage which Green shared with his audience, and which he attempted to preserve in his philosophical teaching. His work had an avowed religious purpose. He sought to replace fundamentalist Evangelicalism by a metaphysical system that would transform Christianity from a historical religion into an undogmatic theology. This would turn the attention of those disciplined in Evangelical families away from the means of personal salvation in the next world to improving the condition of this one. In politics as in theology, the doctrine of citizenship and reform developed by Green can best be understood as a surrogate faith appealing to a transitional generation.

As a theology, Evangelicalism taught a simpler doctrine than that of the first Protestant reformers. Originally, the Wesleys preached a creed that came to little more than that doctrine of justification by faith which Protestantism claimed to be the essence of the Pauline Epistles and St Augustine. Caring little for theological subtleties, Evangelicals made an essentially emotional appeal. Contrasting nature with grace, the eternal suffering that follows from unredeemed original sin with the eternal bliss that God in His mercy will confer upon those who call on Him, they summoned sinners to repent and to surrender themselves to that saving grace. The fruit of conversion was said to be a direct sense of assurance that all has been forgiven, followed by deep peace. All this was held in varying shades of opinion: some Evangelicals believed in predestination, others, not. But most typical was the reaction of Hannah More. 'How I hate the little narrowing names of Arminian and Calvinist. . . . *Bible* Christianity is what I love; that does not insist on opinions indifferent in themselves.'[22] All agreed in basing their belief on the literal inspiration of the Bible and the reality of their religious experience. That the Revival was first directed at non-intellectual classes became the source of its immediate strength and ultimate weakness: its power to stir, its concentration upon philanthropy always counted in its favour; its extremely simplified theology, indispensable during the period of conversion, proved to be its eventual undoing.

The origin of the Revival explains also why Wesley preached active philanthropy as a religious duty. On this matter his thought differed altogether from that of the Puritans, who regarded poverty as a sign of sin, and charity as the immoral encouragement of those who had chosen the way of improvidence and laziness. The late Professor Tawney in a famous chapter identified the Puritan attitude with that of Nonconformity and traced the genesis of the New Poor Law of 1834 to the views taken in the seventeenth-century Puritan pamphlets.[23] There is much evidence for believing that Puritanism was a middle and lower middle-class movement; Wesley, on the contrary, did not preach to the middle class, nor for that matter to the most debauched or poverty-stricken. Rather his interest lay in reaching the industrious workman in town and country.[24]

A movement so rooted cannot take the middle-class view that circumstances mean nothing compared to character. Wesley's experience showed him that good men were often turned into poor men by circumstances. When he visited the poor in London he found them in hovels and garrets,

> half-starved both with cold and hunger, added to weakness and pain. But I found not one of them unemployed who was able to crawl about the room. So wickedly, devilishly false is that common objection, 'They are poor only because they are idle'.[25]

Thus Wesley knew well the handicaps and the potentialities of his followers. He had no illusion that they could live as an ascetic community in the midst of a commercial society. His position was stated in a sermon 'On the Use of Money' which he repeated on innumerable occasions. Love of money for its own sake is evil; wealth in itself, but 'thick clay'. Yet money, when properly used, can do great good. Thus he preached three precepts: Gain all you can; Save all you can; and Give all you can. The first two can be justified only by the third. While it is now all too apparent how these first two might become autonomous, nevertheless in Wesley's time philanthropy was not only preached but practised. One man records how of his £47 per annum, he had spent but £28 on personal expenses, the rest being given to the poor. During the twenty years from 1770 to 1789, when membership in the Methodist Societies of London averaged about 2,500, £15,000 was given to the poor.[26] This is a remarkable figure when it is remembered that subscriptions were the only source of funds, that many of the members were themselves poor enough to be helped from this fund, and that much was given in kind. During the same period expenditure for the maintenance of 'Preachers and Families' both inside and outside of London came to about £11,250. In short, money paid to preachers came to only 75 per cent of the sum contributed to the poor.

The significance of this philanthropy lay not in its success in alleviating poverty, nor in any revolutionary deductions from the judgment that the poor were not personally responsible for their condition. For Wesley was a Tory, who like Blackstone and Paley, thought that the English Constitution could not be improved. In his view England enjoyed 'entire civil and religious liberty'.[27] He denounced the American Revolution. As an official body, the Methodists remained Tory in sympathy until two-thirds of the nineteenth century had passed. Wilberforce, the leader of the Evangelicals in the early nineteenth century, was an extreme Tory, as was Lord Shaftesbury. But the Revival was more emotional than reasoning, and so too was its philanthropy. Methodists and Evangelicals championed particular causes without any careful calculation of their effects, without any explicit political or economic theory. In the case of the anti-slavery campaign or Lord Shaftesbury's agitation for factory acts, precedents were set for state interference without any appreciation by the reformers of their implications. For action of this kind seemed, like evangelising, to follow from the assertion that religion alone regenerates. And if regeneration is the only road to salvation, then he who has been saved is obliged to save his neighbour.

So long as Methodism remained concentrated in the upper working class, Wesley's doctrine of charity was feasible and even necessary. But the essence of conversion is the transformation of character. The virtues prescribed by Wesley's religion led to the economic virtues of industry, initiative and thrift. Indeed when Wesley preached 'Gain all you can' as the condition of 'Give all you can', he recommended the economic virtues quite explicitly.

> Gain all you can, by common sense, by using in your business all the understanding which God has given you. It is amazing to observe, how few do this; how men run on in the same dull track with their forefathers. But whatever they do who know not God, this is no rule for you. It is a shame for a Christian not to improve upon *them* in whatever he takes in hand.[28]

Even within Wesley's lifetime, this doctrine produced consequences which he himself analysed. For he saw clearly that his converts were menaced by worldly success. Methodism 'must necessarily produce both industry and frugality, and these cannot but produce riches. But as riches increase, so will pride, anger, and love of the world in all its branches.' The spirit of 'pure religion' would thus pass away, leaving only its empty form.[29] And what should be done? Here Wesley's remedy fell short of destroying the evil he had diagnosed, for he felt that he should not prevent people from being diligent and frugal, and so becoming rich. Rather the way he chose was to make them aware of their duty to continue practising philanthropy.

What Wesley foresaw as a danger did in fact occur; what he prescribed as a remedy could not in the long run prevail against the secularising influence of wealth. As Methodists rose in the world, their attitudes towards charity altered. Many ceased to be Methodists and went over to a more stylish and less exacting Church, perhaps eventually to the Establishment. But what should be noticed here is that members of a rising class are likely to look with contempt upon those they have left below them. Such an attitude was altogether incompatible with the spirit of Wesley's teaching. As Methodism in the nineteenth century became more and more a Nonconformist middle and lower middle-class church, it dropped Wesley's social gospel. There returned that austere individualism in matters of economics and charity which had characterised seventeenth-century Puritanism. Once again middle-class Protestantism tended to identify poverty with sin. The poor and weak, so far from being viewed as the victims of circumstance, were now held to be realising the deserved consequences of their own laziness or improvidence.

While this view of charity was due partially to the perspective of those who had recently emerged from the lower classes, it was reinforced by the older Nonconformist sects who in at least this matter adhered to their Puritan heritage. Their social experience had been that of an isolated, but middle-class group. Their Puritan ancestors had been able to feel so harshly towards the poor because 'the Protestant sects and the strict Puritan communities actually did not know any begging in their own midst'.[30] Lack of charity and profound individualism are the attitudes of a rising middle class.

The Victorian form of this individualism received its classic portrait in 1869 when Matthew Arnold wrote *Culture and Anarchy*. For thirty-five years HM Inspector of Schools, he came to know the Nonconformist lower middle class of small shopkeepers and employers who managed the schools he inspected and were parents of the children attending them. There he met 'the life imaged in such a newspaper as the *Nonconformist*—a life of jealousy of the Establishment, disputes, tea-meetings, openings of chapels, sermons'.[31] The lower middle class and middle class believed on both theological and economic grounds in individualism, in every man's being free to do what he likes with no obligation to any other man beyond that of not harming him. Representing trade and Dissent with their maxims of every man for himself in business, every man for himself in religion, these groups dreaded a powerful administration which might interfere with them. Of this stern individualism, Arnold found a telling instance. The newspapers had recently taken up the suicide of a Mr Smith, the secretary to an insurance company. This poor man, it was said, could endure no longer his two obsessive fears—that he would become a pauper, and that his soul was damned to eternity. Reflecting on this case, Arnold began to see in Mr Smith a symbol, 'by the selection of his two grand objects of concern, by their isolation from everything else, and their juxtaposition to one another, of all the strongest, most respectable, and most representative part of our nation'.[32] For by this time Nonconformist England had but two main concerns, making money and achieving personal salvation.

This side of the 'dissidence of dissent' was systematised by Herbert Spencer who was born and bred a Nonconformist, and published his first writings in the very journal Arnold had singled out. Spencer's elaborate system marks the extreme limit of concern for gain and the denial of obligation between man and man. Thus the Wesleyan revival produced two very different attitudes towards charity: the first, prescribing philanthropy;

Green
+

the second, interdicting it. The Evangelical tradition contained, therefore, a fundamental ambivalence towards charity and its objects. Those deeply touched by this religious impulse, as was Green, tended to alternate between the older and newer positions. If the creed in which he was raised led him to give a religious tone to politics, it also made it impossible for him to be either a clear-cut individualist or collectivist.

Green and his generation encountered Evangelicalism at a relatively late stage of its development, and this defined their image of it. In 1850 the Evangelicals had behind them a notable series of victories. Allied with the Whigs and using the power of the State, they had won their campaign against plural livings and had helped invigorate parish life; it was their energy that had largely made possible a very considerable missionary activity overseas.[33] At home, allied at different times with the most various parties—Dissenters, Philosophical Radicals, and even on occasion with the Tories—they could claim such triumphs in Parliament as prison reform, the beginning of factory acts, and the abolition of slavery. There was even a second wave of successful Evangelical revival after 1858. Yet by the end of the nineteenth century, the movement was no longer the force it had been. Already in mid-century, there had been danger signals, which did not go undetected by the observing. Its competitors in the Establishment, the Broad Church and High Church parties, were adding to their strength at the cost of the Evangelicals. Their failure to employ fully its intellectual talent, such as that of the Clapham Sect, or to adapt its doctrine to the age, meant that the new currents of thought—Comtism, rationalism, agnosticism, materialism, above all, the worship of science and progress—all made dramatic headway with the rising generation.*

But in 1855, when T. H. Green entered Balliol College, the movement was still strong enough to define intellectual questions by their relation to religious issues. John Stuart Mill, perhaps the most genuinely cosmopolitan of the British thinkers of his day, wrote in his diary:

> I sometimes think that those who, like us, keep up with the European movement, are by that circumstance thrown out of the stream of

* 'It is not perhaps too much to say that the major phenomenon in the religious history of England in the latter half of the nineteenth century was the spread of Agnosticism. This is traceable, in part, to the fact that the Evangelical Revival had set too high a pace for the clergy in the discharge of their parochial duties . . . to leave sufficient time for the work of study, of keeping abreast of the new intellectual and social currents of the age. . . .' This is the judgment of Charles Smyth, 'The Evangelical Movement in Perspective,' *Cambridge Historical Journal* (1943), p. 162.

English opinion. . . . What is it that occupies the minds of three-fourths of those in England who care about any public interest or any controverted question? The quarrel between Protestant and Catholic; or that between Puseyite and Evangelical.[34]

3

In Green's Oxford, religion was the obsessive issue that eclipsed all others. In the memoirs of his more articulate contemporaries again and again the same note is struck: always the recurring, undermining doubt raised by science and scholarship at war with the will to believe. The claims of Christianity pressed upon men with an urgency that precluded indifference. Yet educated men could not ignore the attacks that were being launched upon the unmediated interpretation of the Bible that constituted the theology of Evangelicalism. Religious belief was being sapped by two separate types of inquiry: science and the higher criticism of the Bible. The results of these researches were especially damaging to those who had been brought up on the literal interpretation of the Bible. For Christianity seemed to most believers to involve four propositions: 'the transcendence of God; the origin of the material world in an act of creation in time; the claim of Scripture to be an authoritative revelation of truth otherwise unobtainable by man; the happiness and salvation of individual souls. . . .'[35] Obviously the Book of Genesis, as earlier interpreted by Evangelical Protestantism, did not stand up before the geologists, nor at first could Darwin be interpreted otherwise than as an unambiguous alternative to the Biblical account of creation. As for the higher criticism of the Bible such as Strauss's, whose *Life of Jesus* had been translated by George Eliot, its close scrutiny of texts combined with a critical turn of mind tended to discredit belief in miracles on the basis of authority. Roman Catholicism, because of its theology, was much less susceptible to attack. But the strong Protestantism of the British tradition set up prejudices that were not easily overcome. The conversion of Newman to Roman Catholicism was to be imitated by relatively few.

To most mid-Victorians, it seemed that men were forced to choose between faith and reason. The way to agnosticism and atheism lay open, but before this prospect many quailed. For what could life be without faith in God? And yet did one have the right to fly in the face of the best knowledge of the age? Something of the pain inherent in this choice emerges from a letter written by one of Green's students to another. The author voicing his

doubts was to become a philosopher, his correspondent a clergyman in the Church of England:

> I have thought a great deal . . . on . . . our religious differences. . . .
> It would be a terrible thought . . . that we who are so knit together
> in all else should have that one link in the chain missing on which all
> the others must really hang. . . . Other sympathies, many others, we
> have: I hardly know any real interest of either which we do not both
> sympathise in: but they meet and have their focus in this—in the
> common love of Christ and God—in the struggle side by side to live a
> higher life—to find the Truth wherever it is—to overcome the flesh—
> to become members of Christ and temples of the Holy Ghost.[36]

Green, like his students, had been much too closely bound to
Christianity to disregard its traditional answers to the all-important
questions of 'What shall we do and how shall we live?' Such
problems as the nature and destiny of man, the meaning of
human existence, and man's relation to God were to them what
William James called 'forced options', issues which had to be
met. Upon their resolution everything depended. This Green
understood and he faced his task with full recognition of its
seriousness; 'When the old questions about God, freedom, and
immortality are being put by each man to himself in the direct
and popular form which they have now assumed, as questions
bearing upon his own life, it is idle to deny that he is a different
man according to the answer which he gives to them'.[37]

Two main strategies lay open to the defenders of belief. Either
they could repudiate the new knowledge or they could attempt to
accommodate Christianity to it. The gap between these two views
was very great, and at Oxford constituted one of the major issues
dividing the High Church party of the Church of England from
the latitudinarian Liberals known as the Broad Churchmen. Their
animosity dated back to the days of the Oxford Movement when
the famous Tracts written for the most part by Newman, were
suspended at the instigation of the Broad Church party. The High
Churchmen led by Pusey and Liddon, although they had not
followed Newman into the Church of Rome, continued to argue
as he had done that the truths of Revelation are simply not
accessible to human reason. Hence the miracles reported in the
Scriptures as well as the Biblical account of the creation must be
believed on the basis of authority.[38] Seen from this point of view,
the Broad Churchmen were guilty of what Newman called
Liberalism, 'the mistake of subjecting to human judgment those
revealed doctrines which are in their nature beyond and independent of it, and of claiming to determine on intrinsic grounds the

truth and value of propositions which rest for their reception simply on the external authority of the Divine Word'.[39]

The Broad Churchmen led by Benjamin Jowett argued that Christianity must adapt itself to the best knowledge of the age. The essential truths of Christianity are valid for all time but the intellectual formulae in which they are phrased must from time to time be altered. Green's Broad Churchmanship is to be found in his attempt to drop the traditional dogmatic theology of Christianity which was phrased in historical terms in favour of a restatement based upon Idealist metaphysics. By this means, he thought that he could remove the ostensible conflict between the truths of science and the truths of religion; that he could provide through his philosophy an unassailable foundation for belief.

Here, then, were two quite disparate attitudes towards the crisis of belief at Oxford: the High Church party, orthodox, insisting on the claims of authority; the Broad Church party, Liberal, modernist, asserting what it called the claims of reason. Newman described the High Churchman *par excellence* in Keble (and all this is said in praise), 'Keble was a man who guided himself and formed his judgments, not by processes of reason, by inquiry or by argument, but, to use the word in a broad sense, by authority. . . . What he hated instinctively was heresy, insubordination, resistance to things established, claims of independence, disloyalty, innovation, a critical, censorious spirit.'[40] But Green felt that such an attitude had become impossible for thinking men. If this were to be the fixed and unyielding position of the Church, then thinking men would be drawn to materialism and atheism. 'Once let the conflict be presented as one between reason and authority, and just those nobler elements of character which it is feared that popular materialism will undermine will be enlisted in its defence.'[41]

Thus the conflict between religion and science was no more intense than theological disagreements within the camp of religion's defenders. Although the centre of controversy was at Oxford, the whole nation became involved in this dispute. One of the best-selling novels of the nineteenth century, Mrs Humphry Ward's *Robert Elsmere*, emphasises these theological differences.[42] The book is dedicated to Green and, thinly disguised as Professor Grey, he plays a prominent part. Mrs Ward was herself a protagonist of the Broad Church party, and her novel had its origin in a pamphlet where she sketched two types, 'the character that either knows no doubts or has suppressed them, and the character that fights its stormy way to truth'.[43]

The central character is a young man, Robert Elsmere, who

comes up to Oxford in the early 1870's to a College which is unmistakably Balliol. Coming under the influence of Grey, Elsmere is carried away by one of his sermons, and contrary to the effect Grey intended, decides to take orders as a clergyman of the Church of England. Then he meets and marries a devoutly Evangelical girl and takes up a country parish in which he lives a life of strenuous pastoral activity, combining sanitary reform with preaching and boys' clubs with saving souls. This idyllic combination of religion and vague reform is not to last. Elsmere comes to know the local squire, Roger Wendover, a renowned and very learned rationalist. By a series of exhausting theological arguments, he manages to undermine Elsmere's faith. These arguments turn largely on the nature of Christian evidence, and run on for an astounding number of pages. Elsmere *in extremis*, half maddened by his perilous condition of disbelief, goes off to seek Grey's counsel at Oxford.

Then comes the turning point. Taking Grey's advice, he resigns his living and goes off to London to work with a tiny group. There in the East End slums the Established Church had no power with the embittered working men who were drifting into atheism and materialism. Elsmere, teaching a creed based on ethics without dogma or miracles, begins to make great progress. Finally, he establishes a new Church of his own, 'The New Brotherhood of Christ'. But before long, Elsmere dies of tuberculosis, drained of life by the extraordinary effort of the work he will not abandon. At the end, he refuses to call upon Christ. Mrs Ward describes his death in language and symbolism more usually reserved for the lives of saints.

The novel's success was astounding, certain proof that Green's message popularised had much consolation for those perplexed by problems of belief. Mrs Ward wrote:

> As to the circulation of 'Robert Elsmere', I have never been able to ascertain the exact figures in America, but it is probable from the data I have that about half a million copies were sold in the States within a year of the book's publication. In England, an edition of 5,000 copies a fortnight was the rule for many months after the one-volume edition appeared; hundreds of thousands have been circulated in the sixpenny and sevenpenny editions; it has been translated into most foreign tongues.[44]

Gladstone dropped his political activities to defend the Church of England against the book in *The Nineteenth Century*. Oliver Wendell Holmes, Sr., wrote from America that 'it is, I think, beyond question the most effective and popular novel we have had since "Uncle Tom's Cabin".'[45]

Two themes dominate the novel: the crisis of conscience and its resolution in a form that applies religious energies to the secular problems of modern life. Elsmere settles his theological difficulties by translating orthodox Christianity into what he considers a creed consonant with reason. The duties prescribed by this new faith are activist rather than contemplative. It teaches the duties of applied altruism rather than personal piety. Thus Liberalism in theology leads to Liberalism in social and political life, a connection inherent not in logic but in the special conditions of Oxford controversy. This is the alignment so keenly analysed by Newman: the alliance between reform in politics and modernist theology on the one side, and between Toryism and orthodoxy on the other. But whereas he attacked Liberalism as the anti-dogmatic principle equally subversive of Church and State, Mrs Ward in her memoirs saw in the political and social activities of Liberalism, the realisation of the true meaning of Christianity through the activities of citizenship. This is how she described the Broad Church party at Oxford:

> Mr Green was not only a leading Balliol tutor, but an energetic Liberal, a member both of the Oxford Town Council and of various University bodies; a helper in all the great steps taken for the higher education of women at Oxford, and keenly attracted by the project of a High School for the town boys of Oxford—a man . . . pre-occupied . . . with the need of leading 'a useful life'.
>
> Let me pause to think how much that phrase meant in the mouths of the best men whom Balliol produced in the days when I knew Oxford. The Master [Jowett], Green, Toynbee—their minds were full . . . of the 'condition of the people' question, of temperance, housing, wages, electoral reform; and within the University, and by the help of the weapons of thought and teaching, they regarded themselves as the natural allies of the Liberal party which was striving for these things through politics and Parliament. 'Usefulness', 'social reform', the bettering of daily life for the many—these ideas are stamped on all their work. . . .
>
> And the significance of it all is only to be realised when we turn to the rival group, to Christ Church and the religious party which that name stood for. Read the lives of Liddon, of Pusey, or—to go further back—of the great Newman himself. Nobody will question the personal goodness and charity of any of the three. But how little the leading ideas of that seething time of social and industrial reform, from the appearance of *Sibyl* in 1843 to the Education Bill of 1870, mattered either to Pusey or to Liddon, compared with the date of the Book of Daniel, or the retention of the Athanasian Creed![46]

From this last passage, the outlines of Green's view of the world begin to appear. The connection between Liberalism in theology and Liberalism in politics is not accidental. Green's theology, like Elsmere's, offers an ethic based on humanism. Gone are dogma, miracle and Church. Green's theology is pre-eminently of this world. Good works and altruism, amelioration of the lot of others—these are the marks of genuine faith. Citizenship becomes a religious vocation. Private religious experience is denigrated as a subtle form of self-indulgence. All this, together with an intense hate for Roman Catholicism, appears in a letter from Green to Henry Scott Holland. The occasion of the letter was nothing less than the conversion of Gerard Manley Hopkins to Catholicism. Hopkins had been a Balliol undergraduate when he wrote in 1866 his now famous letter to Newman asking to be received into the Church of Rome. Green writes:

> I am glad that you and Nettleship saw Hopkins. A step such as he has taken, tho' I can't quite admit it to be heroic, must needs be painful, and its pain should not be aggravated—as it is pretty sure to be—by separation from old friends. I never had his intimacy, but always liked him very much.* I imagine him—perhaps uncharitably—to be one of those, like his ideal J. H. Newman, who instead of simply opening themselves to the revelation of God in the reasonable world, are fain to put themselves into an attitude—saintly, it is true, but still an attitude. True citizenship 'as unto the Lord' (which includes all morality) I reckon higher than 'saintliness' in the technical sense. The 'superior young man' of these days, however, does not seem to understand it, but hugs his own 'refined pleasures' or (which is but a higher form of the same) his personal sanctity. Whence, and not from heterodoxy, ruin threatens Christian society. . . . It vexes me to the heart to think of a fine nature being victimised by a system which in my 'historic conscience' I hold to be subversive of the Family and the State, and which puts the service of

* It appears that Hopkins at first detested Green, but later modified his view. 'They have cut down the beautiful beech in the Garden Quad, which stood in the angle of Fisher's buildings, because it was said to darken their rooms. This is a wicked thing; such a beech no doubt has not its like in Oxford, beech being a rare tree here. Its destruction is owing to the Fellows Green and Newman [W. L.]. The former is of a rather offensive style of infidelity, and naturally dislikes the beauties of nature.' (Letter from Gerard Manley Hopkins to his mother, 19 October, 1863, *Further Letters of Gerard Manley Hopkins*, ed. Claude Colleer Abbott [2d ed. rev.; London: Oxford University Press, 1956], p. 83.) But after Green tutored Hopkins in philosophy, they became more friendly. Hopkins then left Oxford, and the two men did not meet again until 1879. (*Further Letters*, p. 152.) After the death of his tutor, Hopkins wrote: 'I always liked and admired poor Green. He seemed to me upright in mind and in life. . . . His fortune fell first on Knox and then on Hegel and he was meant for better things. Probably if he had lived longer he would have written something that wd. have done the same.' (Letter from Hopkins to A. W. M. Baillie, 6 May, 1882, [*Further Letters*, p. 249.])

an exceptional institution, or the saving of the individual soul, in opposition to loyal service to society.[47]

Green returns to this theme in his next letter. He attacks first monasticism and then Catholicism and all other religious beliefs which he believed to emphasise salvation in the future life in preference to social reform in this world. His objections here are aimed as much against the High Churchmen as the Roman Catholics. These he lumps together as basing religion on blind, unreasoning authority and a selfish concern for personal salvation at any cost. Worst of all, they ignore the basic disorganisation of society. Religion, if it is to have any reality, must begin its real task of working with genuine humanising effect upon the great mass of men living brutal and deprived lives. Its task, in Green's significant phrase, is 'to moralise masses'. What do Catholics and High Churchmen do towards that end? Green hints prophetically at a new religion such as Robert Elsmere's:

If, then, I question the monastic form of co-operation, it is because... it does nothing to organise life. The real movement of the world has passed it by. It lets the muddy tide have its way, and merely picks up a few stones thrown on the shore, which will take the saintly polish—not without satisfaction that the tide should be as muddy as it is by way of contrast. Nor is this weakness accidental. It results from the wrong principle, on which, historically, monasticism rests, of the antithesis between Church and World, the religious and the secular, etc. This antithesis, doubtless, had its work to do, but the rational movement of mankind has got beyond it. Just so far as ordinary religion, 'Catholic' or 'Protestant' is governed by it, it loses its interest for the fully educated citizen of the European common-wealth, to lapse into, it seems to me, at best, a piece of spiritual invalidishness. Catholicism embodies the antithesis in its most objectionable form, inasmuch as it fixes the Divine, falsely opposed to the human, in a definite institution claiming supremacy over secular and civil interests, and represents the 'objective presence' of the incarnate God as a sensual presence in the sacraments instead of a moral one in the Christian society, and makes Him speak authoritatively thro' the priest instead of rationally thro' the educated conscience. . . .

Does it not appear that *mere* religious agency does but touch the surface of our modern rottenness: that the people who cry 'Lord, Lord' do no wonderful works and never get nearer to any organisation of life; that the only hope lies in such 'secular' agency and 'human' philosophy as requires a religious zeal, not less self-denying and much more laboriously thoughtful than that of the monk, to bring into action? . . .

Whether the outcome will be new forms of religious society or a gradual absorption of all such forms in simple religious citizenship,

I do not predict: but I have faith that the new Christianity, because not claiming to be special or exceptional or miraculous, will do more for mankind than in its 'Catholic' form hampered by false antagonisms it has ever been able to do.[48]

These little-known letters contain Green's most explicit statement of the relationship between his theology and his politics. But they were private communications. Green's public effect—and he made a very considerable impression upon religious thought at Oxford—came from two lay sermons upon 'The Witness of God' and 'Faith' which he delivered in the Balliol College Chapel.[49] Occupying fewer than fifty pages in Green's collected works, they now go unread by those who seek to understand the impact of his *Principles of Political Obligation*. And yet the meaning of that work is incomprehensible apart from Green's theology and the atmosphere which created it. His Oxford was in the midst of a painful transition from an institution that had changed little since the Middle Ages to the great secular university that it is today. And when Green came up to Balliol in 1855, he found himself at the very storm centre of theological controversy. It was his religious background and personal intellectual experience that made him feel so strongly the points in issue.

CHAPTER TWO

THREE FAMILIES AND THEIR FAITHS

I

G. M. YOUNG REMARKED THAT THE Victorian Age in Great Britain was but the insular phase of a movement felt everywhere in the western world. 'Ways and habits, fashions and prejudices, doctrines, ideas, and even phrases which we think of as typically Victorian, are really part of a general European pattern.'[1] Of this international development, no part was more important than the *Ersatz* theologies, the all-inclusive philosophies of life so dear to the nineteenth century. Idealist philosophy and Comtist positivism, heroic vitalism and social Darwinism, nationalism, liberal and integral, socialism, utopian and scientific—all in their separate ways attempted to enlist religious impulsions in the service of worldly causes. J. L. Talmon in his analysis of the Jewish element in the Saint Simonian movement has described the spiritual void of youthful and recently emancipated Jews who, under the impact of rationalism, had quickly shed their religious heritage.

> 'The accumulated intensity was suddenly left without object, as it were. In such a situation men are driven sometimes to idealistic sainthood, sometimes to ruthless and shameless self-assertion. . . . In the case of spiritual and idealistic sublimation, the age-old Jewish tradition of solidarity and imaginative compassion with the sufferings of others was able to find a kindred disposition in socialism. . . .'[2]

The Jews were but a special case of a general phenomenon. Such a secularisation of religious feeling occured most frequently during the education of middle class children with devout parents who had implanted a taste for self-sacrifice and an uneasiness about luxuriating in the goods of this world. It is striking how many of the thinkers who made or disseminated general systems of ideas came from clerical or rabbinical families. Similarly in Germany, Pietist impulses fed philosophical idealism. This provenance accounts for the vague religiosity which led thinkers as diverse as Hegel in Germany and Durkheim in France to

33

construct secular moralities which they thought would fulfil the
same function for modern society as had traditional religions in
the past. All of these philosophies insisted that the condition of
self-realisation is self-denial. Often their aim was to create a new
and more intimate community animated by common principles
of altruism. Another type of thinker set out to demonstrate that
already existing forms of social organisation presupposed social
solidarity and moral duties of a sort hitherto not recognised.
Whether revolutionary or reactionary, such creeds tended to
brand as irresponsible and egoistic anyone who asserted his
personal will to live without reference to a larger loyalty. These
motifs resound in a dialogue in Turgenev's *On the Eve*. The
year is 1853. Shubin, a young sculptor, is with Bersyenev, a
philosophy student, who has just finished his University examinations. It is a hot summer day, and as they lounge by the river,
they fall into a frank and spirited conversation. Shubin is
speaking:

'. . . But I expect happiness, I demand happiness. . . . So long as we
have life, so long as we have power over our limbs, so long as we're
climbing the hill and not coming down it! Why damn it!' Shubin
went on with a sudden outburst: 'We're young, we're not monsters,
not fools: we'll conquer happiness for ourselves.'
. . . Bersyenev glanced up at him.
'Mightn't there be something higher than happiness?' he said
quietly.
'For example?' Shubin asked and waited.
'Well, for example, you and I . . . each wants happiness for
himself. . . . But this word "happiness," is it the sort of word to
unite us, to fire us, to compel us to join hands in friendship? Isn't it a
selfish word, I mean a word that keeps people apart?'
'And do you know any words that unite?'
'Yes, and they're not rare either; you know them too.'
'Well, then? What are they?'
'Well, art, at any rate—since you're an artist—then motherland,
science, freedom, justice.'
'And love!' Shubin asked.
'Love unites also—but not the love you're thirsting for now: not
love the pleasure, but love the sacrifice.
Shubin frowned.
'That's all right for the Germans: but I want love for myself: I
want to be number one.'
'Number one,' Bersyenev repeated. 'Whereas I feel that one's
whole destiny in life should be to make oneself number two.'[3]

With some few changes, an English author might have set the
same conversation at Oxford in the mid-1850's. There the romantic

egoist would have had to be described as less zestful and more troubled by religious questions. Although Green's undergraduate circle was to include Swinburne, John Addington Symonds and Walter Pater, none of them felt emancipated from all obligation. Just because matters of belief loomed so large, serious young men were more apt to resemble Bersyenev than Shubin. When Oxford and Cambridge graduates went off to live at settlement houses in London's East End, they were responding to the same yearning for 'words that unite' and subordination of self, which in Russia sent well-born young men to seek their larger community among peasants, or for that matter, in Pan-Slavism or social revolution. No doubt everywhere most members of the privileged classes accepted their superior position as just and natural. But among the small minority which thought and read, there were some few who could be touched by appeals to their conscience, their generosity, their repugnance at the prospect of living in a society permanently divided into classes by the barriers of birth or wealth. At Oxford such persons proved to be susceptible to an appeal to their altruism, desire for solidarity and asceticism. Henry Scott Holland, seeking to explain Green's effect upon himself and his generation, remarked: 'He gave us back the language of self-sacrifice and taught us how we belonged to one another in the one life of organic humanity. He filled us again with the breath of high idealism.'[4] In short, post-Kantian Idealism was admirably suited to the needs of Green's Oxford audience.

In his *Phenomenology*, Hegel had anatomised the 'Unhappy Consciousness' of men tortured by doubt and deprived of that unity which alone brings peace. *Das unglückliches Bewusstsein* is the 'Alienated Soul which is the consciousness of self as a divided nature, a doubled and merely contradictory being'.[5] In its most poignant form, 'it is the bitter pain which finds expression in the cruel words, "God is dead" '.[6] Hegel claimed that his philosophy can rescue men from the depressing sense of living in a world foreign to them. Spirit, or *Geist*, is present both in the world and in the minds of men. Reason animates both man and nature. Only a philosophy which can attain 'absolute knowledge' is capable of overcoming the alienation of one aspect of the human spirit from another. Thus Hegel's thought was a disguised theology which pretended to synthesise by reason alone all those aspects of nature and thought which had been represented in Christian theology as permeated by the divine spirit. Within the Hegelian schema, there was a place and justification for every kind of human activity: intellectual, aesthetic and political. History was made clear by the dialectic; the existing social order was declared to be the working out of its rational process. None of this left any room for variety, paradox or unresolved contradictions: these appeared to Hegel as symptoms of spiritual malaise. The purpose of philosophy is to synthesise and reconcile all aspects of human life by showing its ultimate purpose and goal. This definition of the philosophical enterprise was accepted by Green. The first serious group of students to form around him was known as the 'society for looking at things as a whole'.[7]

Yet Kant was an equally strong influence. For one thing, men in reaction against conventional apologists were pleased by Kant's insistence that all claims of religion, as of government, be judged by the 'critical method'; for another, Kant's political preferences were closer to Green's than were Hegel's. Like Marx, although for different reasons, Hegel had a studied contempt for everything which resembled naïve ethical idealism. Thus he gibed at all *Moralisten* and *Menschenfreunde* who would judge politics by moral categories and humanitarian principles.[8] Green, on the contrary, in his ethics was to award the highest place in his moral hierarchy to precisely this type of character, 'the social reformer'. From this point of view, there were limits to how much of Hegel Green could swallow. One eminent student of Hegel has said that his thought may be reduced to three propositions: that reality is spiritual; that reality is systematic; and that reality is rational.[9] Of these, Green accepted the first two. His political beliefs led him, if not to reject the third, at least to sever it from the conservative conclusions of Hegel. Yet the Hegelian impulse with its theological quality of inclusion and reconciliation, with its claim to be altogether rational—this remained as the strongest single element in English Idealism.

The most prominent spokesmen for British Idealism were all sons of Evangelical clergymen within the Church of England.[10] It was an essentially religious concern which first brought Green, Bernard Bosanquet, and F. H. Bradley to the study of philosophy.* This is not to say that their subsequent work was dominated by the same motive. Bradley, who ended as the most antagonistic of the three to organised religion, first encountered Hegel in German theologians such as Baur.[11] In this he repeated Green's experience. Quite literally their interest in philosophy derived

---

* Lord Haldane, an ardent Idealist, came from a family which gave its name to one of the strictest of sects. When Minister for War, he addressed an audience made up largely from clergy of all denominations. 'If that's Hegel we should all be studying him,' said one member. 'No, it's Hegel grafted on to his father and grandfather,' said another Scot, a Highland minister. [Elizabeth S. Haldane, *From One Century to Another* (London, 1937), p. 229.]

from theology. As for Bosanquet, he had left Harrow for Balliol with three friends. All four intended to take orders as Anglican clergymen; none of them did so.[12] Because of Green's teaching and personal example, they gave another form to their original vocation. Bosanquet took up philosophy, but resigned his Oxford fellowship because he felt that his true duty was to do social work in London. His Harrow friend, R. G. Tatton, did likewise, and became the first Warden of the Passmore Edwards Settlement, founded by Mrs Humphry Ward to put into practice those ideas of Green she had celebrated in *Robert Elsmere*.

The search for an object of faith may lead men to very different positions. Green and those among his students who became Idealists did so for a variety of reasons. Some were dominated by the need for a faith; some cared most for the intellectual schema which seemed to order an otherwise inexplicable modern world; still others discovered in the Liberal turn Green gave to his philosophy, a new justification for political ideas already congenial to them.

Philosophical Idealism provided a broadly based set of formulae, which, when filled in with different values, could be used to support a variety of causes. In Green's hands, Idealism became a vehicle of reform, thus reflecting certain aspects of Evangelicalism and Christian Socialism. Bradley, reacting against both, created an aloof conservatism. Green, despite his austere manner, succeeded in transforming the lives of a significant minority of those who heard or read him. Bradley, unable to teach because of illness or hypochondria, cut himself off from all except his family and fellow tutors at Merton. Towards religion, Bradley took a somewhat cooler view than Green, who could write, '. . . if I were only a breeder of heretics, I should suspect my philosophy. If it is sound, it ought to supply intellectual formulae for the religious life whether lived by an "orthodox" clergyman or . . . a follower of Mazzini'.[13] When Bosanquet was a Balliol undergraduate, he and Green belonged to a small society which met for prayer on Sunday.[14] They did not much like worship in College Chapel, and had a reputation for being freethinkers. Yet Bosanquet, although one of the pillars of the English Ethical Culture movement, also attended a Friends' Meeting House towards the end of his life.[15] Green 'would go to Lower Evangelical Churches on Sunday evenings.'[16] Both thought of themselves, not as undermining faith, but rather as providing it with a secure philosophical foundation. As for Bradley, once in the early days of bicycles, he solved his parking problem by leaving his bicycle in the Merton ante-chapel. When other dons described this as desecration, he

37

stated that he had 'no objection to have the beastly thing conse-
crated'.[17] He was annoyed at the report that clergymen had used
his conclusions from *Ethical Studies* for apologetic purposes, and
took care that *Appearance and Reality* should not be used in the
same way.[18]

In part the difference between Green and Bradley was one of
temperament, the one modifying and rephrasing, the other,
rejecting their parental Evangelicalism.* Green always preferred
to comprehend rather than to exclude; Bradley's thought can best
be understood, as Mr Richard Wollheim has convincingly argued,
in terms of a series of negative reactions to positions he found
unsatisfactory.[19] But in Green's case there were more than
personal and psychological forces at work. The histories of his
father's and mother's families, when taken together with that of
his wife, go far towards explaining the values he translated into
philosophy and political action. His version of Philosophical
Idealism in many respects can be viewed as simply giving a new
form to ideas and loyalties long prominent in the Green, Vaughan,
and Symonds families. By examining their history we can better
understand what was typical and what was novel in the life of
their descendants. The Greens and Symonds resembled each
other in that both had been long cut off from the centres of
national life by their stubborn insistence upon maintaining their
Nonconformist faith. Green and his wife were both products of a
characteristic pattern: the evolution from Puritanism through
Evangelicalism to a secular and active morality. Their families
differed in that the Symonds had never entered the Church of
England. The Vaughans, on the other hand, active in Church,
state, public school and university, brought into Green's consciousness a certain corporate element. The duties owed by superiors
to inferiors, the positive functions to be performed by Church
and State, these ideas he was to learn from a Christian Socialist
uncle.

* 'The Reverend Charles Bradley . . . was . . . the mainstay of the well-
known "Clapham sect". He was a Yorkshireman and a not uncommon nineteenth-
century English type: an evangelical clergyman, noted for his polished but
forcible sermons, highly prolific, and a domestic tyrant. He had twenty-two
children by two wives and he bullied them all. Herbert, born in 1846, was the
fourth child of his second marriage and is said to have been the only one of his
offspring who ever stood up to this formidable *paterfamilias*. There is a tale that,
to annoy his father, he taught his brothers and sisters . . . to slide down the
banisters and arrive with a crash outside the study door.' [G. R. G. Mure,
'F. H. Bradley,' *Encounter*, XVI, No. 1 (January, 1961), p. 28.] Green's father
was quite mild and gentle to his children.

2

Green was born in the Yorkshire village of Birkin one year before Victoria's coronation in 1837. His mother, Anna Barbara Vaughan Green, died while giving birth to Thomas, her fourth child in six years of marriage. His father, the Reverend Valentine Green, following a pattern not unusual in an age when the dangers of childbirth were no deterrent to large families, re-married some years later and had three more children by his second wife. Green thus never knew his own mother, and although he was close to his father, very little information is available about the Vicar, who lived and died without making much of an impression on the world. He had married his first wife in Chesterfield Church in December, 1830. An uncle, Thomas' godfather and Vicar of Chesterfield, was patron of the living of Birkin, which he presented to the Reverend Valentine Green when it fell vacant in 1835. The rural vicarage was seven miles from Pontefract, the nearest town. The roads were not good; the railway, when it came to the West Riding, had no station nearer than five miles away. The children lived in a very nearly self-contained world. Except when cousins came, they had no companions to play with them in the large garden where they enjoyed great freedom. Their only schoolmaster was their father, who demanded little from them in their lessons. He was in any case occupied by his parish which stretched for some nine miles away from his house. Almost the only first-hand description which remains of him is that written for Nettleship by Mrs Green, who first saw her father-in-law in 1871. At that time he was very frail, but his keen eyes and beautiful voice were still striking. 'The reality of his religious fervour,' which was a gentle Evangelicalism, did not keep him from telling stories well and displaying the sense of humour he passed on to his son.[20] A deep affection existed between them. After his father's death, Green recalled how his father used to welcome him on his visits: always pretending indifference, but unable to conceal his happiness. A sentence in the lay sermon given by Green at Balliol tells much about him and his father,* whom he seems to have

* No doubt the milieu in which Green was brought up closely resembled that of Mary Paley, the future Mrs Alfred Marshall. Keynes, after reading her recollections of a childhood in a Yorkshire evangelical parsonage, wrote of 'what the world has lost in the atmosphere of plain living and high thinking and strictly restrained beauty and affection, which is the only education worth much. Perhaps no one who was not brought up as an evangelical or a nonconformist is entitled to think freely in due course. . . .' To this tribute, Keynes added: 'But what a very odd, and sometimes terrible, thing are strict principles! Why can an age only be great if it believes, or at least is bred up in believing, what is preposterous?' [J. M. Keynes, *Essays in Biography* (London: Mercury Books, 1961), p. 326.]

had in mind when he wrote it: 'Who can hear an unargumentative and unrhetorical Christian minister appeal to his people to cleanse their hearts and to help each other as sons of God in Christ, without feeling that he touches the deepest and strongest spring of noble conduct in mankind?'[21]

This quiet and inconspicuous quality was typical of the Greens, and one of their descendants has remarked that Thomas Hill Green was the only really able person produced by the family in seven hundred years.[22] Beginning as yeoman farmers at Normanton, Leicestershire, generation by generation, they had improved their position until they at last became squires, not unlike the Cromwell family in the seventeenth century. Thus the Reverend Valentine's elder brother, Robert, owned property at Odstone in Leicestershire and was listed in Burke's *Landed Gentry;* their father, Valentine Green, was squire of Normanton-le-Heath in the same county. But the family's social position was perhaps less significant than its intellectual and religious evolution. Green's sense of identification with the Puritans, so frequently remarked by his Rugby and Balliol contemporaries, turns out to have been based on more than boyhood affection for Carlyle's *Cromwell.* Dorothy Cromwell, daughter of Protector Richard Cromwell, and granddaughter of Oliver Cromwell, was the first wife of John Mortimer (1654-1736). Mortimer's third wife was Elizabeth Sanders, a granddaughter of Colonel Thomas Sanders, one of Cromwell's officers. T. H. Green's paternal grandfather, then the squire of Normanton-le-Heath, married a Miss Mortimer, who was descended from John Mortimer and Elizabeth Sanders.

In addition to this Puritan connection, the Mortimers provided Green with another ancestor of interest, Cromwell Mortimer (d. 1752). A physician and member of the Royal Society, he was the friend, secretary and assistant to Sir Hans Sloane, whose bequest prompted the foundation of the British Museum. Mortimer made himself highly unpopular with his medical colleagues by issuing a circular setting forth in detail the schedule of fees for his medical services.[23] Furthermore, he attempted to put into effect something like a health insurance scheme.

> 'Several persons of fortune', he contended, 'who have the generosity and humanity to take care of their servants when sick, being often at great expense at that account; and many small families, or single persons, finding themselves upon any illness put to great charges; I offer to agree with single persons or families for a certain salary, by the year; computing at about one guinea for each person; for which salary I propose to give them my advice, and attendance when necessary, and to make them a present of the proper medicines.'[24]

Although there is no evidence that Green was influenced by or even knew the works of Cromwell Mortimer, he did display a persistent sympathy for the Puritans and their Nonconformist posterity. This emerged as clearly from his study of the Commonwealth, 'Four Lectures on the English Revolution,' as from the report deploring the still existing discrimination against the Dissenters which he wrote as an Assistant Commissioner investigating the state of secondary education.[25] Of Oliver Cromwell, Green wrote that he gave by his sword 'fifteen years of vigorous growth' to the dissenting sects, thus creating 'a permanent force which no reaction could suppress, and which has since been the great spring of political life in England'.[26] As an ardent member of the Liberal Party, which depended so much upon the Nonconformists, Green saw in that party and in Philosophical Idealism, the fulfilment and correction of Puritanism. It was in the closing paragraph of his lectures on the Commonwealth that Green intimated his own doctrine but put more clearly and systematically that theory of man's nature and his relation to government implicit in the thought of such Puritans as Sir Henry Vane.

By a development not uncommon in families of Green's background, its members had passed into the Evangelical branch of the Church of England. W. L. Newman, who had been a Fellow of Balliol when Green came up, remembered how his impression was confirmed 'that like many other earnest men, he had come from an Evangelical home'.[27] And not only Green's father, but at least two of his sisters were devoutly evangelical. Thus Green's family connected him solidly to Puritanism and Evangelicalism. Through his mother's family, he was to be exposed to the doctrines of Thomas Arnold and Christian Socialism.

Green's mother was the daughter of Edward Thomas Vaughan, Vicar of St Martin's at Leicester. The Vaughans descend from an alchemist, who was a fellow of Jesus College, Oxford, and the twin brother of the poet, Henry Vaughan, the Silurist. By the end of the eighteenth century, the family had already achieved an exceptional eminence. Of five Vaughan brothers, one was President of the Royal College of Physicians and doctor to George II; a second, a prominent judge; a third, Warden of Merton; a fourth, Fellow of All Souls and a diplomat, and the fifth, Reverend E. T. Vaughan, a double first and Fellow of Trinity, Cambridge. The judge's descendants included Henry Halford Vaughan, Regius Professor of Modern History at Oxford, whose son, W. W. Vaughan, headmaster of Wellington and later of Rugby, married a daughter of J. A. Symonds, and whose daughter, Dr Janet Vaughan, became principal of Somerville

College, Oxford. The Reverend E. T. Vaughan married twice. T. H. Green's mother was Vaughan's daughter by his first marriage. By his second wife, he had five sons, three of whom were to succeed him as Vicar of St Martin's, now the Cathedral at Leicester. The elder, Charles John Vaughan (1816-97), was one of Thomas Arnold's prized students and disciples at Rugby, where he shared the honours of the school with the future Dean Stanley, whose sister he later married. After a brilliant career in classics at Trinity College, Cambridge, where he was elected a Fellow, he took orders and became Vicar of St Martin's. After losing to Tait in a contest for the Headmastership of Rugby, Harrow called him to the same post in the hope that he would rehabilitate that ancient foundation, then at the nadir of its fortunes. In this he succeeded and in so doing, placed himself among the great nineteenth century Headmasters who reformed the public schools. After some fifteen years at Harrow, he went on to become Master of the Temple and Dean of Llandaff.[28]

His younger brother, and hence also T. H. Green's uncle, was David James Vaughan (1825-1905). Following his brother to Rugby, he likewise became a Fellow of Trinity, Cambridge. A distinguished classicist, he is the Vaughan of the Davies and Vaughan translation of Plato's *Republic*, which Trinity men have always rated as superior to Jowett's.[29] But in 1860 he left Cambridge to become Vicar of St Martin's, where he remained until 1893. Influenced by his friend, Frederick Denison Maurice, with whom he corresponded on theological questions, to become a Christian Socialist, he is described in the *Dictionary of National Biography* as a 'social reformer'—a term that was to carry a great deal of weight in his nephew's philosophical system. Another intimate friend was the future Bishop Westcott, the first head of the Christian Social Union. Vaughan started at Leicester a working men's college with Sunday morning and evening classes, night classes and advanced classes which at one time took care of 2,300 students. He established a provident society, sick benefit society and book club. On Sunday afternoons he would address in his church, working men including members of the great friendly societies on social and industrial as well as religious themes. The Vaughan Working Men's College is now part of Leicester University. The life and work of his uncle almost persuaded Green to take orders as a clergyman. Although he did not do so, he was never to lose sight of the Reverend David Vaughan's Christian Socialist principles and liberal theology.[30] No doubt it was his uncle who placed Maurice in his nephew's hands while Green was still at Rugby. And the relationship continued: whenever Green travelled North, he always stopped at Leicester. It was there that he gave his lecture on 'Liberal Legislation and Freedom of Contract'.

The third family which must be mentioned in connection with Green is the one into which he married. The Symonds resembled his own father's family more than his mother's. Through the genealogical work done by John Addington Symonds, much is known about the remote origins of his ancestors, their experiences as Nonconformists, and what he described as the 'gradual emergence from narrow intellectual conditions in a Puritan pedigree'.[31] The Symonds descend from the second son of Simon, Seigneur of St Sever in Normandy, who died in 1096. Adam Fitzsimon, as this son was known, acquired lands in Norfolk and Herefordshire. After his death in 1118, his descendants were called Fitzsimon until the beginning of the fourteenth century, when they became known as Symonds. At the Reformation, the family became strict Nonconformists. One of them married John Hampden. Long excluded from the Universities and the traditional careers of the gentry, men of the family became for many generations doctors and occasionally wool-merchants in various parts of England. Despite their middle-class status, the Symonds continued to think of themselves as an ancient family which had sacrificed everything to its religious beliefs.

Presumably it was John Addington Symonds who introduced his sister, Charlotte, to Green. The two men became good friends at Balliol where they were members of the same essay society, went on reading parties with their common friend, Professor Conington, and travelled together in Switzerland. Symonds' health was never good, and he finally had to abandon his father's house in Bristol for a chalet at Davos, Switzerland. Confronted with his family papers, he had to decide what should be done with them. In an autobiographical fragment, he has described how he was so depressed by reading the correspondence left by five generations of his family that he burnt it:

> The perusal of them left a deeply painful impression on my mind. The intense pre-occupation with so-called spiritual interests; the suffocating atmosphere of a narrow sect resembling that of a close parlour; the grim, stern dealing with young souls not properly convinced of sin; the unnatural admixture of this other-worldliness with mundane marrying and giving in marriage and professional affairs, caught me by the throat and throttled me. . . . So I committed an act of vandalism, whereof I am now half-repentant and half-proud.[32]

Their descendant could not but be fascinated with the continuity amidst the changes in succeeding generations. Invariably serious about themselves and their obligations, the Symonds nevertheless gave quite disparate forms to their spiritual concerns.

> Beginning with the ardent faith of the Puritan impulse, passing into earnest but formalised Methodism in the next two generations, feeling the breath of the French Revolution and physical science in my grandfather, but remaining within the limits of strict Puritan orthodoxy; in my father's correspondence with J. Sterling and F. Newman and F. Maurice and Jowett, taking a robust theistic complexion, and in mine . . . expanding finally into a free atmosphere. The spiritual problem was the main matter of all those letters. But how that spiritual problem altered with each generation![33]

J. A. Symonds' grandfather, John Symonds, although remaining a Dissenter, and marrying a Plymouth sister, became what might be called a Christian Stoic. In his son, the father of Green's wife, these moral qualities were 'transfigured and spiritualised' as he attempted to construct a modernist faith. Dr Symonds' place in his family's spiritual evolution is lovingly described by his son in a language that catches the modulations of something part emotion and part idea, which formed as much a part of Green's religiosity as that of the family into which he married:

> My father typified an exceptionally interesting moment of English evolution. He had abandoned the narrow standpoint of Nonconformist or Evangelical orthodoxy, but he retained what was ethically valuable in the religious tradition. He opened his mind to every influence of knowledge and of culture. He relinquished nothing which affected character and principle. . . . Intellectually he had joined the ranks of progress, and belonged to the age of widening thought. Morally he held with them, and exemplified in his own life what was best and noblest in the family tradition. To keep himself unspotted by the world, to admit no transaction with base motives, to live purely and act uprightly, to follow honour, to postpone mundane and selfish interests to duty, to deal mercifully, sympathetically, tenderly, justly with his brother men, to be unsparing in condemnation of rebellious evil, painstaking and long-suffering with struggling good, these were the principles which ruled his conduct. He transfigured in himself the inheritance he had derived from six generations of Puritan ancestors, and he retained something of their rigidity. But he also felt the influence of the age in which he lived. He was open at all pores to culture, to art, to archaeology, to science, to literature. In a large and liberal sense, he yielded his spirit up to beauty, and imbibed the well-springs of modern philosophy.[34]

The sensibility described here is a compound of optimism and humanism, a typically mid-Victorian variety of what William James called the religion of healthy-mindedness. Serious, intellectual, a posture remarkably undisturbed even in the face of death, it can be further studied in the letters Green wrote to his fiancée, Charlotte Symonds, at a time when her father was gravely ill. 'Compare Romans viii 16 and 26, the greatest verses in the bible, very good "to feed on", as Cromwell would have said. You must cultivate a "waiting spirit" as he again would have said. If the last hour is coming, let us try to think of living in years to come as your father would have wished us to live.'[35] These sentences say nothing imcompatible with Christianity, but the sentiment they express is sufficiently attenuated to fit as easily into a purely secular humanism as into an orthodox creed. Green used terms which forced neither himself nor his fiancée to take a clear-cut stand on the question of immortality.* This is the case in the letter written to console his future wife upon her father's death: 'To have been with you during this trial has done me a great deal of good, and in spite of the present sadness gives me more peace in thinking of death. It helps me to see that after all there is no waste in a good man's death. Your father's character, through his death, re-lives more strongly in you than it could during his life, and doubtless through the eyes of God, with whom he is, he sees this. . . .'[36] Metaphysics are here employed to do service for faith, but the style remains curiously homiletic. 'In thinking about a future life you may find it of help to reflect that even in this life sensations are to what we experience through them only as words to the ideas which come to us when we read or hear the words . . . I think the best notion we can form of the state after death is that it is one in which all the spiritual result of our present sensuous life remains in a higher and freer form. . . . Don't you sometimes feel that communion "spirit to spirit" may be purer and freer when it is not "face to face"? Such a feeling soon becomes unreal, and must do so when we are in nature, but it has its value.'[37] These ideas and sensibility may be taken as a fair sample of what Rugby and Balliol could do to a young man of Evangelical origins. And although no thinker of Green's quality is ever the mere subject of external influences, nevertheless it may be instructive to follow his development at two of the most strategic centres of mid-Victorian life.

* 'When a troubled young friend said to her, "If someone is honestly seeking religion and trying to live it, do you think it very much matters about their belonging to a church?" she answered at once "Oh no, I do not"; and faithful attendant as she was in this chapel and in St Giles, she said only a year or two ago, "I seem to want more and more to get to the reality without all that has been built up around the teaching. We can do this if we can keep the spirit alive in us, and all the beauty in nature, and in human beings helps us to do it." '
['In Memoriam Mrs T. H. Green, Balliol College Chapel,' 13 October, 1929.]

3

Educated until the age of fourteen by his father, Green left home for the first time to attend Rugby. Dr Arnold had died eight years before. By a remarkable series of reforms, he had made Rugby into the prototype of the nineteenth century public school, an institution which served both to train the sons of self-made men in the manners and outlook of the ruling class, and to change that class itself by teaching the duties of hard work and leadership. A singular atmosphere, characterised by incessant activity and corporate morality had survived Dr Arnold's death. But young Green was cool towards the organised aspects of life at Rugby. Distinguished from his fellows by a rural, home-bred shyness, he nevertheless was soon to manifest an iron will and unusual independence.[38]

It was not that he sought to make himself conspicuous as a rebel, for he played games out of the desire to have at least that association with his schoolmates, as well as taking a prominent part in the debating society. But he was no ordinary studious type, following the path designated by his teachers. 'He was a plant growing—not a brick being moulded. . . . He was a boy who let school drift round him rather than one who floated on it.'[39] Because he was neither competitive nor natively quick, his masters thought him indolent. It was only with the greatest difficulty that he got himself up in the morning; and he seldom finished assignments by the appointed time. Classical studies, which Arnold, despite other changes, had left in a dominant position, never much interested young Green, who had a dogged way of concentrating upon those subjects he most cared about. Only once did he win a classics prize. Significantly, this was for his Latin translation of Milton's *Areopagitica*. Already he would think things out in his own way and at his own pace, his Puritan heritage and Evangelical upbringing manifesting themselves by what his schoolmate and future philosophical adversary, Henry Sidgwick, recalled as a 'certain solid wilfulness, a certain grave rebeliousness'.[40] Unusually concerned with politics, he was known in the school as an intransigent radical. Perhaps he had himself heard, or knew from his father, the fiery speeches made by agitators of the Anti-Corn Law League as they had gone like Methodist preachers on circuit through the north of England.

It was in his classics that Green first caught a glimpse of philosophy; it attracted him. Sidgwick recalled that as he was out walking one day with Green, they came upon a bridge which his companion attempted to prove was a different bridge for each of them.[41] Even as a schoolboy Green gave evidence of having developed a rare combination of qualities, for together with heterodox opinions he had an integrity that commanded instant respect. In a period notable for its admiration of rugged character, Green stood out. As a connoisseur of a type he knew at first hand from his Clapham Sect family, A. V. Dicey wrote of Green when he first came to Oxford: 'He is one of the few men of my own age of whom I can truly say that his example has tended to keep up one's moral tone'.[42] The same judgment later was phrased by Green's students more facetiously, although still with respect. 'I never go to see Green', said one undergraduate, 'without feeling that I ought to be ashamed of myself, and, by Jove, I am ashamed of myself.'[43] The members of Green's house at Rugby found a striking resemblance between him and his particular hero, Cromwell. In his presence, no one found it possible 'to use a bad word or tell a ribald story'.[44] On Sunday afternoons, he went out by himself, and when teased about it, silenced gibes by saying with a smile that he could best worship God by himself in the green fields.*

This Wordsworthian sentiment reveals that although powerful religious tendencies continued to work within him, he had begun to strike out along paths increasingly divergent from his early training. There is a quality of orthodox unorthodoxy about the faith he constructed, like so many others in his age, out of Wordsworth and Coleridge, Dr Arnold, Carlyle, F. D. Maurice and Kingsley.† Without pretending to greater precision than is possible or necessary, it is not difficult to ascertain what he drew from such sources. Disparate in detail, they were united in their Romantic, Broad Church, or Christian Socialist opposition to what they regarded as undesirable characteristics of the eighteenth century which had persevered as the cardinal errors of their own

* A school friend never forgot an incident which occurred one Sunday soon after Green's arrival at Rugby. He was fourteen. 'Mr Hanbury remembers that . . . stepping into his (Green's) study found him at work. . . . He remonstrated with him. He said that as Mr Hanbury did not like it, he would not work on Sunday, . . . but he added, "I have thought out the subject, and I think it is right".' [MS note by A. C. Bradley, Balliol College Library.]

† 'In the forties we are aware of a new type issuing from the Universities and public schools, somewhat arrogant and somewhat shy, very conscious of their standing as gentlemen but very conscious of their duties, too, men in tweeds who smoke in the streets, disciples of Maurice, willing hearers of Carlyle, passionate for drains and co-operative societies, disposed to bring everything in the State of England to the test of Isaiah and Thucydides, and to find the source of all its defects in . . . the disgusting vice of shopkeeping. These are the Arnoldians.' G. M. Young, *Victorian England* (London: Oxford University Press, 1953), p. 71.

time. Among these were the previous century's mocking spirit, or lack of reverence, its atheism, materialism, hedonism, its mechanical model of the universe, its psychology based upon the association of ideas, and its egoistic individualism. Wordsworth, in one way, Carlyle in another, disposed Green to a pantheistic conception of God as manifest in nature as a spiritual principle, and revealed in history through the lives of great men and the institutions of Church and State by which men are moralised and made peculiarly human. When Green went off to pray by himself in the fields, or when later he found his greatest release in walking through hills and mountains, he followed many another who found in Wordsworth's god:

> a source of inward joy, of sympathetic and imaginative pleasure, which could be shared in by all human beings; which had no connexion with struggle or imperfection, but would be made richer by every improvement in the physical or social condition of mankind.[45]

Carlyle spoke to Green as he did to all those who, discarding with regret the 'Hebrew old clothes' of their parents' creeds, nevertheless held to the morality of Puritanism. Sidgwick wrote that he always associated Green both with the Puritans and with Carlyle: 'he had that religious earnestness in politics which in Carlyle is a kind of revival of Puritanism: and he had also a certain aloofness from his fellows and a sense of unlikeness. . . .'[46] Green's early essays echo Carlyle's fervent appeals made in the name of duty and faith (in what it is not altogether clear) and Carlyle's attacks upon the paralysis of disbelief and materialism. These themes, no less than Carlyle's favourite theory of history as the revelation of God, were to be incorporated by Green into a carefully elaborated system that, however, bore little resemblance to Carlyle's Scottish snorts and frenetic rhapsodies. Altogether excluded would be Carlyle's hero-worship and his latter-day reverence for aristocracy, the other side of the coin of his contempt for the working classes.

On Chartism and the 'condition of England' question, Green found F. D. Maurice and Kingsley more congenial than Carlyle. The example of his uncle was no doubt critical. The Christian Socialists not only believed that the workmen had legitimate grievances against their employers; they admitted that the Church had taken a position opposed to Christian justice. 'We have told you that the Bible preached to you patience, while we have not told you that it promised you freedom,' wrote Kingsley.[47] Although opposed to adult suffrage and paid parliamentary representatives, the movement attempted to convince the working class that they should prepare themselves for citizenship by joining friendly societies and forming co-operative organisations, and that they should educate themselves by attending working men's colleges. The Christian Socialists attempted to avoid revolution by opposing to the *laissez-faire* of the middle classes, older principles of the positive functions to be performed by Church and State. Instead of individualism and competition, they preached a theory of corporate obligation and co-operation. Denying that there is any dichotomy between the interests of the individual and those of the State, they contended that individuals expand and develop through their participation in the State and voluntary associations. Indeed the proper function of the State is precisely to reconcile the interest of each with the interests of all. Green found much to admire in a position that on spiritual grounds urged political and social reform. This, too, he was to translate into the formal language of German philosophy.

The Christian Socialism which Green thus took in was precise in its statement neither of Socialism, nor of Christianity. On the one side its religious teaching derived from Coleridge through Maurice, who had to resign his professorship at King's College, London, because of allegedly dangerous views on eternal punishment; on the other, through Dr Arnold, whose influence made itself felt upon Christian Socialism via his student, Thomas Hughes, author of the Rugby Iliad, *Tom Brown's Schooldays.* Green's religious beliefs closely resembled those of Dr Arnold, a fact which no doubt stemmed from that persistent influence of German philosophy and theology on the Broad Church movement which has been so thoroughly documented by Professor Klaus Dockhorn.[48] Arnold argued that the quality of a church is to be measured, not by its dogma or ritual, but by its practical capacity to Christianise the nation and introduce the principles of its teaching into men's social and civil relations. The great failure of religion in modern times had been the radical separation of things secular from things spiritual. The Evangelicals had erred in making religion too exclusively a transaction between the individual and his God; the High Churchmen and Roman Catholics had confined the highest form of religious life to the clergy and made too much of mere forms. Although he censured the Evangelicals in this general indictment, he nevertheless shared their notion that the essence of Christianity is that of personal holiness. In a letter directing how his children should be brought up in the event of his own death, he wrote:

> Remember always that although Evangelicalism . . . be not the perfection of Christianity, yet it is Christianity, vital and essential.

I would rather not have my sons narrow minded and silly, but this will be merely the wood, hay and stubble, which will be swept off the foundation at the Day of Account.[49]

But there was no need to choose among the extremes of parties. Indeed, Arnold like Maurice would not admit that he held a point of view which could exclude any truly religious person. To restore the Church to its proper function, all religious bodies should be united within the Anglican Church under the condition that they could maintain their separate rites and creeds. Only by such extraordinary action could the Church become what it was meant to be, ' a society for the purpose of making men like Christ—earth like heaven—the kingdoms of the world the Kingdom of Christ. . . .'[50] In this emphasis on realising Christianity in the social relations of this world, Arnold, like the Christian Socialists, attacked the doctrine of *laissez-faire*.

Here, then, are some of the authors whom Green was reading at Rugby. Politics, metaphysics, religion—these were weighty concerns for a schoolboy, and it is small wonder that he made but few friends. When he himself reached the sixth form, he found himself virtually isolated, for those he liked best had departed with the class ahead of him. All at once, his schoolmates began to appear to him not only as children, but as disagreeable children.* Calamities began to descend: his one close friend became ill and then permanently insane. From Oxford came the news that his older brother had been sent down from Merton, where he had shut himself up in his room and refused to take his examinations. He had been drinking heavily, and his brother became involved in what was to be a long and losing struggle to rescue him from alcoholism.[51] It was in this atmosphere of darkening gloom that he left Rugby for his first trip to Oxford. If prematurely advanced in his ideas, he knew little of the world he was entering, and what he knew, he dreaded. His Evangelical sensibility was not sanguine, and shy, countrified, he shrank back from Oxford, then still unreformed and manifesting strong class distinctions. Noblemen paraded proudly, marked by the gold tassels in their caps; scholars, commoners, servitors, each was distinguished by a special dress. With this side of Oxford, Green never made his peace. He was pleased neither by the rough sporting types, nor by the elegant young men accustomed to dazzle and charm with their geniality and aristocratic flippancy.

* He was no kinder in his judgments of himself; from his home, he wrote a friend: 'My life here is as monotonous as usual, spent chiefly in eating, drinking, and sleeping, very much in fact, the life of a pig.' [Copy of a letter from T. H. Green to David Hanbury, 6 July, 1853, Balliol College Library.]

To his father, anxious for his son's first impressions, the schoolboy wrote:

> The insides of the colleges are strangely incongruous with the outside. The finest colleges are the most corrupt, the functionaries from the heads to the servants being wholly given to quiet dishonesty, and the undergraduates to sensual idleness. . . . I shall be happy there if I can work hard. But the temptations to idleness seem innumerable.[52]

If there were Oxford colleges that in fact corresponded to Green's description, Balliol was not among them. Indeed it was the centre of reform—University, theological and political. As for the difficulties of working there, Green's tutor was to be Benjamin Jowett.

CHAPTER THREE

BALLIOL AND JOWETT

THE COLLEGE GREEN ENTERED in 1855, although distinguished, had not yet entered that period of dazzling pre-eminence associated with Jowett's rule. Balliol had begun the century in none too spectacular a fashion. But gradually it developed the qualities requisite for success and was rewarded by a golden age when it swept all before it. By the 1830's, it had already demonstrated its willingness to reckon with the *Zeitgeist*, its capacity to merge noble birth with new wealth and ability. Its energetic tutors somehow taught aristocrats how to work, while not neglecting to instruct young men of the middle classes that they must take seriously those responsibilities imposed by their admission to the nation's leadership. Balliol's cautious radicalism, its liberal conscience which usually stopped short of social democracy, its taste for efficiency, and its didactic tone—all harmonised with the age. Indeed as the century went into its final quarter, and Jowett at last became Master, Balliol achieved a reputation which brought, and still brings to it, future potentates and notables from India, Japan, darkest Africa, and the United States, all in search of its secret (perhaps not unjustly connected in their minds with that of Empire). At the close of the Victorian Age, one-sixth of the Indian Civil Service was drawn from Balliol men, as were three consecutive Governor-Generals.[1] Not long before nine Oxford colleges in succession elected graduates of Balliol to head them.[2] In the Oxford Union Balliol again threatened to monopolise the Presidency. 'If we had a little more money,' said Jowett, 'we could absorb the University.'[3]

Members of other colleges could scarcely be blamed if they assumed that expansion for its own sake was the Balliol ideal. But its own members conceived of it otherwise. Jowett's successor, Edward Caird, declared the College to be a little Republic, the end of which, as in Plato, was the complete development of those human capacities worth realising. Within its walls flourished a

genuine community which 'binds together the social and intellectual life, and mingles work with pleasure. . . .'[4] One who knew
its joys just before the First World War, has recently written in
the same vein: 'I have sometimes thought that the life we led at
Balliol half a century ago was a pattern, in miniature, of what a
civilised western community ought to provide for us all'.[5] But
Balliol had another distinctive aspect, for as the same person
recalled, he was taught by A. L. Smith and A. D. Lindsay to
believe that Balliol existed, not only for Balliol men, but for the
country.[6] And this, in the view of these future Masters of the
College meant more than succeeding in the competition for power
in public life. It positively implied the duty to initiate reform for
the benefit of those disadvantaged by birth and poverty. This
current ran strong and was as significant a strand in Balliol's
tradition as Jowett's penchant for power and success. The first
great exponent of social conscience in the College was Green,
and A. L. Smith and the future Lord Lindsay had both taken his
gospel to heart.

Yet a corporate institution rarely owes its distinctive qualities
to a single person. It would be as misleading to attribute Balliol's
concern for social reform to Green alone, as it would be to give
Jowett exclusive credit for its meteoric rise in reputation and
influence. Indeed any study, however cursory, of modern Balliol
ought to begin by a consideration of the work done by two of
Jowett's predecessors: Dr Parsons in the period linking the end
of the eighteenth century with the beginning of the nineteenth,
and Dr Jenkyns from 1819 to 1854.[7] It was they who had
inaugurated those policies which were to be improved and fulfilled
by Jowett, first as tutor and then as Master.

Dr Jenkyns, a crusty Tory eccentric, nevertheless took the
unprecedented course of making individual merit, if not the
exclusive criterion of admission to College, at least that of award-
ing fellowships and scholarships.* When selecting candidates for
admission, Jenkyns favoured two types: those with high family

---

* The number of anecdotes circulated about Dr Jenkyns rivalled in number
those connected with Jowett. Edmund Warre, who took a First at the same time
as Green, claimed that the same stories he had originally heard about Parsons
and Jenkyns were later told about Jowett. No doubt, his biographer surmised,
they had first been attributed to Wyclif. [C. R. L. Fletcher, *Edmund Warre*
(London, 1922), p. 23.]

At the height of the Oxford Movement, W. G. Ward wrote a pamphlet
which caused some pain to the Master of Balliol. 'I wish that Mr Ward would
not write such pamphlets,' sighed Dr Jenkyns. And then in the same breath,
'I wish Mrs Jenkyns would take care of the flowers instead of the cabbages.'
(Mallet, *Oxford*, III, 269, 269 n.)

connections and those of marked personal ability. This second source of strength was tapped by competitive examination, a device so familiar today that it hardly seems plausible that the Victorians had to discover it in China. And yet Balliol was among the few Oxford colleges in the first half of the nineteenth century to use this method systematically. Elsewhere in the University, provisions unchanged for centuries awarded what should have been the recognition of scholarship or piety to persons who were donors' kin, or who happened to come from certain favoured localities or schools. Before the state forced change upon Oxford, out of 572 fellowships, only twenty-two were awarded by competitive examination.[8] At Christ Church, the Canons in rotation quite arbitrarily awarded sixty-one studentships which, although ostensibly granted for excellence, were more often sinecures. Balliol, long afflicted by an ancient provision favouring persons from Blundell's School and Tiverton in Devon, reformed itself in 1828 by throwing its scholarships open to competition.* Its success was unequivocal: between 1841 and 1850 Balliol won twenty-two first class degrees; Christ Church, more than twice its size, but still under the old régime, won thirteen. At one time All Souls had been chiefly recruited from Christ Church, while Balliol men rarely won prize fellowships there. But between 1844 and 1857 the number of those elected from Balliol was almost twice that from Christ Church. The moral was clear to see, and Jowett, along with certain others of his temperament, Broad Church and Liberal, had already begun a more general attack upon the organisation of the University as then constituted.

Their task was not to be easy, and to understand their difficulties, as well as those later encountered by Green, something must be said about the main lines of Oxford's history insofar as it is relevant to the story being told here. For Green's thought would not possess its distinguishing characteristics had he not spent his career at Oxford amidst the forces Cardinal Newman analysed: the alliance between reformers in politics, in university organisation, and in theology on the one side; and Toryism, High Church orthodoxy, and resistance to any change in the University on the other. It will soon be seen how Green was given his chance to make philosophy into an influential and autonomous field of study by the Broad Church party in the name of reason; it will become no less clear that Green's philosophical method, which is at the

---

* Dr Jenkyns is reported to have said to the future Archbishop of Canterbury, Frederick Temple, who was a Blundell Scholar, 'Coming up as you do, very *inferior* men, into the society of *very superior* men, some of you are improved by it, and some are not.' (Mallet, *Oxford*, III, 286-7.)

heart of his political theory, was fixed, some might say vitiated, by considerations essentially theological in nature. Although ostensibly welcoming the findings of science and history, Green sought to build his new foundations for belief on ground which could not be undermined by any empirical evidence whatever. The intellectual style he constructed was in part a rebellion against the Oxford modes of thought which he first learned as an undergraduate and then taught as a Balliol tutor; but in its teleological emphasis, its definition of political philosophy as essentially a moral study, he also reaffirmed the teaching of Aristotle and a kind of didacticism long associated with Oxford teaching. Like his master, Jowett, in the field of university organisation, the limits of Green's rebellion in philosophy were decisively fixed by his experience at Oxford. Anyone who spends his adult life in Oxford will be permanently marked by its contemporary controversies and the powerful traditions of its past.

2

'Oxford,' it has been said, 'likes the taste of old wine too well; is too fearful of losing some subtle unanalysed residual value, to throw it away.'⁹ Styles of thinking and ideals of human perfection have a way of persisting there despite the most profound changes in English politics and society, in the governance of Oxford itself, and in its teaching. Yet there is a danger, when emphasising this continuity, of passing over such innovation as has taken place. For more than a hundred years, the University has been pressed from both outside and inside to move faster than, left alone, it would have done. This has brought striking results, and Oxford today has travelled as far from what it was in Green's day, as the University, at his death in 1882, had progressed from the low point to which it had sunk in the eighteenth century. But the great modern University cannot concern us here, although it is still said that to be a reformer at Oxford is a frustrating occupation. And small wonder, if we consider, even as schematically as must be done, the principal lines of its development until the recent past: its emphasis upon a curriculum deliberately narrow in scope and centred on Aristotle; its identification, from the Renaissance on, of liberal education with that of a gentleman-amateur, proficient in Greek and Latin; the close ties linking the University to the centre of political power in London and to the governing class; the continuing significance of the Church; and its conservatism, which some might prefer to call piety.

In attempting to grasp the extraordinary continuity of Oxford's intellectual tradition from the time of its foundation until Green's time, it may be useful to recall the words of a great historian of political ideas, who, meditating upon his experience at both Oxford and Cambridge, 'those most noble and most equal sisters,'[10] had this to say about the *genius loci* of each: 'Oxford, as early as the thirteenth century, accepted the sovereignty of Aristotle and the authority of antiquity; it pursued a general and encyclopaedic wisdom, and it discovered the fountain of that wisdom in the past. Cambridge was later in finding a single acknowledged master; but that master, when he came, was one of its own sons, Isaac Newton, and he was a master of deep and ascertained knowledge in the one field of natural philosophy.'[11]

John Henry Newman, in the lectures he delivered on *The Idea of a University* long after he had left Oxford, proved how strong was its imprint by his remarks on Aristotle: 'While we are men, we cannot help, to a great extent, being Aristotelians, for the great Master does but analyse the thoughts, feelings, views, and opinions of human kind. . . . In many subject-matters, to think correctly, is to think like Aristotle; and we are his disciples whether we will or no, though we may not know it.'[12] These remarks delivered in 1852 at about the time Green entered Oxford indicate how persistent was Aristotle's influence. This had begun early. Like most universities founded in the middle ages, Oxford insisted that all students study for their BAs the trivium (grammar, logic and rhetoric) and the quadrivium (arithmetic, geometry, music and astronomy). The grammar was Latin, the universal language of educated men, and the key to further study as a Master. Rhetoric taught composition, and the arts of persuasion; logic, which in time came virtually to annex these two other fields, provided the means for argumentation and training in rigorous deductive thought: 'To analyse, to subdivide, to know the *pros* and *cons* of every argument, to be alert in disputation, in posing questions and in suggesting replies—these were the arts which appealed to teacher and scholar alike'.[13] Outstanding ability in disputation might open a brilliant career to the student; skill in debate and polished ease in presenting a case were highly prized. The undergraduate, forced to spend at least four years at his studies, had to master not only the seven arts but also the three philosophies: natural, moral and metaphysical. In each of these fields, as in so many of the arts, the established authority was Aristotle. Although most students terminated their work after they became BAs, some persevered for three more years in order to gain the Master's degree which would allow them to teach. Professional schools existed for the study of medicine, law and theology, long and difficult courses. For Doctors of Theology sixteen to nineteen years of training were not thought excessive.[14] But few chose to take the DD. Contrary to the usual impression, the university offered most men who became priests little religious training. Yet a high proportion of students did take orders. There was a tradition of service, for the mediaeval university took care to assure, in the language of an ancient prayer, 'that there may never be wanting a supply of persons duly qualified to serve God both in church and in state'.[15] But the feudal nobility with its own system of chivalric education almost never appeared at the universities.

Although Oxford was fundamentally changed during the sixteenth and seventeenth centuries, the study of Aristotle and stress upon logic remained. But Renaissance humanism taught Greek and rhetoric in a new style, and grammar, freed from its mediaeval subordination to logic, was increasingly studied through classical authors. Oxford, after it ceased to be controlled by the Roman Catholic Church, found that it had come under the closer scrutiny of the Crown. Archbishop Laud in 1636 completely revised and codified the mediaeval statutes of the University. The new science, although it found no place in the instruction prescribed by statute, nevertheless was often taught by college tutors to their students. The same was done with Machiavelli, Bodin and other political theorists.[16] During this period the social composition of the University was transformed. For the first time the nobility and gentry began to regard a university education as necessary and desirable. There arose a type, from this time on very influential, but hitherto unknown in the higher classes of society, the virtuoso or amateur gentleman of cultivation, 'a man for whom learning is the means to dispose of wealth or leisure in the happiest fashion—and with the comforting assurance that he may also be serving the desiderants of philosophy, history, or art'.[17] This ideal was to be one of the reasons why hereafter the British upper classes would scorn professional and scientific training. The Renaissance gentleman had a lasting effect on the definition of liberal education.

The eighteenth century is by common if not universal consent the nadir of Oxford's long existence. If the testimony of Gibbon, Adam Smith and Bentham is to be believed, Oxford in this period ought to be studied as a case of institutional atrophy, an example of how a university may become decadent, ceasing to perform its traditional functions without replacing them by any positive contributions. Outside its walls, momentous changes were recreating society and knowledge as well; but the industrial revolution produced no echoes in Oxford, nor did the scientific revolution, which had been so advanced by Englishmen outside the universities, receive any aid or recognition from the ancient foundation. The enlightenment failed to arouse it, Oxford slept on, Tory in politics, high and dry in theology. The University as such had virtually ceased to exist for, beginning in the Renaissance, power over both the course of study and finances had fallen into the hands of the college tutors, who provided instruction for all subjects wanted for the BA. As far as graduate instruction went, the situation had deteriorated considerably from that prevailing during the Middle Ages. Although the faculties of theology, medicine, and law still continued in name, and further professorships had been added at various times by the Crown and private benefactors, this aspect of Oxford was pitiable in its futility. Often professorships were treated as sinecures to be held along with one or more parishes by some clergyman who had political or ecclesiastical influence. Sometimes he did not even deliver his statutory lectures; if unusually conscientious, he would hire a substitute at a fraction of his own salary. Even when professors were qualified and serious, audiences were not easy to come by. As late as 1852, the Regius Professor of Medicine had to abandon his lectures after the number of his hearers dropped from ten to four. In any case, even after nineteenth century reforms, undergraduates could not have been more indifferent since they knew that their degrees in no way depended upon their attending professorial lectures. But most striking of all, undergraduates received their degrees without examination. The mediaeval procedures that were supposed to govern such matters had so fallen into neglect that some of their terms were no longer even understood. The tangle of precedents, regulations, and bequests defied description, for the statutes had last been completely revised during the reign of Charles 1. The colleges varied greatly in the resources and style of life available to their tutors. Even when colleges contemplated improvement, they were usually obliged to choose their scholars and fellows on the basis of considerations completely apart from merit. All college fellows, the faculty in practice, had to be celibate clergymen. The university was an Anglican preserve, which, by denying degrees to Dissenters, Roman Catholics and Jews, excluded much of the nation, and in particular the increasingly powerful middle class. Needless to say, Oxford students contemplated few careers outside the Church of England, public life, the University or the public schools, the bar, or that traditional aristocratic occupation designated by the Balliol College Register simply as 'landowner'.

58

Noblemen wore a special gold tassel on their caps until 1870; a class of poor students called servitors rendered at small cost menial duties to 'Gentleman Commoners'.[18]

Much of this picture holds true of nineteenth century Oxford as well. There were important reforms within, and in time these were reinforced by the Royal Commissions which, beginning in 1850, prompted Parliamentary revision of Oxford's statutes. But religious discriminations were not removed until 1870, and every change in the old order was bitterly resisted. There were many who opposed any intervention by Parliament, some no doubt to protect their interests and privileges, others because they believed that Oxford was well on the way to doing what had to be done, and would suffer more in the long run if the hand of the state were allowed to be laid upon the University.

What were the changes which could be cited as evidence of Oxford's spontaneous reformation? In 1800, the University for the first time produced a system of examinations mandatory upon everyone taking his BA, and provided as well the opportunity for exceptional students to receive honours, also by this previously unknown means of public and competitive trial of their abilities. But the spirit of innovation stopped here. This revolution in administration restored Aristotle's pre-eminence. This is worth noting not only as a further example of Oxford reliance on that author, but as an indication that the use of the word 'reform' still retained at this time its old meaning of restoring an institution to an earlier excellence by the removal of abuses. No one dreamed of improving the University by any radical addition or transformation, of raising it to a level unattained in the past. The subject remained what tradition had sanctified: grammar, rhetoric, logic, and rudimentary mathematics. The classics received their due in the emphasis placed upon knowledge of Latin and Greek; at least three authors from these languages had to be presented for sight translation. Some religious matter was also obligatory. This body of studies was known as *Literae Humaniores*, or 'Greats'. During the nineteenth century it was steadily expanded to include first ancient history, moral and political philosophy ('in so far as they may be drawn from the writers of antiquity'), and a paper in the history of philosophy.[19]

In the early nineteenth century, a School of Mathematics and Physics appeared, although its standard was low until the last quarter of the century. After such sweeping change, Oxford had to wait fifty years before the creation of a School of Natural Science and another of Law and Modern History. But no candidate could take any of these subjects without passing through *Literae*

Humaniores. Not until 1911 was the Greek requirement waived for those taking science or mathematics. On the whole the University improved in the first half of the nineteenth century. The intellectual life, especially of honours candidates, became more lively and industrious. For the 'pass men', a majority of the students, life at Oxford meant, in the words of a great social historian: 'much unscientific cricket and rowing, a fair amount of riding and hunting, occasional street fighting, some wenching, and much drinking'.[20] The same authority remarks of the best men produced by the reformed Greats School, that although none of them 'could have talked science with Prince Albert, many of them were competent scholars, several were excellent scholars, and the imprint of a thorough, if narrow, classical education is visible in Hansard whenever the speaker is Peel or Lord John Russell, Gladstone or Derby'.[21]

What were the consequences of the type of education provided by the Greats School? Whitehead has speculated that the schools and universities which gave such a training contributed much to both the failures and successes of nineteenth century England.[22] Science, technology, specialised learning of the kind perfected in Germany, all this was as unknown to this ruling class with its classical education as was modern competitive society and its problems. But they thought logically and saw clearly what they saw at all. Classical emphasis on moderation 'entered into our philosophy of statesmanship, sometimes reinforcing our natural stupidity, sometimes moderating our national arrogance'.[23] The landowners, the most successful men in business and commerce, and the professional men who made up the ruling group were educated, either by private tutors or at public schools and then passed on to Oxford or Cambridge. What they learned was based on the assumption that the classics were the one thing a gentleman ought to study. To the extent that a rational foundation existed for this course of study, it was argued that the world, human nature and politics were pretty much what they had always been. Whitehead's description of his own training in a small public school of the 1870's probably reflects the university training of his masters of the previous generation, 'a curious mixture of imaginative appeal and precise, detailed knowledge'.[24] There was no attention given to foreign languages; Latin and Greek did not fall into that category, but were simply the indispensable means for learning everything of importance that had ever been said. Ancient history was seen through the predispositions shared equally by Liberal schoolmasters, Tory parents and students. 'We did not want to explain the origin of anything. We wanted to read about people like ourselves, and to imbibe their ideals.'[25] Roman history stopped with the murder of Julius Caesar, because freedom ended at that time. But Athens was the ideal city. Not that Periclean Athens was exactly like mid-Victorian England; historical pedantry was not the issue. Rather the Athenian navy and the British navy were seen as the bastions of freedom. Russia in the nineteenth century looked rather like the Persia of Darius, and India was seen in terms of what the Greeks said about the barbarians. Of all this Whitehead concluded:

> 'Altogether we were a happy set of boys, receiving a deplorably narrow education to fit us for the modern world. But I will disclose one private conviction, based upon no confusing research, that, as a training in political imagination, the Harvard School of Politics and of Government cannot hold a candle to the old-fashioned English classical education. . . .'[26]

Whitehead's case for the type of education offered in the Greats School in part resembles the position taken by those inside Oxford who opposed Parliamentary reform of the University. Two arguments were employed by them: the first, a defence of *Literae Humaniores* as the best means of educating men into their *humanitas*, their true form, their essential human nature, was eloquently put by Newman in *The Idea of a University;* the second, was Dr Pusey's contention that the historic purpose of Oxford would be destroyed if it ceased to be an exclusively Anglican institution. In this respect, the High Churchmen applied to the issue of University reform the Oxford Movement's dominant principle: 'a passionate assertion that the Church must rule or society cease to be Christian'.[27] This lay behind Dr Pusey's conception of the University:

> 'The problem and special work of an University, is not how to advance science, not how to make discoveries, not to form new schools of mental philosophy, nor to invent new modes of analysis, not to produce works in Medicine, Jurisprudence or even Theology; but to form minds religiously, morally, intellectually, which shall discharge aright whatever duties God, in his Providence, shall appoint to them?[28]

The notion that truth has been discovered, and that its authoritative form is to be found in the teaching of the Church, has seldom been put more sternly than this. And the political overtones are conservative in the extreme. They were dangerously out of keeping with developments in the country. But none of this meant anything to Dr Pusey. To him it appeared that University reform was but an aspect of liberal theology, for was not Jowett the leader of both causes?

In the 1840's Oxford, so long protected from the reform movements of the century, began to feel pressure from outside, and the middle classes had an increasing power to make their demands met. Elated by the passage of the First Reform Bill and the repeal of the Corn Laws, they began to take notice of proposals that would open Oxford and Cambridge to more than the fraction for whom they had been reserved. Principles of liberalism, utilitarianism, science and specialisation were in the air. Since that liberalism was pledged to remove the disabilities imposed upon Dissenters, to uproot ancient privileges and aristocratic monopolies, it could be predicted that the exclusive position of the Anglican Church would not be maintained indefinitely. Within Oxford itself, a new group of men, often themselves the products of colleges such as Balliol which now chose fellows on the basis of merit, began to advocate changes. Jowett and his party argued that there was but one defence against wholesale change imposed from outside: Oxford must reform itself and thus anticipate more drastic criticism. The main issue in their view was precisely the same in university organisation as in the religious crisis. How could ancient institutions be adapted to those developments which over the last two centuries had transformed the nation and the state of man's knowledge? Insistence on maintaining antiquated forms would mean the loss of everything valuable in the essential spirit. If the relations of social classes in the nation had been considerably altered, if learning and science were no longer what they had been, if faith had to be defended on grounds other than those which were traditional, then Oxford must adjust itself to the new situation. But of course prudence prescribed that change must not go too fast or go too far. Jowett was most concerned to put the teaching of *Literae Humaniores* on an efficient basis. He was himself so much the product of it that he cared little about the natural sciences and development of specialised and advanced studies, nor did he favour any drastic change in the prevalent system which assigned primary responsibility for teaching to the colleges rather than to university professors, as on the Continent. Jowett was a man who could see up to a given point what ought to be changed in the institution which formed him, but who was not willing to go past that point. He set himself against the position taken up by his former partner in reform, Mark Pattison, who wrote in his *Suggestions on Academical Organisation*, published in 1868: 'There remains but one possible pattern on which a University, as an establishment for science, can be constructed, and that is the graduated Professoriate. This is sometimes called the German type. . . . What I wish to contend is, that the Professor of a modern University ought to regard himself primarily as a learner, and a teacher only secondarily. . . . But we must go further than this: . . . No teacher who is a teacher only, and not himself a daily student . . . can be competent to treat any of the higher parts of any moral or speculative science.'[29]

3

If the limits of Jowett's liberalism in University reform are relatively clear, the same cannot be said about his religious beliefs. What meant most to Jowett in Christianity, he thought could be expressed in modern language and in the terms of modern thought. For miracles, ritual and dogmatic theology he cared next to nothing. Like other Broad Churchmen he believed that the greatest danger to religion was to be found, not in reason or science, but rather in the possibility that intelligent and good men might reject what is true in Christianity because of the implausible form in which it was presented to them, because they were repelled by the ' . . . involution of self-deceit, the half-sincerity of hypocrisy, the almost animal form which religious emotion may sometimes take'.[30] His own positive beliefs were more difficult to determine.

Towards the end of his life Jowett wrote:

> Can there be prayer if the personality of God is no longer believed? I think so; prayer may be conceived as (1) communion with God; (2) recognition of the highest good within us; (3) intense resignation to law, i.e., to the will of God; (4) intense aspiration within the limits of our own powers.[31]

Although this was never published during his lifetime, such a statement was not far from what Jowett's critics took him to mean. What did he mean to say? Did it include or exclude the belief in the real personality of the Christian God? The place of grace in his theology, the meaningfulness of prayer, as understood by the Church, seemed vague indeed. Could a person who held Jowett's view honestly subscribe to the Thirty-nine Articles or take priest's orders? Of this last act, Jowett had written to Stanley that his ordination was 'not unpleasing, if you will resign yourself to being semi-humbugged by a semi-humbug'.[32] It was Sir Leslie Stephen's judgment that Jowett was intellectually dishonest. 'A Christianity without the supernatural, without doctrines, without immortality, and without a "personal God" seems to be merely an alias for morality.'[33] But Sir Geoffrey Faber nevertheless maintained that Jowett did believe in God as the divine governor of the world and the divine companion of mankind, beliefs which may have been simple but, for all that, were strong and unshakeable.[34] This claim will scarcely convince anyone who believes that religion involves at once a more precise statement and a more passionate set of concerns than those confessed by Jowett. Yet Sir Geoffrey's view was not altogether without foundation. It must be remembered that Jowett was better placed than his critics to observe the obstacles to belief encountered by young men. He thought that such difficulties ought not to be allowed to obscure what remained valid in religious experience as he understood it. Here is Jowett in a characteristic role, counselling a Balliol man at a time when his career hung in the balance. He is suggesting that his pupil consider the virtues his mentor recommended as part of essential religion:

> 'Your kindness leads you to think that I have done more for you than I have. I know, from long experience, that I can do hardly anything for others. But they can do much for themselves. . . .
> Eccentricity is a difficult thing to correct; we never see it ourselves, and persons familiar with us hardly observe it. It is often mistaken for character; but eccentricity is a mere blind weakness, character is strength. . . . Some would speak also of humility "not thinking of ourselves more highly than we ought to think" as the reverse of isolation, and "of casting all our care upon Him who careth for us" as the opposite of that anxious temper of mind in which ill-health often makes us indulge. I believe firmly in these things, and feel that I have need of them. If they ever occur to you, I would strongly urge you not to cast them aside as without meaning or profit, for sometimes (notwithstanding all the self-deception there is in the world about Religion) they may be the springs of a new life.'[36]

Jowett was an unusually complex figure, and it is no easy matter to sum up the man and his opinions, some of which altered a good deal between his years of adversity and his later position as an all-conquering celebrity. The one cause he never gave up was Balliol.* As Sir Leslie Stephen remarked, Jowett was one of the last and finest products of the old school of dons who took his college in place of a family and made it the object of his intense devotion.[37] In such a man the ancient obligation of celibacy was almost justified in its effects upon students and college alike, for such dedicated bachelors were certainly preferable to the other

---

* Even here Jowett thought in terms of practical effects. On one occasion he attempted to dissuade a young man from going into journalism: 'You are making a great mistake, Mr Steevens,' said the Master. 'No man leaves so deep a mark on human life as the man who is connected with a great organisation.' [David S. Cairns, *Life and Times of Alexander Robertson MacEwen, DD* (London, 1925), p.21.]

dominant type of don, the young clergyman who regarded his college fellowship as but a phase that had to be endured before marrying and acquiring a living.* Jowett took extraordinary pains with Balliol men, whether his students or not. He coached them for examinations and his rooms were open every evening to anyone who needed aid. But his rarest gift was surely his capacity to make undergraduates work. One of his students wrote in his journal:

> I have just come from . . . Jowett. . . . He gave me hope, blowing a trumpet-blast of determination. Such a man was never found, so great to inspire confidence and to rouse to efforts. . . . By a single word, with no argument but a slight appeal to the natural powers of most men, and a plea for work as work, he makes one feel that to be successful is the only thing short of dishonour.[38]

More than anyone else, Jowett was responsible for the steady stream of firsts produced by Balliol.

Success, success for his College, success for the undergraduates who would magnify its name outside Oxford—this called for knowledge of the ways of the world and the direction history was taking. If the fortunes of Balliol, of Oxford, of the nation and Christianity itself were to prosper, all must make accommodations to the spirit of the age. Long after Jowett became disillusioned with German thought in general and Hegel in particular, he never swerved from their 'moral futurism', the assumption that value attaches only to those individuals and causes which win out because they have accepted what are said to be the inevitable laws of history. Adherence to a losing cause, an unworldly character that insists upon principle, these were not admirable qualities in Jowett's eyes if accompanied by failure. Ineffectiveness was for him no mark of spiritual distinction. This doctrine he imposed upon many and diverse personages. Asquith and the Marquess of Lansdowne, the two great adversaries in the struggle between

* How the Jowett tradition persisted at Balliol can be illustrated by a story told about J. L. Strachan-Davidson (Fellow 1866-1907; Master 1907-16) by Dr Arnold J. Toynbee. Strachan-Davidson believed that a College Tutor could not serve the College effectively unless he lived in and was accessible all hours of the day and night. Because of this view he opposed marriage for his tutors. Dr Toynbee tells how extraordinarily difficult it was to announce his own engagement. But later, he heard that the Master had said that he hoped Toynbee and the other junior fellow (aged twenty-two and twenty-three) would be crossed in love. 'If tutors were crossed in love at an early age, they settled down and devoted themselves to the College. Benevolent though he was . . . I do not think it would have been possible to make him understand what an inhuman wish he had uttered. After that, I felt that we were quits.' (J. W. Mackail, *James Leigh Strachan-Davidson* [Oxford, 1925], pp. 56-59.)

the Liberal Party and the House of Lords in 1910, had both learned this lesson from Jowett.* Like him, Asquith could never understand 'how an intelligent man should not desire the capacity to influence events—the bigger the events the better'.[39] Jowett had found the future Marquess of Lansdowne as an undergraduate to be at once shy and indolent. For him to assume a distinguished place in life, he needed to acquire more force and a heightened sense of political reality. The correspondence between Jowett and the Lansdowne family reveals both the bracing and the corrupting elements of Jowett's creed. Although his protégé in this case just missed the highest honours available, the tutor had scored an essential point: from now on Lansdowne would see the great question of life as whether one was to be first, second, or third class. This was no small victory, for great aristocrats had not been accustomed to think in terms of merit and hard work. In this vein, Lord Lansdowne wrote his mother:

> I cannot help feeling that a very great prize has been almost within reach, and been missed by my own fault. It would have been such a great ending to my life here. . . . As it is I have a feeling that my career at Oxford has manqué. . . .
>
> I can't look at these sort of things from the point of view of those who, when they get their 2nd, pity the poor devils in the 3rd. . . .[40]

Jowett's letter stated the moral to be learned: Lansdowne could still make his first in life:

> I was very sorry about the Class List, both for your sake and Lady Lansdowne's, and also for the sake of Oxford and Balliol. . . .
>
> But I should be much more sorry if I thought that you were going to settle down 'second class' for life. Don't allow yourself to think this for a moment. You have certainly far greater ability than many First Classmen, and by good management, with your opportunities, you may make every year a progress on the one before.
>
> I want you to have objects and dreams of ambition and energy and industry enough to carry it out. A new era of politics is beginning and unless a man would be a cipher or a paradox, he should fit himself for it. Time will show him how to shape his course. . . . Knowledge of the world and of political subjects; reticence, self-control, freedom from personal feeling, are the qualities to be aimed at. I don't object to a touch of idealism or speculation also if kept in its proper place. But how few statesmen have these qualities in any degree?[41]

---

* The two men were not unaware of this. Lady Oxford recalled that, despite their political differences, they had a genuine affection for each other, as well as a devotion to Jowett's memory. 'Had it not been for him,' he [Lord Lansdowne] said, 'I would have done little with my life.' [Margot Oxford, *More Memories* (London, 1933), pp. 186-7.]

In this letter (unmentioned by Sir Geoffrey Faber), Jowett nowhere considers the possibility of applying Christian or ethical principles through politics. What he emphasises is pure technique. Surely this is curious advice for a clergyman to give a young man entrusted to his care.

Jowett usually concealed his manipulative attitude, but one day J. A. Symonds, when still quite young, heard and recorded a conversation on this theme between his own father and Jowett.[42] The Balliol tutor, as he was then, seemed to view his students as remarkably pliant raw material. It was his task to determine in each case what could be made out of the unsuspecting undergraduate, and then to convince him that his first duty in life was to work unceasingly towards the objective Jowett had decided upon. His achievements along these lines were already notable, but on occasion he encountered a young man who balked at the blueprint. Perhaps because he knew Jowett's method, Symonds himself rejected the directive prepared for his life's work: to be called to the Bar, to achieve an intellectual reputation by translating Zeller's *History of Philosophy*, to acquire a useful association with philanthropy by taking on volunteer hospital visiting, while all the time keeping his eye open for potential opportunities in politics.[43] In more than one sense a deviant from Balliol morality, Symonds in time rebelled, abandoned Zeller to two more obedient disciples of Jowett, and made his own mark by a prodigious number of literary and historical works, including the first extended treatment in English of the Italian Renaissance. Symonds married and lived in Switzerland with his wife and four daughters, but had another aspect to his character which led him to keep a Venetian gondolier as his personal servant. Yet Jowett never repudiated him; indeed Jowett came often to stay with the Symonds at their villa, Am Hof, at Davos. Campbell, Jowett's biographer commented on this. For the Master 'had a "horror naturalis" of sentimental feelings between men ("diabolical" I have heard him call them). . . . Nothing is more remarkable than his persistent attachment to J.A.S., though they differed so profoundly about this. . . .'[44] The relationship was indeed curious, for on the one side Symonds struggled for a long time to complete Zeller, his assigned task, and on the other Jowett could never bring himself to recognise that his old student no longer cared to be urged on. Once, the Master in an unusual moment of candour confessed to Symonds that his ambitions for himself and his former students had their origin in something more than the sane and cool wish that they make the most of themselves: ' . . . I have an insane desire to lift, if possible, myself and at any rate my old pupils, to a peg higher in their literary work, forgetting sometimes that the old relations no longer subsist between us.'[45]

This insight was not enough to restrain him from spurring on the man who thirty years before had been his charge. Long after Symonds, despite his bad health, had written enough to make the reputation of two men, Jowett went on in the same vein as before. In 1887, Symonds then having attained the age of forty-six, Jowett wrote:

> 'You have great stores of knowledge and a wonderful facility and grace of style. But I want you to write something stronger and better and in which the desire to get at the truth is more distinctly expressed. . . . Let me add, what I am equally convinced of, that you may not only "rise to eminence"—that is already accomplished—but that you have natural gifts which would place you among the first of English contemporary writers if you studied carefully how to use them.'[46]

Needless to say, Symonds was outraged, and he dashed off a furious letter to Jowett, which he described to a friend:

> 'Jowett writes *more suo* that I have reached "eminence"; but that now is the time to win a permanent place among the first writers of my generation . . . which I am still considerably far away from. His well-meaning exhortations reached me when I was half frantic with pain in the joints, wholly to bits in nerves, and terribly depressed by the sense of the difficulties under which I have to labour as author at Davos. So I exploded a fantastic firework of words on this *tema*: "Damn success! *A bas la gloire*! . . ." I don't know how he will have liked it. But I am an old panting cab-horse; and can't bear to be flogged up the last hill. . . .'[47]

The letter was never sent.

In what will probably remain the definitive biography of Jowett, the late Sir Geoffrey Faber was concerned to refute recurrent criticisms made by those unsympathetic to his subject. To those who found Jowett's concern with success repellent, Sir Geoffrey replied that they misrepresented the reasons for Jowett's emphasis upon work and worldly recognition. What Jowett found attractive in power was not the opportunity it offered for domination, but for self-realisation. What Jowett exalted to his students was 'power over self: power in a man to control and direct his own life, instead of drifting on the currents of fortune and self-indulgence'.[48] Thus the habit of strenuous work implanted by the Master was in fact a unique gift, and one which goes far towards explaining why he left so great a mark upon his students, his College and his country. What Sir Geoffrey wished above all to demonstrate was that Jowett was a great man. Certainly the Master was a most unusual man, but does it really matter very much how many points he compiled towards whatever hypothetical score would entitle him to be called 'great'? From at least one point of view, Jowett's attitudes are now most significant when considered, not as the subject of approval or censure, but as a final phase of that movement described by Max Weber in his study of the Protestant ethic and its dissolution into a secular asceticism. The emphasis upon hard labour as a duty, the importance of the will, the obligation to destroy all sensual impulse by methodical discipline, the investing of one's calling with religious sanctions—these were all aspects of Jowett's gospel of work.* He gave it a meaning with no moral or religious significance whatever. As Jowett phrased his teaching, it was a doctrine of self-realisation in which there was no discussion of what ought to be realised. Means thus became ends in themselves. Jowett's pronouncements on work invariably left open the question of what it was that he sought and convinced so many others to seek. About his own translation of Plato, he confides, 'The load of the book is a terrible burden to me. I suppose this world was meant for a place of work, and that we were meant to be at work in it.'[49] Or consider his praise when tasks were achieved and the stamp of success placed upon them: 'I congratulate you on having finished your *magnum opus*. . . . For the happiness of life is work, and you are able to do more than anyone else.'[50]

Was it that Jowett's life-long responsibility for undergraduates led him to accept the examination system and all other means of evaluation which brought general approval? After all he did not originate the rôle he played so well. Dr Jenkyns who had preceded him as Master had been described as 'an unfailing judge of a clever man, as a jockey might be of a horse'.[51] And Jowett's deification of success was but a symptom of a secularisation, a profound change in the College and the nation. From 1833-4 to 1844-5, nearly one half of Balliol BA's were ordained; in the next ten years, one in three; during Scott's mastership, one in five; under Jowett, one in ten; and in the 1890's, one in twenty-five.[52]

* Here is Jowett justifying his role: 'The greatest influence which is exerted over the mind and character is the personal influence of other men. . . . Most of us can trace the makings of ourselves to one or two persons, . . . who told us plainly of some flagrant defect in our behaviour, . . . who raised our standard of knowledge, . . . who made us feel the value of purity and unselfishness and sincerity in our daily walk. A word spoken in season, how good was it! They taught us to see ourselves as others see us; they dispelled our nervous fancies. . . . These were the true friends of our youth. . . .' Where were these words spoken? In a sermon on John Wesley. (*Benjamin Jowett, Sermons*, Biographical, p. 108).

Of all the judgments on Jowett's personal character, none exceeded in balance and justice the verdict of J. A. Symonds' daughter, Margaret. She remarked that the Master ' . . . loved my Father for himself, but he certainly loved him better for being successful in his work'.[53] But she also refers to the opinion of the cultivated Swiss governess of the Symonds who knew Jowett for many years, had talked with him, and been with him during grave illness:

> 'The thing I shall always remember about him was his great kindness to other people, and his gratitude for any kindness shown towards himself.'[54]

This would seem to belie that sadistic image so celebrated in anecdote of the punishing silences by which the Master terrorised the young.* Margaret Vaughan, however, suggested that Jowett behaved quite differently in his public and private rôles:

> 'As girls we were extremely devoted to him—we were indeed his slaves. I fancy that it was young men, and older and more worldly people who became his critics, and as a matter of fact I believe that Mr Jowett had one set of rules for men and quite another for women. If he was tolerant of women—if he loved them for their charm, their brilliancy or loveableness, ignoring something of their want of concentrated thought and training; . . .—he was completely different in his attitude towards young men. Of young men he seemed to ask and expect nothing but hard work and ceaseless effort; and marked and almost awful was the manner of his aloofness if a stray undergraduate appeared upon the scene. The Master would then stiffen into a completely different person, and leaving the alluring manner of a soft and fluffy owl, he could assume that of a prickly porcupine; and he would snub the stammering questions of some unhappy young man by complete silence or swift rebuke. To walk as bodkin between him and an undergraduate for an afternoon, as it once was the miserable destiny of one of my sisters to do, was a nightmare. Her account of it remains with me for ever.'[55]

Jowett's worldliness, even in his old age, should not be allowed to obscure his other qualities. In the 1840's and 1850's, he was no opportunist, for again and again he had endangered his career by the causes he championed. Much later both John Nichol and Green used to say to critics, 'Ah, you never knew Jowett in his prime, when he was fighting the world'.[56] As a young man, he was an

---

* This is a description of Jowett at breakfast with his undergraduates: 'Here they met stiff, awkward, shy, from their very reverence for Jowett. He sat, sipped tea, ate little, stared vacantly. Few spoke. The toast was heard crumbling under desperate jaws of youths exasperated by their helplessness and silence.' (Brown, *Symonds*, p. 132.)

important figure in the movement to reform the civil service, so as to put it on the basis of merit. The same was true of University reform. And he was one of the very few dons at Oxford who could read German and knew Kant and Hegel at first hand, who had intimately acquainted himself with the momentous discoveries of the historical school, its new methods in philology and the higher criticism of the Bible. By calling attention to these developments, Jowett helped break down Oxford's insularity. It was largely due to Jowett's lectures and translations that Plato began to be studied seriously. Jowett was not himself a great classicist, judged by German and Cambridge standards, or for that matter, Oxford standards by the time he died in 1893. And he was to tire of Hegel, dismissing that august figure with the remark that like most German philosophers, anything which came into his head was straightaway elevated into a law of thought.[57] But earlier Jowett had encouraged Green and others to make their way through the German theologians as well as going directly to the texts of the philosophical idealists. Such first-hand knowledge provided a new standard of philosophical scholarship, for most educated Englishmen accepted the versions of German thought which derived from Coleridge and Carlyle, neither of whom had in fact mastered the German philosophers whose works they claimed to admire.

At the time when Green was about to come up to Balliol, his future tutor was entering a period of trials. In 1854 when old Dr Jenkyns died, Jowett anticipated that he would become Master of Balliol, the post he coveted above any other. But even in his own college, his theological views were suspect and Dr Scott (of the Liddell and Scott Greek lexicon) was elected instead. The very next year, the Whig Government, which controlled nominations to the Regius Professorships, named Jowett Professor of Greek. Green was a freshman when Jowett published a two volume work on the Pauline Epistles which vigorously attacked the doctrine of the Atonement. Jowett found himself summoned before the Vice-Chancellor of the University on the charge of heresy. To keep his place, he had to subscribe again to the Thirty-nine Articles, a humiliation in which his enemies rejoiced. Moreover, his foes were able to deny him his salary as Professor of Greek. Then in 1860 Jowett took the lead in publishing *Essays and Reviews*, a volume by seven authors, which became one of the *causes célèbres* of the period along with the works of Darwin and Bishop Colenso. Jowett's own essay 'On the Interpretation of Scripture' argued that the Bible must be interpreted like any other book, if it is to be understood properly. A storm of protest from the orthodox greeted this volume. Another attempt was made to condemn Jowett for 'infringing the Statutes and privileges of the University' by publishing 'strange and erroneous doctrines'. Eventually the proceedings collapsed, and in time Jowett was able to obtain his pay as Regius Professor. But for many years after, devout families, such as R. B. Haldane's, refused to send their sons to the college of the 'arch-heretic'.*

Jowett at this time was more disposed to encourage the eccentric and nonconforming than he ever would again. Sometimes he even doubted whether he had not erred in his decision to stay in Oxford. Walking one day with an undergraduate with whom he was discussing the University, the need to reform it and the entrenched resistance to change, Jowett suddenly throwing down his walking stick to the ground, exclaimed, 'I hate the place'.[58] But, as he later wrote the same man, any one who chooses to be unconventional because of his principles, must not expect life to be sweet and pleasant. Here is Jowett at his most attractive:

'You and I are in the same difficulty. We can look for no external help, but must fashion our lives for ourselves, and that ought to unite us. If opportunities don't come, we must look at life calmly, and make them. It is no use complaining of having public opinion against us. We have challenged that, although perhaps undesignedly, and now we must fight it out, and make a place for ourselves. . . .'[59]

With such counsel, Green was later to be brought out of his isolation, and rallied to constructive causes.

4

The grave freshman who arrived at Balliol in Trinity Term, 1855, at first created a not altogether favourable impression. Even to those destined to become life-long friends, he seemed to have rather more than his share of Evangelical seriousness and the 'earnest' quality associated with Rugby. 'Maturity, ripeness, almost over-ripeness,' went one judgment.[60] 'Excessively austere,' commented his future brother-in-law,† 'expecting from others no

* Jowett did not much favour conspicuous changes of allegiance. A Scot who had begun to think of becoming a communicant of the Church of England made this known to the Master with the following result: 'Jowett sent for me one day, and after staring into the fire for an unusually long time, turned his blinking eyes full upon me and said, "A man is most likely to be useful in the Church in which he was brought up in".' [Cairns, Life . . . of . . . MacEwen, p. 48.]

† Symonds never forgot, although he forgave, an episode on a reading party: 'Conington and Green were conversing in the paved kitchen . . . and perhaps they were not conscious of my presence. . . . Conington said—"Barnes will not

less than himself an ascetic rule of life and speaking with . . .
scorn of what was alien to his own conception of manly, sober
citizenship.'[61] His penchant for plain-speaking became all too
well-known. A. V. Dicey, glowing after winning a university
prize, was suddenly cut down by Green's dictum that such
pleasures never last long. On another occasion when Dicey had
become worried about forthcoming examinations, he was told by
Green that no one who devoted so much time to the debates of
the Oxford Union could expect first class honours.[62] Such a
manner did not make great numbers of friends. For sports Green
cared nothing, and as a matter of principle he would not drink
anything stronger than coffee. Such eccentric virtue marked him
out, and the future Lord Bryce records that the first time he found
himself seated next to Green, he felt awe not unmixed with alarm.[63]

But no one who knew Green at all well would have thought of
calling him a prig. Not only was his external grimness compatible
with a redeeming sense of humour, but he could not resist telling
an anecdote, even if it involved, as his brother-in-law put it, 'a
point of gross nature'. Symonds went on to describe 'the impression of his vigour, humour, health of soul and gentleness combined
with rough, masculine force. He had a quite inimitable way of
telling racy stories'.[64] A school friend remarked that with unusual
speed the boy, half-unnoticed at Rugby, became at Balliol a 'broad
and genial man'.[65] There was general agreement about the quality
of Green's mind. 'You never talked to him without carrying away
something to remember and ponder over.'[66] Yet it seemed highly
unlikely that he would accommodate himself to university life
any better than he had done to Rugby. The classical philology
that bulked so large in the Greats curriculum bored him. In his
first trial by examination, he failed to distinguish himself. Absorbed
in his efforts to articulate views unusually personal and deeply
felt, he was notorious for puzzling on Monday over essays that
had been due the previous Friday. None of this augured well for a
successful university career. And yet the class of degree achieved
by a poor clergyman's son might fix the course of his future life.
With First Class Honours doors would be opened to him, beyond
which he otherwise could not hope to penetrate. Left to himself,
Green's character might have manifested itself in a mediocre

---

get his First." (They called me Barnes then and I liked the name because they
chose it.) "No," said Green, "I do not think he has any chance of doing so."
Then they proceeded to speak about my aesthetical and literary qualities, and
the languor of my temperament. . . . Though I cared little enough for first-
classes, I then and there resolved that I would win the best first of my year.'
(Brown, *J. A. Symonds*, p. 80.)

record which would have condemned him to eking out an existence as a schoolmaster, or to burying himself in an obscure government post. But Green fortunately profited from the ministrations of his tutor, that Pascal of the undergraduate heart.

Jowett saw something worth stimulating in this gauche freshman. No doubt Green shared the experience of a close friend who reported home: 'Jowett is, I think, the best of them all; certainly the wisest. He took me today to some broad meadow on the eastern side of the town, and tried to find out what I was; found out a good deal not much to his satisfaction, and told me a great deal of truth.'[67] What did Jowett find in Green? As he said many years later, the only person in his experience who at all resembled this singular young man was another Rugbeian who had entered Balliol twenty years before, Arthur Hugh Clough. Of course the two men were not exactly alike. Green's mind was far more abstract. Clough had been formed by Dr Arnold personally; Green had been left alone at Rugby to read by himself. Clough had been at once 'more poetical and more indolently dreamy than Green'. (To which Dicey noted in his journal, 'If this is true, Clough must have been oppressed by a large amount of "Schwärmerei" for Green's most patent peculiarity is a special kind of indolence. No man is driven with greater difficulty to work not to his taste.')[69] But in other respects, Clough and Green were associated in Jowett's mind. Reserved and self-contained, they moved in a detached sphere of almost inhumanly high principle. Society and politics were to them intimate realities, the great problems of which it had fallen to them personally to resolve.

Jowett, a life-long correspondent of Clough, believed that the older Rugbeian's career had been blighted by his high-minded unworldliness. First it had led to a Second in Greats despite the fact that Clough had one of the best minds of his day, and this failure had been but partially redeemed in Balliol eyes by his later election to an Oriel fellowship. And then for reasons of conscience that had seemed absurd to the Broad Church Jowett, Clough had resigned his fellowship and botched his career, first going to America and then returning to take up an insignificant post in the Education Office. About the time that Green was recalling the older Rugbeian to Jowett's mind, Clough was acting as a kind of factotum to Florence Nightingale, for whom he wrote notes, delivered letters, and wrapped endless parcels in brown paper. Much as Jowett admired Dr Arnold, who had trained Clough, and Florence Nightingale, who exacted from him 'the work of a cab-horse', he was determined that none of *his* students should be permitted to make a similar mess of life.[70]

74

If Green were to be made to work, add to the College's glory, and be guided to a place appropriate to his abilities, Jowett would have to gain his full confidence. Clearly this could not be achieved by the same strategy that had enticed Lord Lansdowne. Visions of power did not attract Green, nor was there in his case any need to combat luxurious habits or aristocratic friends. Instead Jowett conquered Green by treating him from the very beginning as an intellectual equal. 'My tutor is most kind to me, and I like him exceedingly,' wrote Green to his father during his first term. 'I breakfast with him occasionally, when he talks to me freely, and not the commonplaces which such men generally do to their pupils.'[71] As the older man came to know his student better, he diagnosed his inability to apply himself. Temperamentally and physiologically lethargic, Green also suffered from more than usual difficulties in making himself understood. Thus he was apt to be rated far below his real abilities. In addition, his independence led him to scorn academic prizes indispensable to his success.

Jowett decided that it was only through his Puritan sense of duty that Green could be made to work. And so particularly after Green disappointed his friends and family by his Second in Moderations, his tutor began to prod. Green's essays, he remarked were much too dry and dull, a fault which might be repaired by reading poetry. But Jowett's major stroke was yet to come. One day he said casually: 'If you do not get your First, Green, *I* shall have a good deal to answer for'.[72] This remark Green later recalled as the turning-point of his life. Knowing how much the prestige of the College meant to his tutor, Green's sense of duty was called into play: the gospel of work taught by Carlyle, Dr Arnold and Jowett had now to be applied to himself and his condition. And so he plunged into the task ahead.

To cope successfully with the Greats examination schools, systematic cramming was necessary. As did most students going in seriously for the highest honours, Green took on a private coach, C. S. Parker. By a happy chance, tutor and student got on, and Green settled down to the stern routine of a 'reading man'. Parker, grasping that Green's interest in philosophy was essentially religious, used this as a means of enlivening the set authors. It was to Jowett, Parker, and the University Professor of Latin, John Conington, that Green credited his subsequent transformation. 'But for their constantly stirring me up, I should have sunk into permanent lethargy.'[73]

Conington was an oddity at Oxford, as much for his political opinions, as for the circle of undergraduates he collected around him, choosing them on the basis of their intellectual qualities, although not exclusively so.* Himself a product of Rugby, he had the reputation of being an extreme radical. In the revolutionary year of 1848, he had been accused of nothing less than wearing trousers cut on a Christian Socialist pattern. At that time, he ardently championed the Chartists in particular and the working classes in general, loyalties alleged by senior common-room wits, to have been based upon a rash generalisation from his college servant. It may have been Conington's influence which led Green to view with such hostility the formation of a University volunteer rifle corps: 'Fools talk at Oxford of its being desirable, in order that the gentry may keep down the Chartists in the possible contingency of a rising. I should like to learn the use of the arm that I might be able to desert to the people, if it came to such a pass.'[74] As for University reform, Conington proposed nothing less than the abolition of the Colleges and a fresh start.

As though such heresies were not enough to distinguish him, he was a picturesquely eccentric and quaintly methodical man, known as the 'sick vulture' because of his appearance. Conington's 'extraordinary visage, with its green-cheese hue, gleaming spectacles, quivering protrusive lips might be encountered every day at 2 o'clock on his way to a constitutional which, he would have liked, he said, to conduct between two high walls shutting out all irrelevant topics such as surroundings and scenery might suggest'.[75] His companions were undergraduates who had passed a trying set of tests:

> First came the invitation to breakfast; then if the undergraduate pleased him, an invitation to walk: then more breakfasts and more walks: then, if the young man had survived this ordeal . . . perhaps an invitation to join a reading party in the Long. The final stage of intimacy was the fixing of a particular day in the week to walk with a particular man. To this last both Green and I at length attained, Green's day being Monday and mine Wednesday.[76]

Conington had a serious side and a deep culture. What especially attracted Green to him was their common interest in metaphysics, derived perhaps from their religious background. 'Both

---

* Symonds, like Green, was one of Conington's favourites, although perhaps not for the same reasons. Symonds wrote: 'The association with Conington was almost wholly good. It is true that I sat up till midnight with him nearly every evening drinking cup after cup of strong tea. . . . This excited and fatigued my nerves. But his conversation was itself a liberal education. . . .' (Brown, *J. A. Symonds*, p. 70.) Jowett seems to have thought that Conington corrupted at least one student. (Faber, *Jowett*, p.90.) As for Green, 'he thought it a weakness in Conington to be so dependent on the friendship of young men—a man must stand alone and be selbst-ständig.' (MS letter from J. A. Symonds to Mrs Green, postmarked 10 October, 1882, Balliol College Library.)

moreover had been nursed in the Evangelical form of Christian piety, and their religious views therefore from early life probably took the same tone.'[77]

Every summer Conington led a 'reading party', a peculiarly Oxford compound of country holiday combined with concerted study under the direction of a College tutor. For four years Green spent his long vacations in this way: digesting what he had heard and read during term time, discussing his own theories, helping others in the subjects he knew most about, and being helped by them in their specialities. Symonds wrote home that he was being coached in Plato by Green, who knew an immense amount about Greek, as well as modern, systems. However, he was so original a thinker, that he did not express himself as clearly as a beginner might have liked. Nevertheless the members of Conington's reading parties had little to complain about. The quality of the conversation was high, and when mind flagged, there were always walks amidst striking scenery to revive the hard-working. With such friends and natural surroundings, Green began to expand. Some of his censoriousness left him, and he became increasingly genial. He thrived in the countryside, and particularly among hills and mountains, where his Wordsworthian God seemed near.

There was another reason for his happiness when well away from Oxford. With country people he felt none of the barriers which impeded his relationships with public school men of the conventional kind. Green was among those few English thinkers of his time who held a mystical belief in the capacities of all men, including the working classes. Not only did he believe that the entire adult population should be encouraged to develop and express its opinions, but he also maintained that the views thus obtained would be generally superior to the alleged wisdom of the ruling class as found in the foreign policy of Palmerston or Lord John Russell. Further and better education was badly needed, but its proper goal should be preparation for full citizenship and the elimination of that snobbery which he felt blighted British life. He was prepared to argue that national prestige mattered much less than the standard of living of the labouring classes. And this concern set him apart even from most others who considered themselves radicals. For many such, although quite prepared to denounce aristocratic landowners, were themselves Malthusians and strict devotees of orthodox political economy. Of this pervasive viewpoint, Green was not altogether free, as a later discussion of his theories of philanthropy and property will show. But it was more than outbalanced by the faith he confessed in man's 'elemental reason, in virtue of which man is properly a law to himself'.[78]

Later in his career, he sought to establish that the spiritual origin of modern democracy is to be found in the disdained religious mystics, and even the Levellers of the Commonwealth. Western democracy, in his view, was religious in its beginnings. This was perhaps the beginning of what might be called the Balliol theory of the Commonwealth.

Green had a grave confidence in labourers and common men, and his disapproval of upper-class manners later led him to use the term 'diner-out' as a synonym for *débauché*, and 'club life' as a shorthand description of everything calloused and ignorant in aristocratic circles.* Something of this sturdy republican virtue is to be seen in a striking group photograph of the Old Mortality.[79] In it Green stands short, upright, looking resolutely ahead over another young man. His neighbour was Swinburne of whom more will be said below. This portrait of Green as an undergraduate reveals that already he bore the distinctive appearance by which he would be remembered after his premature death in 1882. A solid man with massive head and thick black hair, his heavy dark eyebrows accented eyes which gave the impression of unusual steadiness and quiet strength. His characteristic expression was one of slight fatigue, attributed by friends to consistently strenuous thought, and by those less than friends to excessive concern with the cares of the world. At no stage of life did he communicate with facility, and never in lectures, tutorials, conversation, or writing was Green what Lord Melbourne would have called an 'easy man'.[80] Yet his personal severity concealed a kindness, which if undemonstrative, seldom failed when called upon. Later in his career, it was often remarked that he gave himself no airs. Curiously down to earth for an Idealist in philosophy and a reformer in politics, he insisted upon taking men as he found them. He was to win the respect of even the most cynical of his associates by his patience and thoroughness in mastering the hard details of college business and local politics. In day-to-day life his reticence concealed the depth of his moral commitments, and his manner was deceptively businesslike and even casual. Counting his words, he spoke rarely, and then only on matters he knew after long study. What he said was apt to carry unusual, even overpowering weight. On but a few occasions

---

* A similar judgment was made by a fellow member of the Old Mortality Society: 'How dangerous is the luxury of the Club life and society of London! It most surely saps a high degree of virtue. I like to dine now and then in a Common Room—a much simpler place of luxury—but I would not dine there often. Dinner parties are, I am sure, great enemies to simple virtue.' (Lucy Crump. [ed.], *Letters of George Birkbeck Hill* [London, 1906], p. 176.)

was he ever to express his most personal beliefs, as distinguished from the purely intellectual statement of his position. The reader who wishes to seek out this aspect of the man will find it in his two lay sermons, a few scattered and quite exceptional passages in his philosophical lectures, and some political speeches he delivered with a deliberate Puritan violence that recalls his much admired model, John Bright.

When Mrs Ward needed a pseudonym for Green in *Robert Elsmere*, she chose to call him Professor Grey, surely echoing that portrait sketched by one of his oldest acquaintances:

> 'His habitual dress of black and grey suited him well and was true to his character. He was drawn to plain people, to people of the middle and lower class rather than to the upper, to the puritans of the past and the nonconformists of the present, to Germans, to all that is sober-suited and steady-going. One judged from his feeling for homely, unadorned and solid worth what he must feel for things showy, brilliant and hollow.'[81]

As for his clothes, a student remarked that Green was so careless about them that in anyone else it would have seemed an affectation. A farmer he knew near his home in Yorkshire was at first a little in awe of him when Green returned home upon his election some years later as Fellow of Balliol. Looking over the curate's son as they went through the farm, the old man stopped in the midst of a ploughed field and exclaimed: 'Why, Tom, you're not a bit like one of those scholar fellows. You look like a cattle-dealer'.[82]

Clearly Green's character was altogether distinctive and cannot be explained away simply as the result of exposure to Rugby and Balliol. Yet he grew a good deal in the exciting and embattled atmosphere of Oxford. He came to be identified as the leader of a numerically small but intellectually distinguished faction. With his friends, he attended the lectures of Matthew Arnold, the celebrated debate between Huxley and Wilberforce, and the sermons preached by men of all clerical parties. He predicted the storm which would be aroused by *Essays and Reviews;* he loyally stood by Jowett when it came. For the first time in his life, he found listeners sympathetic enough to give him a fair hearing, and intelligent enough to stimulate him to further thought by their objections. Invited to select breakfasts by members of his circle, he was a centre of interest whenever he chose to speak.*

---

* 'Yesterday I had a very intellectual breakfast: Conington, Rutson, Green, Tollemache, Dicey, Lyulph Stanley and Puller. I find these breakfasts formidable things; for there is a succession of meats, all of which I have to dispense, to change plates and keep people going with fresh forks and knives, etc. It is not the custom for any scout to be in attendance, so that the host has to do all

Needless to say, this was not the case on the occasions when he summoned the courage to take the floor of the Oxford Union, that training ground for future politicians. The truth was that he had to struggle with himself on such occasions. For he was a bad speaker, and his views impressed his audience as audaciously radical. He was hooted and interrupted. Once in the face of frantic opposition, he presumed to propose a motion supporting the Tories' *bête noire*, John Bright. The ensuing debate lasted two days, at the end of which time, the vote revealed Green to have convinced one other member. From this disapproval he found refuge in the Old Mortality Society, which included some of the ablest men of his day: Bryce, Dicey, Swinburne, Walter Pater, Symonds, Edward Caird, Ingram Bywater, and T. E. Holland.[83] Although not as secret or influential as the 'Apostles' at Cambridge, the Old Mortality and its publication, *Undergraduate Papers*, holds a small but secure place in the history of mid-Victorian letters and thought.

The founder of the Old Mortality was John Nichol, a Snell Scholar, from Glasgow, and although but a few years older than his English friends, much more worldly and confident than they. Not only was the Scottish University much less protective than the English public school, but Nichol already could count himself a friend of Kossuth and Mazzini, and an acquaintance of John Stuart Mill and Carlyle. He was already interested in German thought before his arrival at Balliol. More than anyone else he was responsible for the tone of the Old Mortality: philosophical, radical, even republican. There were no aristocrats among the members. In some circles they were known as 'a revolutionary set, and read Browning'.[84] Prominent among their number was Swinburne, never ordinary either in his appearance or behaviour. He had come to Balliol from Eton with a curious combination of republican ideas derived from his grandfather, and an inclination towards High Church ritualism which soon disappeared under the influence of Nichol. Swinburne was tiny, with a large head crowned by flaming red hair. He had broad eyebrows and fine eyes; his weak chin was not yet hidden by the scraggly beard he later developed. At first ignored at Balliol, almost his first friend was Green, with whom he would often go on the country walks

---

the menial offices. You would be amused to see these intellectual men begin with fried soles and sauces, proceed to a cutlet, then taste a few sausages or some savoury omelette, and then finish up with buttered toast and marmalade. Up to the sweet finale coffee is the beverage; and tea, coming when hunger has abated, prolongs breakfast.' (J. A. Symonds to his sister Charlotte, 11 March, 1860. [Brown, *Symonds*, p. 72.])

of which they were both fond. It was their political views which brought them together, and Nichol spurred both of them to support his favourite causes: the abolition of all University tests, the supreme merit of national self-determination as a principle and frantic opposition to the régime of Louis Napoleon. Under Nichol's influence, Swinburne placed in his rooms portraits, first of Mazzini, and then of Orsini, the Carbonaro who attempted unsuccessfully to assassinate Louis Napoleon. Before these icons, Swinburne declaimed revolutionary verse and made extravagant supplications. Green, rather self-consciously, followed him in these rites.[85] Other members of the Society judged such enthusiasm about foreigners to be merely foolish. But Green wrote his father that the Emperor of France was no better than a successful brigand, and *Undergraduate Papers* announced a Union Debate on the topic: 'That this country is bound to protest, under present circumstances, any alteration in the Laws relating to Refugees or Conspiracy'.[86] It was Green who had brought forward the motion condemning the Conspiracy Bill, the prospect of which almost kept him from eating. Some years later, Green felt called upon to defend Mazzini in the Union. Swinburne, meanwhile, danced around the table in his rooms, screamed abuse and advocated the murder of the Emperor. Long after, when Jowett was Master of Balliol, he turned to Swinburne at a dinner party and jocularly accused him of having advocated regicide when a member of the Old Mortality. Swinburne turned grave. 'There was not one of us,' he replied, 'who would have questioned for a moment that sacred duty.'[87]

Although Green acquiesced in much of the youthful exuberance of the Old Mortality, he was not swept away by its romantic preoccupation with national revolutions abroad. His political judgment was already surprisingly informed and responsible. What concerned him most was the condition of the working class in England, and his knowledge may well have been developed from his frequent visits to Leicester, where his uncle, the Reverend David Vaughan was well-placed to see what the Industrial Revolution was doing to so many lives. Not many of his fellow students at Oxford, even those of the Old Mortality, knew or cared. Dicey, in a passage written in a tone rather different from that he adopted later in his attacks on 'collectivism', recalled how advanced he found Green's views in the late 1850's and early 60's:

He [Green] was as enthusiastic as we all were about Italian freedom, but objected to every scheme of intervention. . . . What makes me especially note this is, that the more I think the matter over, the more I am struck with the fact of his having when so young thought so much more than most of us about the state of the poorer classes and the necessity of making their material and moral welfare a main object of politics. . . . At a time when we were thinking of what one may call romantic politics, he kept constantly pointing out to us the evil of pauperism. I suppose that both his sympathies and his power of imagination led him to realise much more clearly than most of us the actual sufferings of the poor. I never knew any man who so constantly had their position before his mind. This certainly was the case when he was hardly grown up.[88]

Already Green was a devotee of the great political meetings connected with radical and reforming agitations. He thought nothing of travelling to London to be present on such occasions, and at least once he organised an expedition to Birmingham to hear Bright. This constituted the introduction to actual politics for Dicey and Bryce.

Bryce had an intimate relationship to Green, indeed Mrs Green long after her husband's death, wrote, 'You knew and understood him in many ways better than anyone else'.[89] Bryce was Secretary of the Old Mortality, and most energetic in hunting down members to deliver essays. As a joke, Green used to avoid him for this reason. It was most difficult to get Green to perform despite the congenial atmosphere of the society. What was it like? Its members subsequently fell into rhetoric when they recalled those days. From the usually reserved Edward Caird, there came these words: 'The free discussion of everything in heaven or earth, the fresh enjoyment of intellectual sympathy, the fearless intercommunion of spirits, the youthful faith that the key of truth lies very near to our hands, give a unique zest and charm to those meetings of students with students, before the inevitable parting of the ways of manhood has come.'[90] Others remembered the extravagance of Nichol, modelling himself on Carlyle. Swinburne occasioned a wondering letter home from Hill, who spoke of the poet as 'the most enthusiastic fellow I ever met, and one of the cleverest'.[91] It was said of Walter Pater that 'his speculative imagination seemed to make the lights burn blue. T. H. Green preached Hegel, with the accent of a Puritan. And what solemnity of authority could resist the edge of Dicey's epigram.'[92] The papers read were almost invariably grave: Nichol delivered essays on Hume's 'Essay in Defence of Suicide', Wycliffe as a reformer, and 'The danger of unduly exalting Strength and Success, with particular reference to the tone of feeling pervading Carlyle's History of Prussia'. Green himself contributed essays on 'National Life', 'Political Idealism,' and an essay on the development of Christian dogma. From much of this Swinburne was already estranged. Much later Green used to tell how on the occasion of giving his theological paper, he 'happened to look up once from his paper, and nearly burst out laughing at the sight of Swinburne, whose face wore an expression compounded out of unutterable ennui and naïf astonishment that men whom he respected could take interest in such a subject'.[93]

The society developed its own set of favourites in the arts, as in politics. Tennyson, then Laureate, was valued far below Browning; Matthew Arnold, appointed Professor of Poetry at Oxford, disappointed the Old Mortality by his lectures. The very first issue of *Undergraduate Papers* contained an attack upon 'Modern Hellenism', written by Nichol. As in a good many other such groups, a certain cliquishness developed and Jowett duly warned its members that their characters might suffer if they did not expand their friendships beyond its circle. Not surprisingly, the Society developed little rituals and taboos. At the meetings, perhaps out of deference to Green's views on drink, only coffee was served (although apparently on other occasions, Nichol led Swinburne to begin drinking heavy quantities of brandy).[94] Every year the members made an excursion, one year to Godstow, another to Edgehill. In 1859, Swinburne, being confined to College for disciplinary reasons, could not come along. Upon the return of the other members, they went as a body to Swinburne's rooms, where he regaled them with a magnificent display of invective, for which he had a genuine gift. It seems that the Old Mortality ceased to meet in the 1860's, as its members took their degrees, left Oxford or assumed new responsibilities. In any case, their relations could not remain what they had been. For example, the once intimate connection between Green and Swinburne had been broken by the publication of *Poems and Ballads* in 1866. Although Green's politics remained as radical as before, his Puritanism was deeply offended by Swinburne's revolt against the limits on frankness set by contemporary morality. A. C. Bradley recalled that from then on, 'Green adopted a very hostile and contemptuous attitude to Swinburne'.[95] The old members of the Society, however, continued to have reunions at intervals until at least the late 1870's.

At the same time that Green was a member of the Old Mortality, he attended regularly every Sunday meeting of a group for reading the Bible and prayer, which convened at Balliol. In part, there was a convergence with the Old Mortality, for Luke, Nichol and Grenfell belonged to both. This was a curious atmosphere, Balliol in the 50's of the last century. A place was somehow found for this sensibility, unorthodox in religion and radical in politics:

One of his associates recalled Green's place in this prayer meeting.

'Some were narrowish Evangelicals—one or two High Churchmen, but all earnest men. I remember he [Green] startled some by the breadth of thought which he at once brought to the criticism of the New Testament. But I also remember that his breadth was accompanied by such reverence and manifest earnestness that it had no repellent effect on anybody and no disintegrating effect on the little society. Nothing to my mind could have been better than his influence on Balliol men of the same generation.[96]

Despite these absorbing associations, Green did not escape the constant surveillance of Jowett, who would not allow his promising students to lose sight of their examinations. A good deal of drill, memorising, and advance preparation of essays likely to be set— these were established techniques at Balliol for men seeking honours. With all this Green dutifully complied, although not without much inner struggle. Other members of the Society did the same, for several of them were to take their Schools in 1859. The result was recorded by Nichol, who had been ill: 'To Cumnor with Swinburne. Edgar Poe and green leaves. Chaucer in the evening. Jowett sends for me to his inner room; rest on the sofa. Shouts without announce Riddell and the Class List. 1st class— Green, Luke, Nichol ("Old Mortality"), Warner, and Warre.'[97]

Jowett had worked his spell again. The examiners had found Green to be the most distinguished candidate of his group. His tutor, still guiding his every step, told him that although Balliol had no opening for a philosophy tutor, it would soon require a College lecturer in the newly created school of Modern History and Law. The thing to do was to read for that school for six months. Green did so, and when he was examined, took only a third class. That mattered little, for he had already proved himself in the older and more respected curriculum. In 1860 he began to lecture for the first time. Greek history was his subject for the Greats School, and early European history for the School of Law and Modern History. That same year he was elected to a Balliol Fellowship. Success followed upon success. The Oxford Union, where once he had been hooted, chose him to be its President in 1861. Shortly thereafter he was told that he need no longer confine himself to history, and began to lecture on Aristotle, whose work then constituted the core of philosophical studies. And Jowett further showed his trust in Green by entrusting him with the preparation of a pamphlet designed to present Jowett's theological views at a time when he was under heavy fire.[98]

From the viewpoint of conventional success, Green was as happily placed as anyone of his age and tastes might hope to be.

But his real situation was very different. He was in fact entering a period of deep depression and inner conflict. For his initial elation at his hard-won prestige gave way to the realisation that his tutorial work did not satisfy him. Teaching did not come easily, and the undergraduates he had to instruct in the rudiments of philosophy wanted for a pass degree, seemed for the most part 'an obnoxious breed'. And to face an endless prospect of presenting Aristotle in simple comprehensible form—was this really what he wanted to do? He had, quite without being prepared for it, arrived at a critical point where he saw himself confronted by questions to which he had no answer. Because of Jowett he had for some years been given a limited and clearly defined task. But now he would have to find new motives rooted in his own deepest needs. Doubts beset him, and he wondered whether he had a vocation to teach. For the first time in his life, he had difficulty in sleeping. Every time he had to prepare a lecture, he could do so only after a struggle with himself. Once it was done, he felt reluctant to deliver what he had written. Had the time come to leave Oxford? If so, where should he go?

For a time he considered a teaching position in the more congenial Nonconformist and Manchester atmosphere of Owens College. Or perhaps he might attempt to become a school-inspector as had Matthew Arnold. Then suddenly he was offered the editorship of the *Times of India* which was about to begin publication in Bombay. The salary was £1,200 per annum. This seemed an exciting project, for it meant a call to action in a new experience drastically unlike anything he had known. He could both get to know India at first hand and save a good deal of money. But Jowett advised against it, and this influential judgment combined with family objections and fears for his health decided the issue.

Looking back at this turn in the road which he had refused to take, he grieved: 'It will very likely turn out to be the only chance I shall have of saving myself from being a stick for life'. Now twenty-seven, he examined gloomily the prospect before him:

'Ultimately there seem to be three courses open to me: (1) to persevere in Oxford life . . . with a bare possibility of one day getting a professorship, but with more probability of writing a heterodox book and becoming a dissenting preacher; (2) to get on the staff of a daily paper, and make £500 a year by squeezing my brain into five leaders a week; (3) to get an educational appointment of some sort under government. The last course seems to me the most unworthy, the first least so, though it would require much resolution and involve celibacy.'[99]

At this same time, Green apparently considered entering the Church. But it is characteristic both of him and the Broad Church movement that he could not decide whether he should become a Nonconformist preacher, a Unitarian minister or be ordained in the Church of England. Already he felt the first stirrings of a desire to have a 'stump' from which he could preach his beliefs to the world. Despite talking of a Dissenter's pulpit, and even saying that a modified Unitarianism suited him, he was nevertheless advised to take orders in the Established Church. His counsellor has not been identified. It may have been Jowett, but such an opinion was not necessarily that of a Broad Churchman. It was a not uncommon view that serious young men who had irritating doubts about their faith should nevertheless take orders and busy themselves in pastoral work, after which their earlier questions might very well seem academic in retrospect. So Keble had advised Thomas Arnold in his time, and so many a clergyman still saw the issue.

Practically, the question imposed itself in two ways: to take his degree of MA, he would have to subscribe again to the Thirty-nine Articles of the Church of England; and if he decided that he could in good conscience do so, ought he then go on to take deacon's orders? The situation in relation to University Tests between 1854 and 1874 was that although a student could take his BA without any religious profession, he could not become an MA, the almost invariable condition of holding a fellowship, without signing the Articles. Green, like Jowett, and, as Dicey tells us, all but one of the Old Mortality, 'treated the signature of the Articles as a way of stating that we were members of the Church of England, and did not belong to any other body'.[100] By contrast Leslie Stephen and Henry Sidgwick at Cambridge took the line that the Articles were a creed that ought to be interpreted at their face value. This meant, in their view, that no one should adhere to the Anglican Church if he felt any doubt whatever about its statement of belief. On this matter of principle, both these Cambridge agnostics resigned their fellowships. And nearer home, John Nichol, by refusing outright to sign, sacrificed the Oxford fellowship which most likely would have been his. Nevertheless Green persevered in doing what Jowett and his other friends judged suitable. Now a further decision imposed itself: whether he ought to take orders. Henry Sidgwick was shocked to hear that Green could even consider 'diaconising', and commented: 'It is only in such a *milieu* as Oxford that a high-minded man could think of it'.[101]

Was it possible to live an active and genuinely useful life within

the Church of England as one of its clergymen? This question
which is the very centre of Robert Elsmere's dilemma, apparently
for a time engaged Green's attention. Indeed he loved and much
admired his Christian Socialist uncle, the Reverend David Vaughan.
But deeper forces proved to be decisive over this personal influence.
For Green had a strong streak of republicanism, and a Puritan
distrust both of the hierarchical structure of the Church of
England and of the privileges given to its clergy. As Nettleship
finely remarks, Green felt that he could not share what the
Established Church enjoyed to the exclusion of the Nonconformists and rationalists.[102] Nor did he feel closer to the dissenting
sects or to the unorthodox. Ultimately he found the first too narrow,
and the second too shallow, in their spiritual commitments. He
could not become a clergyman. Agnosticism and positivism were
no more satisfying. The proper balance between modern knowledge and faith had yet to be found. And he himself did not know
where he should search for a solution that would satisfy. Certainly
no English school of thought held any attraction for him. All the
leading thinkers in his own country seemed to him trapped in a
cul de sac. In one way or another, they were patching up obsolescent
theories which reduced thought to the principle of association in
epistemology. Moral and political philosophy were arid variations
on the 'greater-happiness' principle. As for the few rebels against
this tradition, Coleridge and Carlyle were incoherent and un-
systematic. Nor was the situation any better in theology, where an
unpalatable choice existed among an unlearned fundamentalism,
or the High Church doctrine of submission to authority, or the
arid rationalism of Unitarianism.

In the early 1860's, just after his election as a Fellow of Balliol,
Green, apparently as the result of a visit to Germany, took up the
study of some theologians who had been recommended to him
some time ago by Jowett. This Tübingen school, which had been
much impressed by Hegel, caught his imagination. F. C. Baur
particularly attracted him. From this beginning, Green felt
moved to reconsider the great modern German thinkers. As he
made his way through the complex arguments of Kant, Fichte, and
Hegel, he began to experience something as close to a conversion
as his temperament would permit. It now seemed to him that
modern philosophy had arrived at a method which preserved
everything he found of permanent value in Christian experience,
but did so on the basis of reason alone. This meant that it broke
definitively with all mythological forms and historical assertions
imposed by primitive Christianity. From one point of view, this
offered the advantage of disengaging matters of belief from

scientific discussion about matters of fact; from another, it posed real difficulties. German philosophy bore an uncertain relation to the official creeds of the Christian churches. To abandon Christian symbolism with all its ancient and venerated forms, to put in its place a purely philosophical statement—these were not trifling steps.

Did Green at this time pass through a period of painful religious doubt? Nettleship, in his admirable memoir of Green, goes to some lengths to deny this possibility.[103] All too well acquainted from personal experience with such agony, Nettleship could find no trace of it in the man who as teacher and friend had shown him the way out of the maze. But Nettleship knew Green as a formed and powerful character, and this long after he had taken the decisive step and felt invigorated by it. In a letter written after R. L. Nettleship had finished his work, Mrs Humphry Ward told Gladstone of a conversation with Green which she had made into a central episode in *Robert Elsmere*:

> The parting with the Christian mythology is the rending asunder of bones and marrow '—words which I have put into Grey's mouth— were words of Mr Green's to me. It was the only thing of the sort I ever heard him say—he was a man who never spoke of his feelings— but it was said with a penetrating force and sincerity which I still remember keenly. A long intellectual travail had convinced him that the miraculous Christian story was untenable; but speculatively he gave it up with grief and difficulty, and practically, to his last hour, he clung to all the forms and associations of the old belief with a wonderful affection.'[104]

Where is the truth to be found? R. L. Nettleship would appear to be a more reliable source than Mrs Ward. And yet her statement has a quality which gives it credibility. Were there nothing more available as evidence than these discrepant statements, we could not know. But among the materials Nettleship used was a letter from his brother, Professor Henry Nettleship. Of this extremely detailed account of Green's theological opinions, his biographer cited only those extracts relating to his subject's religious temperament. This may have been due simply to the need for selection; on the other hand, Professor Nettleship's account may have been too explicit for his brother's taste. Broad Churchmen always preferred to have theological statements veiled in ambiguity. In any case, Professor Nettleship's account appears to carry conviction and is not ultimately incompatible with Mrs Ward's account. This passage is meant to describe Green, as he was in 1862, when he visited Germany:

> He had, I think, at this time definitely abandoned his belief in the

miraculous, and therefore in the commonly-accepted historical groundwork of Christianity. Many men go through this stage, but the peculiarity, as it seemed to me, of Green's mind was that the fact in no way affected the basis of evangelical piety which lay at the root of his whole life. I have known only two or three cases of the same kind. At no time did Green lose . . . his effective desire for spiritual advancement in the ordinary Christian sense, and his complete belief in the code of ethics universally accepted as Christian as a practical guide. All this he retained in full force to the day of his death. His steadiness of mind was, in so speculative a man, quite remarkable; he knew nothing of mental cataclysms, and had none of the qualities which make interesting converts. . . . His religion was always . . . of the Protestant and Evangelical type, and . . . for Catholicism or Anglicanism he never had the smallest sympathy.[105]

It was above all to German thought that Green looked for guidance on how to reconstruct his belief. This high estimate is now not easy to comprehend. Elie Halévy, in one of his rare deviations from objectivity, attributed Green's admiration for things German to the Prussian victories over the French in 1870-1, 'Then Thomas Hill Green . . . at the moment when the Prussians were victorious at Sadowa and Sedan had inaugurated in the Anglo-Saxon Universities the tradition of what was known as Hegelian "Neo-Kantism" '.[106] But Green, as a member of the Old Mortality and an admirer of Bright and Cobden, was the last person in the world to be convinced of the moral virtue of a nation by its success in war. In fact his Germanophilia was based on two images which long antedated Bismarck: the first being a contrast made by the Manchester School between rational and efficient Prussia as compared to traditional and corrupt England; the second, the identification of German culture with Goethe, Schiller, Kant and his successors, and the golden age of the universities. As early as 1838 Richard Cobden had denounced the 'great juggle of the *English Constitution*—a thing of monopolies, and Church-craft, and sinecures, armorial hocus-pocus, primo-geniture, and pageantry,' and gone on to suggest that 'for the great mass of the people, Prussia possesses the best government in Europe. I would gladly give up my taste for talking politics to secure such a state of things in England.'[107] As for the respect felt by educated Englishmen for things German before 1870, this was demonstrated by Carlyle's Teufelsdrück and Matthew Arnold's Arminius, the two most obvious examples of didactic lessons directed to the English by fictitious Teutonic preceptors. In the eighteenth century, they would have been given Persian or Chinese sobriquets.

Green's attitudes towards Germany clearly belong to the period before its unification, when it was still possible to conceive of its people as the most spiritual and unworldly in Europe. His own personal knowledge came from the summer visits he made in 1862 and 1863 with such friends as Henry Sidgwick and H. G. Dakyns from Cambridge, and Dicey, Bryce, and Symonds from his own university. Taciturn in Oxford, Green became rhapsodic in Germany, where he delighted in the peasants with their 'homely patriarchal ways, their care for animals, the pious legends carved upon their chalets, the primitive love-making of their young men and maidens'. Dresden impressed him by its social equality and apparent absence of vice and distress. He was heard to say that he preferred Germany to England. This judgment he applied even to the women, who were 'of unquestionable and universal ugliness . . . but to make up for this they seem much more sensible, and more companionable for the men'. Clearly the Germans put first things first. In the art galleries, Green turned away from the Renaissance painters to Rembrandt, Holbein and Dürer because they, in contrast to the pagan interests of the Italians, 'grasped the Idea of Christianity'. It is true that in politics, his personal beliefs were challenged when in 1863 Bismarck enacted the ordinances further restricting the freedom of the press. But ultimately, he decided, Prussia could be trusted because the soldiers could all read, and the artisans, 'free from the worse forms of socialism,' had developed schemes of co-operation and self-help.[108] Kingsley, Maurice, Cobden, and Bright did not much help Green in penetrating to the direction and meaning of Bismarck's Prussia.

All this unwonted enthusiasm reflects Green's exhilaration at the intellectual discoveries he was making. From this time on his writing would for a time glow with a subdued excitement at the possibilities which seemed to open up before him. And his enthusiasm was contagious. On his way back to England after his second holiday spent abroad, he burst in on J. A. Symonds at Davos, 'full of German philosophy, politics, and the higher poetry'. Listening to Green reciting Goethe, Symonds experienced a personal illumination about how he might henceforth live. But if it was out of poetry and art that Symonds would fashion his own creed, Green at this time cared more about theology and philosophy. It was his intention to translate immediately a work by Baur, whom he found 'nearly the most instructive writer I ever met with'.[109] Nor was his enthusiasm dampened by his travelling companion, Henry Sidgwick, who for his part did not put much stock 'in this Hegelian Christ'.

This summer was a turning point, for now Green began for the first time to see that Oxford offered him some exceptional opportunities. To rehash Aristotle to the end of one's days was, to be sure, not the most alluring of tasks. But perhaps his life might be so arranged that he could begin to introduce his countrymen to the spiritual impulse he had found so dominant in every department of German thought. He found a new zest in contemplating what changes would follow from the systematic investigation of experience by the Idealist method. For art, religion, and even the operative political ideas of British life could not be accounted for by the theories used by Utilitarian and Evolutionist thinkers. Even political liberalism and reform suffered from such out-moded formulations. Only German thinkers had thus far understood that the first task which must be performed by modern philosophy is to find 'formulae adequate to the action of reason as exhibited in nature and human society, in art and religion'. But the German Idealists had never made themselves sufficiently intelligible, and in any case, the political applications they made of their philosophy seemed altogether irrelevant to British institutions. Yet on the intellectual foundations which had been already laid in Germany, it was, he thought, possible to build a philosophy of life which would incorporate everything he believed true in theology and politics. These two parts of the enterprise went together: the theology would be connected to the political philosophy by the conception of citizenship. His brother-in-law thought that it was this vision that became the mainspring of Green's subsequent life: 'He thought it all important to saturate the English with German ideas—to hold fast the essential solid qualities of the English mind in politics and piety, but to give them a new vigour and intensity, adapt them to a *Begriffsphilosophie*'.[110]

This programme was not easy to achieve. Quite apart from other difficulties, there was the matter of his older brother, who now was a chronic alcoholic. After having been sent down from Merton, he obtained a scholarship from Magdalene College, Cambridge which, however, expelled him almost immediately. Thereupon he went out to India, but returned in 1861 after an absence of five years. His brother then asked him to live in Oxford, where they shared rooms. This experiment was no less dismaying because its failure was predictable. It cannot be determined what happened thereafter, but Green was much depressed by the fact that he was powerless to aid his brother.

All this had involved much time and effort just when he had begun to make progress on the translation of Baur. After his brother's departure, he was about to return to this piece of work, when he received an offer to edit the *Nichomachean Ethics* in conjunction with Edward Caird. This he could not refuse, and so that his work on Baur thus far should not be wasted he wrote an essay on dogma, a version of which was delivered to the Old Mortality. Then he forced himself to spend a not inconsiderable amount of time and effort on the edition of Aristotle. It in turn came to nothing because of a disagreement with the publisher. Again attempting to salvage something from his work, he published an essay on Aristotle in the *North British Review*. This almost immediately affected his career. Upon Jowett's advice, Green had decided to stand as a candidate for the chair in moral philosophy at St Andrews. When another man was chosen, Green attributed his defeat to malicious rumours that he was a dangerous radical, a Comtist and a materialist unfit to instruct young men. But Jowett, who may have been better informed, told Green that in fact he had destroyed his chance by the essay on Aristotle, written in a Hegelian jargon unintelligible to the committee making the selection.* What Jowett told Green on this point may be inferred from the older man's antagonism to obscurity of any kind. No doubt he gave more than advice on style, for to Nichol, who himself had just failed election to another chair, Jowett wrote in pungent phrases:

'Green's failure is a great disappointment. He is doing very well here with a class of pupils.

I think that persons who take up an independent line cannot expect to succeed in early life, and if at all only by great energy and force of character. Do not let us choose the stronger part and find ourselves unequal to it. The sooner men like yourself and Green get to acquiesce in this, and look forward to some higher good, the better.'[117]

Thus goaded, Green gradually overcame his depression at his brother's fate, and his own defeat at St Andrews. His teaching became less mechanical and more individual; and he saw the justice of Jowett's view that anyone who scorns received opinion cannot complain if he is hardly treated. He found consolation in the fact that his status at Balliol seemed to offer him opportunities which he had not previously appreciated. Although he continued

---

* Jowett's view of Green's style in this essay was shared by Mr Justice Holmes: 'I will try to finish Green on the philosophy of Aristotle, expressing in, a phraseology that I imperfectly understand, ideas that I don't believe. His ideas never are difficult—but the damned technical language of each new discussion keeps me in a fuzzle.' [Mark DeWolfe Howe (ed.), *The Correspondence of Mr Justice Holmes and Harold J. Laski, 1916-1935* (2 vols. Cambridge, Mass.: Harvard University Press, 1953), I, 188. Letter from Holmes to Laski, 28 February, 1919.]

to have trouble communicating with the Etonians and future peers, he did make an increasing mark on the 'reading-men' in the College. Balliol was unique among Oxford colleges for its Scottish connection: the Snell exhibitions, which had supported Adam Smith in the eighteenth century and Nichol and Caird in Green's own time, continued to send a significant number of Scots, sometimes poor, reared as Calvinists, always older and more serious than the English students. Among such men, together with those who had backgrounds similar to his own, Green began to find a number of devoted followers, and these were to increase even more rapidly, once the restrictions against Nonconformists were removed in 1871. Even before this the tide had been going his way; Manchester and Owens College no longer seemed so inviting now that he had discovered his vocation as a teacher of philosophy. Thus he wrote Bryce:

> 'I have felt drawings towards Owens College, but Jowett urges me to stop here. In the teaching way, I suspect I can do more here. Manchester clerks would want some shorter cut than my Hegelian philosophy, whereas here I anticipate increasing success with pupils. I am beginning to be sought after by men reading for fellowships, with whom I can expatiate. . . . The practical openings at Manchester are the great attraction, but they wd. be poor compensation for failure in one's proper line as a teacher.'[112]

It was true that by now he had the reputation for being 'an extreme man, an ultra-radical in politics, an ultra-liberal in religious opinion'.[113] But he had learned not to retreat. This was the time of the American Civil War, and if sympathy with the North and belief in its political institutions were marks of radicalism in politics, Green did not shirk the label. His deep conviction that upper-class Englishmen thought in sophistical terms was rein-forced by their arguments in favour of the Southern cause. Speaking in the Oxford Union, he angrily disputed Tory assertions that the Federal Government had precipitated the war and that in any case secession was inevitable because of the anarchy inherent in republican institutions. To this last charge, he responded in the accents of Bright, 'It is not a republic that is answerable for this war, but a slave-holding, slave-breeding, and slave-burning olig-archy, on whom the curse of God and humanity rests'. As for the allegation that it was not secession but the Union's reply to secession that had brought on the fighting, he answered by telling one of his country stories: A farm hand had defended himself against an attacking dog by using the prongs of his pitchfork. When reprimanded for not having used the handle to ward off the animal, he retorted, 'I would have done, if the dog had come at me with the other end'. Green was among the first in Oxford to recognise the genius for democratic leadership that lay hidden under 'the rough exterior and Yankee humour of Lincoln', and later called his assassination, the 'greatest political crime of modern times'.[114] Despite the principled pacificism of his beliefs as later expressed in the lectures on *Political Obligation*, and his opposition to the Crimean War, at this time he cheered every Northern victory without apparent pangs of conscience. On at least two occasions he travelled to London so that he could demonstrate his support. In 1863 he was present at the great meeting of trade unionists where John Bright defended the Northern cause to the entire satisfaction of Henry Adams; and when William Lloyd Garrison, the abolitionist, was honoured in 1865, Green again came down.[115] Just after the Civil War, came the great scandal about Governor Eyre's cruel actions in Jamaica. Green joined the Jamaica Committee, formed in protest against Eyre.[116]

Little of his personal views on politics was revealed in his teaching. He prided himself on his reserve in such matters. Nevertheless he did not allow to pass unchallenged even unconsciously condescending references to the classes still excluded from Oxford or the franchise. In an undergraduate essay he read to Green, Bernard Bosanquet expressed his belief that it was essential for the British to develop a ladder of learning extending from elementary school to university, and enlisting the most capable young people, regardless of class. As was common in those days, he implied that such reform in education was necessary before the franchise could be safely extended. Such sentiments might have been expected to elicit approval from Green. But all that he said was, 'If you imply that no one is fit to have a vote who has not had a university education, I don't agree with you.' This made such an impression that his student used it to illustrate a point in a book written fifty years later.[117]

Such a relationship appears to have been typical even with those students who were most drawn to him, and after he had become far more sociable than before. For after 1868, when for the first time he invited two undergraduates to spend some time out of term with him, he often led reading parties during the Long Vacation. He had begun to acquire the reputation of having a good sense of humour with his students. Rather indifferent to the variety and quality of food, he used to be teased by the question whether herrings and mutton were related as cause and effect, or only as following each other in time. On another occasion, when the party was caught on a Scottish loch by a fierce storm, the undergraduates reassured their mentor by telling him that if the worst came to the worst, he would only be absorbed into the absolute. His rôle was not so much the schoolmaster, which was that of Jowett, but that of an 'elder brother, in whose society we were ashamed to be selfish or mean, and who taught rather by example rather than precept'.[118] Yet Green did not give up the disconcerting frankness of his youth. This weapon he used on those closer to him, persons, who in his view, were Liberals in mind alone, when they should have transformed their personal and social attitudes. Snobbery he regarded as completely indefensible, as one of the great barriers in England to the development of a healthy political society. For his investigation of education had convinced him that there was a political purpose behind the exclusive manners and schools of the upper classes which kept the rest of the nation at a distance. This line of thought deeply impressed itself upon one of his students, who later recalled travelling with Green:

> When he used to insist that we should travel by third class on our excursions and when I held out for second, he would say, 'You will be an aristocrat as soon as you get your Fellowship and will want to travel first.' The day we were at Tintern Abbey, while we were climbing to Wyndcliff, some young women came running down, and one of them said to me in rather an off-hand way, 'What's the time?' I did not make any answer but walked on. He said. 'Why didn't you answer the young woman?' I said, 'Because she didn't ask properly.' He looked quite vexed and said, 'That's what comes of being at Oxford. Up at Oxford we entirely lose the ordinary power of communication with our fellows, and think they mean to be rude when they do not speak like ourselves. It is you who were rude.'[119]

To put Oxford in communication with the rest of the nation, to open the University to classes hitherto excluded from it, and to make its students aware that their privileged status implied corresponding duties to those less fortunate: these ideas were later to rank high in the programme of Green, Arnold Toynbee and their circle. Except for the emphasis upon atonement for social injustice, none of these notions was new, for they had been long associated with the influential Rugby-Balliol connection, within which Green was beginning to play an increasingly important rôle. He was singled out in 1864 and offered a post as assistant commissioner in an inquiry which engaged much of his energies for the next three years. The Royal Commission of 1864 was charged with investigating those schools 'attended by the children of such of the gentry, clergy, professional and commercial men as are of limited means, and of farmers and tradesmen'.[120] His appointment Green owed to Frederick Temple and Jowett, who shared a belief in the necessity of reform from within, a line not always appreciated by those from other schools and colleges. Green's report, for example, was to be sharply attacked by Robert Lowe, the leader of the opposition to the Second Reform Bill. But Rugby and Balliol constituted a powerful line of force. After the death of Dr Arnold, three successive headmasters of Rugby—Goulburn, Tait and Temple—were recruited from the Balliol tutors who had supported the much-imitated innovations of their College. Tait and Temple both were to become Archbishops of Canterbury. A contributor to *Essays and Reviews*, Temple had also been among the most effective witnesses calling for extensive reform before the First University Commission. He had long had a distinguished part in the improvement of public education, and he had collaborated with his Balliol tutor, Jowett, in developing the Indian Civil Service. When through Temple's agency, Green became an assistant commissioner, he found himself associated with two other men whose distinction underlined the significance of his own choice. One was his old friend from the Old Mortality Society, James Bryce; the other, Matthew Arnold.

Within Balliol itself, Green's position became increasingly important. In 1866 he was named senior dean, and by 1870 when Jowett was elected Master, Green, in addition to his teaching duties, virtually had to administer the College single-handed. He made one attempt to attain a position which would free him to do philosophical work, but after his unsuccessful candidacy for the Waynflete professorship in moral and metaphysical philosophy, he became reconciled to his demanding duties in the College. But he no longer lived within its walls, for in 1871 he married Charlotte Symonds, and became an Oxford householder. In this capacity, he became eligible to participate in the political life of the town; he also now had in his wife and his home a new and attractive rallying-point for his increasing number of students and admirers. He and his wife were at home to them fortnightly, and these occasions became a part of Oxford's philosophical and political life. A new phase of his life had begun. If Jowett as Master still dominated Balliol, Green was more of a force with the most vigorous and intellectual students both inside and outside the College. By his innovations in philosophy, his increasingly active participation in reform politics, and his theology, Green made himself a powerful figure in Oxford.

CHAPTER FOUR

TOWARDS A THEOLOGY

I

MUCH OF THE SECRET intellectual history of an age is made not so much by the formal treatises of its outstanding thinkers, as by some one of their lesser known but more telling works. Thus Mr J. P. Mayer has described how a generation of German scholars were sustained throughout their wanderings of the 1930's and '40's by the two yellow-covered pamphlets containing Max Weber's lectures on science and politics as vocation.[1] Similarly, across the gulf which separates us from Green's time, we can catch an occasional glimpse of his religious ideas at work through the slim volume which reprinted his lay sermons: Jowett reading from it to the future Lady Oxford and her sisters; Mrs Humphry Ward sending her prized copy to Gladstone in the hope of convincing him of the spiritual worth of Professor Grey-Green.* Perhaps more than anything else he ever said or wrote, these fewer than fifty pages contain his esoteric doctrine, and the key to his appeal.[2]

It was these lay sermons rather than their popularisation in *Robert Elsmere* which gave Green his reputation as a theologian. This was not inconsiderable. In a survey of religious life at Oxford, written two decades after Green's death, is the judgment that he 'had an influence upon the religious thought of his time, which it would be difficult to over-rate, and which has affected men of all parties'.[3] As late as 1917, R. W. Macan, then Master of University College, wrote: 'At least none will challenge the title of Thomas Hill Green as a master mind in our spiritual building. Even if his lay sermons and theological lectures were not there to claim it, his whole philosophical influence and his ever-memorable personality—so intense, so sincere, so lofty—declare him a

* The sequel to the Jowett episode is somewhat unexpected. Margot Tennant, as she was then, asked Jowett, after he had finished reading, how much he had loved Green? His answer came back, 'I did not love him at all.' (*The Autobiography of Margot Asquith* [London, 1920], p. 35.)

missionary of the Spirit.'[4] No doubt Green would have cared little for the title of 'a missionary of the Spirit'. But the language of Macan's claim, as much as its content, serves as a reminder of the distance it is necessary for the reader to travel in order to understand this theology and its success. For the most part Green's philosophical texts are dry enough, and yet in some few places the note of affirmation sounds. But it is not long sustained, and it is necessary to go to the lay sermons for a fuller specimen. There Green's prose, usually so impersonal and abstract, attained the peculiar rhythm and intensity of the Evangelical sermon.* For the reader of a later age there is no danger of missing the distinctive rhetoric and emotion. Yet the precise tone is difficult to identify. Certainly in Green's case there is something edifying about this call for sacrifice of self, this denunciation of materialism and hedonism. But just what was being said, and how did Green come to be saying it? The answers are by no means self-evident.

In several senses Green bridged two worlds. For he was the first layman in Balliol history to hold a Fellowship. Prior to reform such an office could be held only by ordained clergymen of the Church of England. Green was also a tutor, and being the man he was, he could not but feel responsible for the welfare of his students. He recognised that in his own case, his tutor had quite altered his life, both by setting him on to his career, and by indicating how he might reconcile his faith with reason. Nor was this the only source of his concern. An older and highly perceptive Fellow noticed in Green 'a half-suppressed wish, very rarely and slightly indicated,' to receive a hearing for his own religious views.[5] This he felt debarred from doing in his philosophical teaching by strong professional scruples. But now the question posed itself in another form. It had long been the custom of Balliol tutors to address their students on the evening before the Sundays on which communion was to be administered. When Green became a tutor, he had as a layman to consider whether he should continue this practice. A precedent existed, not in the Church of England with its requirement of ordination, but among the Nonconformists and especially the Methodists who made much use of lay preachers. Only twice did Green in fact deliver lay sermons at Balliol: the first time in 1870 on 'The Witness of God'; the second time in 1871 on 'Faith'. In them Green proposed to

* G. M. Young estimated that 'a young man brought up in a careful home might have heard, whether delivered or read aloud, a thousand sermons.' Thus he accounts for the 'homiletic cadence so persistent in mid-Victorian oratory and letters.' (Young, *Victorian England*, p. 14.)

make so few concessions to the language of the Church that even Jowett had his doubts, which he confided to his journal:

> 'G[reen] wants to write a sermon in which the language of theology is omitted—a Christian discourse meaning the same thing in other words.
> The attempt is worth making, but it requires great genius to execute it. The words will seem thin, moral, unitarian. . . . Yet something like this is what the better mind of the age is seeking—a religion independent of the accidents of time and place.'[6]

Jowett turned out to have overestimated the dryness, the rationalism of the doctrine Green taught. For in fact his theology turned out to possess formidable attractions. Mrs Humphry Ward, although not invariably the best of guides, did feel and convey the emotional pathos of the lay sermons in *Robert Elsmere*. Although some of the details she added for effect, such as Green's alleged Midland accent, do not square with the historical record, it would be over-scrupulous to pass over her vivid account of Professor Grey's sermon and the impression it produced upon young Elsmere. It is true that the passage cannot have the same reverberations today that it once produced upon the mass audience of the 1880's and 1890's, but it nevertheless communicates more of the atmosphere than a bare statement would do. In the novel, Elsmere is a freshman invited to the lay sermon by his tutor who, although himself not sympathetic to Professor Grey's message, has divined that Robert would be touched by it.

> 'At eight o'clock that evening Robert found himself crossing the quadrangle . . . on the way to one of the larger lecture rooms, which was to be the scene of the address. The room when they got in was already nearly full, all the working fellows of the college were present, and a body of some thirty men besides, most of whom already far on in their University career. A minute or two afterwards Mr Grey entered. The door opening on to the quadrangle, where the trees, undeterred by east wind, were just bursting into leaf, was shut; and the little assembly knelt, while Mr Grey's voice with its broad intonation, in which a strong native homeliness lingered under the gentleness of accent, recited the collect "Lord of all power and might", a silent pause following the last words. Then the audience settled itself, and Mr Grey, standing by a small deal table with the gaslight behind him, began his address.
> All the main points of the experience which followed stamped themselves on Robert's mind with extraordinary intensity. Nor did he ever lose the memory of the outward scene. In after years, memory could always recall to him at will the face and figure of the speaker, the massive head, the deep eyes sunk under the brows, the Midland

accent, the make of limb and feature which seemed to have some suggestion in them of the rude strength and simplicity of a peasant ancestry; and then the nobility, the fire, the spiritual beauty flashing through it all! Here, indeed, was a man on whom his fellows might lean, a man in whom the generation of spiritual force was so strong and continuous that it overflowed of necessity into the poorer, barrener lives around him, kindling and enriching. Robert felt himself seized and penetrated, filled with a fervour and an admiration which he was too young and immature to analyse, but which was to be none the less potent and lasting.

Much of the sermon, itself indeed, was beyond him. . . . It was not, therefore, the argument, or the logical structure of the sermon, which so profoundly affected young Elsmere. It was the speaker himself, and the occasional passages in which, addressing himself to the practical needs of his hearers, he put before them the claims and conditions of the higher life with a pregnant simplicity and rugged beauty of phrase. Conceit, selfishness, vice—how, as he spoke of them, they seemed to wither from his presence! How the "pitiful, earthy self" with its passions and its cravings sank into nothingness beside the "great ideas" and the "great causes" for which, as Christians and as men, he claimed their devotion.

To the boy sitting among the crowd at the back of the room, his face supported in his hands and his gleaming eyes fixed on the speaker, it seemed as if all the poetry and history through which a restless curiosity and ideality had carried him so far, took a new meaning from this experience. It was by men like this that the moral progress of the world had been shaped and inspired; he felt brought near to the great primal forces breathing through the divine workshop; and in place of natural disposition and reverent compliance, there sprang up in him suddenly an actual burning certainty of belief. "Axioms are not axioms," said poor Keats, "till they have been proved upon our pulses;" and the old familiar figure of the Divine combat, of the struggle in which man and God are one, was proved once more upon a human pulse on that May night, in the hush of that quiet lecture room.'[7]

As Mrs Ward's text reveals, these sermons produced their effect by the tonality Green struck, by his expression of a temper that fitted the requirements of an audience, so considerable in his time, so shrunken in our own, of serious-minded persons who demanded a view of the world combining intellectual adequacy with moral direction. The terms in which science and philosophy were then posed had not produced our present despair about understanding the world we live in, nor had history as yet taken the violent and bewildering turns which have created in the twentieth century a new Protestant fundamentalism that Green's generation would have found irrational and authoritarian.

2

Green's theology is couched in terms which make it difficult to determine his exact meaning. Some have understood him to care little about creeds or churches because, in his view, religion consists of a direct relationship between the believer and his God;* others have understood him to say that religion is morality or citizenship; the sacrifice of one's own selfish concerns to some higher ideal. In his specifically theological work, Green found the centre of Christian life in the notion that within the individual soul there takes place a perpetual renewal of the death and resurrection of Christ: 'As the primary Christian idea is that of a moral death into life, as wrought for us and in us by God, so its realisation, which is the evidence of its truth, lies in Christian love—a realisation never complete, because for ever embracing new matter, yet constantly gaining in fulness.'

It is this which is the essential quality of Christianity, not creeds, nor dogmatic theology, nor the authority of the Church. Religion, so conceived, is independent of miracles and of all statements presented as historical or scientific within the Bible. God is to be sought not in nature but in his transactions with man. 'You cannot find a verification of the idea of God or duty; you can only make it. God is not something outside and beyond the consciousness of him. . . . The true verification of the consciousness is the life of prayer and self-denial which expresses it.'[9] Such a theology must minimise adherence to any statement of belief: 'The glory of Christianity is not that it excludes, but that it comprehends; not that it came of a sudden into the world, or that it is given complete in a particular institution, or can be stated complete in a particular form of words; but that it is the expression of a common spirit, which is gathering together all things in one.'[10] This spirit cannot be identified with any past event. Accounts of the life of Christ and of the doctrine he taught can be found only through a series of fluctuating interpretations, which will always be but a shadow of what in fact occurred or what was said. What is real is the idea of a Christian life which was created then and still lives. 'Faith is a personal and conscious relation of man to God, forming the principle of a new life.'[11] The Incarnation and Resurrection can

---

* When Green was appointed an examiner, R. W. Macan, then about to take his Schools, asked his tutor, Ingram Bywater, once a member of the Old Mortality, and later Jowett's successor as Professor of Greek, whether he might prepare an essay on 'mysticism'. Bywater thought that the subject was not likely to appear on a philosophical paper set by Green. However, it was the first question in the examination. (William Walrond Jackson, *Ingram Bywater* [Oxford, 1917], p. 64 n.)

THE POLITICS OF CONSCIENCE

only mean that the divine spirit manifests itself under various forms in all that is good in human experience.

Green deliberately chose to seek the rationale of religious belief in philosophy. He believed that he had found in Philosophical Idealism a profound method which enabled him to translate the language of Christianity without losing its true meaning. Like Hegel, he saw its method as the final result of a process in which religion evolved into philosophy after transcending an intermediate stage of theology. Thus he felt no doubts about abandoning the doctrine of God's transcendence for that of God's immanence. By the use of Idealist concepts, Green claimed to retain in his theology all that men had valued in what previously had been believed to be communion with a transcendent God. But he translated that communion into a new language which gave special technical meanings to the terms familiar to the average believer. By this means Green builds up the theory that God is immanent in the universe, in the sense of being its constitutive principle; immanent in men, in the sense of being the principle of reason and morality within them.

In the 'Essay on Christian Dogma',[12] which crystallised his study of Baur, he maintained that Christianity was at first the immediate intuition of a small group of uneducated men. But as it gradually expanded, it entered a second phase, in which by a kind of dialectical necessity, it had to become a Church spreading over great expanses of territory and including all classes of society. For the first time the highly cultured had to be taken into account. To do so successfully required the translation of the original immediate intuition into the terms of the intellect, into dogma. And as heresies arose and had to be combatted, a further intellectual development took place. It was inevitable that the theologians, in their attempts to rationalise this ever-growing set of theories, became increasingly abstract and all the more removed from the original intuition of Jesus and the Primitive Church. All of this was necessary at this stage. Otherwise Christianity could not have become a permanent and universal religion.

Yet the modern mind cannot accept the dogmatic theology which shows so clearly the marks of the local circumstances and outmoded categories in which it was formed. Does this mean that the proper course is a return to a purely subjective conception of each man's relation to God? This Green denies. Pure intuition will not do any more than will a purely abstract 'idea' of Christianity. The Quaker doctrine of the 'inward light' illustrates the peril of an exclusive emphasis on direct experience, which carries with it the categorical refusal to formulate any definite doctrine. For this is as unsatisfactory as a purely dogmatic theology. The individual must formulate his Christian experience in his own mind, and, if left to himself will do so inadequately.

To overcome the difficulties which can be resolved neither by immediate intuition nor by authoritative dogma, Green proposes to use the resources of his philosophical method. This alone, he thought, could do justice to the wholeness of religious experience, which has been mutilated by earlier concepts. From the new heights attained by modern thought, the philosopher, by the use of reason alone, can transcend previous limitations, penetrate to what is eternally true, and point out how it may be applied to his own society. For what once was a personal revelation now can acquire a greater scope by being embodied in social and political institutions. The true philosopher can find room in his scheme of things for the saint, although the reverse is not true. In short, everything significant in traditional Christianity can be better put by Idealism. And it is highly practical, for it makes into a religious obligation the improvement of this world by the application of Christian love and charity. All men, on religious grounds, should be considered as citizens, as ends in themselves rather than as means to an end. And Green terminates in a paean to the philosopher, who:

> 'drinks the juice of the wine-press which others have trodden. . . .
> He sees that which the prophets of the past in vain desired to see: he sees through their eyes that which they saw not themselves. . . . The eternal objectification of God in the world has for its temporal side the realisation of the divine unity in the perfect art of living. The development of this art consists in the gradual application to wider spheres of a type first realised under special conditions.'[13]

Of course there will be those among the orthodox who will reject this translation of dogmatic theology into Idealism. But they are like those who stoned the prophets, 'like them, in their zeal for the truth once delivered to the saints, they shut the door upon that power of infinite expansion in virtue of which alone it can claim to be absolute truth at all'.[14]

3

Although the details of Green's theology are phrased in a highly technical philosophical language, his conclusions appear with relative clarity in his lay sermons. There he claims that the rôle of the philosopher is to begin with those facts which we know and act upon. Such a fact is man's consciousness that there exists an authoritative standard for moral behaviour which often is at variance with his desires. 'It is the authority of what he is apt to call his conscience, the authority of his own moral nature. Of this, however incompletely it may be actualised in himself, he in a sense feels the possibilities.'[15] And thus men distinguish their 'actual self' from their 'better', 'higher', 'possible' self. How can we explain this consciousness of difference between the self as it is and might be? Green's answer is that 'the "possible self", the realisation of which is the source of all action that can properly be called moral or immoral, is God, and that in our identity with it lies the true unity with God'.[16]

When Green states that the 'possible self' is God, he intends that this proposition be understood in terms of teleological process. Man's present condition is only one phase in his moral development which ultimately has been determined by his idea of his better self. Thus understood, this process of development is to be understood by its *telos* or end.

> Our formula then is that God is identical with the self of every man in the sense of being the realisation of its determinate possibilities, the completion of that which, as merely in it, is incomplete and therefore unreal; that in being conscious of himself man is conscious of God, and thus knows that God is . . .[17]

Thus the meaning of 'realisation' like that of 'identity' is defined within this teleological framework. In this sense, Green's theology and ethics are doctrines of self-realisation and so too, is his theory of political obligation. 'Self-realisation' is a term not without ambiguity. From the last passage cited, it is clear that 'realise' is being used in two different senses: (1) 'to become conscious of'; (2) 'to make real'. Man realises himself by (1) being conscious of his 'higher' or 'better' self; (2) the effort to make that self real, that is by seeking to make his actual character identical with the idea he has of his 'better' self.

So far, the theory maintains that God is identical with the higher self of individual men. But now it may be asked whether God realises himself in either of these two senses in society and institutions. This is Green's claim: 'God has . . . realised himself in all the particularities of moral life'.[19] Or more specifically, 'God's revelation of himself in the human consciousness has thus issued in the institutions by which our elementary moralisation is brought about'.[20] God realises himself in the world by making real his spirit in human institutions, customs and laws. But what can this mean? In what sense could there occur such a realisation of God in the world? Green attempts to answer these questions in his two lay sermons.

In 'The Witness of God' Green turns to St Paul to show what kind of evidence there can be for the reality of God. St Paul sought the proof of Christ's spirit and power in the new life being lived by the body of Christians. 'In the Christian society a new life was being really lived. To this evidence, not to his visions and revelations, St Paul constantly reverts; and it is one good for all time.'[21] From this follows a maxim which further sharpens the meaning of 'self-realisation'. 'For the truth of any practical idea, the only possible evidence is its realisation.'[22] The most convincing evidence of God's reality is in this power manifesting itself in the individual and corporate life of Christians. Thus is God immanent in men. Real faith has real effects.

Green applies to human society the conception of God as immanent in the institutions, aspirations and customs of men just as He is in individuals. Realisation is gradual and growing, developing itself in time. This part of the theory became Green's philosophy of history, which is a theory of progress. Thus man's consciousness of God

> has in manifold forms been the moralising agent in human society, nay, the formative principle of that society itself. The existence of specific duties and the recognition of them, the spirit of self-sacrifice, the moral law and the reverence for it in its most abstract and absolute form, all no doubt presuppose society; but society, of a kind to render them possible, is not the creature of appetite and fear, or of the most complicated and indirect results of these. It implies the action in man of a principle in virtue of which he projects himself into the future . . . as some more perfect being than he actually is, and thus seeks not merely to satisfy momentary wants but to become 'another man,' to become more nearly as this more perfect being.[23]

This passage shows beyond any doubt the theological basis of Green's chapter in *Political Obligation* on 'Will not force is the basis of the state'. To be sure, Green says 'will' and not 'God', but as can be seen in the *Prolegomena to Ethics*, 'will' is also identified with the idea of the 'higher' self and hence God. The formative principle of society itself is divine. And the principle is not static but progressive. Gradually it transforms wants and desires that had their origin in man's animal organism.

> Under this influence wants and desires that have their root in the animal nature become an impulse of improvement (*Besserungstrieb*), which forms, enlarges, and re-casts societies; always keeping before man in various guises, according to the degree of his development, an unrealised ideal of a best which is his God, and giving divine authority to the customs or laws by which some likeness of this ideal is wrought into the actuality of life.[24]

The realisation of God in history takes places in discrete but progressive stages. Man is presented with the idea of God in various guises, according to the degree of his development. At an early stage of God's manifestation in society, man lives by habit and custom. Later it becomes possible to distinguish the concept, the divine spiritual principle making possible society. When the idea of God can be recognised, He can be worshipped. God is immanent in this teleological process of development from the very beginning. Green used this argument against the application of evolutionary theories to ethics and politics. Green's philosophy of history traces God's revelation of himself through men's institutions.[25] Human history is that progressive development of man in society made possible by God. It is not mysterious, because God is reasonable.

4

One peculiarity of Green's position is his insistence that belief involves no sacrifice of reason. Indeed he specifically condemned two arguments frequently used by religious apologists: first, that faith must be based on a leap beyond reason, the *credo non quod sed quia absurdum*; second, that morality and civil obedience would collapse if men generally refused to believe in Christianity. Anyone who is a member of the Church on such grounds is taking a route which in the long run is apt to end in disbelief.

> 'We are not on this account to assume, as hasty and passionate theologians would do, that God reveals himself to man in some other form than reason, or that he suddenly set up the Christian Church as a miraculous institution owing nothing to the other influences of the world, within which all is light, without it all darkness.'[26]

It is this passage which Mrs Ward took out of Green's actual text to become Robert Elsmere's essential article of faith after losing faith in the authoritative defences of Christianity that had thus far served him. 'Christianity is cheaply honoured, when it is made exceptional: God is not wisely trusted when declared unintelligible. . . . God is for ever reason; and his communication, his revelation, is reason.'[27]

It is not frivolity or idle curiosity to inquire into the relation between the life of faith and the order of the world. The human spirit is one and indivisible. The desire to know what nature is and means, the scientific impulse, is but a different relation of faith, the consciousness of God and the longing for reconciliation with him. Philosophy for Green is to be the arbiter between science and religion, demonstrating that there is no inherent conflict, no real competition, between them. Only because men base Christianity on miracles or the dogmatic interpretation of historical events can their faith be challenged. If religion were removed from the realm of history and dogma, then philosophy could prevent its being called into question by every advance in historical criticism and scientific research. This is the basis of Green's statement that:

> The position of dogmatic theology is that true ideas about God and things spiritual are derived from miraculous events. . . . To me the philosophic condition of Theism is that there is nothing real apart from thought, whereas the doctrine of miracles implies that there is something real apart from thought, viz. 'nature,' but that thought has once or twice miraculously interfered with it.[28]

The orthodox apologist insists upon just that theory of the basis of faith which brings it and science into competition on the same ground. 'He will have it that faith stands or falls with the admission or rejection of certain propositions concerning matters of fact, concerning the causation of events which are strictly within the domain of science and which *it* must inevitably reject.'[29]

The scientist must reject all intrusion of the supernatural within the natural. 'The scientific impulse goes on its own way and yields its own result. It traces the determination of event by event in a series to which it finds neither beginning nor end.'[30] But this procedure, perfectly appropriate to the study of the natural, has its limits as well. It is misapplied when the scientist seeks to apply the same process to the spiritual. The scientist tends to be positivistic; that is, he denies the existence of, or, at least, any basis for, our concern with anything which is not strictly an object of science or matter of fact. When confronted with the facts of man's moral or religious life, he is apt to interpret this type of experience in his usual way as a natural history. He naturally attempts a type of reduction which explains human thought and behaviour as analogous to those of animals. Political and social behaviour he derives from appetite and fear, or as the result of their complicated and indirect results. This type of explanation is erroneous because founded on the attempt to apply the methods of science to a realm where they explain nothing. The spiritual life of man has its own principles which are just as reasonable as those of science, although based on a different mode of explanation. The details of this position depend upon a complicated philosophical argument developed in the *Prolegomena to Ethics*. At any rate, this consideration of what science can and cannot explain leads to the conclusion:

> . . . that God is not to be sought in nature, nor in any beginning or

end of nature, but in man himself. It warns us against trying to make statements about God as we might about any matter of fact . . . but it does not touch that relation of the inner man to a higher form of itself of which the expression is to be found, not in the propositions of theology, but in prayer and praise . . . and in that effort after an ideal perfection which is the spring of the moral life.[31]

Faith does not mean submission to authority. Its real foundation is not historical propositions depending on evidence of uncertain origin and value, but a personal and conscious relation of men to God forming the principle of a new life. Again, Green's intention was positive, as Arnold Toynbee insisted:

> Other thinkers have assailed the orthodox foundations of religion to overthrow it. Mr Green assailed them to save it. . . . Christian ideas are the result of certain primary facts of man's spiritual being, the truth of which must be tested by mental analysis instead of historical analysis.[32]

In the modern age, religious men must understand by the light of philosophy the essential spirit of Christianity. A proper philosophical inquiry will not depend upon historical evidence for miracles; it will cut deeper than the evidence of evolutionists. With such a theory as Idealist philosophy can supply, there need be no warfare between science and theology, no gulf between the best knowledge of men and their worship of God. This belief in the sufficiency of the unaided human reason connects Green's theology to his philosophy, or more exactly, comes very close to identifying the fate of Christianity as an intelligible doctrine with the fortunes of Idealist philosophy. Green's confidence in this matter has not been confirmed by the course of philosophy since his time. Behind his espousal of Idealism was a calm confidence in progress and human reason. He saw no ultimate paradoxes about the world; no demonic forces, nothing in the nature of man that needed miraculous redemption. That so high a place should be given to the unaided natural reason indicates how sanguine was its author's view of human nature.

Once Green has described God as identical with that conception of the higher self, possessed by every human being, he cannot possibly accept any version of original sin. The very conception seems barbaric to him, involving the paradox 'of guilt without free agency'.[33] And yet some shadow of that austere dogma lingers on in his own theory. The spiritual principle must realise itself in the animal organism, but it can never do so completely. Hence the faint tragedy, such as it is, of human existence. Man's destiny is to strive after perfection but he can never quite attain it. Sin is the illusion that perfection has been reached, the confusion of any given condition attained by man with his ideal potentialities which remain yet to be realised. But there is none of the sadness and crushing finality of the dogma of original sin. The pathos of Green's view of human nature is that of 'Excelsior!', which is all very robust and hopeful. 'Es irrt der Mensch so lang er strebt' says Goethe's God of Faust. The errors which come from striving are not sins. Sin is complacency, sin consists in 'the effort to actualise one's possibilities in that in which they cannot be actualised, viz. in pleasure'.[34]

In 'The Witness of God' Green considers the sins separating man from God. If these are removed as they can and should be, 'Christ the revealed God, will gradually find his way into our souls. . . . We must be clear from vice, clear from self-indulgence, clear from self-conceit.' All of these are forms of selfishness. That is the root of the matter. The difficulties of the spiritual life are perfectly obvious to anyone who cares to see them. 'They are manifold, doubtless, but their source is simple, and subtlety is wasted in their unravelment.' Perhaps what is worst to be feared is a 'refined self-indulgence, from habits of luxury or indolence, and from nameless desires after all things sweet and pleasant'. To eradicate these vices may be difficult. 'To do so indeed, may be the work of years; but once let the higher resolve be in force and the discipline of life will gradually neutralise or transmute the passions which thwart the single mind.'[35] This is very far from the notion of radical evil. And it presupposes that type of character formed by an Evangelical upbringing.

Green's optimistic conception of human nature was in tune with his age. There is no great individuality in his mild rationalistic optimism. About Green there was 'nothing ecstatic or stormy or mysterious, nothing of the air of a man who had a "new religion" to communicate'.[36] A friend said of him 'For rules of ascetic discipline he had no need. The view of life suggested by so much of the best French literature, that thinking men are generally in a practical dilemma between the extremes of sensual excess and of spiritual exaltation, did not commend itself to him in the least.'[37] He himself was not like this nor were his students. J. A. Symonds reports that à propos of someone's feeling an acute sense of being wicked. Green remarked, 'Poor fellow, the sense of Sin is very much an illusion. People are not as bad as they fancy themselves.'[38] This last remark is significant because it indicates Green's suspicion that such radical judgments of the human condition are meant to prove that strenuous moral efforts in this world are in vain. This would have made nonsense of his own notion of what constituted a genuinely religious life.

If Green's theology were to provide the frame for that' simple religious citizenship' which he had predicted would be the religion of the future, then clearly there was no place for the other-worldly aspects of traditional Christianity. One of the deepest strains in Christianity had been the strong sense of the inherent inferiority of life on earth to life in the next world, 'the belief that both the genuinely "real" and the truly good are radically antithetic in their essential characteristics to anything to be found in man's natural life, in the ordinary course of human experience, however normal, however intelligent, and however fortunate'.[39] Mediaeval Christianity saw human life in the ultimate perspective of its eschatology: death, judgment, heaven and hell. If these are the truths by which men are to govern their lives, then secular activity in this world has but a limited value. Nor has this conclusion been unique to Christianity. Confronted with the transience of human happiness, life's disasters and cruel violence, the baffling spectacle of evil going unpunished and virtue unrewarded, all *clichés* of the human condition, many other religions have likewise rejected this world.[40]

But Green had no sympathy for such abnegations, which in his view are but pretentious excuses for evading duty. Citizenship is preferable to concern for personal sanctity. He saw nothing holy about that type of saint who, finding the world a threat to his conception of the religious life, withdraws to the solitude which enables him to live as he wishes. Such an attitude is individualistic and what Hegel called 'abstract', inappropriate, that is, to an age which, recognising that man's spiritual qualities are God-given, demands that actual institutions be made to correspond to its own standard. Self-realisation now implied positive action. The highest religious duty is the union of theory and practice. Judged by this criterion, monasticism, personal asceticism not directed to improving society, in short, all religious practices oriented away from this world must stand condemned. If Christianity means anything, it means the organisation of a society according to its own highest principles. The logical outcome of other-worldly holiness is a religion of annihilation.

> In the religions of the east the idea of a death to the fleshly self, as the end of the merely human, and the beginning of a divine life, has not been wanting ... But there it has never been realised in action, either intellectually or morally. The idea of the withdrawal from sense has remained abstract. .... In like manner that of self-renunciation has never emerged from the esoteric state. It has had no

outlet into the life of charity, but a back-way always open into the life of sensual licence, and has been finally mechanised in the artificial vacancy of the dervish or fakir.[41]

To this Green contrasted his own notion of a God who has realised himself in the particularities of nature and man's moral life. Gone is the antithesis between the divine and the human. No church is needed to mediate between God and man. Green speaks of

> God, not as 'far off' but 'nigh,' not as a master but as a father, not as a terrible outward power, forcing us we know not whither, but as one of whom we may say that we are reason of his reason and spirit of his spirit; who lives in our moral life, and for whom we live in living for the brethren, even as in so living we live freely, because in obedience to a spirit which is our self.[42]

If there is no gulf between the human and the divine, if in man a divine principle is recognised as the source of truth and moral conduct, then fall all conceptions of the world especially designed to maintain the distance between man and his God. With it as well goes the doctrine of mankind's absolute corruption through original sin and any need for a heavenly world where there will be deliverance from corruption. Therefore life in this world acquires the highest value. Since the ends of human life can be nowhere else, the transformation of this world for the better becomes the chief goal.

The goals of religion have been placed solidly in this life. No unbridgeable distance separates man from God. Sin has no final reality. And human reason unaided by dogma is sufficient to explain all religious truth. Green scarcely seems to feel the need for a theodicy. The problem, as defined by Max Weber, arises out of the question of:

> How it is that a power which is said to be at once omnipotent and kind could have created such an irrational world of undeserved suffering, unpunished injustice, and hopeless stupidity. Either this power is not omnipotent or not kind, or, entirely different principles of compensation and reward govern our lives—principles we may interpret metaphysically, or even principles that forever escape our comprehension.[43]

To this question each of the world religions has evolved its own answer, from which follow significant consequences for the rest of their doctrine.

> One can explain suffering and injustice by referring to individual sin committed in a former life (the transmigration of souls), to the

guilt of ancestors, which is avenged down to the third and fourth generation, or—the most principled—to the wickedness of all creatures *per se*. As compensatory promises, one can refer to hopes of the individual for a better life in the future in this world (transmigration of souls) or to hopes for the sucessors (Messianic realm), or to a better life in the hereafter (paradise).[44]

None of these alternatives can serve Green's purposes. He cannot explain suffering and injustice in this world by original sin any more than he can offer hope of compensation in the next. And there is no comfort for him in the suggestion that human lives are governed by incomprehensible principles. His contention, after all, is that faith must be rational, that there are no mysteries beyond human reason. Further: since God realises himself in this world, the divine power cannot be described as unkind or unjust.

Are there any alternatives left to Green? He can say with Hegel that while from a limited point of view within the process which is being developed, there seems to be evil and injustice, these are but moments in the dialectical progress of history. Seen from the proper teleological perspective, evil and injustice are finally understood to be means to a good end, God's design. Thus Hegel writes in his introduction to *The Philosophy of History*:

> Our mode of treating the subject is, in this aspect, a Theodicy—a justification of the ways of God,—which Leibnitz attempted metaphysically in his method, *i.e.* in indefinite abstract categories,— so that the ill that is found in the World may be comprehended, and the thinking Spirit reconciled with the fact of the existence of evil. Indeed, nowhere is such a harmonising view more pressingly demanded than in Universal History; and it can be attained only by recognising the *positive* existence, in which that negative element is a subordinate, and vanquished nullity. On the one hand, the ulti- mate design of the World must be perceived; and, on the other hand, the fact that this design has been actually realised in it, and that evil has not been able permanently to assert a competing position.[45]

Hegel does not deny evil in history, but claims that it can be seen as necessary to good. Hence it is not arbitrary or capricious, nor does it exist in and for itself. Seen in ultimate perspective, evil is negative, 'a subordinate and vanquished nullity,' vanquished by the 'cunning of reason' working in and through men whether or not they are conscious of its purposes.

Green's theodicy resembles that of Hegel. But for his own reasons, as a reformer in politics, as an enemy of complacency in morals, as a believer in the importance of striving after the good, Green emphasises less the certainty of the outcome than the element of struggle in the process. His optimism is more veiled. He prefers to speak of the 'struggle of mankind towards perfection' rather than of the fulfillment of the world's ultimate design. Green was eminently aware of those political and moral consequences which follow from the various conceptions of theodicy. For this reason, his emphasis falls quite differently from that of Hegel's theory, although it is clearly related to it. Hegel smoothes away too much of history even for Green who detects a potential danger to his own theory of moral and political obligation. The inference could be drawn from Hegel that violence and fraud may be justified as the means employed by divine agency.

On this point Green is a good deal more tender-minded than Hegel. Although in *Political Obligation* Green claims in Hegelian language that 'the actions of men, whom in themselves we reckon bad, are "overruled" for good', he hastens to add that this is true only in a limited sense.[46] The whole discussion of Napoleon's morality in *Political Obligation* is inexplicable without considering the relation of Green's politics to his theology. What is involved is the problem of theodicy and its implications for the theory of political obligation. The theory Green wishes to defend is that good comes only from good; from evil follows only evil. Napoleon and Caesar did good only because their selfish passions had to operate through institutions which embodied a high degree of morality. Napoleon could add to his own power only by increasing the power of France. The French national spirit 'had so much of what may be called the spirit of humanity in it, that it required satisfaction in the belief that it was serving mankind. Hence the aggrandisement of France . . . had to take at least the semblance of a delivery of oppressed peoples, and in taking the semblance it to a great extent performed the reality.'[47] Yet Napoleon's selfishness gave a particular character to his pursuit of those ends and to the extent that it did so, had an evil effect. Thus leaders and heroes are as morally responsible as all other men.

The problem of theodicy was seldom discussed explicitly by Green in his theological writings. Rather the issue was displaced into politics and ethics where Green has to answer the question of whether his is a theory which defines good by the motives of the agent or by the results of the action. In effect, Green's answer to the problem of evil is to deny its existence. Other theories have admitted that evil exists but have introduced some kind of vindication of God's justice. Traditional Christianity has it that justice is done in the next world. Both Hegel and Green attempt to solve the problem within this world. Their theories differ only in emphasis. Hegel's argument is that God is seen to be just when evil is shown to be a vanquished nullity in the course of realising the divine design. Green contends that inevitably passion and selfishness are combined with good, but they can be sorted out. On final analysis, from good comes only good, from evil follows only evil.

This article of faith was closely linked to Green's theory of progress. Both assumptions were to play an important part in his moral and political philosophy. His theology committed him to the belief in an immanent God gradually realising Himself in the world through the idea of human perfection. Acting on this conception of their better selves, men seek to become more nearly perfect. Thus the abstract idea becomes increasingly concrete in 'a complex organisation of life, with laws and institutions, with relationships, courtesies, and charities, with arts and graces through which the perfection is to be attained'.[48] This was neither a static theory nor an encouragement of complacency. Rather it anticipated an unending prospect of struggle as the condition of extending the idea of perfection. This is particularly evident in Green's redefinition of sin as 'the individual's making his own self his object', accepting 'the limitation of momentary appetite or interest', while at the same time ignoring 'the possible expansion in which it becomes that true will of humanity's which is also God's'.[49]

Although in his theology, Green merely implied such theories, or asserted them without attempting to prove their truth, he did feel compelled to attempt this task in Book III of his *Prolegomena to Ethics*. Human progress, he argued, is true *a priori*. As a theory, it cannot be validated or invalidated by reference to any observed facts. Thus he declared no historical or anthropological evidence was relevant to a discussion of their validity. Since Green reserved this privileged sanctuary for those matters such as religious belief which mattered most to him, it is clear that his theory of progress and his neatly moralistic theodicy were unexamined major premises which had a peculiar significance for his theory of Christian citizenship.

5

'Christian citizenship'—this is a phrase which recurs in the work of Green and those affected by him. Yet it is still not altogether clear just how much of a Christian Green was. On the one hand, he produced a strong impression of personal holiness; on the other, his theology left much open to the judgment of his readers and listeners. Chavasse, himself the strictest of Evangelicals, said of his Oxford years, 'The man who made the deepest impression upon me was the late Professor Green, who seemed to have more of the prophet about him than any man I have had the honour of meeting'.[50] Hugh Price Hughes, among the leading Methodists of his day, called Green 'the most splendid Christian that I ever knew'.[51] Hughes attended Green's lectures and insisted that the key point of the latter's Idealism was 'the philosophical expression of the good old Methodist doctrine of entire sanctification'.[52] Such testimonials are, however, not altogether conclusive, if Green's theology is to be judged by its effects. Many of his students became rationalists who cited their master; still others revived the High Church and Tractarian wing of the Anglican Church by the use of Idealist modes of thought. Not infrequently Green's teaching was considered to corrode belief, and yet his lectures were attended by 'a good many of us [who] at that time cherished the hope of confirming our shaken religious faith'.[53] What did his theology mean to Green himself? Was his ambiguity deliberate or otherwise?

It is easier to state what he was against than what he positively affirmed. Green set himself against dogmatic theology and the creeds used by churches claiming to be the authoritative organ for interpreting the objective revelation of God in his sacred writings. He refused to assign more than symbolic significance to any miracles or historical events reported in the Bible. Jesus he regarded as the original stimulator of the Christian consciousness. God is the idea of one's self as it might be. This idea is progressively realising itself in the experience of mankind, both in its social and political units, and in individuals. Such a mode of thought made it possible for him to consider both the political action of citizenship and the individual act of faith as religious. Although in his politics he emphasised the significance of men's membership in corporate groups, in his theology, he defined religious experience as essentially individual, a relation between a man and his God, the evidence for which is the sacrifice of an interest or passionate impulse. That there are grave ambiguities in his form of statement is evident from the defence of Green's theology offered by Nettleship. To the question, 'Was Green a Christian?,' his biographer replied:

> The answer must depend on what 'to be a christian' means. If it means to believe that every man has God in him, that religion is the continual death of a lower and coming to life of a higher self, and that these truths were more vividly realised in thought and life by Jesus of Nazareth and some of his followers than by any other known men, then without doubt he was a Christian. If it means to believe that the above truths depend upon the fact that Jesus was born and died under conditions impossible to other human beings, then equally without doubt he was not a Christian. If he had been asked, why then

he so habitually used the language of orthodox christianity, he would probably have answered that language is not the private property of any man or set of men, and that much of the phraseology of Paul and the fourth gospel . . . is quite incompatible with some of the doctrines of orthodoxy. But the truth is that . . . he cared about the reality of religion and not about its accessories, and was convinced that its reality does not depend upon its dogmatic expression.[54]

From this statement no one can say whether Green believed in the real personality of the God he described in Idealist terms, or whether he thought of God in any of the senses essential to Christian worship. This ambiguity seems to have been deliberate and intended to sustain a variety of interpretations. It is not as though we are dealing with a clear-cut theistic conception of God which happened to be blurred by Green's personal difficulties in expressing himself. Rather he felt strongly an emotion which he thought he could phrase more adequately in Idealist language than in any other terms. He thought that he was being purely constructive in his substitution of philosophy for dogmatic theology. Yet it must be noticed that he was doing more than translating traditional Christian language into its nearest Idealist equivalent. He insisted on his right to continue using that language while construing its meaning in a way altogether different from that ever intended by orthodox believers, or the men who devised Christian creeds.[4] At the end of his sermon on 'Faith' he advises those of his hearers who can no longer 'adopt the received dogmatic expression of Christian faith', that

> Inability to adopt the creeds of Christendom . . . need not disqualify us from using its prayers. A creed is meant to serve either as an article of agreement with other men, or as a basis of theological argument; and from each point of view there are objections to using its words in any other meaning than that which they are ordinarily understood to bear.[55]

But prayers are not meant to be heard by men. 'So long as our prayers express the effort after a higher life, recognised as proceeding from, and only to be satisfied by, the grace of God, the theological formulae in which they are clothed are of little importance.'[56]

Green wished to be not merely critical, but constructive and reasonable as well. From Evangelicalism he had inherited earnestness and pious purpose; from Idealism the tendency to retain the names of old beliefs for views which bore but a shadowy resemblance to their originals. This, as Santayana has remarked, enabled German philosophers to transform the concepts of God, freedom, and immortality into their opposites, while claiming that these new meanings represented not change, but merely superior understanding.[57] This mode of thought today seems to have combined arrogance with a disingenuous lack of candour. Yet it is important, just because we lack sympathy with it, to make certain that we comprehend what Green thought himself to be doing. There was a remarkably explicit exchange between him and Scott Holland on the occasion of the latter's ordination. Holland was among the first of Green's disciples to become a High Church clergyman, and he felt the need to explain himself. He could not see that he was doing anything inconsistent with what he had learned from Green: 'It seemed to me as if all the meaning I could put into my theology and certainly my ethics was still the old thing. Only, the religious form seemed to me to cap it all, and the cap seemed to me to fit.'[58]

Green answered that so far from being displeased, he could have no greater satisfaction than the knowledge that he had helped lay the intellectual platform for Holland's religious life. He would rather not express his own ideas at all, if by doing so he weakened anyone's faith. To become a clergyman offered an opening to a nobler life than was offered by most other professions. All the best influences in his own life stemmed from clergymen, and he himself had been powerfully attracted to that calling. As for his own conception of the relation between philosophy and religion:

> I never dreamt of philosophy doing instead of religion. My own interest in it, I believe, is wholly religious; in the sense that it is . . . the reasoned intellectual expression of the effort to get to God. . . . But tho' I reckon religion and morality properly identical, and religion and philosophy to be in such different planes that they cannot compete, I do recognise a competition between philosophy and dogmatic theology each claiming to be the true *rationale* of religion; and . . . I have definitely rejected dogmatic theology for a certain sort of philosophy.[59]

Green has effectively reversed his earlier statement that he never dreamt of philosophy doing instead of religion. His actual meaning is what he said in his sermon on 'Faith': that so long as men make the effort after a higher life, the theological formulae are of little importance. He acknowledges that this view is incompatible with orthodox Christianity.

> This does not to my own consciousness essentially separate me from orthodox Xtians, but I fear it must (if known) do so to theirs. . . . The result is that from orthodox Christianity, as expressed in prayer, and in the ordinances of Protestant worship, I find no alienation, while I could not subscribe to one of the creeds.'[60]

Green hoped to meet the needs of his students by supplying to them intellectual formulae which would be as appropriate for orthodox clergymen as for rationalists. In short, he thought it worth his while to sketch out what philosophy could offer as a least common denominator of belief for those who searched for moral principles by which to govern their lives. His enterprise may now appear to be quite strange, and certainly few today would think it possible to succeed in it. Yet we ought not dismiss Green's effort as doomed from the beginning. It did have the effect he sought to achieve—among his own students. His early death, and the difficulty of his concepts and his language no less than the transitional quality of his message, limited the impression he was to make on opinion outside Oxford. But for some time within the University and its intellectual orbit which stretched as far as Scotland,[10] Green's theology satisfied a variety of groups. On the one side, the tendency towards a secular ethical culture movement appeared among Green's followers; on the other, his thought was exploited by men like Holland who regarded themselves as Tractarians. Both wings showed their debt to Green by their active concern with movements designed to better the lot of the lower classes. The rationalists were for the most part associated with the London Ethical Society and its offshoots; The High Churchmen, with the *Lux Mundi* movement in theology, and the Christian Social Union in reform. In London, Toynbee Hall was the natural centre for those outside the Church; Oxford House, for those within it. The effect of *Robert Elsmere* certainly was to strengthen the hand of those who thought that the Church of England was not the place for anyone who held Green's views about the meaning of religion. Mrs Ward did her part to give an institutional basis to the 'New Brotherhood of Christ' by establishing the Passmore Edwards Settlement in London, and naming the Library for Green, a lectureship for Jowett, and choosing a former student of Green's to head the settlement.

The London Ethical Society had its origin in a group of Green's students at work in and about Toynbee Hall, the pioneer settlement house in the East End of London. The Reverend Samuel Barnett, who presided over Toynbee Hall, was an empiricist who kept his eyes on practical enterprises. And this did not please those who felt '. . . the neglect of the philosophical view of the nature and ends of human life which Arnold Toynbee himself had learned from Green'.[62] Although the founders were willing to take the name of their society from the American Ethical Culture movement founded by Felix Adler, the English thought of themselves as philosophers first, and ethical or religious teachers second. Their inspiration came from Green's theology as they interpreted it: the 'faith in the reality beyond sight of the things that make life worth living'.[63] Its devotees were not theists, nor were they Comtean positivists. Rather they emphasised their belief that in nature there is 'one onward-moving, self-differentiating, self-comprehending life. This . . . spirit of nature . . . is something we did not make, but of which we have all received. In so far as we understand its meaning and enter into its purposes we obey its law, which is also our law—our morality.'[64] Among the most significant of those who established the movement was another of Green's students, J. H. Muirhead, who made it clear that the Ethical Society distinguished between Jesus as an object of worship and as a teacher of what is lovable and admirable. He added that the followers of Jesus were not called Christians at the beginning, and might not be at the end. In another 'ethical sermon', Bernard Bosanquet stated even more bluntly that when men had first to learn to behave themselves, they could do so only by imagining that they had to obey some kind of parent or schoolmaster. But modern man must get the matter straight on the proper rational basis:

> We must know what is right, what we call God's will, by finding it in our own will. And we must do what is right, what we call God's will, because we find that it is our own will. . . .
> I do not think it matters whether we call the community in which we have our station a Christian community. If we keep the substance of Christianity, we may let the shadow, the name, take care of itself. . . .
> Thus, in everyday life, we need the belief that the good is a reality. If we hold this belief more distinctly and more intensely, it amounts to this, that *nothing but good is* a reality.
> This faith is what people mean by religion. . . .
> The difference between morality and religion seems then to be that in morality we know that the good purpose is real, in religion we believe that nothing else is real. . . .
> An all-important truth follows from this—from religion and morality being the same in principle. The *duties of religion are the same as the duties of morality*. If we speak of duties to God, we mean the same duties as duties to man. Worship or prayer, in the sense of meditation, are good things if they help us to do our real duties. But it is a sad degradation of words to speak of a ceremony in a church as Divine Service.[65]

What is surprising about this movement is not the number of its adherents, which was never considerable, but the broad spread of prominent and influential persons who rallied to it. Its committee for the approximately fifteen years that it held together, from

1886 to 1897, included a curious mixture of members of the Fabian and Charity Organisation Societies, as well as civil servants, economists, businessmen, and many who taught in university or school. An 'Ethical Library' was published by Swan Sonnenschein & Co., with Muirhead as editor. Among the Presidents of the Ethical Society were Edward Caird and William Wallace, both of whom might have been anticipated since they were leading Oxford Idealists. But the list also included such less likely names as Henry Sidgwick, Leslie Stephen and Sir John Seeley. The presence of Sidgwick and Stephen indicates that the alleged differences between Oxford and Cambridge men of this generation may be easily exaggerated. Stephen published two volumes of addresses to Ethical Societies under the title of *Social Rights and Duties*. And this reference to F. H. Bradley's *Ethical Studies* was repeated in Sidgwick's presidential address, which he later published under the title of 'My Station and its Duties'.

Apparently Cambridge men felt the need for an untheological humanism based on ethics just as much as did Oxford men of the same generation. Certainly Stephen, Sidgwick, Green, and many of his followers, had all felt the same religious impulse, the value of which they never denied even when most impressed by the intellectual objections to it. Thus they were led to seek a reasonable view of the world by which the best knowledge and the highest morality might be reconciled. In their views of duty and truth, in their devotion to their separate tasks as they defined them, they all showed themselves marked by their Evangelical heritage. Although both Sidgwick and Stephen resigned their fellowships at Cambridge because they considered themselves to be Rationalists, they were not able to put completely behind them the teaching of self-sacrifice, or renounce altogether interest in theological questions. Both knew and admired George Eliot, as did Green, who cited her in a crucial place in his *Prolegomena to Ethics*. All three would have identified themselves with her as she spoke with 'terrible earnestness' of God, Immortality and Duty, explaining 'how inconceivable was the *first*, how unbelievable the *second*, and yet how peremptory and absolute the *third*'.[66] Indeed Sidgwick once approached Green in the hope of finding Oxford supporters for a projected 'Free Christian Union', which had as its object an invitation to common action by

'. . . all who deem men responsible, not for the attainment of Divine truth, but only for the serious search for it; and who rely, for the religious improvement of human life, on filial Piety and brotherly Charity, with or without more particular agreement in matters of doctrinal theology.'[67]

Later in life, Sidgwick was one of the founders of the Society for Psychical Research, in which he remained active until his death. By almost any criterion Sidgwick was a curious rationalist, seeking communion in a 'Free Christian Union', and a scientific proof of immortality. Provided only that the language of Idealist metaphysics were not used, he and Stephen were perfectly willing to collaborate in the effort 'to set moral, social and religious problems in the light of philosophical principles'.[68] And this consensus about objectives combined with caution about insisting on any one formula was reflected in the General Principles of the Ethical Society.*

At its best, the Ethical Society served as a common meeting-ground for men from the various universities who found themselves working in London, and for the younger men to get into touch with some of the most prominent thinkers of the generation before. Its effort to attain a common denominator of belief necessarily depended upon the ambivalent attitudes towards religion that have already been discussed at such length. It played a part in the world of London reform, and brought together men otherwise as diverse as C. S. Loch and J. A. Hobson, Graham Wallas and Bernard Bosanquet. In 1897, the Society was transformed into a 'School of Ethics and Social Philosophy' under the direction of E. J. Urwick. When the University of London was reconstituted, the School was absorbed by the London School of Economics, where Urwick became the first professor of Social Philosophy. And so, like the Fellowship of the New Life, which turned into the Fabian Society, and like the institution of the Charity Organisation Society for social workers, which was taken over by the Department of Social Science formed by the London School of Economics, there was a transition from a voluntary group designed to promote a moral objective to an efficient organisation for playing a rôle in the continuing development of British social policy.

---

* Muirhead commented that the Oxford Idealists took care not to carry their essential ideas on their sleeves, lest they alienate others. Hence the language of the General Principles as stated in the Annual Report for 1888-9:
  1. The good life has a claim upon us in virtue of its supreme worthiness and this claim is the highest it can have.
  2. It is therefore in no way dependent upon belief in a system of supernatural rewards and punishments.
  3. In practice it is to be realised by accepting and acting in the spirit of such common obligations as are enjoined by the relationships of family and society in so far as these are means to the fullest development of our nature as man. (Muirhead, *Reflections*, p.76.)

6

Of all the diverse effects produced by Green's thought, none was more unanticipated than that upon the High Church party at Oxford and elsewhere. In 1889, seven years after his death, some of Green's students, a group of theologians for the most part teaching at Oxford, published *Lux Mundi: A Series of Studies in the Religion of the Incarnation*.[69] This volume of essays speedily became the most controversial work of its kind since *Essays and Reviews;* but, more constructive than that plea for freedom of religious thought, it began the trend which came to dominate Anglican theology, as the present Archbishop of Canterbury tells us, from the last decade of the Victorian era until well into the twentieth century.[70] The *Lux Mundi* movement, Dean Inge remarked, gave a new lease of life to the High Churchmen.[71] And even more extraordinary, the leaders of this group in theology, Charles Gore and Scott Holland, founded, as the direct political and social consequence of its teaching, the Christian Social Union. Although this organisation never established an effective relationship with the working classes, nevertheless it did much to make the Church aware of the degree of justice present in the claims of the democratic and socialist movements. The testimony of the *New Statesman*, although not conclusive, may serve as an approximate measure of the CSU's achievement:

> 'Charles Gore did more than any one man, except perhaps Westcott, to change the official attitude of the Church to the problem of Labour; it is due to him, and to men like Stanton, Dolling, Headlam, and Scott Holland, that the assumption usually made on the Continent that Christianity and Socialism are incompatible has never been accepted in England.'[72]

That Green should have affected both the religious thought and the political objectives of the group within the Anglican Church which he personally found least sympathetic—this is a story which requires both exposition and explanation. For the earlier Tractarians cared little for what concerned him in theology. Froude, Newman, Ward, Keble, and Pusey laid their emphasis upon the Catholicity of the Church of England. That it was a substantive body independent of the State, that its origins were divine, that through its continuity with the apostolic Church, it had supreme authority over the minds and consciences of its members who were bound to observe its ancient rituals—these were themes that the first generation of High Churchmen never tired of repeating. To the challenges raised so frequently by natural scientists and practitioners of historical criticism, the Tractarians who remained within the Anglican Church tended to respond by the repetition of ancient dogmatic formulae and injunctions to obey ecclesiastical authority. Insofar as their theology had a distinctive character, its accent fell on the Atonement, a doctrine which in their minds had much to do with personal holiness, and rather less with the circumstances of the actual life of most men in the society within which their Church was placed. The Oxford Movement thus remained within the terms of Evangelical thought—the soul, sin, redemption. It is true that Tractarians conceived of 'the Church as the sphere, the sacraments as the means, of Redemption; but still only the redemption of *the soul*, not the redemption in the full sense of man, nor the redemption of the world'.[73] In short, freedom of thought, attention to the discoveries of scientists and scholars, active concern for the social welfare of those within its religious jurisdiction did not rank high among the concerns of High Churchmen.

All this was changed by the *Lux Mundi* movement. Like so many other Victorian controversies, the stir occasioned by its publication today seems remote. But it is perhaps worth recapitulating here a story told in greater detail elsewhere. Charles Gore, who had emerged apparently unscathed from the instruction first of Westcott and then of Green and Jowett, was the rising hope of High Church theology at Oxford. Liddon himself chose Gore to be the first head of the house at Oxford founded in honour of Pusey's memory. But when the book appeared, Liddon was appalled by its contents. To him it appeared little less than a betrayal of trust, 'a proclamation of revolt against the spirit and principles of Dr Pusey and Mr Keble,'[74] a capitulation to all that was rationalistic and pelagianising in Idealist thought. It is obvious why Liddon was so provoked and shocked. He thought that Green's teaching had transformed the outlook of these young theologians who still called themselves High Churchmen.

It must be said immediately that, although certain of Green's orientations were taken over by this school, it remained in all other respects Tractarian and ritualistic. Its members to a man believed that dogma, sacrament and Church are essential to Christianity. Nor was the sense of mystery denigrated any more than the reality of sin denied. Even Scott Holland, close as he was to Green, was distinguished from him by a passionate emphasis on the doctrine of redemption.[75] This miraculous element, like other Tractarian aspects of his theology, represents those points on which he would not yield to his teacher's views, Green had had no effect when he warned against 'the tendency . . . to substitute for the moral presence of God in the Church, a miraculous and mystical one, in other words against "Sacerdotalism and Sacramentalism". Opinions about evidence don't affect the essence of Christianity; but these demoralise it.'[76] No doubt had Green lived to read *Lux Mundi*, he would have disapproved of the use it made of his theology. Jowett, at least, was not pleased:

> 'The point on which the High Church party tend to give way is Scripture, and especially the Old Testament. They feel that as the Bible is seen more and more to be like other books, the greater the need of the Church, an aspect of the question which is not wholly unpleasing to them.
> I have read a considerable portion of *Lux Mundi*, but am a good deal disappointed in it. It has a more friendly and Christian tone than High Church theology used to have, but it is the same old haze or maze—no nearer approach of religion either to morality or to historical truth.'[77]

Yet Green would have been more impressed by the social philosophy of the *Lux Mundi* group. For although Green shared many of Jowett's Broad Church opinions in theology, he had added to them his own distinctive note: that a Church unconcerned with its effect upon the political justice and social welfare of its society cannot be said to be the bearer of the gospel taught by Jesus. This had not gone unheeded by the essayists. Nor did they reject his notion that the Christian message was a progressive revelation which could be seen at work in movements outside the Church. Like Green they believed that the great forces operating in modern culture were beneficent, and ought to be regarded as the fulfilment of Christianity. Principal among these were democracy and the new kind of citizenship it made possible in a State moralised by the values immanent in Christian teaching. In this respect as in others, religion could not be separated from ethics.

Despite such resemblances, some commentators have played down Green's influence upon the essayists, who, it is said, cared more about what he criticised than about his philosophical method and the results it yielded. No doubt Green's repudiation of materialism, hedonism, and empiricism appealed to these young clergymen, but their debt to him was greater than that. J. R. Illingworth, who was among the strongest intellectually of the contributors, wrote in a letter the year before publication: 'Someone is wanted on our side to keep up the touch of abstract thinking—as circumstances seem driving most of us to one form or another of "applied" thought, and the only people who are doing the other seem to be the Greenites of the Left (Bosanquet, Bradley). And yet we know the Greenites of the Right are the only

true interpreters.'[78] Indeed in the preface to *Lux Mundi* that drew
Liddon's fire the dominant note sounded by Gore could have come
almost verbatim from Green. The apparently harmless declaration
by the writers that their aim was 'to put the Catholic faith into its
right relation to modern intellectual and moral problems',[79]
brought the almost immediate question whether High Churchmen
should not proceed in precisely the opposite fashion, that is, by
evaluating proposed contributions of modern knowledge in the
light of the Church's teaching. But this was simply a failure to
understand that *Lux Mundi* was an attempt to mount an apologist
counter-offensive with the aid of new categories of thought
hitherto monopolised by the enemies of Tractarianism. After
sitting in Green's classes and then teaching undergraduates on the
scent of the Idealist concepts that were becoming so powerful,
the essayists were convinced that the success of the Church with the
new generation would depend upon its capacity to confront, with
all the intelligence it could muster, the major intellectual problems
of the age. And, on the basis of Green's analysis, they agreed that
science and historical criticism, if properly understood, would
restore rather than annihilate the prospects of faith.

In its theology, the school deliberately shifted emphasis from the
Atonement and cross to the Incarnation. This they regarded not
only as an unique and miraculous event, but as one that has continued to have effects upon man's historical development. 'He
who became incarnate is the Logos who has been at work in the
whole created world, in nature and in man, in art and in science,
in culture and in progress, and all in such wise that contemporary
trends of thought, like evolution or socialism, are not enemies to
be fought, but friends who can provide new illuminations of the
truth that is in Christ.'[80] This conception of the world as the
realisation of a spiritual principle is clearly taken from Green. His
conception of the relation between science and philosophy was
translated into theological terms by two of the more enthusiastic
Greenites of the right, Illingworth himself and Aubrey Moore.
The latter, writing on the 'Christian Doctrine of God', began with
the leading theme of Green's lay sermons: that a God who
appears but occasionally in history, intervening by miracle in the
chain of causation, is incredible in the light of modern science.
Indeed from the point of view of High Church theology, this
consequence of scientific work was to be welcomed as dooming
whatever was left of Deism or natural religion. The proper conception of God is that he is at once transcendent and immanent
and, when understood properly, the theory of Evolution provides
an indication of how this immanence has worked itself out.

Illingworth, likewise welcoming evolution as a confirmation of Christian teaching, declared that Darwin had made it possible to see the true significance of the Incarnation. It had been understood by the Church Fathers to mean that the divine world had ordered creation, and thereafter served as the guiding light of mankind. And so the final effect of Darwinism upon theology will be other than was at first anticipated: 'Our Creator will be known to have worked otherwise indeed than we had thought, but in a way quite as conceivable, and to the imagination more magnificent'.[81] In his discussion of the 'The Incarnation and Development', Illingworth went from optimism about the effects of science upon faith to an even more striking expression of Green's notion that modern western civilization is but the progressive working out of principles immanent in Christianity from the beginning: 'It is true that secular civilization has co-operated with Christianity to produce the modern world. But secular civilization is, as we have seen, in the Christian view, nothing less than the providential correlative and counterpart of the Incarnation.'[82] Scott Holland in his essay on 'Faith' again exhibits the characteristic device of adapting one of Green's key concepts for the purposes of this group. What is involved here is the definition of faith as the total effort of a man to realise his conception of an ideal perfection. Holland, for his part, defined faith as 'an active principle, a source of energy, a spring of movement: and, as such, its verification can never take place through passive introspection. It verifies itself only in actions: its reality can only be made evident through experience of its living work.'[83]

In the eyes of some at least of the *Lux Mundi* group, their theology had direct political and sociological consequences. No doubt, as in all such matters, the question of influences is complex and impossible to resolve conclusively. Certainly the notion that the Church should regulate and order any society which calls itself Christian is to be found in many authors; Maurice cannot be ignored in this connection, and Westcott, the first President of the Christian Social Union, taught Gore at school. Yet the tone and argument of the *Lux Mundi* school, when it came to the social question cannot but suggest Green's powerful emphasis on citizenship and reform. Just as the essayists listened when Green told them that faith to survive must take the line that science is not irreligious, nor religion hostile to knowledge so too they heeded his words that a Christianity that concentrates exclusively on personal piety will have nothing to say to the great majority of men in an unjust industrial society. In the private correspondence of Scott Holland there are vivid passages testifying to the marks left upon him by the biting language Green used in describing clerical indifference to suffering and injustice. And even after the passage of many years, Gore in recollecting the circumstances in which the Christian Social Union was founded, caught the authentic accent of Green and Arnold Toynbee:

'Its motive was the sense that Christianity and especially the Church of England, had lamentably failed to bear its social witness—its witness to the principles of divine justice and human brotherhood which lie at its heart. It had left the economic and industrial world to build itself up on quite fundamentally unchristian premisses, as if Christianity had got nothing to do with the matter. And now that a widespread rebellion of Labour was organising itself against the economic slavery of the workers, and against a condition of the law which seemed to regard property as more sacrosanct than persons, it was essential that at least by a tardy act of repentance the Christian Church should bestir itself to reconsider and assert its own principles and let the contending parties and the apathetic churchgoers see that it was nothing less than essential Christianity that was at stake.'[84]

The responsibility outlined by Gore and actively propagated by the Christian Social Union was based on their new emphasis on the Incarnation. The *logos* has become flesh to fulfil and redeem the world He has originally created. His body, the Church, must express the universal brotherhood of mankind. Democracy and socialism, as historical movements which are working to that end, should be welcomed and assisted. Personality, to be fully realised, must not be subjected to the so-called iron laws of economics, but to the moral requirements of the Church. On this implication, Binyon commented: ' "Lux Mundi" is of as much importance for the Christian Socialist Movement as "Fabian Essays" for Socialism itself'.[85]

When the Christian Social Union was founded in 1889, its first president was Westcott and its first secretary, Scott Holland. Its declared principles were marked by a certain generality and moralism, which some of its later critics detected in all of its later activities:

'1 To claim for the Christian law the ultimate authority to rule social practice.

2 To study in common how to apply the moral truths and principles of Christianity to the social and economic difficulties of the present time.

3 To present Christ in practical life as the living Master and King, the enemy of wrong and selfishness, the power of righteousness and love.'[86]

The leaders of the CSU proposed to do their work by careful

inquiry and investigation of social problems to be followed by the application of the Christian solution. The CSU at various times took part in campaigns against slums and denounced the use of leaded glaze in the manufacture of pottery; it compiled lists of approved trades, and organised study groups to develop what it called a Christian sociology. Several volumes emerged from such projects and the views of eminent contributors can be found in *Property: Its Rights and Duties* and *Good Citizenship.*[87] What the CSU really intended to do was to change the thinking of the Anglican Church on social and economic questions so that it should not be a foregone conclusion that its authorities should without exception support employers against employees. To this end, it restricted membership to Anglicans, organised study groups in the Universities where candidates for ordination were preparing themselves, and set up a number of branches which also sponsored public meetings. Connected with it were three journals: the *Economic Review, Goodwill* and *Commonwealth.* The average membership from 1910 to 1920 was probably about 6,000.[88] During that period, friends and critics agree, the CSU failed to reach the working class with anything like the success of the Christian Socialism of Maurice and Kingsley. And, by its refusal to work with either the Fabians or the Independent Labour Party, it antagonised those members of the clergy who expected most from it.[89] On the other hand, the CSU did achieve its objective of transforming the attitudes of the Anglican clergy in part and those of the Bishops almost completely. One member who was in a position to know, thought that by its method of group discussion among ordination candidates at Oxford, the CSU changed the minds of the younger generation there and, to a lesser degree, the same was true at Cambridge.[90] The declarations of the Bishops on social questions had, by 1908, come around to the viewpoint of the CSU after having been at the opposite pole. In addition, out of its work had come the first Interdenominational Conference of Social Service Unions, for the dissenters had within their own churches emulated the conception of the CSU. This lasted until 1920 when it merged with the Navy League and took the new name of the Industrial Christian Fellowship. The founders of the CSU shared Green's ambivalence about state interference because they had been convinced by him that the improvement of character by the removal of obstacles is the only sound criterion for legislation. Yet it can be said about Green's former students, whether in the CSU or in the London Ethical Society, that they accepted the responsibilities of citizenship as an essential part of their view of the world. If a philosophy of religion is to be judged by its fruits, then many of the allegations that have been made about the conservative implications of Idealism will have to be reconsidered in the light of what Green and his students made of it.

7

As a reformer, Green wished to invest political activity with the strongest possible sanction. Society, permeated by God, disciplines and moralises man. Hence through activity in his community, man realises his ethical potentialities. Faith reveals itself in good works; active citizenship is the highest attainable morality. This is how the reason and the conscience may cease to be merely individual and intellectual. A proper view of the world will teach men how much they owe to forces outside themselves: to God, and to the social and political groups of which they are members. Reason, the source of rights, is also the source of obligations.

This was Green's 'philosophy of life', his alternative to Evangelical Christianity. Just as Roman Catholicism had defined for him what must be excluded from his philosophy, so Evangelicalism had delimited what must be carried over and translated. Its emphasis upon individual religious experience, the minimising of priest or minister, the revival of justification by faith, the methodical life dedicated unconditionally to the highest of pursuits—these seemed to him worth preserving. Thus Arnold Toynbee in explaining the meaning of Green's metaphysical paraphrase of God tells us that, 'The ideal self is in fact the God of the Psalms and the Christ of evangelical religion'.[91] But Green's sympathies with Evangelicalism did not extend to its vivid concern with salvation. His own interests were rather more secular and ethical than other-worldly. What he sought was a type of character and a mode of life. Yet as Scott Holland remarked, 'It was his profound Evangelical heart which made all that he taught us intellectually become spiritual and religious in its effect.'[92] Green's religious interests have meaning in terms of this tension with an antecedent state of belief. Unquestionably, he admired the seriousness, the certitude of the older generation in their stern faith. Taken over from them were his criteria for determining what constituted a worthwhile life. But the fervent zeal for salvation had disappeared. In its place was a restless altruism, a drive to incessant activity in the name of some ideal. Evangelical discipline had left its mark upon the characters of the faithless. They were never to be quite nonchalant in their graceless state, for their dominant quality was, 'what the Evangelicals called seriousness, the Arnoldians, earnestness; and Bagehot, most happily, eagerness . . .'[93] A student said of Green: 'His dark and serious face expressed the earnestness, the almost sombreness, of his character. He was not gloomy nor pessimistic, but he seemed to dwell much on the evil in the world and in his own country, and on the obligation incumbent on him and all men to do something to mitigate inequality and misery and vice.'[94]

This background makes explicable Green's transposition of religious values. From Evangelicalism, he derived his belief that faith reveals itself in the transformation of individuals and society. What makes man's life dignified and peculiarly human is the sinking of individuality in something higher and better than the fleshly self. To reject selfish pleasures, to overcome indolence and apathy, and by this discipline to methodise one's life in the service of the higher ideal—these were the values taken from the rigid tradition and 'transformed and spiritualised'.

But these continuities should not obscure the changes. The older theology had put at the very centre of man's life the struggle to attain salvation and eternal life in the next world. With the abandonment of belief in a future life, struggle became an end in itself; and optimism, the doctrine of a theodicy which must balance its accounts in this world without bringing in the next. Of all human destinies, the most exalted is to strive on in the service of the common good of humanity. The peculiar twist of the doctrine, its pathos, is in its abnegation. Its heroes may not themselves live to enjoy the fruits of their labours.

Green was not overly given to literary illustrations, but he selected two passages to end his *Prolegomena to Ethics:* one from George Eliot, the other from Browning. The George Eliot passage is full of ascetic altruism and disciplined sacrifice. It comes very close to expressing Green's conviction that men will respond, if called upon, to the painful ideal rather than the selfish pleasure.

> We can only have the highest happiness, such as goes along with being a great man, by having wide thoughts, and much feeling for the rest of the world as well as ourselves; and this sort of happiness often brings so much pain with it, that we can only tell it from pain by its being what we would choose before anything else, because our souls see it is good.[95]

The passage from Browning's 'Rabbi Ben Ezra' combines the same sentiment about pain with the glorification of striving for its own sake.

> Then, welcome each rebuff
> That turns earth's smoothness rough,
> Each sting that bids nor sit nor stand but go!

Be our joys three-parts pain!
Strive, and hold cheap the strain;
Learn, nor account the pang; dare, never grudge the throe![96]

These two passages, like so many others in Green himself, express an emotion dear to the Victorians, and one which recurs in thinkers and schools otherwise diverse. Men, in the midst of a swing away from Christianity, felt strongly the need for something to replace it. Perhaps it was the half-conscious realisation of this condition which brought Green to perceive that a great reservoir of energy and fervour might be diverted to secular altruism from a crumbling faith focused upon the next world. This insight is at the bottom of that remarkable final book of the *Prolegomena*, which might be called an essay in the social psychology of reform. There he criticises the Utilitarians, not for being bad men, nor even for teaching a doctrine that produced bad effects, but because a much better strategy than theirs was available to the social reformer. Hedonism, materialism, the flat denial of the value of self-sacrifice, could not attract large sectors of this new public. Nor could Utilitarianism be successfully transformed from egoistic hedonism to altruistic hedonism. Those who, like J. S. Mill and Henry Sidgwick, attempted to do so became entrapped in a conflict between their logical premises and their philanthropic motives. Thus Green concluded that the philosopher who sought reform should provide not directions on how to use the felicific calculus but a doctrine of self-sacrifice in the interest of altruism.

Green believed that he had found in Idealism a profound truth, the ignoring of which had led astray his predecessors in British philosophy and the discovery of which at last rendered it possible to give the right answer to the great question of the age: how to reconcile right thought with right conduct. At the heart of his own teaching is the exaltation of an integral and ever-active altruism. Through continued and purposeful striving, there may be realised progressively, if never completely, a type of character and an organisation of society which is altruistic, subordinating personal pleasures to the common good. Clearly these values are secular transpositions of the certitude, perseverance, and dedication of the Evangelical believer.

The emotional dynamic formerly directed to attaining salvation is now switched to the service of man in this world. And this is done in Green's theology by a re-definition of the human situation. Beatrice Webb describes this process as 'the emotion which, like the warp before the woof, gives strength and direction to the activities of the intellect. I suggest it was during the middle decades of the nineteenth century that, in England, the impulse of self-subordinating service was transferred, consciously and overtly, from God to man.'[97]

'Self-subordinating' is a significant phrase. To subordinate one's self to the service of other men seemed obviously analogous to the surrender of self in divine worship. Both might be called religious, because abnegating personal desire for a principle outside the fleshly self. Perhaps the sanctity of the citizen may be even nobler than the sanctity of the individual believer concerned only with his personal salvation. 'True citizenship "as unto the Lord" ... I reckon higher than "saintliness" in the technical sense.'[98] In this sentence, passed in judgment against Gerard Manley Hopkins, is summed up the most powerful tendency of Green's religious ideas. He would direct the zeal of Christianity into a religion of citizenship.

Yet it has been suggested that his choice was a mistake. Repeated attempts have been made to prove that if Idealist theory is taken seriously, it leads logically to passive acquiescence in things as they are.[99] If progress is the law of history, if God gradually is revealing himself in man's institutions, then this process began without human agency and proceeds independently of man's moral actions. If the world is so good, why change it? If it is getting better because of some inevitable development, why should anyone waste his time on what is already assured? This is the substance of Hobhouse's charge that:

> ... when we are taught to think of the world which we know as a good world, to think of its injustices, wrongs and miseries as necessary elements in a perfect ideal, then, if we accept these arguments, our power of revolt is atrophied, our reason is hypnotised, our efforts to improve life and remedy wrong fade away into a passive acquiescence in things as they are; or, still worse, into a slavish adultation of the Absolute in whose hands we are mere pawns.[100]

However applicable this criticism may be to Hegel's form of Idealism, it does not affect Green's. At the very heart of his metaphysics, there is the pathos of the imperfect. God realises himself gradually, but never perfectly in human customs, laws, institutions. Man must struggle to attain perfection, but never can quite do so. This Faustian motif links virtue with the incessant attempt to attain what by its nature is unattainable.*

As for Green's optimistic philosophy of history, it did not foster

---

* Green had been much affected by Goethe's *Faust*. He once told a student that reading it was 'an epoch in a man's life.' (MS letter from A. G. C. Liddell to Mrs Green, in her copybook, Balliol College Library.)

complacency, but in the circumstances served as a call to action. From the Germans, many men had caught a kind of historical *Weltschmerz*, and were convinced that their age was inferior to the great periods of the past. Thus Lionel Trilling describes Matthew Arnold: 'Like Wordsworth before him, like T. S. Eliot after, he wrote primarily for a small group of saddened intellectuals for whom the dominant world was a wasteland, men who felt heartsick and deprived of some part of their energy by their civilization.'[101] Arnold in 'Stanzas from the Grande Chartreuse' addresses the Carthusian monks who once lived there.

> Wandering between two worlds, one dead,
> The other powerless to be born,
> With nowhere yet to rest my head,
> Like these, on earth I wait forlorn.
> Their faith, my tears, the world deride—
> I come to shed them at their side.[102]

Green's theory of progress was meant to brace up those who were paralysed by such feelings. One of the most vehement passages in his sermon on 'The Witness of God' used this theory of the progressive realisation of God on earth as a call to action.

We talk, perhaps, half-sorrowfully, half-complacently, of the demoralising, or unchristianising, tendencies of modern life. Opinion, it is said, is fundamentally unsettled; science keeps encroaching on the old faith; the lineaments of the God whom our fathers worshipped are blurred by philosophy; and meanwhile an enlightened hedonism seems competent to answer all practical questions. It is no fault of the individual if, amid such influences, he loses the thought of God's presence and the consciousness of his love, which indeed can only be retained by taking refuge in mysteries or going out of the world.

This is the foppery of men who want new excuses for old sins. . . . Philosophy and science, to those who seek not to talk of them but to know their power, do but render his clearness more clear. . . . His witness grows with time. In great books and great examples, in the gathering fulness of spiritual utterance which we trace through the history of literature . . . in the moralising influences of civil life . . . one spirit still speaks—here God's sunshine is shed abroad. . . .[103]

Green's contemporaries were willing to strive after an ideal, if only they could be assured of its meaning and efficacy. The theory of progress provided a sense of significance. It did not always produce quietism or complacency. It is easy to forget that a belief in progress seemed to be a necessary part of the reformer's rationale. As Lord Lindsay said with much insight about Marx, 'A belief in thoroughgoing determinism and a vigorous call to action are logically incompatible, but, if the call to action comes first, they are psychologically compatible.'[104]

And so, the ideas of Green's theology, when considered in relation to his religious interests and the contemporary crisis of belief, turn out to have oriented men towards active citizenship and reform. This is a civic religion which Green taught. Its great influence can be explained in no other way. Accurately aimed and powerfully argued, Green's theology enlisted emotions essentially religious in the cause of social reform. Even when his students embraced the High Church position, they did so with a difference. His faith of citizenship appealed to a strong sense of sin combined with an equally strong sense of duty. Essentially its message was directed at the middle classes, at men with philanthropic impulses, with consciences to be touched, and with a guilt about their ebbing faith that could be turned into a guilt about their privileges. But even those who turned Green's Idealism to apologetic purposes for which he had little affection, responded to his call to all those with advantages to renounce them. When the claims of all men to be treated as members of the community are acknowledged, then a new and more demanding self-denial becomes morally obligatory upon those few who enjoy privileges not open to the rest. Thus Green pointed out to his audience how they might attain a new way of life. His theology was an effort to designate a supreme good to which they might devote themselves secure at last from the paralysing disjunction between reason and faith. But there was a price to be paid for their release. They must sacrifice their personal pleasures and atone by social service for the elegant life they lived as Oxford students while so many of their countrymen were denied the chance to realise their potentialities as human beings.

Thus Green worked upon his young men, reaching a way of life that linked religious fulfilment with social reform. In contrast to Marx and the philosophical radicals, Green began his agitation for change, not by denouncing asceticism and the official Christian values of charity and justice as sham, but by re-affirming their validity. And this once done, he found no difficulty whatever in denouncing such abuses as the London slums as intolerable evils in a society which professed to believe in the moral dignity of the individual. In short, Green believed that the strongest motive for reform was to be found not in anger but in guilt. The reformer should not seek to condemn completely this society which tolerated such injustice, but rather to arouse guilt at the clear discrepancy between its avowed ideals and its actual performance. Marx believed that only the under-privileged would act. This assumption makes it necessary for him to prove the total depravity of capitalist society and its values. Green, brought up in a tradition of Evangelical philanthropy, believed that reform could come from above, as well as from below, if the standards of Christianity could be applied to social and economic life.

In this attempt to arouse a sense of guilt among the upper classes, Green became a great and influential spokesman for a new movement of the Evangelical impulse. In the 70's and 80's, a noticeable change occurred in public opinion about the social and economic structure of Britain. This transformation of opinion began to yield notable results in legislation. But it did not begin among the manual workers.

> The origin of the ferment is to be discovered in a new consciousness of sin among men of intellect and men of property. . . . When I say the consciousness of sin, I do not mean the consciousness of personal sin. . . . The consciousness of sin was a collective or class consciousness; a growing uneasiness, amounting to conviction, that the industrial organisation, which had yielded rent, interest and profits on a stupendous scale, had failed to provide a decent livelihood and tolerable conditions for a majority of the inhabitants of Great Britain.[105]

Here is Green's strategy for reform. He asked the privileged to sacrifice their selfish advantages so that the poor and weak might be given the chance to realise their potentialities. In return, the privileged would gain the release from bad conscience and more: that moral development which comes from living in a moral society where all men are treated as agents, each of whom is an end equally to himself and to others. This appeal was both to the intellect and to the emotions. To those who sought a whole view of life there was offered a rational theory of man and society, a theory neither hedonist nor materialist. And upon those tormented by conscience Green pressed his theory of reform, not as an academic alternative among other academic alternatives, but as a moral obligation which could not be ignored by the conscientious Christian citizen.

CHAPTER FIVE

PHILOSOPHY AS A PROFESSION

I

TASTE FLUCTUATES IN PHILOSOPHY, as in other things, and it can be safely predicted that fifty years after the greatest vogue attained by a school, its reputation will fall to a record low. Certainly that has been the fate of Philosophical Idealism in Great Britain. Green is no longer read except by students of political theory. Nor have philosophers shown much interest in determining why such a manifestly wrong-headed doctrine was once widely accepted. Mr. T. D. Weldon's judgment is typical of analytical philosophers: Idealism was 'a highly sophisticated language game' used 'to give an *a priori* endorsement to the moral and political principles which the educational system inaugurated by Dr Arnold impressed on the minds of those who were destined to be rulers'.[1] The average reader would take this passage to say that Idealism taught a set of justifications for received ideas, that it was the doctrine of the Establishment in its day. Professor Ryle, in a more perceptive but still not altogether accurate essay, has explained the recent 'revolution in philosophy' by two great changes: first, that between the period of Idealism and the 1920's, the population of 'academic intellectuals' shifted from being predominantly clerical to being almost entirely lay in its make-up; second, philosophy itself became a subject independent from classical scholarship, theology, and psychology. During the Idealist dominance, he asserts, all issues revolved around the question of faith or doubt; the only significant differences were between theologians and anti-theologians or among competing schools of theologians. By the 1920's such concern with religious belief had quite passed. The way was clear for the 'professionalising of philosophy'. Teachers of philosophy became concerned with matters of technical interest; their passion was for 'ratiocinative rigour'.[2] After the First World War, then, amateurism was replaced by a stringent academic discipline. If the accounts of Professor Ryle and Mr Weldon are combined, Idealism emerges as a com-

136

bination of theology with an ideological defence of the then existing order.

Another portrait of Oxford Idealism appeared in Mr Noël Annan's brilliant study of Sir Leslie Stephen. In reviving the Cambridge view of the school, Mr Annan has placed Green in the succession of preachers produced by nineteenth-century Oxford: Whately, Thomas Arnold, Keble, Jowett, Ruskin, and Pater. To these names Cambridge presented no analogues. There thinkers formed by mathematics, science, and the rationalism of their University preferred to keep the soul in its place. Fearing fads and enthusiasm, the Cambridge philosopher consoles himself for his lack of followers by the thought that 'prophets are half humbug and produce disciples who will be wholly humbug'.[3] This estimate has a long pedigree. It echoes C. D. Broad who, writing long after the deaths of Green and his severest critic at Cambridge, still felt strongly enough to say: 'Even a thoroughly second-rate thinker like T. H. Green, by diffusing a grateful and comforting aroma of ethical "uplift", has probably made far more under-graduates into prigs than Sidgwick will ever make into philo-sophers.'[4] Before Broad, Sidgwick in his personal journal had copied out a passage to describe the way he felt about himself and his relationship to Green:

> 'Though without much fame, he had no envy. But he had a strong realism. He saw what it is considered cynical to see—the absurdities of many persons, the pomposities of many creeds, the splendid zeal with which missionaries rush on to teach what they do not know, the wonderful earnestness with which most incomplete solutions of the universe are thrust upon us as complete and satisfying.' (This repre-sents my relation to T. H. G. and his work.)[5]

Even more severe is the treatment of Green in Sir Geoffrey Faber's biography of Benjamin Jowett. Although Sir Geoffrey was neither an analytical philosopher nor a Cambridge man, his charges were damning. Green, along with the first Arnold Toyn-bee, is said to have believed in the right of a tutor to instil his own beliefs into the minds of students not yet capable of critical resis-tance to their teachers' views. To this alleged proselytising is contrasted the nobler position taken up by the Master of Balliol:

> Jowett had proposed to himself, and had followed in his own tutor-ship, a wider principle . . . ; that the true aim of the teacher is to make his pupil think for himself, not to make him think what his teacher thinks. After he became Master, some of the Balliol tutors found this principle altogether unsatisfying. Green and Toynbee, especially, discarded it. They did not hesitate to use every opportunity of

framing and fixing the mind of any worthwhile young man who swam into their tutorial nets. Teach him to think for himself? Teach him, rather, to think the right way, *my* way.[6]

These characterisations of Green and Idealism differ somewhat in their tone and content. Mr Weldon's remarks are for the most part *obiter dicta*. Why bother to produce any evidence for what is perfectly clear to everyone: that between Hume and Russell there is nothing whatever of interest in British philosophy? Hence all authors of this period may be treated sociologically, that is to say, loosely. Professor Ryle's account is sounder, and he believes that at least one Idealist, F. H. Bradley, deserves study. Yet the version of events given by Professor Ryle renders less than justice to the battles fought and won by Green on behalf of philosophy as an autonomous professional discipline. As for Mr Annan's chapter setting off Cambridge rationalism against Oxford mysticism, it no doubt succeeds in demonstrating that these two universities differ in subtle but significant ways. Yet can all these differences be reduced to the single contrast between reason and emotion? Mr Annan's unrivalled portrayal of Victorian Cambridge may be allowed to stand without our accepting everything he has to say about Oxford Idealism. In any case we have found his Cambridge rationalists, Sidgwick and Stephen, working in almost complete agreement with one wing of Green's students in the London Ethical Society. And Lord Keynes, whom the present Provost of King's cities as the finest product of that newer Cambridge rationalism known as the Bloomsbury Set, was almost as hard on poor Sidgwick as Broad was on Green.* This suggests that a man's generation may affect his thought at least as much as his university.

As for the vehement attack mounted by Sir Geoffrey on Green and Toynbee, any defence of them is complicated by the fact that Jowett's biographer cited nothing whatever in the way of evidence to support his assertions. One suspects that Sir Geoffrey felt he needed some rhetorical targets so that he could better set off the distinctive virtues of his subject. There was indeed a serious clash

* 'Have you read Sidgwick's Life? . . . Very interesting and depressing. . . . He never did anything but wonder whether Christianity was true and prove that it wasn't and hope that it was. . . . And then his conscience—incredible. There is no doubt about his moral goodness. And yet it is all so dreadfully depressing— no intimacy, no clear-cut crisp boldness. Oh, I suppose he was intimate but he didn't seem to have anything to be intimate about except his religious doubts. And he really ought to have got over that a little sooner; because he knew that the thing wasn't true perfectly well from the beginning.' (Letter from J. M. Keynes to B. W. Swithinbank, 27 March, 1906, R. F. Harrod, *The Life of John Maynard Keynes* [London: Macmillan and Co., 1951], pp. 116-17.)

between Jowett and Green, but it did not turn on the issue of flagrant proselytising. It will be argued that Jowett did not enjoy any moral or educational advantage in this matter. His latest admirer cannot be said to have discovered the facts of the case.

What is striking about these recent treatments of Green and his school is the unanimity in detail and tone of their composite portrait: the Idealists are represented as prigs, earnest preachers who forced their edifying views on students who should have been taught to reason rigorously and independently. In all these judgments upon Idealism there is a quality of self-satisfaction which renders them suspect. Such a condemnation recalls the undiscriminating attacks upon the Victorian Age which were so popular before Lytton Strachey's *Eminent Victorians* began to be challenged, and before Mr T. S. Eliot's more subtle disparagement of liberalism and humanism were understood to reflect his own theological preferences rather more than detailed and objective study. The critics of Idealism thus far examined seem to attribute to it all the undesirable qualities once attributed to the Victorian Age as a whole. There is a gap here between the most recent work done by scholars on that period, which no longer is thought to constitute a seamless web, and the view of Idealism held by philosophers and intellectual historians. Surely as we gain in knowledge of individuals placed so imprecisely under the once pejorative rubric of 'Victorian', it ought to become possible to consider them as human, and even, in some rare cases, as sympathetic. And so they should appear. To believe that we are somehow superior because we no longer have troubled consciences; to feel that, because we are rather more frank about some matters, we are invariably conscious about our real impulsions in every aspect of life; to judge that we have progressed morally because we no longer believe in progress—this is to substitute one kind of complacency for another.

In fact this collective indictment confuses two quite distinguishable issues: first, did Green actually proselytise his students? Second, did his theological and political commitments intrude themselves upon his technical work as a philosopher? Each of these questions requires the examination of evidence, but the materials in point are not of the same order. The documents which bear on Green's relationship to his tutorial students and lecture audiences will be treated in this chapter; the other and more complex issue must await the detailed study of his philosophical work which will be made below. But it is perhaps not premature to say here that the evidence indicates a verdict of 'not guilty' on the first count, and 'guilty' on the second. Such findings may seem paradoxical, but they offer a closer approximation to the determinable truth than the blanket condemnations of Idealism which have become fashionable. The fact is that Green, far more than anyone else during his time at Oxford, championed the claims of philosophy as a discipline which should be subject only to the criteria imposed by its qualified practitioners. That is to say, he thought his subject required specialised training on the part of those who taught it; that it had real value beyond whatever part it played in training the minds of those taking the Greats School; that its potential contributions to knowledge justified post-graduate study and teaching. Green was certainly the first Fellow of his College, and possibly the first in his University, to conceive of himself as a professional philosopher. As Ensor has remarked, 'Whatever be thought of the English Idealist school, which Green did so much to found, they at least conceived their task as one for fully trained and organised professionals, not for gifted but isolated amateurs.'[7] We shall see how the changes ascribed by Professor Ryle to the 1920's were in fact begun by Green in the 1870's. As far as he himself was concerned, Green felt that he was bound to follow the 'critical method' of Kant wherever it might lead him. Systematic doubt, he believed, is indispensable to the technique of every modern philosopher—no matter how corrosive its effects upon received opinion. He was no mere apologist for religious belief. Had he chosen to seek popularity by such means, he could have much more easily acquiesced in some one of the conventional modes of thought available to him. His refusal to do so was altogether inexplicable to Gladstone.*

Green's intentions were one thing; his actual performance, quite another. The balance he sought to establish between faith and reason now seems to represent more of the aspiration of theology than the rigour Green himself thought proper to philosophy. Nor is this surprising. Few thinkers have been altogether immune from the temptation to identify the nature of reality, or knowledge or language with precisely those conclusions which support or do not disturb their view of the world. In balance, given the standards of his time and situation, Green cannot be said to have made things easy for himself. He was a man who

---

* During their controversy about *Robert Elsmere*, Gladstone wrote Mrs Ward: 'And my meaning about Mr Green was to hint at what seems to me the unutterable strangeness of his passionately beseeching philosophy to open to him the communion for which he thirsted, when he had a better source nearer hand.

It is like a farmer under the agricultural difficulty who has to migrate from England and plants himself in the middle of the Sahara.' (Letter from Gladstone to Mrs Ward, 16 April, 1888, Trevelyan, *Mrs Humphry Ward*, p. 62.)

specialised in philosophical scruple, although this was more manifest in his criticisms of others than in his own attempts at positive construction. Of Hegelianism, he said for example, that 'men unbiassed by Positivism or materialism or the current materialistic theology will still suspect that there is some intellectual jugglery about it'.[8] Such remarks, indicating that Hegel's work would have to be done over again by men less impatient and more thorough, did much to produce in his students the consciousness of how curiously high technical standards were combined in Green with an ultimate spiritual affirmation. In part this contradiction was the result of his own needs; in part, the result of the changing place held by the study of philosophy in the Oxford course of study.

2

At the time Green came up to Oxford in mid-century, the course of study prescribed in the School of *Literae Humaniores* included books which by any criterion would be counted as philosophical. Certain of Aristotle's works had long dominated the curriculum, and G. M. Young in a passage which only he could have written, analysed the effects of such study upon the style of a First Class scholar like Gladstone who belonged to the generation just preceding Green's.[9] But whatever were the benefits of the old order, it now came under sharp attack from the would-be reformers within Oxford. The Greats School as then constituted was said to encourage an unthinking acceptance of authority. The method used to teach philosophy was denounced as degrading the subject into an old-fashioned type of philology. The treatment of philosophical topics in any case was too exclusively 'rhetorical' and 'literary'. Just what were these critics saying? In the case of philology, their meaning was relatively clear: that so much attention went into the study of Latin or Greek texts that little time was left for discussion of the substantive issues discussed in them. And, it was added, these books were too often read as mere illustrations of logic, which was still studied when Green was an undergraduate by Dean Aldrich's textbook (described to the First University Commission as 'an epitome of almost every possible blunder').[10] Even after Aldrich was replaced by Mill's *Logic*, philosophical instruction still left itself open to charges that it accomplished far less than it should do. For the pass-men such texts did little more than to serve as a source of commonplaces or tags which would one day adorn the public pronouncements of statesmen or divines. What was worse, the best students were taught to treat their philosophical texts as nothing more than quarries from which there might be hewed passages useful in examination questions. For the final schools required essays which, if taken seriously, so far exceeded the philosophical knowledge of undergraduates that successful answers depended upon essays prepared and memorised in advance by students with the collaboration of their tutors or coaches. And these papers were set and marked by examiners, who might be amateurs in philosophy, open to the charge that they knew little about technical developments since the time they took their own BA's. Thus not only the philosophical instruction but the method of examining in the Greats School was said to blight originality among students and teachers alike. It was highly exceptional for undergraduates to be taught that there were better and worse ways of using the basic concepts they used in discussing knowledge and conduct. Nor did such instruction as was given in the history of philosophy suggest that the student ought to make a principled choice among alternative systems. Rather all was grist for the essay mill. And in the 1850's the required reading was still so narrow in range as to exclude modern thought almost completely. J. A. Symonds, who took a First in Greats at the same time as Green, had this to say about the course of study:

> At Oxford . . . philosophy was studied mainly from the rhetorical point of view. We were taught to write upon a vast variety of debatable topics, and to acquire some smatterings of what the several schools had uttered on them; but there was no robust mental training, no process by which the man was compelled to think. Worse than that, aspirants after honours were habituated to deal cleverly with words and phrases, and to criticise without substantial knowledge. . . .
> There was an almost total defect of discipline in tough studies. . . . In a sort of blundering way the docile among us were made to recognise the force of duty; and that was pretty nearly all we gained. . . . Yet . . . this great educational defect had . . . its educational quality. This quality was freedom of choice. . . . We were comparatively unspoiled by drill of any kind. Our minds were made less by the curriculum than by our friends, the subjects we were instinctively adapted for, and our spontaneously selected lines of reading.[11]

The first substantial changes in this method of teaching were introduced by Jowett and Mark Pattison, who began to induct their students into the history of philosophy. In the study of this subject, they saw a potent weapon against those arguments from authority and tradition that were so dear to High Churchmen. For a time Jowett assigned to Green the task of developing a kind of philosophy that could thus be used against Dr Pusey and his allies. Philosophy became an autonomous subject at Oxford for the same reason that sociology later became established in the French university system—as the result of a deliberate attempt to develop out of German thought a rational and unecclesiastical ethics of citizenship. For it was Jowett, who by a shrewd political stroke introduced significant changes into the Greats course of study. Philosophy was thus to serve the purposes of the Broad Church movement. To Florence Nightingale, Jowett wrote:

> Any religious movement should be also, like that of the Jesuits, an educational movement. . . . And there is a great change in education at the Universities, especially at Oxford. When I was an undergraduate we were fed upon Bishop Butler and Aristotle's *Ethics*, and almost all teaching leaned to the support of doctrines of authority. Now there are new subjects, Modern History and Physical Science, and more important than these, perhaps, is the real study of metaphysics in the Literae Humaniores school—every man for the last ten years who goes in for honours has read Bacon, and probably Locke, Mill's *Logic*, Plato, Aristotle, and the history of ancient philosophy. See how impossible this makes a return to the old doctrines of authority.
>
> The 'Hebrew Conservative' [Dr Pusey] has just found this out, which he ought to have found out long ago, and is going to try to upset all this by appointing what he calls a Board of Studies, which would be nominated by him and his friends. But I think that we can hinder him. . . .[12]

Jowett's enthusiasm for 'the real study of metaphysics' did not last long. What he believed in was the value of teaching the history of thought which, by revealing the failure of all previous systems, had the effect of freeing young men from their prejudices without putting any new and inconvenient convictions in their place. This aspect of Jowett was thrown into sharp relief during the last part of his career. For in 1870 Jowett's Liberal friends managed to convince Gladstone that he should nominate Dr Scott, then Master of Balliol, as Dean of Rochester, thus clearing the way for Jowett's elevation to the position denied him at Dr Jenkyns' death. As Master, Jowett showed no further taste for controversy, he came to accept the world and to be accepted by it, and even rose in his turn to become Vice-Chancellor of the University where once he was prosecuted for heresy. Despite his earlier reputation as a champion of modern thought, he actually did not move far from the older Oxford ideal of using the undergraduate years to develop just that blend of strong character with logical training deemed

necessary for men destined to rule. Jowett once described someone to a student as 'over-educated'. When his pupil, puzzled,
asked what that phrase might mean, his preceptor answered that
'the intellect might be developed beyond the character and will. It
happens in the case of Germans mostly.'[13] Pure knowledge held
few attractions for the Master of Balliol, who refused to support
the endowment of research at Oxford and strongly opposed any
step likely to weaken the colleges and strengthen the University.
Nor did he see any valid reason for teaching any more than the
handful of post-graduate students already doing advanced work
at Oxford. In short Jowett's aspirations did not go beyond making
the old system less authoritarian in its matter and more efficient
in its teaching. Students were to be tested by a thoroughly
competitive examination system, which would reward those who
could write persuasive essays on either side of any general issue
as well as coping with sight translations from Latin and Greek.

Once Jowett and Pattison had won a partial victory over the
High Churchmen, the differences between the Master of Balliol
and the Rector of Lincoln became increasingly more evident. For
these two powerful individuals did not agree on what direction the
reformed University ought to take. Pattison had an admiration for
the German ideal of *Wissenschaft* that was not shared by Jowett.
Whereas the first championed research, the advancement of knowledge, and post-graduate study, the second thought that the skilful
teaching of undergraduates and the formation of their characters
were all that Oxford should aspire to. Nor has Jowett's ideal of a
reformed and strengthened Greats curriculum lacked defenders.
R. G. Collingwood was among the most eloquent of those who have
cited the numerous benefits conferred by this course of study upon
innumerable generations of undergraduates who have sharpened
their wits by the detailed reading of, commenting upon, and
expounding of, a few well-tried texts.[14] And consider the testimony
of Logan Pearsall Smith who came directly from Harvard to take
a degree at Balliol during the height of the Jowett era, and who
still thought many years later, that the Greats School was the best
scheme of education he had ever heard of:

'It is based upon an accurate knowledge of Greek and Latin texts,
especially the texts of Plato and Aristotle and Thucydides and
Tacitus, and the subjects studied in it are the eternal problems of
thought, of conduct, and of social organisation. These are discussed,
not by means of contemporary catchwords, but by translating them
back into another world and another language. Nor could anything
be more profitable from the pupil's point of view than the way in
which this scheme of education was carried out.'[15]

This last reference is to the tutorial system, as perfected by Jowett and the other Balliol tutors. For those who have not themselves undergone it, there are few better accounts of its operation than Smith's:

> These discussions were carried on much in the spirit of the Socratic dialogues; and the Socratic irony and assumed ignorance of the instructors, their deferential questions, as if the pupil were the teacher and they the learners, was a method which I found it hard at first to understand.
>
> I remember, for instance, in reading a paper to Nettleship, I mentioned the distinction between form and matter. 'Excuse me for interrupting you,' Nettleship said, 'but this distinction you make, though it is no doubt most important, is one that I find a little difficult to grasp. If it is not troubling you too much, it would be a real kindness if you would try to explain it to me.'
>
> 'Oh, it's quite simple,' I answered patronisingly, 'There's the idea, say, in a poem, and there's the way in which it is expressed.'
>
> Nettleship still seemed puzzled. 'Could you give me an instance?' he pleaded.
>
> 'Oh, nothing easier,' I answered. 'Take the lines, for instance, when Lovelace says:
>
> "I could not love thee, dear, so much,
> Loved I not honour more".
>
> Now he might have said, "I couldn't be nearly so fond of you, my dear, if I didn't care still more for my reputation." The form, you see, is very different in both these sentences, but the subject of them— what they mean—is exactly the same.'
>
> Nettleship seemed greatly discouraged. 'I'm afraid,' he said, 'I can't see that the meaning of the two sentences is the same. I'm afraid I'm very stupid, but to me they seem to say quite different things.'
>
> He was, I thought, curiously stupid; but in my patient attempt to make my meaning clearer to him a dim suspicion began to waken in me that perhaps it was not Nettleship but I myself who was playing the part of the fool in this dialogue.[16]

For Jowett this method of teaching, when combined with the competitive examination, seemed the pinnacle of educational wisdom. Did it not teach men how to think without telling them what to think? And did not the discipline imposed upon the ambitious in their carefully planned campaign for First-Class Honours later serve them well in whatever place they were called upon to fill in society? Others, including Pattison and Green were less content. For it was possible to doubt from the use Jowett himself made of the classics whether his own work was as free from any positive teaching as he himself imagined. And apart from any personal considerations, is it in fact the case that a tutor by the Socratic method does nothing more than elicit in a more rigorous form ideas that are already present in the student's mind? Were this so, it could be argued that such midwifery is the best of all teaching methods because it but aims at self-realisation on the intellectual level. This surely is what Jowett believed and what Sir Geoffrey Faber uncritically accepted as the truth: that dogmatism and the undue influence of teacher upon student may be eliminated by following the Socratic rules of the game. What the tutor does is to introduce his charge to the spirit of criticism, and from this process there emerges nothing didactic, but only a stricter statement of the original ideas and presuppositions. Jowett's theory of the tutorial process may be questioned on several grounds, some of which were explicitly voiced by Green, and others not. Among the most telling of these criticisms is that recently made by Professor Ernest Gellner in his provocative book on linguistic analysis: namely, that a theory may be taught by means other than direct statement; it may be insinuated by what the tutor lets pass as against what he cross-questions. The beginning student must learn the rules of the philosophical game from someone who subtly communicates a conception of what is permissible and what not.[17] Depending upon the attitude of the older man, the neophyte may gather that common sense is to be avoided or the contrary impression that, in everyday modes of expression, there is to be found all that we know or need to know. Green, for his part, thought that such issues should be discussed explicitly and that there existed a body of accumulated learning to which the student should be directly exposed. This method was of course precluded by the more traditional procedure of emphasising the texts and playing down all discussion of philosophical issues.

Another objection to the mode of philosophical instruction stemmed, not from the tutorial system, but from that of examination. None of its critics stated their case more pungently than did Pattison in his article published in 1876 as his contribution to the first number of *Mind*. Green later made very similar charges in his testimony before the Oxford University Commission of 1877. All philosophical initiative in Oxford, Pattison declared, was crushed between two millstones: the upper consisting of the reign of ecclesiastical terror carried on by High Churchmen; the lower, the competition machine which sucked into it dons and honour candidates alike. In the struggle for freedom of thought, Jowett, Pattison and Green were at one. This was scarcely the case when it came to the second point. Pattison, pointing an accusing finger at the much-imitated Balliol apparatus for producing First Class degrees, argued that its effects were baneful. Teaching at Oxford was effectively in the hands of the college tutors. As a group, these men, when they began to teach, abounded in energy, ability and the ambition to affect their students. But the zeal to teach well had been contaminated by the competition among colleges and individual tutors to produce the largest possible number of successes in the schools. For the enthusiasm of such teachers is not that of the scientist who has mastered a technique for making progress in a subject and who wishes to share this means of advancing knowledge with younger men. Rather the young teacher, as turned out by Oxford, has been trained only to compete successfully for the purely artificial and arbitrary goals of the place. 'He is an honour-man and a prize-man; *voilà tout!*' Once embarked on a teaching career at the age of twenty-five, he finds himself the slave of a great teaching-machine which has formed him and now allows him no time for study, research, and any progression past the point he has attained as an undergraduate. Once involved in the great competitive struggle, it is superfluous and even dangerous for the welfare of his pupils for their teacher to say anything about the foundations of a subject, or to suggest that thoroughness and love of learning are the marks of true scholarship. Rather he must crowd into a year and a half or two years at the most an assortment of ready-made propositions on the topics of philosophy, history, politics, and literature upon which the examinations are based. 'Our system has gradually become one which carefully excludes thoroughness. It is the exaltation of "smattering" into a method.' What it trains to do is aimed not at producing intellectual discipline or at teaching how to carry out an investigation, but rather at producing a clever answer to a question on a subject of which one has no real knowledge.

That the papers produced by such training were impressive, Pattison was prepared to admit; that the Oxford First-Class in Greats knew anything about philosophy seemed dubious to him. In a passage of great polemical brilliance, he summed up his case against Jowett's ideal:

I have never, in the capacity of examiner, analysed the paper . . . without astonishment at the combination of scholarship, varied knowledge, command of topic and scientific vocabulary which the candidates can bring to bear on the questions! I have felt a thrill of awe at standing in the presence of such matured intellectual development. . . ! The thought has been inevitably forced upon me: If these minds are already arrived at this stage at twenty-one, where will they be at forty? Surely these young men have used their time well, who . . . have exhausted the process of human thought from Thales to Hegel; they can have nothing more to learn!

A nearer acquaintance, however, with the whole result of the system dispels the illusion. If from the papers we turn to the minds from which all this clever writing has emanated, we shall find no trace of any philosophical culture in them. The question . . . is on a philosophical subject, but the process by which the question has been answered has been not a philosophical action of mind, but a purely literary or compositional process. . . . Memory is really almost the only quality called into play. Were they facts with which the memory is thus charged, the inadequacy of the system would be apparent at once. But in the preparation for this examination, instead of facts, the memory is charged with generalised formulas, with expressions and solutions which are derived ready-made from the tutor. The first principle of philosophical, nay, of intellectual, training, viz, that all should be educed from the pupil's own mind, is here inverted; all is poured into him by his teacher. . . . The utmost that the student can acquire from the system is that he has learned to write in the newest style of thought. . . .

Out of this training some few stronger natures may emerge unscathed. A still smaller number of the most vigorous may even be braced by re-action against the oppression to which their minds have been subjected.* But in the average Oxford prizeman we too plainly recognise the symptoms which indicate that he has suffered from the forcing-house; mental pallor, moral indifferentism, the cynical sneer at others' effort, the absence in himself of any high ideal. He knows of everything, and truly knows nothing. For him intellectual enjoyment is passed away; the taste for reading which he brought to college he has lost there; he has lost reverence without acquiring insight; he remains an intellectual *roué*, having forfeited the native instinct of curiosity, of which, as Aristotle says, Philosophy was born.[18]

3

It is against the background sketched by Pattison that Green's falling out with Jowett must be viewed. Philosophy for the earnest young man meant rather more than the essentially critical instru-

* It would not do to leave the impression that Pattison and Green held the same views on philosophy. Pattison, although a considerable scholar, had no particular interest or training in the technical questions of philosophy. Himself an empiricist of the English school, he did not understand why anyone considering himself as a Liberal should criticise the great Locke and the intellectual tradition which spawned him. In his article, Pattison commended in part Green's treatment of Empiricism in the edition of Hume, but he cannot really tolerate the suggestion that the school is no longer intellectually defensible. And in his *Memoirs* Pattison attributes to Green 'a certain puzzle-headedness' that he, 'a staunch Liberal' should have imported into Oxford, 'an *a priori* philosophy, which, under various disguises, aims at exempting Man from the order of nature, and erecting him into a unique being whose organism is not to be subject to the uniform laws which govern all other Being that is known to us.' [Mark Pattison, *Memoirs* (London, 1885), pp. 167, 242-3.]

ment Jowett thought it to be. Although his old tutor had first put him on to German ideas and theology, Green now found himself in a position which tried his highly developed sense of duty. Loyalty to Balliol, to Jowett, to the pupils entrusted to him—these obligations increasingly conflicted with the sort of work needed to develop the philosophical discipline for which he had high hopes. After being elected Fellow in 1860, he for six years had filled in wherever a subject needed to be taught, including the new School of Law and Modern History. Then, beginning in 1866, he was assigned to lecture exclusively on subjects required by the Greats curriculum, and as a tutor, to see a number of students every week, read their essays, and assist them in their preparations for their terminal examinations. There was a powerful tradition of tutorial responsibility at Balliol. Green felt that when he took up his Fellowship he had accepted the primary obligation to teach as conscientiously as he had himself been taught by Jowett. Yet to do so carried with it distinct disadvantages for his own philo-sophical work. In addition to the amount of time taken up by his tutorial functions and college lectures, he found himself forced to do much of his teaching on Aristotle, whose works still comprised the single most important section of the Greats School. And even further from his own concerns were the other required subjects on which he found himself required to lecture: the New Testament, Plato and the history of early Greek thought. Thus the scope of his College lectures was determined, not by what he himself regarded as the most significant issues of his chosen speciality, but by the questions likely to appear on examination papers. Not until 1878 when he was elected Whyte's Professor of Moral Philosophy was he to be freed to state his own theories in the sequence and form of his choice. But even before his election Green had begun an unprecedented series of advanced classes in philosophy. And so great was his renown that even in an atmosphere where students characteristically judged the value of teaching by its potential value for their Schools, Green managed to attract and hold some of the best young men. Green's growing influence upon under-graduates, upon the young tutors of Balliol, such as Nettleship and A. C. Bradley, the antagonism stirred up by his Idealism in examiners otherwise trained—all this contributed to tension between him and Jowett. The Master's antagonism to Green put him in curious company.

In 1874 the Whyte's Professorship of Moral Philosophy had become vacant. The two leading candidates were Green, unques-tionably the leading philosopher at Oxford, and the Reverend John Eaton, once an Oxford tutor and the author of a commentary on Aristotle's *Politics*. But Eaton had accepted a living ten years before, and had not been seen in Oxford since that time. The electors charged with choosing the Professor were not themselves named because of any qualification in philosophy. In any case, so great was their opposition both to Green's unorthodoxy and German metaphysics that, by a two-thirds majority, they elected Eaton. Soon he found that philosophy at Oxford was not as he had left it; his clerical friends who had persuaded him to stand had left him in an untenable position. After publishing two lectures which failed to mollify his still indignant students, Eaton resigned in 1877, and Green finally was elected. Even then one of his competitors wrote a tract which quite overtly appealed for his own election on the basis of his theological opinions.[19]

This experience of an opposition, which was as intolerant as it was amateur, is clearly evident in the testimony Green gave to the Oxford University Commission of 1877. He came out in favour of making the University much more learned and specialised, views clearly incompatible with those of Jowett. For Green argued that the undergraduate had for too long monopolised the University's attention at the cost of sacrificing a function at least as significant: that of advancing knowledge. The existing system for choosing college fellows took no account of research. It was surely an advance that examinations were now almost universally employed instead of patronage and favouritism. But the candidates were not expected to have progressed past the point attained in their BA's. Indeed nowhere in the University was there any opportunity for them to gain advanced training, nor were there enough fellowships for anything except teaching. Such a framework was not desirable. The best men produced by Oxford had to go through a period of intensive drill to distinguish themselves in the first phase of their career. Now that they sought fellowships, once again they had to prepare in the same way. Indeed, they were tested even more superficially than in the schools. Rarely were candidates given more than a half-hour or an hour to write on any topic, however complex. In such a trial of abilities, scholarship was actually a disadvantage, for the race was to the glib. 'Success in such an examination naturally falls to the man of most literary skill, who can bring his mind to bear most promptly and neatly on any subject that may be set before him.' Successful candidates would be put to work immediately as a tutor and lecturer to undergraduates, once again producing an exclusive emphasis upon the same unspecialised tasks. Compared to a Continental scholar, the Oxford Fellow lacked technical competence at the age of twenty-five, and ten years later, would fall behind irretrievably. Where under the existing organisation could a man find opportunity or reward for becoming a specialist in his subject? By keeping men at exactly the same work for all their lives, Oxford made it inevitable that in time tutors' lectures would hold the interest neither of themselves nor the men they taught. It was for this reason that students preferred younger teachers to those jaded by repetition without fresh thought. Teaching suffered, just as did research.

And, Green went on, referring to the undesirable position of philosophy in such a scheme of things, 'It is the business of the university not merely to test such attainment of knowledge as can be tested by examination, but to assist in its advancement. If we confine ourselves to the work of helping undergraduates to get up certain books and subjects, and testing the result by examination, the spirit of knowledge will soon die out among us.' Such sentiments could not have endeared Green to Jowett. By way of improving the situation, the younger man went on to propose that a considerable number of readerships be established for those who could write as well as teach. Such posts would build a ladder to the existing professorships. But, Green suggested, it was important to give readers some functions that involved teaching as well as research, for otherwise they would have as little influence upon the colleges as the isolated professors. And so he thought that readers should be charged with the instruction of students who had already taken their BA's, and now wished either to acquire more knowledge of their subject for its own sake, or wished to prepare for fellowship examinations. It followed from this proposal that would-be Fellows ought to be examined on a more advanced level, and that the examiners be experts in the candidate's field, and not, as was then the case, Fellows of the College who might have made no effort to keep in touch with the development of scholarship. What this proposal entailed was nothing less than an extension of the University's power over the colleges. Too much was at stake to allow the colleges to go on setting their own criteria of selection. For fellowships were the only means by which a man without money of his own could devote himself to the advancement of knowledge.

All this was on the level of general University policy, but Green also appeared as a spokesman for his discipline. Until 1875 or 1876, there had been no systematic lecturing in Oxford on any philosophical subject, except occasionally on ethics, or any discussion of philosophical books except those treatises of Plato and Aristotle set for the final Schools. Green, from his testimony, appears to be the first don to have attempted the advanced teaching of his subject, and his classes were attended by students ranging in number from ten to thirty-five. Attendance was voluntary, and about half of the students already had taken their degrees.[20] Thus there were men who had the desire to pursue their interests further than was strictly required of them. Green, in addition to his other duties, had taken upon himself to meet this demand. But Jowett had not welcomed this step. In answer to the chairman's question Green replied that although he was a Fellow of Balliol, and still lectured there, he no longer took part in tutorial work. And this we know was by Jowett's explicit wish. In the Master's view, Green as a tutor was apt to do more harm than good, and the same was true of A. C. Bradley and R. L. Nettleship. What lay behind this active antagonism?

Perhaps what troubled Jowett most was the suspicion that Green might encourage his students rashly to endanger their careers by the use of Idealist language and logic in examinations set and graded by men hostile to such innovations. Jowett's fears were exaggerated. Actually he should have known better than to think that Green should take so light a view of his obligations to his charges. Scott Holland, who took his Schools at the same time as Bradley and Nettleship, prepared under Green's direction, and from their correspondence it can be seen just what Green's most sympathetic pupils heard from him on this score:

> For practical purposes, ie with a view to a first class—which you really must get—you ought to familiarise yourself with the sort of logic and psychology which is familiar to examiners and which perhaps, from the nature of the case, is alone available in examination, since an examination means that one cuts one's mind into scraps. In brief, you must get up Mill. You will find it a very good discipline. You should also keep Schools questions constantly before you and be always thinking how you would answer them. If this is a humiliation, it will only last 7 months. You must also learn to slip the essay style, on occasion, for the 'dodgy' examination style. Finally, be diligent in getting available information about philosophy and history, and keep it together by means of concise summaries and notes.[21]

Despite such loyalty on Green's part to Jowett's method, the Master of Balliol's animosity grew rather than diminished. Bowing to Jowett's wishes Green, for a year or two before he was elected to his Professorship, took but a small part in the teaching of the College. Jowett apparently wished to eliminate Green's influence root and branch. Neither Nettleship, whom Logan Pearsall Smith many years later was to cite as the exemplar of the Socratic tutor, nor A. C. Bradley enjoyed the Master's confidence.[22] Among Green's greatest disappointments just before he died was Bradley's expulsion from Balliol. On the basis of his ability and achievement, as well as his service, Bradley certainly deserved more from the College than this rude blow. Diverted from the teaching of philosophy into the Chair of English at Liverpool, he later returned to Oxford as Professor of Poetry and became one of the most influential literary critics of his day. To Bradley, Green wrote: 'It was but two or three years after I had worked with him (Jowett) in pushing for the definite introduction of philosophy, as independent of ancient books, into the Schools and I was not prepared for the permanence of his desire entirely to expel philosophy from Balliol.'[23]

Why did Jowett reverse himself on the value of the systematic study of philosophy? No doubt he had first adopted his position favouring metaphysics because he thought it undermined uncritical dogmatism. But once he saw what was apt to emerge from thinkers who took Idealism seriously, he came to believe that 'Metaphysics exercise a fatal influence over the mind in destroying the power of observation and of acquiring knowledge'.[24] Detesting obscurity, the Master judged that the 'fuliginous jargon' used by Green's students indicated that both he and they were more likely muddled than profound.

Nor can the possibility be excluded that Jowett felt some jealousy, for now it was Green rather than himself who attracted the most powerful and intellectually mature undergraduates. Jowett was in his fifties; he no longer cared to undertake any further adventures of ideas. Nor would he allow any member of his College to experiment with the minds and lives of undergraduates when his own proven means of instruction were every day producing an unrivalled success for the College. In his refusal to allow Green to teach philosophy to Balliol undergraduates, Jowett was behaving very curiously indeed, although he and his biographers claimed that he was but safeguarding the interests of the College and the students entrusted to it. Abbott and Campbell, in a passage which attempts to smooth over the episode, nevertheless admit a great deal that was unlovely in Jowett's behaviour. Between the two men, despite this one point of strain, there was said to exist the greatest affection possible. But the obligations entailed by this friendship were that, on the one side, Jowett felt free to cut Green off from the teaching which made him a power at Balliol and, on the other, that Green submitted to this arbitrary act. For Jowett was 'sensitive . . . to the influence of metaphysics on the young, and as Master of the College, the young men there were in his charge. Himself a critic of philosophy rather than a philosopher, it gave him real pain to see any of his friends fall, as he thought, under the dominion of a system. . . . On this point he and Green must needs differ, and Green very wisely and generously gave way.'[25] Jowett's biographers thought the episode did credit to both men: to Jowett because he was able to overcome his love for Green when he thought the College's interests were involved; to Green, 'because a man of less noble mind, less loyal to Balliol and Jowett, might have made it the occasion of an open breach, and Green probably would have won the victory'.

That Green felt a strong loyalty to his old tutor and College was demonstrated by his conduct in this affair. He never opposed Jowett unless he felt that his conscience obliged him to do so.* It is questionable whether the Master fully returned this feeling. He was seen at Green's lectures, 'sitting with his back against the table round which the rest of us sat, his legs stretched out over the floor, his vast head sunk on his chest, and his childlike face fixed upon his feet in reverie'. As he went out the Master was overheard to murmur, ostensibly to himself: 'Foolish man! Foolish man!'[26] Even in the memorial sermon he preached in Balliol Chapel after Green's death, something in Jowett drove him to deliver a subtle but unmistakable reproof. The departed, for some reason, had chosen to devote himself to an important, if unfortunately precarious, branch of knowledge. Around him gathered a band of disciples who hoped that from the systematic study of metaphysics might emerge some previously unknown truth which would clear up all the perplexities of the age. And with his characteristic worldliness, Jowett concluded: 'whether this hope would have been altogether realised, or realised in the way in which they expected, or whether any such hope was entertained by himself, I cannot tell'.[27] More was being said here than at first appears, for many of those present at this service had heard earlier in the same chapel another and franker exposition of what Jowett's mature

* 'I have certainly never sought the reputation of a prophet, and if in a small measure and among a small circle I have gained it, I can only wonder why. There is no other way of teaching within my competence than that of trying to satisfy in others the intellectual wants I find in myself, and as I have begun I must go on.

But it is good to be made strongly sensible of the bad side of the effect one is producing, which I take to be a tendency to disregard positive knowledge and to lose the faculty of dealing directly with the ordinary intelligence of men. I find this tendency in myself and can therefore understand that others find it more marked in others who have been much under my influence. It is an effect more difficult to prevent than the obfuscation of the average intellect which I may have sometimes produced by pouring too much metaphysics on it too soon. The latter evil I hope to avoid for the future: but the former is for the time an almost inseparable incident of any bona fide pursuit of philosophy.' [MS Letter from T. H. Green to A. C. Bradley, 16 December, 1880, Balliol College Library.]

judgment of metaphysics came to. Using the dry wit of which he was such a master, Jowett had disposed of Idealist speculation by his reference to Schelling, whom he took to be the archetype of this philosophical school. Jowett recalled that, many years before, he had met the great man whose decline and fall he now proceded to sketch:

> He had already had six systems of philosophy, and was revealing the seventh and newest to a Berlin audience. . . . All his systems of philosophy were the creation of a man of genius, and showed a great deal of thought and insight, but they had no definite relation to history or fact. All of them claimed to be based on first principles and eternal truths. In a few years they were no longer remembered. When I was at Munich a short time since, I asked whether Schnelling had left any disciples. The answer was: 'Yes, he has left *one*, and *he* has no disciple.'[28]

No doubt the sympathies of most readers today will be with Jowett in his dismissal of the value of metaphysics. It may be granted that on this point the Master of Balliol's prejudices were superior to Green's learned arguments. But the central issue of their disagreement in fact was this: Is philosophy a subject to be taught by trained men who are trusted to develop it along whatever lines and by whatever rules they choose to adopt? Or should it be considered as merely one means of developing certain intellectual qualities deemed desirable in young men by a council of wise elders? When put in this light, the merits of Green's own thought became irrelevant.* Jowett made no formal effort to refute his student, and proposed to settle the matter by considerations that were authoritarian as they were unphilosophical. As Master of Balliol, Jowett fell into the posture of the High Churchmen and Evangelicals who had punished him in his youth for having introduced disturbing modes of thought. Jowett's objections to the technical language used by Green closely resemble his advice to Alfred Marshall who, he thought, ought to remove all mathematical proofs from the *Principles of Economics*. Thus Jowett's attitudes were those of a man who refused to recognise the significance of professional studies in the modern world. Although his

---

* F. H. Bradley in this connection remarked: 'Philosophy like other things has a business of its own, and like other things it is bound, and it must be allowed, to go about its own business in its own way. Except within its own limits it claims no supremacy, and, unless outside its own limits, it cannot and must not accept any dictation. Everything to philosophy is a consideration, in the sense that everything has a claim and a right to be considered. But how it is to be considered is the affair of philosophy alone, and here no external consideration can be given even the smallest hearing.' (F. H. Bradley, *Essays on Truth and Reality* [London, 1914], p. 15.)

students were to hold high positions during the zenith of their country's power, they and their teacher were handicapped by a mentality that denied any value to specialisation. This aspect of his character has been assessed by the latest of his successors as Regius Professor of Greek at Oxford:

> 'Jowett was a great teacher; he had a magnetic influence over the young; but we think of him as tutor, and as master, never as Professor. The young Housman wrote home that he had absented himself from Jowett's lectures in disgust at the Professor's gross ignorance of Greek. . . . Even if one could forgive Jowett's deficiencies as a scholar and his reluctance to take steps to amend them, what can we say of his openly expressed aversion to research, of his opposition to every scheme calculated to advance sound learning in the University, of his not only failing to perform what are usually held to be the duties of a Professor, but actually coming forward as the main adversary of the interests he might have been expected to protect?'[29]

Jowett, in his abrupt and unjust series of actions against A. C. Bradley and Green, behaved like a man who suddenly saw endangered everything for which he had lived. To lose his dominance over the most intellectual men of his College, to submit to having metaphysical chimeras put into the heads of students who ought to be immunised by their education against any mystification —this situation struck him as so intolerable that he reacted with an unwonted passion and resentment. Yet there is reason to believe that the Master underestimated his own capacity to counteract Green. For he failed to see how healthy and stimulating was the atmosphere of intellectual tension between the distinctive method of teaching he himself had introduced and that followed by Green in his lectures. The memoirs of Balliol men during this period refer again and again to the challenging situation produced by the simultaneous presence of two minds so strikingly disparate. H. W. C. Davies, looking back at this great epoch of the College, concluded that 'there are many who still think that no better place of education can be imagined than one in which the "Credo" of Green should be constantly opposed to the "Quaero" of Jowett'.[30] Within this framework, Green had effects which were on the whole desirable: he made ideas exciting to some who otherwise might not have been touched by any type of abstract speculation; and, what was more, by his example of sustained intellectual effort, he launched many along independent investigations which in time reached conclusions far removed from his own. No doubt he did befuddle some students, who never subsequently made themselves understood; but surely every school of philosophy produces a certain number of living caricatures of its leading figures. At the very least, Philosophical Idealism accustomed Oxford men to the notion that they should not shun intellectually difficult problems. And the testimony of many who underwent such a training suggests that it served as well as a way of sharpening men's wits as the ancient texts on the one side and the latest revelations of our time on the other.*

Green's case for the advantages of teaching philosophy was to prevail over Jowett's doubts. By the time of his death, Green had pretty much won approval by his personal example for the proposition that the subject requires professional competence and cannot be adequately conveyed to undergraduates by the amateur efforts of tutors called upon to take care of all aspects of the Greats curriculum. And it came to be generally recognised that it was not a valid objection against philosophers that their concerns are less accessible to the common reader than the controversies fought earlier in the nineteenth century reviews by thinkers of the previous generation. This step was made first with Jowett's co-operation, and then against his will. The battle that followed made Green a disturbing and original force who attracted students delighting in fearlessness. Their devotion to philosophy, carried to the point of endangering their careers, cannot be accurately described as a bland rationalisation of the status quo.

4

Green's significance for the development of philosophy at Oxford can scarcely be exaggerated. Asquith, who although a student of Green's nevertheless sided with Jowett, wrote:

* A judicious verdict was that of Farnell:

'It somewhat surprises me, considering the mental force I put into it, that now I cannot remember a single definite phrase or judgment; nor . . . can I recall anything except a vague impression as of one running unceasingly round the same lamp-post and never advancing. . . .

It may seem deplorable that four years of such tense study should leave no harvest. . . . But something else may have abided, other than definite theorising or ratiocination. And a long and severe philosophic training leaves its impress on any later work. . . .

Looking back wonderingly at it, I feel convinced that all this intellectual travail, whatever was its fruit, was eminently worth while; and was the best thing that could then have happened to us. Nor did this part at least of the Greats course deserve the strictures that were sometimes passed at that time on the humanistic schools of Oxford, namely that the students were spoon-fed and were slaves to the examination. Toiling after Green in his Hegelian furrows was not indeed research-work in Mark Pattison's sense, but it was certainly not like being fed with a spoon, and the mental effort was almost creative. And in these fascinating throes I was entirely unconscious of any examination.' (Farnell, *An Oxonian Looks Back*, pp. 45-47.)

'Between 1870 and 1880 Green was undoubtedly the greatest personal force in the real life of Oxford. . . . It is not too much to say that by the time of his premature death . . . he had transformed both the atmosphere and the methods of philosophical thought and study at Oxford.'[31]

Green produced this result by means which cannot be said to have stemmed either from his qualities as a preacher or from an altogether inappropriate injection of his views into the minds of unsuspecting undergraduates. There survive numerous memoirs and auto-biographies of men who studied under Green, who was a sufficiently notable figure for them to devote some space to their recollections of him. And none of their accounts of his performance as a teacher lend credence to the charge that he proselytised. Rather they agreed in emphasising his personal reserve and intellectual austerity. So far from adapting his ideas or his language to the level of his hearers, his failure to compromise alienated many who came eager to be convinced. Even his admirers had to admit wryly in later years: 'Green was cruelly inarticulate: and his message was tough and tangled: and the Hegelian jargon was teeth-breaking . . .'[32] Nor did he give any signs of encouraging intimacy or wishing to attract disciples. The truth seems to be that in his attack on empiricism as well as in his positive attempt to put together an Idealist system, Green's efforts impressed his audience as being altogether novel. These accounts by men who were to go such different ways pay tribute to the excitement engendered by following a thinking mind along tracks all the more fascinating because they seemed unpredictable. That his ideas were in fact less original than they at first appeared may be conceded. Green's reputation profited from the isolation of English intellectual life from that of Europe. And no doubt the impact made by his use of Idealism must in the long run be explained by the religious situation. Yet it must be emphasised that many of the best young men attracted to Green would have rejected a mere preacher, a type which most of them knew all too well, and found unattractive. In short, it required a considerable intellectual effort to comprehend Green's theories. Upon most of the undergraduates exposed to him he produced little more than the impression that here was a most difficult subject which an otherwise estimable man for some reason found worth pursuing.*

* This mixture of affection with bafflement appears in the Apocrypha to the *Ballad of Balliol*:

> I'm the self-distinguishing
> consciousness in everything;
> the synthetic unity
> one in multiplicity,

Like most other movements, Idealism went through a number of phases. The sorts of persons apt to be attracted at the beginning when the doctrine seemed bold and unconventional were not at all the same as its typical adherents when, after Green's death, it became itself an Oxford orthodoxy. At the outset there was an inner group of followers, some of whom went on to achieve great eminence in their own right. What was there about Green and his conception of his philosophy that drew them to him? Did they expect from him, as Jowett suggested, some complete and unprecedented revelation? Some light on these questions is cast by a petition to Green from a group of students who wished him to lead them in an essay society, one of those esoteric discussion groups, which at Oxford is always to be found at the heart of any significant movement.[33] Certainly this document, drawn up by its then youthful members, deserves close attention as an indication of the relationship between Green and his students. If, indeed, this was one between proselytiser and proselytes, then the petition ought to reveal it.

What some people feel the need of now in Oxford: (1) belief in principles, instead of the present eclecticism; (2) earnest effort to bring speculation into relation with modern life instead of making it an intellectual luxury, and to deal with various branches of science, physical, social, political, metaphysical, theological, aesthetic, as part of a whole instead of in abstract separation; (3) co-operation instead of the present suspicious isolation; (4) fearlessness in expression of opinions amongst men who really have opinions, instead of the present deadly reserve.

Feeling these views strongly among ourselves, we wish to know whether you do the same, and if so, whether you are sufficiently convinced of their importance to do something towards supplying them by joining us in an essay society.

We have formed ourselves into an Essay Society to do what we can towards the objects described in the paper you have seen. We do not represent, or wish to represent, any specific philosophical principles, except so far as common belief in the possibility of philosophy constitutes a principle. But we are all in one way or another your debtors, and look to you as the man who does more than anyone else in Oxford to teach men to think. We therefore write to ask you whether you sympathise with our attempt, and, if so, whether you would give it a start next term by reading us something in connection with it.

---

the unseen nexus of the seen,
sometimes known as TOMMY GREEN.
(W. G. Hiscock [ed.], *Balliol Rhymes* [Oxford: Printed for the editor, 1955], p. 27.)

Signed for R. L. Nettleship   H. S. Theobald
             F. H. Bradley   J. R. Sturgis
             A. C. Bradley   A. Goodwin[34]
             F. H. Peters

The text of this proposal casts some light upon the history of Idealism in England, for here is the first proof of the close connection that once existed between Green and F. H. Bradley.* But more significant for the questions being put here, is the coolness of its tone. Quite explicitly it asserts that the signers of the petition were united, not by any one creed, but rather by their mutual confidence that it was worthwhile to study philosophy as a subject apart from classics. What they did share was impatience with the superficiality and amateurism then characteristic of the teaching of philosophy. Nor did they have any tolerance for aristocratic flippancy or the type of scepticism apt to be induced by the use Jowett made of the history of thought. Their use of 'luxury' in a thoroughly pejorative sense indicates the ascetic assumptions and background of its authors. Their call for fearlessness was directed against what Pattison later called 'the terrorism of an ecclesiastical Ring', which first replaced discussion by controversy, and then controversy by denunciation.[35] As for bringing speculation into relation with modern life, this demand meant two things: first that theologians had failed to provide a meaningful answer to questions of meaning and conduct ever since Christianity had been challenged by science and historical criticism; second, that philosophy as taught at Oxford was cut off from all the great questions men felt called upon to answer in their personal lives as well as in defining their obligations to society. Here then in this modest manifesto are the two paradoxical elements that have appeared in Green's own thought: on the one hand, a confidence in reason and in whatever conclusions follow from unconfined thought and discussion; on the other, the confidence that the practice of philosophy will produce answers to questions which had long been defined as religious. These young men did not deceive themselves about their motivations. Nettleship described himself and his fellows as belonging to those relatively few undergraduates to whom personal experience had made real problems ordinarily regarded as merely abstract. Perhaps he had his own crisis of belief in mind; but he went on to

* When the second edition of *Ethical Studies* was prepared for publication after F. H. Bradley's death by his sister and brother, Mrs de Glehn wished to claim priority for it as the first formulation of Idealist ethics in England. (It was published in 1876, whereas Green's *Prolegomena to Ethics* appeared posthumously only in 1883.) But A. C. Bradley refused to allow this claim to be made since he knew of his brother's exposure to Green's views.

characterise the other members of the essay society as 'men who, having in them some strain of idealism, had found a difficulty in adjusting their lives to it; men in whom radicalism was seeking a meeting-point with loyalty or whose acceptance of a moral principle or a religious idea was crossed by a half-understood scientific theory or a half-disguised selfish impulse'.[36]

Although the petitioners were disposed to believe that ideas ought to be taken seriously, and that philosophy ought to help men to build up a set of organising principles on which they might act, nevertheless they did not attribute to Green the actual achievement of such a system. They were grateful to him, not because he had provided them once and for all with ready-made answers, but because he had done more than anyone else in Oxford to teach them how to think.* Another student later wrote in this same vein:

> 'In teaching . . . he was great . . . because he made one feel that truth was to him, and ought to be for anyone who pretended an interest in learning, the one essential thing . . . It was so obvious that truth was a serious thing to him . . . that it was hard to be with him and not to be driven on to learn with a purer interest than one was likely to have had before.'[37]

This aspect of Green much impressed not only his inner circle but also the other students he taught at Balliol. In his lectures on Aristotle he had great difficulty in expressing himself. Yet his hearers liked him because he was working out an original meaning for the text instead of repeating what others had written.† 'The men in fact took a sort of pride in the difficult process which he went through before he got things clear, as if it were in some way the joint action of us all.'[38] His lecture style never much improved, for he always read from a manuscript characterised by an uncompromising abstraction which left no room for concrete illustrations or imaginative flights. So far from eliciting comforting morals, Green was criticised by T. H. Huxley because he seemed most convincing when he found fault with other philosophers. He cared not at all for biographical detail or even the placing of a

---

* Sixty years later, one of the original members stated: 'He did not supply his pupils with thought, but he made them think; he did not give them philosophy but he made them philosophise.' [Sir Henry Studdy Theobald, *Remembrance of Things Past* (Oxford, 1935), p. 47.]

† 'His first pupils found that in conversation he did not bewilder them, as . . . in his lectures. Nothing gave him greater pleasure than to be asked those awkward questions which children in philosophy, like other children, often ask. Never perhaps was he seen to laugh more delightedly—for he could laugh at the right time—than when it occurred to a pupil leaving the room with his hand on the half-opened door to put the trifling question, "What, then, is the origin of our ideas?" ' (Wright-Henderson, *Glasgow and Balliol*, p. 45.)

thinker against the background of his age. Each philosopher was treated as nothing more than the exponent of a position. None of this was done with fluency or charm. Asquith's memories of Green express the usual view of his students:

> His lectures were not easy to follow: his manner was apt to be jerky; and his style abounded in what Burke calls 'nodosities'. It was a familiar gibe of those who looked on from outside the fold that, by the end of the hour, he had become so contorted that he had to be untied by friendly hands.[39]

Self-criticism he practiced increasingly. As he grew older, he became less and less satisfied with his own formulation of Idealism. In 1879 he wrote in a letter that 'writing now is very different from what it was ten years ago. Then . . . I thought I had got hold of a key which I find now will not unlock so much as I fancied it would. . . .'[40] It was this professional integrity that repelled eager young men seeking conversion. His contemporaries remarked that he would send away his tutorial students who brought essays to him with the sense that he was equally dissatisfied both with what they had written and his own attempts to improve it. Here is the experience of a good, but not distinguished student:

> I had the privilege of taking a few essays to Mr Green. . . . I went to his home with my work, and he used to sit over the fire, 'tying himself into knots'. He beat out his music with some difficulty, and the music itself was not an ordinary melody. I once said I was afraid that some phrase of mine was not very clear. 'I am afraid,' he said with a rueful smile, 'that in philosophy clearness of thought is often in inverse proportion to clearness of expression';* and then seeing me a little dashed, said in his pleasant way, 'But, never mind, come, and have some tea downstairs'. All that term he continued to criticise. At last I produced an essay of which he said, 'Well, I think that is a good essay'; and that is the highest praise I ever got from him—but it is still precious.[41]

If, by his manner, Green belied the impression that he thought himself in possession of the truth, he took care in his lectures and writing to distinguish the rôle of the philosopher from that of the preacher. When the philosopher understands his business, he does not attempt to create moral standards but to understand them, analysing their nature and demonstrating their implications. The

* This phrase deserves some explication. No doubt what Green meant to say was that his students should not overestimate the intellectual worth of glib formulae calculated to impress examiners. Yet some element of *hubris* may also have been present. Green's undergraduate coach remarked: 'Even in after years . . . he cared less than most men do to be easily understood. Of an article he had written for the North British Review, he remarked, "I flatter myself no lady will read it." ' (MS letter from C. S. Parker to Nettleship, 26 September, 1882, Balliol College Library.)

philosopher can aid the practice of morality only indirectly and this by doing his work of analysis. Only in cases of *bona fide* perplexity, when the usually accepted authorities seem to conflict and make it difficult for men to see their duties, can he help at all. Such circumstances are exceptional. Ordinarily men's duties are clear enough. 'The function of bringing home these duties to the consciences of men—of helping them to be honest with themselves in their recognition and interpretation of them—is rather that of the preacher than of the philosopher.'[42] When the philosopher can render a service, it is rather 'of the defensive and negative than of the actively inciting kind'.[43] Green makes no claim for the philosopher as seer or law-giver.* Yet, while the philosopher in most circumstances, has an essentially critical and negative rôle, he cannot, 'in a speculative and dialectical age,' disregard the nihilism apt to be produced by the apparent lack of intellectual justification for all values.[44] In a period of intellectual confusion, as Green thought of his own time, philosophy can be a constructive force by re-formulating the principles on which the good citizen, if he could think the matter out, would find that he had already been acting. Once this implicit set of principles is articulated, men can again see their duties and act upon them. Green's image of his age, we shall see, was inseparable from his definition of philosophy.

Green believed that his subject was fitted for more than the liberation of men from the pseudo-problems resulting from the earlier work of deceived individuals calling themselves philosophers. He had greater hopes, and the enthusiasm produced by his example did much to produce the situation enjoyed today by some of his critics. But it has not been the purpose of this chapter either to defend him or to assail him. Rather this has been an attempt to discover what sort of teacher he in fact was. If any one summary of the impression he produced is to be remembered, it ought to be the anonymous and remarkably detached estimate which appeared immediately after his death:

> 'Those who have known him as a teacher and friend during the last twelve years feel, now that he is gone, that he was the man who most made Oxford what it was to them. Yet they would find it hard to say why they felt this. Professor Green was in no sense a popular teacher.

* J. A. Symonds particularly emphasised the difficulty of getting Green to discuss his own philosophical beliefs. To all inquiries, 'he used to repeat that Philosophy is not a Mystery, that the Philosopher cannot be expected to know more for certain than the rest of men about such things as Immortality, that his superiority consists in knowing his own thoughts, what man must think, that the old religious language receives through exact thinking a new vitality, that it is our prime business to take account of what and how we think. . . .' [MS Letter from J. A. Symonds to Mrs Green, undated, but postmarked 10 October, 1882.]

The subjects on which he liked to dwell were such as appeal only to a limited audience; and the difficulties which he found in expressing himself tended to make them even more obscure than they really were. Still less was he a philosophical propagandist. He never had or wished to have a school, or even a following; to be "a third-rate prophet", as he used to say, was the last thing he was ambitious of. On the contrary, he shrunk, almost to excess, from imposing his ideas upon others, and even from expressing them unless called upon to do so by his position. Those who knew him most intimately re-member . . . how hard it was to get him to speak upon the subjects upon which he had most right to speak. Yet it remains a fact that his influence in Oxford as a teacher has been greater than that of any other man of his generation. One of the causes of this was the intense reality of his teaching. Those who heard him lecture or talk felt that whatever he said was a part of his very self. In lecturing, especially, though he habitually used written notes, he seemed as it were to be thinking over again—one might almost say to be living over again—the mental experiences which he was trying to express. Each sentence was literally pregnant with thought. . . . It is true that he never put out his ideas in a system; he was even careless about the form in which he presented them; and this sometimes made them difficult to assimilate. But upon those who had the patience to follow him, there gradually impressed itself the sense of a single and dominant principle —a principle which underlay his views of the most different and apparently unconnected things, and which got its strength and con-sistency from the strength and consistency of his own personality. It was here that so many men began to feel for the first time that philosophy (to use his own words again) was not a "method or a dodge", but a spirit pervading and unifying life . . . he was one of those men to whom human life is emphatically divine and spiritual. The conviction that the every day affairs of the world, its politics and history as well as its religion, are all in some way a growing pro-clamation of a divine order gave a kind of religious fervour to his expression of the most secular ideas and his performance of the most common duties. Yet he never gave the impression of feeling himself to be on a pedestal. His talk, even on the highest matters, was very homely, and even prosaic.'[45]

No one who has followed Green's closely-spaced criticism of Hume and his critics will deny that this is the work of a man who spurns easy conclusions and is enforcing upon himself and his readers the demands of an inexorable procedure. His task involved for him an arduous analysis, detailed proof and sustained reason-ing along with the necessity for meticulous rejoinders to the ob-jections made by unfriendly critics. Such was his standard, and he has the right to be judged by it. But this is only to open the question of how adequately he squared his will to believe with the high demands of his chosen subject; it is not to foreclose the answer.

CHAPTER SIX

METAPHYSICAL FOUNDATIONS

I

NOW THAT GREEN IS no longer read by philosophers, he may gain a new status as one of the most representative mid-Victorian thinkers. His obscure style and technical interests have long concealed the extent to which his ideas coincided with those of his better-known contemporaries. And no less deceptive was his polemic, direct and indirect, against John Stuart Mill, Matthew Arnold, Herbert Spencer and Henry Sidgwick. In this connection it is well to recall Whitehead's warning against accepting at face value the formal differences among the competing schools of any given period. For ostensible rivals tend to share assumptions which restrict the range of disagreement. Often there is a tacit consensus upon the questions to be examined as well as upon the terms in which they are put. Recurrent words and obsessive issues may thus unite the work of authors classified as antagonists by themselves and textbooks.

Philosophers of Green's vintage thought that their task was dictated by the special characteristics of their age, which they considered unique in human history. Never before had a society changed so rapidly. On the whole, this was considered a proof of progress, but few cared to dispute the fact of a general unsettlement in religious and moral opinion. This was not a situation which thinking men could ignore. Every aspect of human thought would have to be brought into harmony with the spirit of the age. This conception dominated Green's Broad Church theology: religion could be kept alive only by giving to old beliefs that rational form appropriate to the level civilisation was said to have attained.

There was nothing original about these ideas. Green was but following the well-marked trail of Coleridge and Carlyle and, for that matter, of those Utilitarians like Leslie Stephen and the younger Mill, who had learned from the German or French to divide history into discrete periods: ages of vigour and decadence; ages of faith and those of bleak disillusionment or corrupt cynicism. Faith was said to be the condition of vigour. Man can be 'whole' only when conscious that his fundamental beliefs are consistent with the best knowledge of the day. All great epochs were said to have achieved such a unity. It was commonly conceded that England had not yet arrived at this state of felicity. More optimistic thinkers thought that they had within their grasp the intellectual key to a golden age. Both Green and J. S. Mill had moments of great hope. Others like Carlyle thought that all was lost; perhaps most symptomatic was Matthew Arnold, whose lyric poetry and private sensibility expressed an uncertainty which contrasted with his more robust public utterances as a Victorian sage. The first mood, of doubt and the sense of what had been lost, evoked in Arnold his familiar lines from 'Dover Beach':

> The sea of faith
> Was once, too, at the full, and round earth's shore
> Lay like the folds of a bright girdle furl'd;
> But now I only hear
> Its melancholy, long, withdrawing roar,
> Retreating to the breath
> Of the night-wind down the vast edges drear
> And naked shingles of the world.[1]

His programme of reconstruction provided the theme of his inaugural lecture in 1857 when he took up the chair as Professor of Poetry at Oxford: it was not untypical of the Rugby-Balliol connection.

To his audience, which no doubt included Green and the Old Mortality, Arnold spoke of the modern age as 'copious and complex', characterised by a 'vast multitude of facts awaiting and inviting [man's] comprehension'.[2] Unprecedented difficulties challenged the poet, and the ancient touchstones could no longer serve as a guide. What criterion of worth ought to be adopted? Arnold proposed that literature be tested by its adequacy to the age. Modern society must judge everything by reason. Its authors should observe facts with a critical spirit and seek to discover the basic laws underlying this multiplicity. To produce a sense of 'adequacy', literature must be not only reasonable but 'whole'. Arnold declared: 'We are in an epoch of expansion; and the essence of an epoch of expansion is a movement of ideas, and the one salvation of an epoch of expansion is a harmony of ideas.'[3] This craving for integration was connected with the crisis of conscience. J. A. Symonds wrote to Henry Sidgwick in the same vein: 'At all events, I feel, let us not acquiesce in anything but Wholes; let us feebly gasp, or powerfully bear, displaying strength in our weakness; until the Whole is made clear to us'.[4]

Green agreed with Arnold's diagnosis, but quarrelled with his remedy. Poetry and literary criticism were powerless to deal with the root of the matter. In his view, the very concepts in which Englishmen thought were bankrupt, because hopelessly entangled in the paradoxes Hume had bequeathed to all who followed him in the tradition of empiricism and hedonism. Green's first major work was an effort ' to show that the philosophy based on the abstraction of feeling, in regard to morals no less than to nature, was with Hume played out, and that the next step forward in speculation could only be an effort to re-think the process of nature and human action from its true beginning in thought'.[5] His cry was 'On to Kant and Hegel.' Poetry, which had to accept ordinary language and the concepts of common sense was not sufficiently critical; the disposition of educated men to turn to Tennyson's *In Memoriam* or Browning's *Rabbi Ben Ezra* for a statement of belief indicated only that philosophers had failed to meet their obligations. The frequent pronouncements of literary men on the great problems of life were due to the needs of 'the multitude of the educated, who have wearied of the formulas of a stereotyped theology, but still demand free indulgence for the appetite which that theology supplied with a regulation-diet'.[6] Green thought of himself as doing something very different. As a philosopher he was carrying out a meticulous examination of human knowledge and its presuppositions. In this way only could it be demonstrated that reason supports the belief in a meaningful and spiritual order.

The appeal to Kant was significant, reflecting both great respect for criticism and the confidence that the most rigorous procedure would sustain all that the philosopher and his public most cherished. 'Criticism' had a broader and a narrower connotation: the first being an attitude of mind; the second, a philosophical method. Kant's great statement of the critical attitude was one of Green's sacred texts:

> 'Our age is, in especial degree, the age of criticism, and to criticism everything must submit. Religion through its sanctity, and law-giving through its majesty, may seek to exempt themselves from it. But they then awaken just suspicion, and cannot claim the sincere respect which reason accords only to that which has been able to sustain the test of free and open examination.'[7]

Green also thought of criticism as providing the ideal for philosophical investigation. In contrast to dogmatism on one side and scepticism on the other, criticism offered the way to lead men out of contradiction and doubt into a reasoned certainty based on the determination of the bounds between our necessary knowledge and our equally necessary ignorance. 'Not the conclusions of reason but reason itself must be submitted to critical evaluation.'[8] This distinction of a third and more excellent way between dogmatism and scepticism carried a powerful appeal.

Already in his undergraduate essays Green addressed himself to 'that peculiar characteristic of our times, the scepticism of our best men'. Although this quality is scarcely what would be expected by those who still take *Eminent Victorians* as a definitive portrait of the age, Green was not untypical in both his questioning attitude and his concern about the absence of standards which could be accepted by the thinking. Yet if his generation was perplexed, it was also confident that something could be done to put things right. It doubted, so much so that authors of the period occasionally give the impression of striking a pose. But there was also a respect for reason. An easy faith was regarded as not worth having if its price was the abandoning of inquiry. And so they inquired in the spirit eloquently described in Bishop Gore's memorial talk on Henry Sidgwick:

'That was what was so remarkable in Henry Sidgwick—the perpetual hopefulness of his inquiry. He always seemed to expect that some new turn of argument, some new phase of thought, might arise and put a new aspect upon the intellectual scenery, or give a new weight in the balance of argument. There was in him an extraordinary belief in *following reason*—a belief and a hopefulness which continued up to the last . . . Though he was expressing doubt and then doubting the expressed doubt, and then doubting the doubt about the doubt—yet the quality of his mind was profoundly different from ordinary scepticism: for it was inspired by a fundamental belief in the attainableness of positive truth. At the bottom of his mind was the profound desire to find an adequate basis on which to rest a positive construction of a worthy life.'[9]

Once again there is a reference to 'adequacy', a disclaimer of 'ordinary scepticism'. This rationalism is ultimately confident because backed by the belief in progress.

The faith shared with his school friend was what Green had in common with Matthew Arnold and J. S. Mill—all of them conceived of their age as awaiting a view of the world which was rational, progressive and secular. Such a *Weltanschauung* they did not hesitate to substitute for belief in God, since they thought that it would perform the functions in their age that traditional religions had done during the great periods of faith. As T. S. Eliot has remarked, 'From this proposition two different types of man can extract two different types of conclusion: 1 that Religion is Morals, 2 that Religion is Art.'[10] The first was the way of Sidgwick,

Mill, and Green; the second, the way of Arnold. In both cases, the demand came to the same thing—for 'a philosophy of life'. This phrase, with all that it meant as a definition of philosophy, occurred in Mill's diary at the time when he was considering the claims of Comte's religion of humanity:

'A Philosophy of Life, in harmony with the noblest feelings and cleared of superstition, is the great want of these times. There has always been talent enough in the world when there was earnestness enough, and always earnestness enough when there were strong convictions. There seems to be so little talent now, only because there is universal uncertainty about the great questions. . . . Ages of belief, as Goethe says, have been the only ages in which great things have been done. Ages of belief have hitherto always been religious ages: but Goethe did not mean that they must necessarily be so in future. Religion, of one sort or another, has been at once the spring and the regulator of energetic action, chiefly because religion has hitherto supplied the only Philosophy of Life, or the only one which differed from a mere theory of self-indulgence. Let it be generally known what life is and might be, and how to make it what it might be, and there will be as much enthusiasm and as much energy as there has ever been.'[11]

These sentiments were virtually indistinguishable from Green's. But if these two agreed that the age needed an integrating creed, they differed sharply about what it should be. Green gave Mill credit for good intentions, but he judged the Utilitarians as he had Bishop Berkeley: 'When the most pious theological purpose expresses itself in a doctrine resting on an inadequate philosophical principle, it is the principle and not the purpose that will regulate the permanent effect of the doctrine'.[12] In Green's view, the hedonism and empiricism, central to Utilitarian theory had the effect of encouraging selfishness and political complacency. As Green saw the philosophical situation, the dominant trend of English thought in the 1850's and 60's was empiricism, whether in the form of J. S. Mill or in the modification of Herbert Spencer's evolutionary theory.[13] The empirical school derived all knowledge from sensation, and described the mind as the passive recipient of impressions from the material world. Its logic denied the reality of 'Universals', the objects to which general names refer. These were described, not as independent features of the real world, but as mere abstractions including a number of wholly distinct individuals simply on the basis of one point of resemblance. As Professor C. C. J. Webb has pointed out, this school left no room for religion. Spiritual truths could never be proved, but only asserted and this by the claim that the heart has its own truth or by the authority of revelation attested by the evidence of miracles, a claim and authority which this philosophy could not admit. In short, the empirical school left 'man without a Father in heaven, without real freedom to will and to act, without an outlook beyond the grave'.[14] Green and his school argued that the unchallenged predominance of these ideas was undesirable from every point of view:

> 'Adapted to the requirements of public spirit, and illogically modified in the adaptation, they have become, under the name "Utilitarianism", the permanent practical theory of men of the world. . . . They have been wrought into the rhetoricised philosophy of the press, the pulpit and the platform, to become the source of much undemonstrative agony at the times when speculation comes home to life.'[15]

Utilitarianism once had helped to demolish the special claims of those classes which asserted tradition to constitute a valid title to privilege. But now Utilitarianism no longer was a liberating force. Its principles, as Green argued in his political theory, now had the practical effect of blocking positive reform. In Hegelian language, he contended that the partial truth contained in Utilitarianism had long since fulfilled its special function. And when limited truths have done their work, they must be replaced by a higher synthesis. Utilitarianism failed to take into account that element of God-given reason which is the true spring of moral and political action. Thus its 'popular philosophy' was inadequate to the real position of the age.

What that term meant, Green explained in an essay which gave, in what was, for him, remarkably simple language, his view of the intellectual situation.[16] Philosophy originates in the demand of man, a demand he cannot help making, that he understand himself and his surroundings. Once it was restricted to a small class, but in the modern age, philosophy has become a more general influence. It exerts power because it supplies to men the categories in which they think. If the categories are founded on error, this will produce disastrous results. And in fact this had occurred in England. Hedonism and empiricism had produced a popular philosophy which made men sceptical and destructive: sceptical because of its internal contradictions; destructive, because while purporting to explain the meaning of facts it is too superficial to do more than to dismiss what it cannot understand. Thus the average Englishman, whether educated or not, tended to think in terms of shallow antitheses which made impossible the solution of any of his real problems. In fact there was a dangerous gulf between experience and thought. Englishmen phrased issues in terms which could not account for what is best in human life: the acceptance of limits on desire, not for reasons of prudence but because men acknowledge obligations as right and good. Popular philosophy falsified moral, religious and political action because it represented reason as always separate from and subject to feeling. Good and evil were regarded as nothing more than equivalents for pleasure and pain. Statesmen thus thought and spoke in the language of self-interest rather than moral principle. Hence their abysmal failure during the American Civil War to support the right side. The uneducated working men of the Midlands, despite the economic consequences, had shown themselves superior to their upper-class masters.

How could this be explained? Green's basic optimism no less than his political radicalism asserted themselves in his contention that 'the fabric of European society stands apparently square and strong on a basis of decent actual equity, but no adequate rationale of this equity is generally recognised'.[17] This is a peculiar admission coming from a philosopher arguing the importance of his subject. Either theory affects practice or it does not. If it does, then how could a faulty philosophy produce a society founded on 'decent actual equity'? Green answered that the 'practical reconstruction of moral ideas' in England had not been due to the philosophy or theology taught by members of the upper classes. Rather this had come from the Evangelical revival, the insight of such romantic poets as Wordsworth and the new conceptions of freedom and right popularised by Rousseau. These tendencies has as yet not made themselves felt in popular thought, nor could they until professional philosophers advanced past the point at which Hume had left the subject. 'The result is the diffusion over society of a state of mind analogous to that which we sometimes experience when discussion has carried us a long way from our principles, and we find ourselves maintaining inconsistent propositions, which to us are mere words, yet confuse our views and weaken our hold of the principles from which they seem to follow.'[18]

The remedy Green offered for this situation was to apply to the root problems of philosophy the method developed by Kant and his successors. Once philosophers began to think in such terms, their example, by intellectual necessity, would carry the English forward to those truer notions which, in the development of philosophy, had succeeded Hume. Kant and Hegel had set themselves the task of finding 'formulae adequate to the action of reason as exhibited in nature and human society, in art and religion'.[19] English philosophers could no longer shirk the problems essential to the thinking public. What Green had in mind was a method. As

Edward Caird remarked, he thought that the literal importation
of Kant and Hegel into England was impossible, and in any case
not desirable. Accepting Hegel's criticism of Kant, Green 'yet
regarded the actual Hegelian system with a certain suspicion as
something too ambitious, or, at least, premature'.[20] He never
gave a formal exposition of Hegel's system, but confined himself
to a reconsideration of those elements in Kant which Hegel
developed.[21] Towards the end of his life, he devoted considerable
attention to Lotze, whose works he proposed to edit.[22]

Philosophical Idealism as Green presented it, combined many
of the most characteristic assumptions of its age. As a school, it
claimed to accept the standards of truth provided by science and
scholarship. It argued that the very existence of art, morality,
religion, and even science itself constituted evidence that reality
is something more than the arbitrary intepretation of facts perceived by the senses. Rather, reality for the Idealist cannot be
considered in isolation from the human mind. Reality exemplifies
those forms of sensibility and understanding which belong to the
constitution of the mind itself. 'The world of intelligence and
freedom cannot be different from the world of nature and
necessity; it can only be the same world seen in a new light or
subjected to a further interpretation.'[23]

It was clear to Green's public that his object was to provide that
whole view of life demanded by Matthew Arnold and J. S. Mill.
Upon receiving the privately printed copy of Green's lay sermon
on faith, J. A. Symonds wrote to its author:

> The first thing that struck me . . . was what M. Arnold would call
> the urbanity of your tone—the ἐπιείκεια with which you enter into
> divers points of view, setting Reason, Faith, Science, Religion,
> Ethics, and even passionate revolt, in their right relations, shedding
> light upon them in their several places, and bringing out their
> contours and their harmony.[24]

Thus if philosophy was criticism, it was also synthesis. This dual
conception of the philosophical enterprise explains why so much
of Green's work was an attack upon Hobbes, Locke, Berkeley,
Hume, Mill, and Spencer; why an entire book of the *Prolegomena
to Ethics* is devoted to a polemic against Utilitarianism in all its
forms; why refutation of competing theories takes up a considerable part of the lectures on *Political Obligation*. To set off his own
view of the world, he had to destroy the base of popular philosophy. His audience felt the force of his critique all the more
strongly because Green had a systematic and principled position
of his own. Political theory seemed to demonstrate once again
errors already detected in the metaphysics and epistemology of

Hobbes, Locke, and the Utilitarians. This vindicated all the labour involved in starting with first principles, and understanding where others had gone astray. 'It is the result of such work, and of such work alone, to secure that the foundations are immovably fixed on the rock.'[25] This was Edward Caird's judgment of Green's work, and it came in a volume dedicated to his memory, for which his admirers chose the title, *Essays in Philosophical Criticism*. This represented their conviction of the close affinity between Kant's critical method and Green's. The modern reader may be more impressed by another resemblance:

> 'Kant's view was the beginning of a far-reaching theory of knowledge, later known as the coherence theory, according to which knowledge is organisation into a system and conformity with the system becomes the sole criterion of truth. Kant did not explicitly develop it this far, but he was the first philosopher of importance, to put forward the conception of science as the organisation of our experience rather than the discovery of independent reality. . . .'[26]

2

Green himself called his metaphysics the most difficult and least plausible part of his philosophy. Yet he insisted upon beginning his exposition with it. For in his view the value of his ethical and political theories depended upon their 'foundations' in what he called the metaphysic of morals.[27] This he proposed to investigate by a consideration of the root questions of philosophy, in short, by asking how human knowledge, morality and citizenship are possible. From the consideration of such basic questions, Green hoped to demonstrate that in the everyday life and language of men, there is a power at work which, if they could follow its lead, would lead them to a conception of life as being at once rational and spiritual.

He cautioned against what he considered to be the Philistine view that metaphysics have no practical application. In his own political theory, he argued that the Liberals' difficulties with freedom of contract stemmed from prior assumptions which were metaphysical in just the sense he was concerned to discuss.[28] Among political philosophers, he singled out Burke for praise on the ground that:

> He almost alone among the men of his time caught the intellectual essence of the system which provoked him. He saw that it rested on a metaphysical mistake, on an attempt to abstract the individual from his universal essence, i.e. from the relations embodied in habitudes and institutions which make him what he is; and that thus to unclothe man, if it were possible, would be to animalise him.[29]

Given such an emphasis upon epistemology and metaphysics, it became necessary to understand Green's position. He wrote much on these subjects—and all of it highly technical. In considering his argument, we must choose and adhere to a sharply delineated criterion of relevance lest we be inundated by its details. Green's metaphysics and epistemology will be considered here from two points of view: to the extent that they form the base of his ethical and political theory, and to the extent that they point up the strain between the theologian and the philosopher in his thought. The first point is evident enough; the second may want some clarification. There can be no doubt that the origin of Green's interest in philosophy was religious. But this fact does not in itself affect the validity of his position. It can do so when, and only when, Green's faith leads him into logical contradictions or into drawing untenable conclusions from his argument, or into adopting a method the chief use of which is to bolster certain theological preferences. Any instance of such a tendency to put the will to believe above logical rigour or proper concern for evidence is worth notice.

It has been said that philosophical arguments are essentially simple. Where they become complex and difficult is in their answers to criticisms. These will be omitted in the exposition which follows, for its object is to point up Green's philosophical style, to analyse the characteristic ways in which he puts his problems and offers solutions to them. The positive part of his doctrine falls into recurrent patterns which, once analysed, make their combination in complex notions more nearly intelligible. Professor Lovejoy, who was among the most skilful practitioners of this technique for dealing with the history of ideas, observed that individuals and schools tend to become obsessed with certain formulae, logical devices and methodological assumptions. Once a particular problem has been dealt with in a way which gains approval, there is a strong temptation to extend this strategy to cover a considerable variety of cases, including some far removed from the original starting-point. Just as there is a limited number of plots available to the novelist, so philosophers fix upon a few 'dialectical motifs'.

Three such patterns figure again and again in Green's work: the conceptions of internal relationship in a system, of self-consciousness and of teleological process. What is meant by internal relationship in a system is the theory:

> that, where you have a complex of one or another kind, no element in
> that complex can be understood or can, indeed, be what it is apart

from its relations to all the other components of the system to which it belongs.[30]

Facts are always found embodied in a set of relationships. The world is a system in which every element is correlative with every other. As for the teleological motif, which Green took from Aristotle, it is the familiar conception of an end operative throughout a process and determining its outcome without ever being identical with any stage of its development. The key notion of Green's theology, its only novelty in the rest of his work comes in its use as a defensive weapon against evolutionary theories of mind and obligation. In any process properly called teleological, the *telos* is present in potency and promise from the very beginning. It determines the final stages no less than the earliest. As Green uses this concept, it becomes closely associated with that of self-consciousness. The most primitive principle from which knowledge can be developed is already a perception of fact which implies the action upon successive sensations of a consciousness which holds them in relation. Therefore, this consciousness cannot be said to come before or after these sensations. It is the condition of there being sensation at all.

This dialectical motif, first fashioned in Green's epistemology, became his chief weapon against any naturalistic theory of the origin of morals or the state. Knowledge, ethics, politics, all these are possible only in the presupposition of certain states of mind. Just as facts imply a consciousness holding them in relation, so does a society, however primitive, imply the recognition of rights and a good common to all its members. On the origin of such recognition in the past we speculate in vain. Any society must already imply it. Hence theories about the state being founded by force or compact simply miss the point. No such theory or origins can provide a true explanation of a teleological process.

It is the *Prolegomena to Ethics* which gives the fullest and most reflective account of Green's doctrine. In his introduction, he makes a re-appraisal of the intellectual situation which differs in emphasis from the account he had written eleven years before in 'Popular Philosophy in its Relation to Life'. While the need for an adequate philosophy of life is urged upon the same grounds, his polemical emphasis has shifted. Before he had been most concerned to refute the hedonism and empiricism of the classical English tradition in philosophy; now he saw the principal danger in the claims of science, or more exactly, of popularised philosophies claiming scientific sanction. No less eager than before to refute Utilitarianism, he now saw it as part of a larger movement which included Spencer and the social evolutionists such as Lewes. What these schools shared was the belief in the possibility of a physical science of Ethics.

Such scientism led them to derogate philosophy and systematic metaphysics. And this antipathy to philosophy was strengthened by the vague exaltation of science found in such poets as Tennyson and Browning. What had occurred in theology was now spreading to ethics. Nettleship commented on this parallelism, as Green saw it:

> In religion what most exercised his mind was the prevalent divorce between reason and faith, due as he conceived to a misunderstanding of both, and culminating in scepticism on the one side and superstition on the other, so what he saw with the greatest concern in current theories of conduct was the banishment of all higher aspirations to the region of fancy and sentiment, and the growing claims of natural science to occupy the ground thus left vacant by reason.[31]

The basic assumption of 'scientific ethics' was that all intelligible questions worth asking about human life may be decided by procedures of the kind which had been used so successfully in the natural sciences. Green answered that on the basis of such theories, it can be said only how men act, but not how they ought to act. To someone who is merely the result of natural forces an injunction to conform to their laws is meaningless. A philosopher who has reduced the speculative part of his ethics to a natural science must, if he is consistent with his own principles, abolish the preceptive part. Yet, those who regard moral development as a merely natural process show little reluctance to advise men how they ought to act. They seek to discover the laws by which we have come to be what we are, so that they may then tell us how to seek our happiness by living according to those laws.

But a natural science of ethics can provide no theory of moral obligation. Nor, for that matter, is any genuine theory of political obligation possible on that ground. The critical sections of *Political Obligation* continue this line of argument. Green's point is that no naturalistic explanation can properly account for the use of such terms as 'ought' or 'ought not'. Any philosopher who employs such language, while himself committed to a natural science of morals, does so illegitimately. Of course, such a philosopher will have his own explanation of the language of moral injunction, but this must be of a sort which makes impossible any real theory of obligation.

He will probably trace this language to the joint action of two

1. T. H. Green

2. Colonel Thomas Sanders, an officer in Cromwell's army, and an ancestor of T. H. Green

3. Cromwell Mortimer, pioneer of health insurance, and also a member of Green's family (after a satirical engraving, attributed to Hogarth)

4. Valentine Green (1760–1837) of Normanton-le-Heath, Leicestershire, the grandfather of T. H. Green. From a miniature

5. The Reverend Valentine Green, Rector of Birkin, Yorkshire, father of T. H. Green

6. Birkin Rectory, T. H. Green's birthplace and childhood home

7. The Old Mortality Society
Standing (*from left to right*): J. Payne (Magdalen), Hoole (Queens), T. H. Green
(Balliol), James Bryce (Trinity), Aeneas Mackay (University); sitting: G. R. Luke
(Balliol), A. C. Swinburne (Balliol), John Nichol (Balliol), A. V. Dicey (Balliol),
T. H. Holland (Magdalen)

8. T. H. Green, age 34, at the time of his marriage

9. Mrs Green, age 29, at the time of her marriage

10. Mrs Green, age 84, Drawing by F. A. de Biden Footner, 1925

11. Arnold Toynbee

12. The Balliol Eight, 1869. Three of its members were disciples of Green; R. L. Nettleship and F. H. Peters seated in front, and H. S. Holland, standing at extreme right.

13. Mr and Mrs J. A. Symonds, their daughter, Catherine, and Ció. Taken at Davos, about 1886

14. Benjamin Jowett in 1893. Photographed by H. H. H. Cameron

factors—to the habit of submission to the commands of a physical or political superior, surviving the commands themselves and the memory of them, combined with that constant though ineffectual wish for a condition of life other than his own, which is natural to a being who looks before and after over perpetual alternations of pleasure and pain.[32]

Political Obligation attempts to refute all such theories of obligation in politics; the *Prolegomena* argues that they cannot provide a viable theory of moral obligation.

In its first book, Green set out his reasons for believing that metaphysics is a legitimate field of enquiry dealing with matters not ascertainable by observation and experiment but forming the base for ethics. A being merely the result of natural forces could not form a theory of those forces explaining itself. Science presupposes a principle which is not itself any one or number of such matters of fact or their result.

The first question to be answered is, 'Can the knowledge of nature be itself a part or product of nature, in that sense of nature in which it is said to be an object of knowledge'?[33] If the answer is 'no', then man is not merely a part of nature. Knowledge depends upon a spiritual principle in man which is not natural. And this same principle has another expression in man as the consciousness of a moral ideal which determines human action. All mental functions may be materially conditioned, but if the material conditions are part of the world of experience they cannot originate or explain the conscious principle which makes that world possible.

Human knowledge and moral experience can be understood only on the supposition that a spiritual principle, an eternal consciousness, manifests itself in men. The universe is an eternal activity or energy. Every particular existence is a limited manifestation of it. But in human beings, this activity can be realised only partially because of man's animal organisation. This self-conditioned, free energy acting under limiting conditions makes human experience a continual self-contradiction between what it is and what it might be. To the sense of this contradiction is due the impulse both to knowledge and to goodness.

These conclusions are derived from an examination of nature and human knowledge. Both imply a spiritual principle. Consider what is meant by a fact of experience. This may be the simplest fact, or such a whole complex of facts as science, art or morality. Facts are always found to be embodied in a set of relationships held together by consciousness. Thus the world is a system. Relationship presupposes a self-distinguishing consciousness, because the function which it must fulfil to render the relations of phenomena, and with them, nature possible is one which, on however limited a scale, we ourselves exercise only by means of such a consciousness.

Self-consciousness, then, consciousness of system or relation, of one in many, of identity in difference, is the condition of experience. But this consciousness becomes ours only gradually, piecemeal and by slow degrees. It never becomes ours completely. Insofar as there is a world for us at all, it is because of our consciousness. Yet our idea of system remains only an idea, which gives such form as it has to all our experience, but which recedes as experience fills it up. We are potentially the eternal consciousness which has the world for its object, but we never get far beyond the potentiality. That is what is meant by human limitation. Such knowledge as is possible comes through the spiritual principle realising itself in man.[34]

The details of this epistemological argument are complex. The basic question is how is it possible for us to know what we do in fact know. Experience is in time and space. Knowledge is beyond the transient limitations of perception, for it has an enduring and valid content out of space and time. Therefore both nature and human knowledge imply a principle which is not natural but spiritual. Were we merely phenomena among other phenomena, we could not have knowledge of a world of phenomena.

Everyday perception has a paradoxical character. It is a determination of events in time by a principle that is not in time. This description applies equally well to both fact and the perception of fact. Fact always implies relation determined by other relations in a universe of facts. What such relations imply as the principle of the synthesis which unites them in a single universe is something out of time for which all of the several relations are equally present. This principle can only be consciousness. And yet in man the very consciousness which holds together successive events as equally present has itself a history in time. It seems to vary from moment to moment. Consciousness apprehends processes of becoming in a manner which implies the past stages of this becoming are present to it as known facts. Yet consciousness itself in man changes. How can our consciousness grow? In short, how can we learn?

We can learn, because there is an eternal consciousness which holds facts in relation. And this eternal consciousness *gradually* realises itself in the animal organism of human being. This process is teleological. Two conceptions explain how factors which have been operative from the beginning of the process enable an eternal consciousness to realise itself through a living organism.

One will be the conception of the end, the particular form of life realised in the body—an end real and present, because operative, throughout the development of the body, but which we cannot identify with any stage of that development. The other will be that of the particular body, or complex of material conditions, organic to this end, as on the one hand dependent on an inexhaustible series of other material conditions, on the other progressively modified by results of the action, the life, to which it is organic.[35]

Both of these aspects must be considered in dealing with consciousness. The end, in the form of a completed knowledge, gradually realises itself in the organic process of human life. On the other hand, the organic process has its own history and conditions. It is these which science can study.

Only by such a theory can it be explained how knowledge is possible. Consider what occurs when a man masters some new item of knowledge. This is composed of some relation of facts through consciousness. Surely it cannot be supposed that the relation itself passes through the process by which the individual learns laboriously. Nor does the relation cease to be as the subject forgets or becomes confused. All such relations must exist as part of an eternal universe—and that a spiritual universe or universe of consciousness—during all the changes of the individual's attitude towards them.

We must hold then that there is a consciousness for which the relations of fact, that form the object of our gradually attained knowledge, already and eternally exist; and that the growing knowledge of the individual is a progress towards this consciousness.[36]

This consciousness, further, is itself operative in the process towards its attainment. That is, from the beginning, consciousness is presupposed in the growing knowledge of the individual. Human knowledge cannot be explained by evolution from some lower form of animal without consciousness. Knowledge cannot be derived from anything not knowledge itself. This argument Green directs against any evolutionary or other naturalistic explanation of how knowledge, and progress in knowledge, is possible.

The most primitive germ from which knowledge can be developed is already a perception of fact, which implies the action upon successive sensations of a consciousness which holds them in relation and which therefore cannot itself be before or after them, or exist as a succession at all.[37]

Green's case is argued as true *a priori*. The condition of human knowledge is an eternal consciousness realising itself gradually in the human organism. Can scientific, historical, or anthropological discoveries affect this conclusion?

It is a conclusion which can in no wise be affected by any discovery, or (legitimately) by any speculation, in regard either to the relation between the human organism and other forms of animal structure, or to the development of human intelligence and the connexion of its lower stages with the higher stages of the intelligence of brutes.[38]

Only on philosophical grounds can this theory be shaken. Green argued that only two lines of argument could touch it: first, by showing that a consciousness of the kind he describes as eternal is not involved in knowledge; second, by the demonstration that such a consciousness can in some intelligible way be developed out of those successions of feeling which can properly be treated as functions of the animal system.

This *a priori* foundation of Green's thought was meant to serve as the secure base on which to build a new structure of belief embodying the essentials of Christianity. Human experience has a demonstrable meaning and direction; its very condition is a spiritual principle manifesting itself in men and their societies. These are conclusions said to be derived from reason, from the most scrupulous examination of scientific or historical discoveries. When Green discussed history, it was almost always to provide illustrations of the *a priori* truths of philosophy. At one point, for example, he seems to go to history for proof that whenever men are to be found in society, they are also found to be seeking a common good. But actually the ground for this assertion is not historical but *a priori*. To have reversed this procedure would have meant that the conclusion might be vitiated by some new evidence offered by historian or anthropologist. And this, of course, was the great weakness of historical Christianity— that it risked too much on evidence which was in principle controvertible. This is not to say that Green set out deliberately to provide an apology which violated experience. As he wrote to Holland, 'these opinions . . . present themselves to me as the inevitable result of thinking-together God, the world, and the history of man'.[39] But the process of thinking these together was an examination of the conditions of experience, not its facts.

Green's philosophical method does not admit of verification in any ordinary sense. Of this he was well aware. In Book III of the *Prolegomena*, he made his own statement. The presupposition of all knowledge is the existence of one connected world of relations. This implies the existence of one self-conditioning and self-determining consciousness. Both human knowledge and moral activity are explicable only on the supposition that this eternal consciousness or mind reproduces itself as the self of man.

> Proof of such a doctrine, in the ordinary sense of the word, from the nature of the case there cannot be. It is not a truth deducible from other established or conceded truths. It is not a statement of an event or matter of fact that can be the object of experiment or observation. It represents a conception to which no perceivable or imaginable object can possibly correspond, but one that affords the only means by which, reflecting on our moral and intellectual experience conjointly, taking the world and ourselves into account, we can put the whole thing together and understand how (not *why*, but *how*) we are and do what we consciously are and do. Given this conception, and not without it, we can at any rate express that which it cannot be denied demands expression, the nature of man's reason and man's will, of human progress and human short-coming, of the effort after good and the failure to gain it, of virtue and vice, in their connection and in their distinction, in their essential opposition and in their no less essential unity.[40]

It must be concluded that there is an eternal consciousness, a spiritual principle which progressively realises itself in man.

But consider what counts as 'experience': morality is experience; citizenship is experience; progress is experience. We must ask what are the presuppositions of their existence, for with experience we must begin. Progress is felt to be true and so it must be. Green's attitude towards his theory of progress is worth noticing as an example of how he met evidence unfavourable to his theories. He did not deny that formidable difficulties confront anyone believing in the development of man in time from a less to a more nearly perfect state. Yet men have continued to cling to the belief in progress because of certain permanent demands of the human spirit. 'These demands, having a common ground with the apprehension of facts, are not to be suppressed by it. They are an expression of the same principle of self-objectification without which . . . there could be no such thing as facts for us, for our consciousness at all.' At least part of this argument is highly suspect. Surely the mere survival of a belief whether in progress or its converse tells us nothing about its validity. Nor is the attempt to link the notion of progress to the basis of epistemology more convincing. Ultimately this is a theological assertion masked as philosophy: It is the consciousness of possibilities in ourselves, unrealised but constantly in process of realisation, that alone enables us to read the idea of development into what we observe of natural life, and to conceive that there must be such a thing as a plan of the world.[41]

3

The modern reader at this point can scarcely resist asking whether Green should not have abandoned his theory of progress, if indeed there were so many obstacles to believing it. Nor will it escape very many that Green's method is highly vulnerable to that criterion of meaning known as the verification principle. Whatever the difficulties of sustaining this doctrine, originated in its full rigour by the Vienna Circle after the first World War and naturalised in England by A. J. Ayer in the late 1930's, it seems to have persuaded many already in reaction against Green's method of proceeding. By the verification principle, metaphysics were said to be literally nonsensical:

> The criterion which we use to test the genuineness of apparent statements of fact is the criterion of verifiability. We say that a sentence is factually significant to any given person if, and only if, he knows how to verify the proposition which it purports to express— that is, if he knows what observations would lead him, under certain conditions, to accept the proposition as being true, or reject it as being false. . . .
>
> If a putative proposition fails to satisfy this principle and is not a tautology, then I hold that it is metaphysical, and that, being metaphysical, it is neither true nor false, but literally senseless. It will be found that much of what ordinarily passes for philosophy is metaphysical, according to this criterion; and, in particular, that it can not be significantly asserted that there is a non-empirical world of values, or that men have immortal souls, or that there is a transcendent God.[42]

Although there can be no question of discussing here the issues involved in this chapter of modern philosophy, it must be said that the verification principle seems most plausible whenever unchecked speculations such as Green's are used to arrive at conclusions dear to the author's heart but otherwise unaccountable. As a philosophical method, Green's basic argument is clearly too loose. He had no procedure by which to counter other conclusions than his own, derived from reflecting on our moral and intellectual experience. He constantly claimed that there was no alternative to his own theory. Actually there were a good many, as the number of disagreements among Idealists had demonstrated. And Green's method itself was open to objection on grounds of which G. E. Moore and Bertrand Russell were to give cogent statement.

The apologetic purpose of Green's metaphysics could not be more evident. His *a priori* argument is used to construct a shelter against the potentially hostile conclusions of science and history. Always beneath the formal point being made, there goes on the vindication of Green's theodicy, the assumption that there must be such a thing as a plan of the world.

> That we can adjust all that we observe to this idea is plainly not the case. . . . This we cannot do; but neither our inability to do it, nor the appearance of positive inconsistency between much that we observe and any scheme of universal development, can weaken the authority of the idea, which does not rest on the evidence of observation but expresses an inward demand for the recognition of a unity in the world answering to the unity of ourselves—a demand involved in that self-consciousness which, as we have seen, alone enables us to observe facts as such.[43]

Here, Green was saying to his contemporaries, is a secure philosophical position justifying belief in something higher and nobler than mere materialism and hedonism. A spiritual principle exists, indeed, is the condition of our knowledge, morality, citizenship. This is what can be reasonably meant by the conception of God. There is no need to believe in revelation or authority.

The spokesmen for religious orthodoxy asked what was left if historical Christianity with its account of miracles were abandoned. Green answered, a humanism at once lofty and reasonable, founded securely on the conditions of human experience and dedicated to the realisation of Christian principles in this world. It rested, he claimed, neither on historical claims easily discredited by science and scholarship nor upon the dogmatic assertions of authority. The foundations of Green's philosophy of life were metaphysical and epistemological. And he thought they could not be shaken. By the use of reason alone, he had justified faith.

But was it reason alone that brought Green to his central conclusions rather than this 'will to believe'? On this point, it is of some interest to turn to W. D. Lamont, among the last of Green's defenders, who, in a volume designed to rephrase and rehabilitate his ideas, wrote:

> Strictly speaking, Green should have regarded his Universal self-consciousness as a principle wholly immanent in reality; but certain habits of thought, deriving from early religious influences, predisposed him to think largely in terms of a transcendent creative mind. The 'theistic' and 'pantheistic' ideas which struggled in his mind never quite fought the battle out to a finish. This is shown by the unexpected turn he sometimes gives to an argument and by expression and conceptions occurring at frequent intervals throughout the *Prolegomena*. Unless we keep this fact in mind, we shall be tempted to seek elaborate explanation for these unexpected turns of thought, when their grounds are quite simple and straightforward.[44]

What is being said here? It is the assertion that on purely

philosophical and Idealist grounds Green's theory of personality was incompatible with his theory of relations. His metaphysics, following his theology, used immanentist conceptions. The spiritual principle is present and complete in a 'self' (which Green calls God), that gradually realises itself in individuals. This notion of 'self', Lamont suggests, actually is a residue from the theology of transcendence which Green attempted to paraphrase into a theology of immanence. Now Green claimed to preserve rather than to destroy the great doctrines of Christianity: that of personal relation between man and God and that of immortality. By this paraphrase of immortality is meant the 'eternity of thought' and thus the destruction of thought is 'a contradiction in terms, for destruction has no meaning except in relation to thought'.[45] But what of the personality of God?

This seemingly theological question is crucial to Green's metaphysics. Yet there was no consensus about what he had actually said. Arnold Toynbee, like Professor Lamont after him, thought that Green believed in the real personality of God which was actually present in all men. Only in this way could Green make every person an end in himself. Green's religious ideas were perfectly consistent with his philosophical position, or so Toynbee contended. The ideal self, the existence of which Green, to his own satisfaction, proved to be the presupposition of human knowledge and experience, this self he identified with 'the God of the Psalms and the Christ of evangelical religion'.[46] Now this God must be a personal and living thing and not an abstraction to satisfy Green. For that reason he rejected Comte's religion of humanity. In Toynbee's view, Green refused to identify the 'higher self' with 'humanity' or any other synonym for the object of unselfish emotions. 'Humanity' is an abstraction, created by the intellect. As such it cannot be the object of religion, which requires for worship nothing less than a living personality. Nor would the abstract devotion to self-sacrifice correspond to Green's belief that every individual is sacred.[47]

Other readers outside Green's own circle were not convinced that his position could be identified with Christian belief in the personality of God, the freedom of men and the immortality of the soul. After his death he was criticised on two grounds: first, that consciously or unconsciously he had obscured his views; second, that he held a clear-cut theory, but that it was one riddled with internal contradictions. A fair example of the first type of attack is that of A. W. Benn: Green so defines the 'Eternal Consciousness' that divine personality is silently eliminated. Green was not a pantheist in the same sense as Hegel who conceived of the universe as a self-subsistent, self-contained structure of thought. Rather, Green seems to have considered nature to be constituted by the activity of a spiritual substance. But did he believe that the 'Eternal Consciousness' has a personal existence? 'Unfortunately for our curiosity, Green never seems to have particularly cared about this question, or to have been brought to book about it by his friends; and the passages most nearly connected with it in his writings are so ambiguous that to tie them down to one interpretation seems to involve a sort of logical brutality.' Insofar as his pronouncements give any indication, Benn thought that they lean towards impersonality. As for the idea of immortality, it is even less clear how, on Green's account, the individual can continue to exist after the death of the animal organism in which the divine consciousness is to some extent embodied. Green's metaphysics, Benn further insists, removes the possibility of his giving any adequate justification of individual freedom. By self-consciousness, we identify ourselves with the 'Eternal Consciousness' as subject. Since it is not determined by anything outside itself, neither are we. But this is to ignore the absence of freedom to will actions contrary to those of the 'Eternal Consciousness'.[48]

Toynbee no doubt was in a better position to say what Green himself believed. Yet it must be said that Benn was justified in his complaint about Green's vagueness. This characteristic which has already been remarked in Green's theology was not remedied in his lectures on the metaphysics of morals. There he spoke of 'the one divine mind' which 'through certain *media*, and under certain consequent limitations, but with the constant characteristic of self-consciousness and self-objectification . . . reproduces itself in the human soul'. In his ethics, he claimed this divine principle to be the ground of human will and reason. But is the divine principle a personality? Does it realise itself in personalities? Green answered equivocally:

> If we mean anything else by it [personality] than the quality in a subject of being consciously an object to itself, we are not justified in saying that it necessarily belongs to God and to any being in whom God in any measure reproduces or realises himself.[49]

In this, perhaps his most explicit statement, Green failed to specify whether he thought the eternal consciousness to have an individual personality apart from the humans in which it realises itself. No doubt, he would have insisted that the distinction was not meaningful in his terms. Yet the question remains whether he was not being disingenuous in suggesting that Idealist concepts had enabled him to retain everything valued by ordinary Christians.

Certainly theism was too important to be disposed of as merely a matter of defining terms.

The second of the recurrent criticisms of Green's metaphysics was that, by proceeding from the epistemology of Kant to the metaphysics of Hegel, he had attempted to reconcile two altogether discrepant bodies of thought. This was powerfully argued by the redoubtable 'Tommy' Case, Waynflete Professor from 1889 to 1910, and one of the few philosophers at Oxford to mount a counter-offensive of his own against Idealism at the height of its dominance. According to him, Green was a Kantian to the extent of agreeing that man may gain a knowledge of the natural world only by using the categories of the mind to order sensations. But what is thus learned, according to Kant, is knowledge of *phenomena* only and never *noumena* or things in themselves. This limitation Green disregarded when he argued that, from what man thus knows of nature, it may be inferred that there is a single spiritual principle which alone can explain how each individual knows and behaves. For this eternal intelligence communicates understanding and the things understood—experience and the experienced world. This Case declared to be the Hegelian view that the world is a system of one absolute reason. For Green to embrace this conception was not only a failure to perceive its incongruency with Kant's epistemology, but also made it impossible for him to allow any individual freedom to choose between good and evil. By reducing everything to infinite mind, man's free but infinite personality was absorbed in that of the spiritual principle; evil, like sin, lost all meaning in this context.[50]

Even within the Idealist camp, it came to be conceded that Green's attribution of real and individual personality (if indeed he did so) was in any case scarcely consistent with the rest of his immanentist theory. Thus Professor Lamont claimed that Green should have regarded his universal self-consciousness as a principle wholly immanent in reality, but because of his religious impulse, he thought in terms of a transcendent creative mind. The same criticism had been made by two other Idealist philosophers, Bernard Bosanquet and F. H. Bradley.[51] Both of them denied personality to God and immortality to man. From the point of view of Idealist metaphysics, they argued, personality has no reality.

Even in religion man's relation to God is never experienced as the relation between one finite person and another. For in religion the worshipper finds himself in God and God in him. But the distinction between God and his worshipper which must remain to the end in religion, cannot be regarded as the last word in metaphysics. The ultimate reality which Bosanquet and Bradley call the Absolute cannot be God, if by God is meant Another than us, towards whom we can stand in a personal relation.

If thought is thoroughly criticised, these later Idealists contended, it turns out that Green's notion of a self-conscious higher self is so full of contradictions as to be useless in metaphysics. This judgment was based on another definition of rationality than Green's and one closer to Hegel than to Kant: namely, that rationality means inner coherence and self-consistency, and these constitute the proper criteria of truth and reality. When judged by these standards, Green's notion fails to meet the test. Personality, whether human or divine, lacks ultimate reality. This issue, raised by F. H. Bradley, was treated by him in such a way as to produce the conclusion that:

> The completeness and self-consistency which our ideal requires can be realised only in a form of being in which subject and object, will and desire, no longer stand as exclusive opposites, from which it seemed at once to follow that the finite self could not be a reality or the infinite reality a self.[52]

In short, Bosanquet and Bradley, when forced to choose between the principles of relationship and personality as the ultimate reality, chose relationship. Thus personality was denied to God and rejected as a description of what is most unique and valuable in man.

Even Idealists found Green's metaphysics to have been adversely affected by theological considerations. These were no less evident in his theory of moral and political obligation. For when he maintains that 'there is no such thing really as a conflict of duties', or that 'there is no real reason to doubt that the good or evil in the motive of an action is exactly measured by the good or evil in its consequences', he is asserting a theodicy.[53] And this is extended in both the *Prolegomena* and *Political Obligation* to the assertion that even in politics, 'the good in the effect of the movement will really correspond to the degree of good will which has been exerted in bringing it about; and the effects of any selfishness in its promoters will appear in some limitation to the good which it brings to society'.[54] On this line of reasoning, Professor C. C. J. Webb has remarked,

> That old 'mystical' faith of Green's, that there is a failure or defect in every result of human action corresponding to a moral defect in the agent's motives has always seemed to me to be a pure deduction from general belief in the moral government of the world.[55]

4

When Benn and Case criticised Green for the vagueness or inconsistency of his argument, they did not do so on the ground that all metaphysical speculation is worthless. Although their comments, if conceded to be a fair account of Green's position, were extremely damaging, nothing in the nature of the case barred his followers from attempting a more satisfactory performance of the same tasks Green had set himself. A certain amount of disapproving comment was occasioned by the fact that Bosanquet and F. H. Bradley, although operating in the same tradition of metaphysical Idealism, came to conclusions that were very far from the sort of vindication of God, freedom and immortality which could be inferred from Green. Since such discrepant conclusions could be drawn from the same premises, there seemed to be something arbitrary and uncontrolled about Idealism as a mode of thought. Yet it was not until Russell and Moore had formulated their respective critiques of Idealism at the turn of the century that the school began to lose its impetus. An altogether new wind had begun to blow in philosophy. In part it reflected new technical discoveries in logic and the understanding of language; in part, a new generation in reaction against the type of sensibility voiced by Green.

Russell attacked head on one of the central positions of Idealism, its theory of relationship, certainly a notion of the first importance for Green and no less crucial to Bosanquet and Bradley. At issue was the Idealist theory that everything, whether natural or intellectual, forms part of a system, apart from which it cannot be understood. As Russell understood the Idealists, they were saying that: 'Every apparently separate piece of reality has, as it were, hooks which grapple it to the next piece; the next piece, in turn, has fresh hooks, and so on until the whole universe is reconstructed'. This incompleteness is said to characterise both the world of thought and the world of things. If, in the world of thought, we forget that an idea is incomplete, we become involved in contradictions which may be avoided only by adopting the standpoint of the system as a whole. This, when viewed from the vantage point of the Absolute, turns out to form 'one single harmonious system, not in space or time, not in any degree evil, wholly rational, and wholly spiritual'.[56]

Of this concept, Russell remarked that it is founded on a good many unwarrantable assumptions. Its fundamental tenet is that whatever exists and is incomplete, presupposes by its very nature the existence of other things. But the validity of this procedure depends upon defining the 'nature' of a thing as 'all the truths about that thing'. However, a truth about a thing is not part of the thing itself. Indeed a thing may be known when its 'nature' is not known, or not known completely. Things may be known by acquaintance without any knowledge of their relations. A man may be acquainted with his toothache without knowing what his dentist (who is not acquainted with it) can tell him about its causes or 'nature'. The fact that a thing has relations does not prove that its relations are logically part of its 'nature'. From the fact that it is the thing it is, nothing can be deduced about the relations it actually has.

If this criticism is valid, then it follows that the Idealists cannot prove that the universe constitutes a single harmonious system, free from evil and perfectly just. In short, what this implies, Russell tells us, is that 'we are left to the piecemeal investigation of the world'. Almost nothing can be proved *a priori* from the consideration of what must be. Russell, close to the triumph of *Principia Mathematica*, could announce that the most modern discoveries of mathematics had quite discredited Idealist assertions that the world may be delimited by *a priori* principles:

> The attempt to prescribe to the universe by means of *a priori* principles has broken down; logic, instead of being, as formerly, the bar to possibilities, has become the great liberator of the imagination, presenting innummerable alternatives which are closed to un-reflective common sense, and leaving to experience the task of deciding, where decision is possible, between the many worlds which logic offers our choice.[57]

Thus there is no source of knowledge which is open to philosophy and not to science. 'Philosophy is to be studied, not for the sake of any definite answers to its questions, since no definite answers can, as a rule, be known to be true, but rather for the sake of the questions themselves. . . .'[58]

G. E. Moore, another leader in the movement against Idealism, did so by attacking both the metaphysical and the moral theory in Green's 'metaphysic of morals'. Indeed he denied that the attempt to establish 'foundations' for ethics is legitimate. In his 1903 article called 'The Refutation of Idealism', Moore argued that what really needed doing in philosophy was analysis and distinction. Idealism, for example, asserts that the universe is spiritual. Thus the universe is different from what it seems and possesses many properties it does not seem to have. When the universe is called 'spiritual', by this is meant, Moore reminds us, at the very least, 'that it is intelligent; that it is purposeful; that it is not mechanical'.[59] But the Idealist passes too quickly over the question of what is proper philosophical procedure. He forgets the number of different propositions he must establish before his case may be regarded as proven. And on both sides of the argument, it has been assumed that if one or two points are made the whole case has been won.

THE POLITICS OF CONSCIENCE

His own recommended procedure, as one commentator has summed it up, was: 'to discriminate within the one deceptively simple formula a number of distinct, separate questions. The next is to select one key question on which to begin the intensive examination.'[60] Moore, then, regarded Green's philosophical method as altogether hasty and premature. What was even more damning in Moore's critique of Idealism, was his claim that the ultimate nature of reality can never provide any warrant for ethical rules. The attempt to do so by Green and his followers, he called the 'naturalistic fallacy', by which he meant any effort to derive ethics from the non-ethical, something the Idealists themselves condemned in others.[61]

The criticisms of Russell and Moore are alluded to here, not on the assumption that they are incontrovertible, but rather to indicate what were the principal philosophical arguments used against the Idealist 'metaphysic of morals'. Whether it was the force of logic alone which led to the eventual rejection of Idealism is beyond the scope of what is being attempted here. But the historical record suggests that at some point the tastes of philosophers underwent a striking change. The sort of pleasure derived from philosophy can vary a good deal from period to period, and certainly, as Professor Lovejoy has demonstrated, every mode of philosophising has its own distinctive pathos. Idealists delighted in perceiving the interrelations of things, in deducing every moral duty from some higher good inherent in the nature of reality, of man and of political society. As Mrs Warnock has remarked discerningly of Moore, he did not understand, with his own extraordinary literalness, just what Idealist philosophers were attempting to do by their use of a metaphysical ground for ethics:

> 'The metaphysical pleasure precisely consists in *not* being the centre of the universe, but in seeing familiar problems, such as the problem of how it is right to behave, somehow reduced, and also answered, by being shown to be part of a total scheme of things. This kind of pleasure may be partially aesthetic; it certainly has very little to do with how many of the propositions contained in the system are actually true statements.'[62]

It is not unlikely that the joys of Idealist philosophy were more evident to those searching for a whole view of the world adequate to its complexity. Integration of ideas into a unitary system was an intellectual pleasure; it combined easily in some cases with an equal delight in being taught the reality of human solidarity and the obligations this entailed. It is for this reason that Green's *Prolegomena to Ethics* must be read together with his lay sermons on the one side and with his lectures on *Political Obligation* on the other.

CHAPTER SEVEN

ETHICS

I

IN HIS RECENT AND highly useful anthology of the *Idealist Tradition*, Mr A. C. Ewing expressed the opinion that the school never developed a distinctive ethical theory. While individual Idealists had written on the subject, there was no necessary connection between their views on morals and their epistemology and metaphysics. This judgment, which applies particularly well to F. H. Bradley, would not have been accepted by Green as an accurate description of the place held by ethics in his own thought. For he conceived of this subject as based explicitly upon metaphysics. Since he thought that philosophy ought to supply a comprehensive view of life, he never tired of pointing out what in his view were the continuities between the foundation of ethics on the one side, and its concrete application to the problems of politics and society on the other. In short, his definition of morality was of a kind which would enable him to demonstrate how from the arguments he had developed in his version of Idealist metaphysics there followed a significant set of consequences for individual behaviour and political action. Bradley was much less concerned with political philosophy than was Green who thought that the subject would profit immeasurably from having its problems and concepts recast into the language of Idealism.

Sir Ernest Barker was surely right when he described Green's view of political philosophy as being 'essentially an ethical study which regards the State as a moral society . . . and seeks to determine its relation to the moral constitution and development of man'.[1] Yet it must be emphasised that, to define political philosophy as ethical, Green had to adopt an extremely broad conception of what is involved in the study of morality. Many of the topics treated in the *Prolegomena to Ethics* would not be included in a work bearing the same title written in our own day. To demonstrate that all human societies presuppose an idea, shared by their members, of a good common to them all, to discuss the

191

lessons taught by the philosophy of history—these are not now defined as parts of ethics. Since Green's time, speculation about the ends of politics has ceased to be a concern of philosophers, who now display as great an interest in restricting the scope of their inquiry as he had in enlarging it.

At this date there is little point in a detailed exposition of Green's ethics for its own sake, or even in an assessment of his contribution to that subject. But it is necessary to indicate the place of his moral theory within the economy of his thought taken as a whole, as well as to demonstrate how it may be regarded as a set of responses to Green's Evangelical upbringing, his position within Oxford and his ambitions for English liberalism.

By an accident of publication, what Green had to say about politics became separated from its context in that series of professorial lectures which was for the most part printed in the *Prolegomena to Ethics*. Of his major works, Green saw only his introduction to Hume through the press. All the rest of his work was edited, and very well edited, after his death by Nettleship and A. C. Bradley. But as the study of political theory became increasingly cut off from that of philosophy, most readers of Green have used that edition which reprinted the *Lectures on the Principles of Political Obligation* along with one essay on the meaning of freedom. Yet if his professorial lectures are considered in the order of their delivery, it becomes clear why Nettleship considered Green's lectures on politics to be 'an illustrative comment on the *Prolegomena to Ethics*'.* The failure of most later critics to include the *Prolegomena* in their consideration of Green as a political philosopher has produced a double distortion: first by omitting so much of the material argument, for example, the highly articulated philosophy of history contained there, many of the points made in the *Principles of Political Obligation* have become obscured; second, the philosophical intent and polemical thrust of that work are not altogether intelligible. Often Green's technical terms are not understood at all, or else they are mistaken for what is meant by them in ordinary language. Thus his lectures on politics are

---

* 'The subjects on which he lectured during the four years of his professorship were as follows; *Moral philosophy*, in the summer term of 1878, *The theory of duty* in the three following terms, *The principles of political obligation and the social virtues* in the October term of 1879 and the Hilary term of 1880, *Some metaphysical and psychological questions preliminary to moral philosophy* in the October term of 1880, *Desire, reason and will in their relations to morality, Duty and conscience, The ideal of virtue in Plato and Aristotle compared with that by which we are now influenced*, in the three terms of 1881, *The application of moral philosophy to the guidance of conduct* in the Hilary term of 1882.' (Green, *Works*, III, cxxv.)

not self-contained. At critical points he assumed familiarity with proofs he claimed to have already established in his metaphysics and ethics. This repetition of arguments was deliberate: by it he hoped to demonstrate the comprehensive quality of his thought, its applicability to every aspect of human activity, the most practical as well as the most abstract.

Involved in this method were two ideas, the first of which might be accepted by philosophers of any school, while the second was specifically Idealist. When Green insisted upon the necessity of reconsidering the concepts used in ethical and political discourse, he was on relatively undisputed ground. That such notions should be understood and criticised by their adherents in the light of objections to them, that men's beliefs ought to be internally consistent and follow from their initial premisses—these are assumptions made by anyone who engages in the philosophical discussion of ethics and politics. But Green went on to claim that Idealist language and ways of putting problems are uniquely valuable: they enable men with full critical consciousness to hold substantially the same beliefs as before they were subjected to analysis. What men gain is a new and completely coherent system freeing them from their previous intellectual frustration which they now see to have been due to outmoded philosophical assumptions and scientific evidence irrelevant to their fundamental concerns. And, he further claimed, Idealism aids men to know what they truly value by a consideration of what was involved in their personal behaviour as well as in their relations to the social and political groups of which they are members. Moral and political values cannot be separated from their actual operation; values emerge only upon analysis of the meaningful part of the historical record. Such analysis reveals a law of progress. On the basis of it we can come to perceive the *telos* that underlies our operative beliefs. Once in possession of the proper end of action, we can use it as a guide to behaviour in the present and the future. Just because the method takes men, not abstractly in isolation from their actual membership in groups, but concretely in the full complexity of social and political systems, it enables Idealists to avoid the errors of individualism, whether religious or secular.

Green's application of these principles in the *Prolegomena* cannot but provoke the same objections already raised in connection with his theology and metaphysics: is it the case that ideas, once translated into Idealist language, still mean what they did before? Is it the case that the Idealist method, with its law of progress and teleology, offers an adequate objective means of determining value rather than a mere indication of the analyst's

193

subjective preferences? We may assume Green's good faith in asserting the truth of both propositions; it is considerably more difficult to agree with him after we have examined the results of his method as applied in his ethical work. The actual analysis is anything but objective and inevitable. G. E. Moore's criticisms become increasingly convincing in the light of Green's startling leaps to unproved conclusions. Everywhere there can be seen signs of the pressure exerted by Green's determination to provide a philosophy of life. This is no less evident in his effort to rephrase and defend what he considered worth preserving in Evangelicalism than in his preparation in the *Prolegomena* for a similar reconstruction of Manchester Liberalism in his political philosophy. Both purposes were evident in the Broad Church mentality which characterised Green's Idealism (and was conspicuously lacking from F. H. Bradley's). Green carried over into his philosophical work a Broad Church disregard for clarity when it divided men; thus he preferred ambiguity and vagueness which made easier compromise among men of good will whom he sought to convince that they were separated by imaginary difficulties rather than by stark existential choices. Finding the tendencies of secular society to be benevolent, Green thought it possible to construct a least common denominator of belief applicable to both private and political behaviour. This determination to blur differences and to reconcile opponents was to lead him to attempt the adaptation to liberal purposes of concepts originally developed by conservatives: the emphasis upon history and tradition, upon a good common to all the members of a political community, upon the 'positive theory of freedom'. Like conservative theorists, Green rejected violent revolution and class warfare. All these ideas, he insisted, could be reconciled with liberalism without any danger to its essential beliefs. The supreme value of the individual and his freedom, the obligation to remove all obstacles to merit and fair competition such as class privilege or religious discrimination, the necessity to make moral principle the criterion of political decision—these were articles of the liberal creed which he claimed to have preserved and placed upon an unshakeable foundation. The preparation for this synthesis was undertaken in the *Prolegomena* and given a form congenial to the religious as well as the political needs of his audience.

2

In his ethics Green used two quite different criteria of morality. The first of these reflected his Evangelical origins in its inclusion of ascetic and activist qualities in the definition of any genuinely good moral agent. Self-indulgence is the greatest of sins; the highest virtue involves the subordination of fleshly impulse and worldly interest to a good transcending the individual but also present in him. By sin, Green sometimes meant the refusal to meet the obligations imposed by membership in social and political groups; sometimes, he applied that term to complacency, the confusion of any condition actually attained by a man with those ideal potentialities still remaining to be realised. For virtue, as he defined it, is always characterised by 'moral initiative', the sense of personal responsibility for a further approximation to the good. This attitude is not to be confused with the 'tendency "to be always fingering one's motives" which is "a sign rather of an unwholesome preoccupation with self than of the eagerness in disinterested service which helps forward mankind" '.[2] The mark of the good man is that he constantly acts upon the idea of a perfect life with which his own is contrasted. And such an idea has real effects. It makes a different man of him who has it. Here the Protestant doctrines of justification by faith and the responsibility of the individual believer are translated into the duties of morality.

To translate these attitudes into philosophical terms, Green made much of the notion of the self. Already in his epistemology, he had tried to prove that because of its sensuous conditions knowledge is possible only through categories which sense itself does not supply. Human knowledge can be explained only on the assumption of an eternal spiritual principle which gradually realises itself in man's animal organism. Green builds up his ethics on much the same plan using the same dialectical motifs of self-consciousness, teleology and internal relationship in a system. To begin with self-consciousness: Man's animal organism has not only sensuous perceptions, but certain wants. These wants play the same part in man's willing and desiring that sensations play in knowledge. And there is a distinction between want and a wanted object. To pass from feeling a want to conceiving a wanted object implies the presence of a conscious subject which distinguishes itself from the want. The subject persists through successive stages of the want (just as consciousness persists through a series of events). Hence there arises the possibility of conceiving of a whole system of satisfactions which may be called the self.

Self-consciousness, or reason, is practical or moral to the extent that it seeks satisfaction in giving existence to an object adequate to itself. Just as man is capable of knowledge because he is a being with consciousness of facts, so he is capable of conduct or morality, because he is a being with consciousness of objects. As the primary question in a theory of knowledge must be 'what makes a fact?', so the primary question in a theory of morality must be, 'What makes an object?' Analysis of knowledge leads to the conclusion that all fact is relationship in a system. Within the system there is mutual qualification of facts. This implies a single conscious subject present in, but distinct from, its feelings.

The analysis of practical or moral action leads to analogous results. An object of desire is ultimately an idea of oneself which one seeks to realise. Human desires, in contrast to those of an animal, are not satisfied directly. They are mediated by the human self which is conscious and forms the centre of an integrated system of desires. Even appetites such as hunger are not satisfied instinctively. Contrary to what Hobbes would have us believe, there is a fundamental distinction between men and animals. Animals seek to satisfy an immediate appetite. Men, on the contrary, seek to satisfy a conception of themselves. Hobbes bases morality on appetite. But even appetite, Green now insists, is mediated by reason. Human beings distinguish themselves from their wants. Thus these become more than wants, they are wants of something, acts of a desiring subject. The most objectless human life forms a system in which particular desires meet and are mutually qualified in the conception, however vague and inconstant, of something desirable on the whole. To the extent that even such a relatively purposeless life displays purpose and system, it is an example of moral action.

Moral judgments can be properly applied only to actions of a freely-willing, self-conscious subject. Moral action takes place when the self identifies itself with some object of desire, when in seeking a purpose it makes real the idea of some better state of being and, in satisfying that want, satisfies itself. Taken thus far Green's theory describes all moral action as having the same form: man seeks to realise a conception of himself. This is true of both good acts and bad.

What, then, on this ground, is a good act and how is it to be distinguished from a bad one? What is the distinction between a good will and a bad will? To will means to adopt a certain motive, to originate within oneself the objects which one pursues in action. A motive, therefore, is a desired object, and a desired object is an idea of self-satisfaction. It cannot be said, then, that a motive is something independent of a man which acts upon him from outside. Rather it derives from the conception man holds of himself and his capabilities. Man is a free agent in the sense of originating his own motives. To will is to adopt a certain motive, that is to say, to become something he has willed to be.

Now how can it be decided whether that will is good? Green offers two criteria, the first, formal and psychological; the second substantive and teleological. The first has to do with the agent's sense of the discrepancy between the ideal he wills and the actual state he attains. The second has to do with the substance of what the agent wills and whether this helps realise his essential capabilities which ought to be realised. From the formal point of view, the most that a man can attain is the simultaneous consciousness of possible perfection and of actual imperfection. To the extent that he lives in this double consciousness he lives well. An act is good in proportion as the agent in doing it is conscious that he is doing his best but that there still remains something better to be done. An act is bad in proportion as the agent regards the particular object attained in it as complete, that is, to the extent that he identifies his actual with his possible self and identifies the one with the absoluteness which properly belongs only to the other.

This doctrine is clearly the secularised form of an Evangelical tenet. To reject selfish pleasures, to overcome indolence and complacency, and to methodise one's life in the pursuit of the good—these are the qualities of the good man, the dedicated man. And the struggle to maintain this internal tension, or moral initiative, as Green calls it, is at the root of this part of his ethics. 'The very nature of morality . . . [is] an effort, not an attainment, a progressive construction of what should be, not an enjoyment of what is . . .'[3] The emphasis is on activism. Insofar as man is moral, he pushes on to realise his ideals. An object to himself, because of his capacity to originate motives, he is no passive receptor of sense and pleasure. Quite to the contrary, just the distinguishing characteristic of moral action is this push onward, this permanent drive forward. Yet even a person who is so motivated does not necessarily meet Green's criteria of the good. Whether a will is good must be determined by the nature of the objects in which an agent mainly tends to seek satisfaction. To the extent that these objects conform to the true end of man and society, he may be said to will the good. Thus the second criterion used by Green is teleological, insisting that man has potentialities which ought to be realised in society.

By moral obligation is meant the conviction on the part of men that they are morally bound to do certain actions and not to do certain others. But what is the ground of such obligation? In the form that Green put this question, it might be asked, 'What is the character which an act must possess for it to be one which a man if morally bound to do?' or 'What is the criterion of duty?' Such questions imply the idea that 'we can only be morally bound to do the various acts, which from time to time we are morally bound to do, in virtue of some common character, their possession of this character being what makes us bound to do them: this being what we call the *basis* of our obligation to do them'.[4] This is to say that all obligations share an essential character. A teleological theory of obligation holds that character to be one of purpose. In morally obliged acts we always have a purpose and that purpose is always the same. Therefore the task of discovering what it is that we ought to do consists of two steps. First, it must be ascertained what that purpose or end is; and secondly, which acts would do most to bring about the realisation of that purpose.

What is that purpose or end? Green states that 'The perfection of human character—a perfection of individuals which is also that of society, and of society which is also that of individuals—is for man the only object of absolute or intrinsic value . . .'.[5] Morality is 'in so living that the objects in which self-satisfaction is habitually sought contributes to the realisation of a true idea of what is best for man—such an idea as our reason would have when it had come to all which it has the possibility of becoming, and which, as in God, it is'.[6]

To review the argument thus far: to the question 'Why am I obliged to do this or that?', Green answers first by giving a teleological definition of moral obligation in general, and then deducing the obligation to do a particular act from the general obligation to realise one's moral potentialities. But whence does he derive this general obligation? To this, he responds:

> The question, What is our moral nature or capability? In other words, What do we mean by calling ourselves moral agents? Is one to which a final answer cannot be given without an answer to the question, What is moral good? For the moral good is the realisation of the moral capability, and we cannot fully know what any capability is till we know its ultimate realisation.[7]

'We cannot fully know what any capability is till we know its ultimate realisation;' here is the clue to the line Green's argument will take. The 'witness' or experience from which man's moral capabilities may be deduced is nothing else than the history of human progress. The question is 'What is man's moral capability?' Green answers that if this moral capability had not realised itself at all, nothing could be inferred about it. But man's moral potentiality is not in this wholly undeveloped state. By its actual achievements it had shown what it has in it to become. The philosopher by analysing progress may form some conclusion about its operative principle which he then can make explicit.

In the broad result it is not hard to understand how man has bettered himself through institutions and habits which tend to make the welfare of all the welfare of each, and through the arts which make nature, both as used and as contemplated, the friend of man.[8]

And just so far as this progress is plain, we know enough of ultimate moral good to guide our conduct, enough to judge whether the prevailing interests which make our character are or are not in the direction which tends further to realise the capabilities of the human spirit. Some imperfectly realised, but still operative, idea of there being such a best state of man has been the essential influence in the process by which man has thus far bettered himself. The conviction that there must be such a state, 'may have supreme influence over conduct, in moving us to that effort after the Better which, at least as a conscious effort, implies the conviction of there being a Best'.[9] To the extent that man has bettered himself, it is due to the idea of there being such a higher state to attain. The condition of character and conduct being good in the present and future is that this same idea should continue to operate within us. It will become more definite as it progressively realises itself in man and society and as we reflect upon what is implied by this progress.

What justification does Green offer for such assertions? Essentially the same argument as in his metaphysics—that we cannot explain our experience without bringing in the hypothesis of a self-conditioning, self-determining mind or spiritual principle which realises itself in man and his institutions. As is our knowledge so is our moral activity explicable only on the supposition of this divine mind. Proof of such a proposition there cannot be, if by proof is meant some statement of fact which can be verified by experiment or observation. Once again Green was resting his case on an informative *a priori* proposition. His reliance on metaphysics was complete. For instead of choosing a teleological conception of ethics, which justified duty in terms of purpose, he had the alternative of a deontological theory such as Kant's which taught the obligation of doing one's duty for duty's sake. And Kant also was committed to proving that the basic principles of morality do not rest on self-interest. Green, however, was convinced by Hegel that Kant had been too subjective and 'abstract'. A morality founded on individual duty could not assign intrinsic value to institutions as embodying objective reason.

Morality is possible, Green maintained, only because of the consciousness that there remains a perfection to be attained, a vocation which must be fulfilled, something which is absolutely desirable, no matter what the individual may for the time desire.

It is in ministering to such an end that the agent seeks to satisfy himself. However meagrely the perfection, the vocation, the law may be conceived, the consciousness that there is such a thing, must 'at least keep the man to the path in which human progress has been made. It must keep him loyal in spirit to some established morality, industrious in some work of recognised utility.'

When Green sought 'witness' in progress for man's moral capability, he looked not only to individual experience but to the history of human institutions which tend to make the welfare of all the welfare of each. Just as the divine mind has been described as the pre-condition of individual morality, so the pre-condition of any social grouping, including society, is the manifestation of the same spiritual principle as the idea of the common good of the whole group. Without such a conception, man's social life defies explanation. The idea of a common good must be present in potency and promise for even the most primitive social units to function.

Here is the general outline of a teleological theory of obligation. Obviously, such a theory transforms the ordinary meaning of ethical terms. Freedom and goodness must have very different meanings within such a context from what would ordinarily be understood by them. Simply because a person is free from constraint, or wills what he takes to be the good, it does not follow that he is free or good according to the true end which determines freedom and goodness. In other words, Green held that the only true freedom and the only good will are those which coincide with the fulfilment of man's capabilities according to the divine idea or plan.

The intellectual style used by Green in his ethics was in part a repudiation of the mode of thought he had first learned as an undergraduate and then had to teach as a Balliol tutor. The Idealist metaphysics and epistemology which so offended Jowett and examiners of the older school were prominent in these lectures which were further criticised for their appeal to the audience to act upon their moral principles by taking up the life of philanthropy and citizenship. Yet Green's teaching, in its teleological emphasis, no less than its definition of political philosophy as a branch of ethics, was a reaffirmation of Aristotle, who for so long had dominated the Oxford course of study. That Green retained so much of Aristotle cannot be easily explained. No aspect of Oxford life annoyed him more than its concentration of philosophical instruction upon the Greeks to the exclusion of modern thought. He felt that modern problems could not be met by continuing to repeat that in Aristotle is to be found everything worth saying about ethics and politics. Nor did his own values receive much support from Plato and Aristotle as studied in the Greats School. Their effect was to produce an aristocratic detachment and self-sufficiency which deterred undergraduates from the type of personal commitment to active reform which Green identified with the highest virtue.

Nevertheless he continued to stress teleological arguments in his ethics and politics. Perhaps this may be ascribed to the influence of German Idealists who claimed to complete the work of Plato and Aristotle. It is rather more likely that sustained exposure to Aristotle had set sharp limits upon the intellectual innovations Green could make. Although in conscious revolt against the tradition of Oxford, he could not emancipate himself from its influence. If his religious dynamic and social perspective derived from classes long excluded from the older universities, he for his part learned to view politics from the angle of Oxford's upper-class tradition of public service and to adopt the Aristotelian assumption that there exists a common good which ought to be the object of public policy. Had Green not been at Balliol, everything in his outlook and sympathies would have disposed him to adopt the negative individualism of Nonconformity, its distrust of the state that went along with an insistence upon the voluntary principle even in education. This tension between two perspectives, which had not previously been reconciled or even confronted, was to appear in Green's massive effort to prove that Idealist metaphysics when applied to the sphere of politics did not subordinate the individual to the state. Throughout his ethics there are signs of the strain produced by his merger of conservative concepts with liberal and even radical values. Nowhere was this more evident than in Green's substitution of a 'positive' conception of freedom for that essentially negative statement which had hitherto characterised English liberalism from Locke to John Stuart Mill.

3

Central to the innovation Green introduced was the metaphor of self-mastery or self-government. It was the extension of this notion which is at the bottom of his statement that 'When we speak of freedom as something to be so highly prized, we mean a positive power or capacity of doing or enjoying something worth doing or enjoying'.[10] To will is to seek self-satisfaction in an object.

Freedom depends upon the nature of the object with which the agent identifies himself. One type of object makes true self-satisfaction impossible because interfering with the realisation of the seeker's possibilities, while another type does in fact contribute to self-satisfaction. In the first of these cases, a man might be considered a free agent in identifying himself with a certain desired object simply because he has not been subjected to external coercion. But, in another sense, he is not free, because the objects with which he identifies himself are not those in which he can ever find satisfaction. His will to arrive at self-satisfaction is not adjusted to the law which determines where this self-satisfaction is to be found. Occasionally we speak of a man being a slave to passion or appetite. No instance of such a usage is better known than Rousseau's remark that moral liberty is that which makes man master of himself, 'for the mere impulse of appetite is slavery, while obedience to a law which we prescribe to ourselves is liberty'.[11]

Green admitted that to use 'freedom' in this sense is a metaphor. Indeed he conceded that the term means nothing more than the social relation of one man to another in which he is secured from compulsion. This admission was curious, for it put an obstacle in the way of his positive theory of freedom, which now he had to acknowledge to be based on a 'community of meaning', that is, the analogy between the condition of a citizen in a civilised state and the condition of a man who is inwardly master of himself. This concept of self-government, of being free whenever one's higher self is being asserted, even by compulsion, was to be exploited by Bosanquet and made the central argument of his *Philosophical Theory of the State*. Green, who had a greater sense of political realities, perceptibly hesitated before pushing on to make the deduction from his ethical theory that freedom is more than a man's ability to do as he prefers to do in a given instance. But, finally, he adopted the broader meaning: a man chooses the sort of object which satisfies him because it is in harmony with the law of his being. In a rather academic show of precedents, Green argued that freedom is to be determined by the objects willed:

> It means a particular kind of self-determination; the state of the man who lives indeed for himself, but for the fulfilment of himself as a 'giver of law universal' (Kant); who lives for himself, but only according to the true idea of himself, according to the law of his being, 'according to nature' (the Stoics); who is so taken up into God, to whom God so gives the spirit, that there is no constraint in his obedience to the divine will (St Paul); whose interests, as a loyal citizen, are those of a well-ordered state in which practical reason expresses itself (Hegel).[12]

Readers of Sir Isaiah Berlin's inaugural lecture will perceive clearly enough the grave implications of this deliberate shift from one to another of these two concepts of liberty. In abandoning the older view so long held by liberals, Green gave up a concept which, whatever its other difficulties, was still an effective weapon against dictators and all others who would destroy liberty in the name of some allegedly higher principle called 'positive freedom', or 'self-realisation'. That juggling with such terms comes easily to the enemies of political freedom Green well knew, as can be seen from his caustic remarks about the sophistry of Hegel in theory and Napoleon III in practice. Why, then, did he lend his support to a doctrine which, as he admitted, was previously unknown in English thought?

The answer must be complex and not exclusively philosophical. Certainly Green was more troubled by this theory than by almost anything else in his ethics and politics. Like Kant, he was a Protestant individualist, and although prepared to go some way in Hegel's direction of taking into account man's social and political relationships, Green resisted Hegel's conclusion that the whole is superior to the part, the state to the individual. Indeed Green's vehemence on this point was meant to compensate for the concession made to Hegelianism in his own positive theory of freedom. The fact is that he adopted it for reasons which cannot be divorced from his political outlook and religious origin.

Whenever Green discussed freedom he slipped from the purely philosophical issue to a consideration of the practical effects of holding one or another view, and always in relation to what was then known as the problems of state interference. In short, it was his judgment that individual liberties were in no danger and that the decisive issue of English politics would be the rôle of the state in social and economic life. It may have been his optimistic philosophy of history which persuaded him that civilised states (as he thought of western Europe) could never regress and violate the rights of their citizens. On this supposition, it was safe to concentrate on principles regulating the effects upon personal character of state action. Whether his treatment of this theme was technical, as in a professorial lecture, or popular, as in an address to a Liberal Association, ethical and political issues were treated together. As a philosopher, he took it as self-evident that the natural right argument for personal freedom was intellectually untenable; as a member of the Liberal Party, he thought it impossible for his party to confront the problems of modern legislation while still holding to a doctrine stating that individuals have rights but no duties, and should be left a clear field for competition. Nor did the Utilitarianism of J. S. Mill meet Green's standards. Although, by the end of his life, Mill's practical position differed little from Green's, the younger man thought that if Idealist arguments such as Von Humboldt's were good enough for Mill to incorporate into his revised Utilitarianism, they ought to be used as the basis for a new and coherent structure, rather than as supports temporarily delaying the collapse of the assumptions Mill inherited from his father and Bentham.

The concept of freedom would have to be rethought in Idealist terms, replacing the old formula that a man has the right to do what he wishes so long as his actions do not interfere with the like liberty of others. For quite apart from its philosophical difficulties, this theory could not account for legislation already in the statute book and unchallenged by either party: the use of compulsion by the state to ensure compliance with factory, public health and educational acts. From these actual reconciliations of state action with personal freedom, Green thought he could extricate certain operative principles. What such enactments presupposed, he thought, was the real existence of a good common to all the members of the community, a good definable only in the terms of self-realisation. Thus he told a Leicester audience:

> We shall probably all agree that freedom, rightly understood, is the greatest of blessings; that its attainment is the true end of all our effort as citizens. But when we thus speak of freedom, we should consider carefully what we mean by it. We do not mean merely freedom from restraint or compulsion. We do not mean merely freedom to do as we like irrespective of what it is that we like. We mean the greater power on the part of the citizens as a body to make the most and best of themselves.[13]

Green's use of the term freedom in this way has come under quite justifiable criticism. Sir Isaiah Berlin has denounced its central idea in stinging words: 'This monstrous impersonation, which consists in equating what X would choose if he were something he is not, or at least not yet, with what X actually seeks and chooses, is at the heart of all political theories of self-realisation'.[14] Certainly Green's formulation of 'positive freedom' used just such a distinction between the higher and lower selves, and insisted that only the good will is free. It is difficult to understand why Green thought that the term should be confined to the power of doing what we are obliged to do. For both morally indifferent and criminal acts, if prevented, constitute an interference with the liberty of their would-be agents. A man could not be called free if prevented by the police from smoking, or even oversmoking, even though he has no obligation to do either.[15] It would seem that Green attempted to use the name of freedom for all goods.

Nothing is gained and much is lost by such an extension of a word already too vague. Were the narrow meaning retained, it would be possible to say that some exercises of freedom are undesirable and even ought to be punished; to concede that the exercise of one kind of freedom may entail the deprivation of another; and even that in some circumstances, some social or political purpose may necessitate coercion. But we should not be obliged to call those persons coerced free. Nor should we have to assume, as Green did, that men have but one purpose, that of rational self-direction.

Despite all the explanations thus far offered here, there remains something of a mystery about Green's adoption of the theory of positive freedom. It is true that he shared two vices of Idealist philosophers: their deceptive and self-deceiving way with words, and their passion for system-building. Yet, in matters of politics, he usually remedied these deficiencies by his practical good sense. It may be that his attraction to the metaphor of self-mastery derived from the least understood of all his activities as a re-former: that as temperance worker. Green's pre-occupation with this subject now seems eccentric and even obsessional. Nor will this impression be diminished by the suggestion that he used the problem of drunkenness as a paradigm for his treatment of free-dom.* In his day matters appeared otherwise, and it seemed reasonable for those who had to cope with alcoholism on a large scale to discuss it in terms of autonomy and heteronomy. Mr G. Kitson Clark has recently reminded us of how pervasive a social evil drunkenness was in the middle of the last century. To remedy it much money and energy were devoted to a movement which came to have considerable political significance. It cannot be questioned that Green was struck when working in temperance organisations by the fact that, when popular audiences could be touched at all, it was through their willingness to accept the distinction between a higher and lower self which had to be mastered. This may have been due to the effects of Evangelicalism, but whatever the reason, Green was sufficiently impressed to use the following illustration in the midst of a difficult professorial lecture:

> To any popular audience interested in any work of self-improvement (e.g. to a temperance-meeting seeking to break the bondage to liquor), it is as an effort to attain freedom that such work can be most effectively presented. It is easy to tell such people that the term is being misapplied; that . . . to get drunk is as much an act of free

---

* D. G. Ritchie, *Principles of State Interference*, London, 1891, p. 132. 'His strong opinions on the liquor trade were in his own mind directly connected with his conception of the ethical end and the nature of rights.'

will as anything else. Still the feeling of oppression, which always goes along with the consciousness of unfulfilled possibilities, will always give meaning to the representation of the effort after any kind of self-improvement as a demand for 'freedom'.[16]

Green's analysis here does not strengthen his case as a philosopher, for it shows him inclined to blur distinctions in order to achieve consequences he regarded as desirable. The fact that the urge to self-improvement could be accentuated by calling it freedom tells us something about mid-Victorian social psychology; it does little to convince us that liberty is nothing but the conquering of impulse and conformity to an ideal of character somehow judged to be of the highest value.

It may be that Green's greatest insight and originality did not lie in his formal philosophical work, but in his response to specific conditions and problems which he felt obliged to treat in the crabbed terms of his system. He seems to have suggested in his emphasis upon mastery of self that English liberalism had simply assumed the existence of an ascetic population regulating itself by individual and group action. That is, beginning with thinkers such as Locke, there had been a tendency to play down the need for action on the part of the state, not only because of the belief in self-regulating economic laws, but also because of the assumption that men were self-regulating as well. Whatever truth there was in this theory of human nature, derived from conditions in part religious, in part economic. By the middle of the nineteenth century these conditions could no longer be assumed to exert anything like their former influence. Conduct in the past had been controlled by the norms of religion or tradition; now what was wanted was a rational philosophy retaining what was good in the old creeds but sufficiently flexible to deal with the great transformation of society and politics. The magnitude of change required that the state take on new and positive functions, and no dogma to the contrary could prevent such an expansion. Yet Green thought that it was as absurd to approve all enlargements of the state's field of action as to engage in blanket condemnation of it. What was needed in this area, as in others, was a criterion of value, and this only philosophy could supply by a systematic analysis of man's *telos* as revealed by his moral progress, interpreted as always so as to yield informative propositions *a priori*. Green's professorial lecture bore the title 'On the Different Senses of "Freedom" as applied to Will and to the Moral Progress of Man'. All this had the most direct connection in his mind with the question of what ought to be the field of governmental action. For this was nothing if not a theory of relationship between the part and the whole, between the individual and the state of which he is a member. Here Green's individualism, so strongly rooted in his Protestant and liberal beginnings, reasserted its claims. However vague he allowed himself to be as a theologian in ascribing personality to God, Green as a political theorist was unusually explicit in limiting real personality to individual men, while he denied it to their nationality, humanity or any other abstraction. Whether this conclusion was consistent with his metaphysical premisses and ethical theory remains to be seen.

4

If Green had misgivings about redefining freedom to mean, not absence of constraint, but the power to realise only those capabilities involved in man's *telos*, he was determined to establish proper safeguards against the abuse of this usage. This he thought he could do by making clear his view of the moral obligations created by the relations among the individual and the social and political units to which he belongs. Above all, the freedom in question was that of individuals, not nations or societies. Their effect upon individuals is the sole measure of all such arrangements; the ideal affirmed by Green was one of personal worth. Hitherto he had emphasised the congruities of Idealism, as he construed it, with English liberalism; now he began to confront the fact that some of his central arguments contained implications that he could not very well concede without abandoning his starting point in theology and politics. After all his intellectual strategy was to maintain something approximating to his original beliefs by rephrasing them in more defensible terms. In his moral and political philosophy, many such innovations were taken over from conservatives, Hegel being the most important of these models. The burden of proof fell upon Green to establish that his use of such concepts did not engage him to their original political purpose. This was not an easy task. The theory of internal relations seemed to imply that the system as a whole alone had value, as against the lack of meaning of any one part taken in isolation. To the extent that such a theory had political implications, it seemed to support the organic theory of the state. As for teleology, neither in Aristotle nor in Hegel, who gave it a historical turn, was there any indication of a connection with individualism. The end of the process alone is real, while any phase or vehicle is only a means. Nor was the case much better in the epistemology championed by Green, who made much of the necessity of presupposing a self: this assumption alone could explain how we know what we do. Yet if the society or nation were identified with this self, the individual could be said to realise himself by sacrificing his life in war, or by giving up all claims to rights in peace. And when Green asserted that there exists in every political unit a good common to all its members, he again gave the impression of subordinating individual and group to an overriding value. Thus self-sacrifice, which Green sought to rehabilitate as an ethical concept, bore the stigma, not only of Bentham's ridicule, but of its association with the systems of Hegel and Comte, two thinkers liberals could not easily claim as fellow spirits. Finally, when Green attributed value to tradition, to historical development and existing institutions because they embodied objective reason, when he talked in language of a sort which associated men's duties with their stations, he puzzled radicals and reformers who were not accustomed to accept the past as a measure of right.

Yet Green thought he could vindicate the compatibility of Idealism with liberalism, individualism and the reforming spirit. The divine mind, or spiritual principle, gradually reproduces itself in man under certain limitations, but with the two characteristics of self-consciousness and self-objectification. Man deliberately pursues certain ideal objects. Because the spiritual principle, or reason, is within him, he possesses unique capabilities for good. Only in seeking to realise them can he satisfy himself and attain his true good, which is also freedom. Man does not seek pleasure directly, but rather through realising a conception of himself which, as a self-conscious subject, he has integrated into a system from his ideas and feelings. However individuals within a given society do not construct infinitely varied ideals. They share common assumptions about the nature of the good and thus are ready to acknowledge the legitimacy of duties which may involve the sacrifice of individual inclination or interest. These assumptions, although shaped by society, are also expressions of the same reason which is at work within individuals. Indeed the idea of the good makes itself felt through membership in a society which defines the limits of individual self-realisation. Two consequences follow: first, that the idea of the good 'has been the parent of the institutions and usages, of the social judgments and aspirations, through which human life has been so far bettered'; second, that so far as individual obligations are concerned, 'each has primarily to fulfil the duties of his station'.[17] The individual must accept these duties as bearing the stamp of reason, because his capacity to act outside them is sharply limited. He can realise himself only through being a conscientious child or father, citizen or public servant. Ideals not generally recognised by his society are 'abstract'; the excesses of the French Revolution were said to have resulted from the effort to use such values before their time had come. That such a theory posed a threat to the claims of personality, Green conceded. Its danger was that the individual might be subordinated to society or some other global abstraction. And he further admitted the difficulty of defining personality in the light of his own notion that a divine personality realises itself in the imperfect medium of the human organism. Nevertheless he refused to grant that self-realisation could take place in any entity other than individual human beings.

> It is from this difficulty that we are apt to seek an escape by speaking as if the human spirit fulfilled its idea in the history or development of mankind, as distinct from the persons whose experiences constitute that history . . .; whether in the achievements of great nations at special epochs of their history, or in some progress towards a perfect organisation of society. . . . But . . . there can be nothing in a nation however exalted its mission, or in a society, however perfectly organised, which is not in the persons composing the nation or the society. Our ultimate standard of worth is an ideal of *personal* worth. All other values are relative to value for, of, or in a person. To speak of any progress or improvement or development of a nation or society or mankind, except as relative to some greater worth of persons, is to use words without meaning.[18]

Two arguments underlie this defence of the individual personality: the first, linguistic; the second, metaphysical. To speak of progress in any nation, society or mankind considered as a whole without determining the actual effects upon the individuals composing that unit is 'to use words without meaning'. Such an appeal to common sense and ordinary usage is unusual for Green, and indeed inconsistent with his practice. Since he had chosen to leave ordinary usage behind in his own metaphysics and epistemology, he ought not to have appealed to its authority when confronted with unpalatable political consequences. That he did so indicates how much value he attached to personality. The fact that 'positive freedom' is a violation of ordinary language had not kept him from adopting it. His second line of defence was the assertion that an organic theory of society or a philosophy of history which absorbs the individual in the whole are alike errors in metaphysics. Those who argue that the nation or society are logically prior to the individual because they provide the conditions of his moral life are stating but one side of the relationship. Individual capacities can be realised only through the habits, institutions and laws of a nation or society. But these have no real existence except as the life of the individuals composing the nation or society. A national spirit or will means nothing more than what is felt and thought by persons affected by intercourse with each other and a common historical experience. At the most such a spirit is an ideal shared by individuals. The degree of realisation of their possibilities 'attained by these persons is the measure of the fulfilment which the idea of the human spirit attains in the particular national spirit. If the fulfilment of the idea is necessarily incomplete in them, it can be no more complete in the national spirit, which has no other existence, as national, than that which it has in them.'[19] Self-realisation occurs only in individuals.

Which, then, is prior—the individual or society? Green considered this to be a meaningless question. Each presupposes the other. 'Without society, no persons; this is as true as that without persons . . . there could be no such society as we know.'[20] Thus Green avoided choosing between these two concepts of personality and community, between individuality and system. His premiss was that since reason is the basis both of individual morality and the institutions of society, there can be no true conflict between them. The basis of every society, he will argue next, is the recognition, conscious or unconscious, by its members of one another as ends in themselves. The claim of the individual to have certain rights secured to him by society 'and the counter-claim of society to exercise certain powers over the individual, alike rest on the fact that these powers are necessary to the fulfilment of man's vocation as a moral being, to an effectual self-devotion to the work of developing the perfect character in himself and others'.[21] In short, there is but one end for all men; all the purposes of men which may be called moral are mutually compatible; all conflict is the result solely of the clash of reason with the imperfectly rational or irrational; when properly understood, to follow one's moral duty is to do what is prescribed by one's society or state; hence as the goal of human history is more nearly attained, to be free and to be law-abiding become one and the same thing.[22] Thus Green's teleology put his own most cherished values at the centre of human development, while his philosophy of history declared the increasing convergence of the duties of individual morality and political obligation. Man's progress, as registered in his customs and institutions, reduces almost to the vanishing point the possibility of a genuine conflict of duties.

Such a statement of belief in harmony and progress in the spiritual quality of man's secular life may now appear to be more a theological question than one of political philosophy. Yet these two subjects were never quite distinguished by Green, whose thought undeniably was a political theology. Yet it was a liberal

ETHICS

and humanitarian version of a form which in our own time has
been too exclusively identified with Nazism and Communism.
Like these totalitarian doctrines, Green made use of the notions
of historical inevitability and what Professor Popper has called
moral futurism; also like them, Green believed in the possibility
of a final solution of the problem of human freedom. Was he
merely muddled in thinking that liberalism could be reconstructed
by the use of such concepts? Or did he succeed in establishing
adequate safeguards against possible abuse of the Idealist concepts he urged upon Englishmen?

Certainly Green cannot be said to have done so in the
Prolegomena on the basis of the arguments thus far presented. He
perceived only a few of the dangers to individual liberty contained
in his proposed innovations. Even in dealing with them, he was not
sufficiently thorough. When discussing the necessity of restricting
self-realisation to real individuals, he could not hope to impose
ordinary language upon those he had trained to think in the terms
of Idealism. Although it is clear that Green himself put great
stress on individual political freedoms, he by no means was able
to prove that they could be consistently deduced from his philosophical position. When Bosanquet and F. H. Bradley later denied
that personality could be attributed to any one part of a system of
internal relations, their reasoning was considered by most Idealist
philosophers to be more rigorous than Green's. And given the
premisses Bosanquet shared with Green, it was the younger man
who seemed more consistent in his monistic position that the state
should be placed above its individual members. Green held to a
much vaguer dualism which he claimed to follow from belief in
the theory of internal relations: both the individual and the state
are on the same moral footing; both have valid claims which must
be reconciled and can be, if properly understood.

This Green attempted to do by demonstrating that there exists
in every society a good common both to individuals and to the
whole. It was on this concept and its further application to the
philosophy of history that he placed his hopes of vindicating his
application of Idealism to liberal thought. But radicals in politics
and Nonconformists in religion alike suspected the theory of the
common good to be an ideology of the aristocratic class controlling
the state and Church. These doubts had to be allayed, and in the
process of doing so, Green took the opportunity of differentiating
his own doctrine from those of Comte and Hegel. Comte, who
had some able English disciples to plead the attractions of posi-
tivist altruism, made an impersonal humanity into his religious
surrogate; Hegel's denial of individuality and worship of the state

threatened to discredit Green's own form of Idealism. Hence Green's vehement defence of personality at some cost to his own consistency.

Although ready to reassure liberals on this score, Green disapproved of their characteristic tendency to phrase their political beliefs in negative terms. He wished to take them some distance towards the belief that certain positive functions ought to be fulfilled by the state. To do so he had to argue the theory of the reality of the common good for the first time in the history of English liberalism. Green thought that the attitude of principled objection by Nonconformists and other members of the middle classes to governmental action *per se* was anachronistic. It reflected the past of aristocratic domination and Anglican supremacy, but was inadequate to the actual state of affairs. Universal suffrage was inevitable. To him the extension of the franchise was more than a political manoeuvre; it was the recognition by society of a universalistic ethic of citizenship. With the end of political and religious discrimination, he thought it not only possible but necessary to think of England as a moral community. As such, it must have devotion to the common good as its dominant principle of action. How else could even such pressing matters as the improvement of education be treated on the proper basis? Yet Green conceived of the common good as something compatible with the good and freedom of individuals as previously understood by English liberals. Retaining their respect for the integrity of the individual character, he attempted to reconcile it with a proper recognition of the new obligations imposed by full citizenship. His own emphasis thus fell upon the harmony between the rights and duties of individual citizens and their state. But the terms of discussion were always dualistic and inherently unstable. Green's definition of the common good contained two criteria, each of which could be appealed to in any practical application of it by state action. Later we shall find his followers making the most discrepant deductions from Green's premises. When confronted by proposals to abolish the poor law or to set up government insurance against the disabilities of old age, some liberal Idealists thought only of adverse effects upon self-reliance or personal character; others in terms of the obligations of the community to its members. These two tendencies should be borne in mind when reading Green's attempted proof that a common good really exists.

5

Man is born into an established system of family ties with

reciprocal rights and obligations. He learns to regard himself as a person among other persons. From the dawn of intelligence he is treated as entitled to have a will of his own, provided that he recognises the same title in others. And thus human consciousness makes possible the recognition of rights. 'Some practical recognition of personality by another, of an "I" by a "Thou" and a "Thou" by an "I", is necessary to any practical consciousness of it.'[23] Consciousness thus again is made one of the critical points in the argument. In his epistemology, Green argued that knowledge can be explained only on the supposition that facts are related to other facts in a system held together by consciousness. In ethics, he concluded that even the most objectless human life forms a system in which particular desires meet and are mutually qualified by the conception, however vague and inconstant, of something desirable on the whole. Now society was also represented as a system, depending upon the consciousness of something desirable on the whole, the common good of others which is at the same time the source of the self-satisfaction of the individual. In this way, Green moves from the abstract level of the individual with his idea of personal good to the concrete reality, the individual in society with the idea of the common good which he derives from living in his community. If it is individuals who will and desire and have consciousness, the substance of what they will and desire is supplied by the society in which they live. But the society itself is the vehicle of reason. Just as knowledge and moral action have turned out to rely on reason, so too do social and political action.

Individual moral action presupposes the idea of a self, and thus the existence of a spiritual principle. But the ideas provided to the individual are formal. Distinguishing the lasting self from its transient desires, such moral rules warn against complacency. They call attention to the permanent gap between man as he is and might be. Society, by its laws and authoritative customs, by the aspirations it encourages and the obligations it recognises, provides the content for the formal idea of the self. This might be thought to introduce an element of caprice and unreason. Are not all customs and many laws simply arbitrary? Green answered that their origin and maintenance imply the working of reason.[24] Reason working within the individual meets reason working from without.

The spiritual principle is the source of the idea of a common good just as it is of the individual's idea of a personal good. Man is conscious of himself as an end to himself. Now the self which a man strives to fulfil is not an abstract or empty self. It is a self already affected in the most primitive forms of human life by many interests, notably interests in other persons. Membership in a family is an example. 'The man cannot contemplate himself as in a better state, or on the way to the best, without contemplating others, not merely as a means to that better state, but as sharing it with him.'[25] This is 'a primary fact' which cannot be accounted for by any evolutionary hypothesis. However dependent these social interests may have been upon feelings of animal origin such as sexual feelings, it is not a product of these feelings, nor is it evolved from them. Such social interests have quite another character. They are the feelings of a being who, because he has a consciousness of himself as an end to himself, has also a consciousness of others similarly conceived. 'Having found his pleasures and pains dependent on the pleasures and pains of others, he must be able, in the contemplation of a possible satisfaction of himself, to include the satisfaction of those others, and . . . a satisfaction of them as ends in themselves and not as means to his pleasure. He must, in short, be capable of conceiving and seeking a permanent well-being in which the permanent well-being of others is included.'[26]

Green's argument is here directed against two alternative theories of obligation: that which finds its source in some contract made between individuals in the state of nature; and secondly, that theory of the origin of obligation in conquest by some superior power which subsequently compels obedience by fear of its sanctions. Against them he maintains that 'some sort of community, founded on such unity of self-consciousness, on such capacity for a common idea of permanent good, must be presupposed in any groupings of men from which the society that we know can have been developed'.[27] This supposition is claimed to be true *a priori*. Without it, the fact of society cannot be explained at all. There is an idea which underlies both the conception of moral duty and that of legal right; and in this sense is prior to the distinction between them. Further: this idea must have been at work in the minds of men before they could be capable of recognising any kind of action as one that ought to be done, whether because it is enjoined by law or authoritative custom, or because a man owes it to himself, or to his neighbour, or to God. 'This is the idea of an absolute and a common good; a good common to the person conceiving it with others, and good for him and them, whether at any moment, it answers their likings or no.'[28]

Thus reason is the basis of society, because the source at once of the establishment of equal practical rules in a common interest, and of self-imposed subjection to those rules. This point is being made here at such length because it is the inarticulate major premiss of *Political Obligation*, often alluded to, but never fully developed. The reasoning which supports his argument is never given in *Political Obligation*. There he occasionally gives the impression of arguing empirically from experience and history. But, in fact, he believed, history cannot affect the argument one way or another. All questions of fact—and it is these alone which can be validly raised by historians or social scientists—are alike irrelevant to the sort of proof Green thought was valid. Social union in any of its forms implies a state of mind. Only by 'a contradiction' could this state of mind be represented as different in kind among primitive people from what is the condition of social union as it exists in our own society. Thus Green sealed off his theory from empirical test in two ways: by use of synthetic *a priori* propositions and by teleology.

This notion of the common good, if considered without reference to Green's philosophy of history, would convey far too conservative and static an impression of the meaning he intended. It was a reforming creed of citizenship which he taught. Thus, if reason underlay even the earliest and least humanitarian societies, this was no defence of their abuses of the just claims to rights by all individual human beings. Reason in every society supplies a sense of duty. But the practical answer to the question, 'Who is my neighbour?' has varied in proportion to the realisation of the spiritual principle in human history. The idea of the good has been progressively revealed, and with it the immanent possibilities of man. Here Green moved on to the broader canvas of history. To complete his statement of what follows from the *telos* of human nature, he added his conception of man's destiny. This theory of progress rounded out his 'philosophy of life'. It was a vindication of reason, a secular theodicy explaining away apparent evils, but without reference to anything but this world. Although Aristotle was to be censured on other points, Green thought the *Nicomachean Ethics* a valid model because 'free . . . from debasement by any notion of a compensation which the brave man is to find in pleasures of another world for present endurance'.[29] From his own ethics Green extracted a theory of progress which, he was to argue, imposed greater obligations than had ever before been acknowledged.

6

The possibilities immanent in the operation of reason within man have been increasingly actualised in history and this in two ways. First, progress consists of the range of persons whose good is sought in common with a given individual. In time, the primitive restriction of the idea of mutual interest to a narrow circle gradually widens out into a duty to all men everywhere, to man *qua* man. Secondly, moral progress comes to more than the widening of the range of persons whose common good is sought. The obligations demanded are greater; the good which is sought is richer and fuller than that first sought by early human societies although a development from it.

The first type of development—from a municipal to a universal scope of obligation—follows along the line suggested by Hegel in his *Philosophy of History*. The consciousness of freedom first arose among the Greeks and therefore they were free; but they, and the Romans likewise, knew only that some are free—not man as such. The modern European states, influenced by Christianity, have attained the consciousness that man, as man, is free. Green,[30] applying a similar theory of progress, claims that it is not the sense of duty to a neighbour but the practical answer to the question of 'Who is a neighbour?' which has varied. For the Greek the range of mutual obligation did not extend beyond the *polis* and excluded the class of slaves within the *polis*. 'Among ourselves, on the contrary, . . . there is at least a potential duty of every man to every man.' What is emerging is a 'universal society co-extensive with mankind'.[31]

This process results from the progressive realisation of the 'idea of good, suggested by the consciousness of unfulfilled possibilities of the rational nature common to all men'. As the range of this idea extends itself—as it comes to be understood that no race or religion or status is a bar to self-determined co-operation in its fulfilment—the sense of duty which it yields and which has gained its power over natural desires and aversions through generations of discipline in the family and state becomes a sense of what is due to man as such and not merely to the members of a particular community.

> Given the idea of a common good and of self-determined participators in it—the idea implied, as we have seen, in the most primitive human society—the tendency of the idea in the minds of all capable of it must be to include, as participators of the good, all who have dealings with each other and who can communicate as 'I' and 'Thou'. It is rather the retardation of the acceptance of the theory that the historian has to explain; its retardation by those private interests which have made it inconvenient for powerful men and classes to act upon it. . . .[32]

True there are obstacles in the way of this universal society.

But these obstacles are the same in principle as those which interfere with the maintenance of unity in the family or tribe or commonwealth. There is no necessary limit of numbers or space beyond which the spiritual principle of social relation becomes ineffective. The only impediment to the extension of obligation is the same selfishness which accounts for individual sin in a given society. At the root of all immoral behaviour is this same 'antagonism of the natural to the spiritual man', the 'preference of private pleasure to common good'. Here again is Green's reduction of evil or sin to self-indulgence remediable by an act of will. A theological judgement about human nature has been extended into a philosophy of history.

When Green granted that ignorance and mistrust were impediments to the development of a universal society, when he conceded that force has played a part in the creation of those states which he regarded as the embodiment of reason, he did so only to vindicate the operation of reason in the world. 'But where the selfishness of man has proposed, his better reason has disposed.' Whatever the means, the result has been a gradual removal of obstacles to that recognition of a universal fellowship which the action of reason in man potentially constitutes. Large masses of men have been brought under the control of various systems of law. While each system has embodied the results both of selfish violence and seeming accident, each has been essentially an expression of reason, as embodying an idea of permanent well-being which the individual conceives to be common to his nation and himself. Thus there has arisen, along with an order of life which habituates the individual to the subordination of his likes and dislikes to social requirements, 'a sort of common language of right, in which the idea of universal human fellowship of claims in man as man— itself the outcome of the same reason which has yielded the laws of particular communities—can find the expression necessary to its taking hold on the minds of men'.[33] A universal society is thus the *telos* of the good man following those same principles which make him a good citizen or a good father. Since these principles are alike founded on reason, 'there is no such thing really as a conflict of duties'. And these duties have now become unmistakably explicit:

> Thus in the conscientious citizen of modern Christendom reason without and reason within, reason as objective and reason as subjective, reason as the better spirit of the social order in which he lives and reason as his loyal recognition and interpretation of that spirit— these being but different aspects of one and the same reality, which is the operation of the divine mind in man—combine to yield both the

judgment, and obedience to the judgment, which we variously express by saying that every human person has an absolute value; that humanity in the person of every one is always to be treated as an end, never merely as a means; that in the estimate of that well-being which forms the true good every one is to count for one, and no one for more than one; that every one has a 'suum' which every one else is bound to render him.[34]

7

When Green referred to the superiority of the 'conscientious citizen of modern Christendom', he deliberately challenged what Oxford most esteemed in the classics of the Greats School. Plato's notion that some few by their innate superiority and special training ought to rule all the rest offended Green just as much as Aristotle's ethical ideal of the contemplative life. Nor did he think that ancient Greece was the culmination of human achievement. The fact is that Green stated social and religious values which had been scarcely known at Oxford. John Bright, who ranked high among Matthew Arnold's *bêtes noires* in the ranks of the Philistines, said to a member of the Old Mortality in 1869: 'All that I see and hear of your colleges makes me feel that they are class institutions.'[35] Green, who so much admired Bright, was ready to say the same thing about old Oxford's admiration for Greek thought. There is no doubt about how he ought to be classified in terms of the dichotomy which Matthew Arnold saw in English culture—Hellenism and Hebraism. Arnold described these as two competing philosophies of life, each with a class basis, each possessing distinctive qualities necessary to human perfection:

> The uppermost idea with Hellenism is to see things as they really are; the uppermost idea with Hebraism is conduct and obedience. . . . The Hebrew notion of felicity . . . would not let the Hebrew rest till . . . he had at last got out of the law a network of prescriptions to enwrap his whole life, to govern every moment of it, every impulse, every action. . . . The bent of Hellenism is to follow, with flexible activity, the whole play of the universal order, to be apprehensive of missing any part of it, of sacrificing one part to another, to slip away from resting in this or that intimation of it, however capital. . . . The governing idea of Hellenism is *spontaneity of consciousness;* that of Hebraism *strictness of conscience.*

And clearly, Matthew Arnold, when he thought of Hellenism in England, identified it with the spirit of Oxford—aristocratic, Tory and orthodox Oxford—inalterably opposed to middle-class Liberal nonconformity:

> Oxford, the Oxford of the past, has many faults; and she has heavily

218

paid for them in defeat, in isolation, in want of hold upon the modern world. Yet we in Oxford, brought up amidst the beauty and sweetness of that beautiful place, have not failed to seize one truth—the truth that beauty and sweetness are essential characters of a complete human perfection. When I insist on this, I am all in the faith and tradition of Oxford.[37]

There can be little doubt about which of these two ideals Green preferred. He was a Hebraist who cared little for the cultured gentleman proud of his classics. When Green himself compared the Greek and modern ideals of virtue, he did render homage to Plato and Aristotle. But it is precisely what Arnold most esteemed and associated with Oxford that Green condemned: the intellectualism of the Greeks and, in particular, Aristotle's high estimation of the contemplative man. To the ancient Greeks, the only possible society consisted of a small group of freemen having recognised claims upon each other but using as instruments a much larger number of aliens and slaves with no such recognised claims. Then Christianity proclaimed that men, in a profoundly spiritual sense, are all equally dear to God. Yet historical Christianity failed to create a society organised on its own principles of equality, justice, and mercy. This failure can no longer be tolerated by modern man, who by the immanent logic of his spiritual development now has new and more demanding moral obligations. His own code and the structure of modern society demand greater sacrifices of him than could have been made upon the Greek or mediaeval Christian. Contemplative and leisurely pursuits are not now appropriate:

> It is no time to enjoy the pleasures of eye and ear, of search for knowledge, of friendly intercourse, of applauded speech or writing, while the mass of men whom we call our brethren, and whom we declare to be meant with us for eternal destinies, are left without the chance, which only the help of others can gain for them, of making themselves in act what in possibility we believe them to be.[38]

What is superior in the modern ideal, Green declares, is its secular asceticism and its theory of progress. Progress, Green had concluded in his metaphysics, is one of those *a priori* truths the existence of which is presupposed by the nature of knowledge and morality. It is involved in the nature of self-consciousness; it 'expresses an inward demand for the recognition of a unity in the world answering to the unity of ourselves'.[39] The basis of progress is the Idea of true or absolute good which began to act upon man at the beginning of human history. Potentially this Idea contains the notion that good consists of the full realisation of the soul's capacities. But in his first stages man is not conscious of the Idea, and does not reason about it. Yet even in this phase the idea creates a demand for a self-satisfaction which is not to be confused with mere pleasure. In the most primitive society, this is already for some well-being common to the individual and to the other members of his group. As the Idea develops further in history, the definition of the group included in the common good is extended progressively from the family to the tribe, from the tribe to the state, from the state to humanity. The modern ideal includes all men instead of a small class only. Thus Green has no hesitation in preferring it over that of the Greeks. It is quite wrong, in his view, to believe that the Greek or Roman citizen at the height of their municipal civilisation had a fuller or richer life than that of the modern citizen under a régime of universal freedom and equal rights.

> The realisation of human capacities has, in fact, taken a far wider range with us than in the most advanced of ancient states . . . and every progress achieved opens up a further vista of possibilities.[40]

Progress creates greater obligations than those acknowledged by the most virtuous Greek philosophers. Such moral progress means two things: an increased asceticism, that is, a rise in the degree of self-sacrifice deemed essential to virtue; and an increased democracy, an expansion of the range of persons for whom self-sacrifice ought to be made:

> The hopelessly sick are being tended; the foolish and ignorant are being treated as rational persons; human beings whom a Greek would have looked on as chattels, or as a social encumbrance to be got rid of, are having pains bestowed on them which only a faith in unapparent possibilities of their nature could justify.[41]

Aristotle would not have recognised such service to the sick and lowly as good. And so Green appealed to the asceticism of an audience which had been brought up under Evangelical discipline. He rehabilitated the moral value of asceticism and thus denied the judgment of Utilitarian hedonism, which dismissed self-denial as an absurd survival of mediaevalism. And he made social service and reform into the moral obligation of the conscientious man. Aristotle's 'pleasures of the soul' no longer may be regarded as a proper ideal. Oxford must teach its best young men to leave it and go to the slums, into the schools, or wherever else they can help to bring their society up to its own moral standard.

> There are men, we know, who with the keenest sensibility to such pleasures as those of 'gratified ambition and love of learning' yet deliberately forgo them; who shut themselves out from an abundance of aesthetic enjoyments . . . in order to meet the claims which the work of realising the possibilities of the human soul . . . seems to make upon them. Such sacrifices are made, now, as they were not in the days of the Greek philosophers.[42]

Yet the fact remains that for all his criticism of Plato and Aristotle, Green did not abandon that teleology which is one of the distinguishing characteristics of classical political thought. Even when criticising its ideal, he praised the lasting contributions it made to ethics and politics, and described its rôle in terms which he would have been pleased to accept as his own. For they did not claim to be 'prophets of new truth, but exponents of new principles on which the citizen, if he thought the matter out, would find that he had already been acting'. What they had done was to clarify the end or good of the *bios politikos*, citizen life. This praise of teleology is repeated and intensified in *Political Obligation*, where he declares that whatever their insufficiencies Plato and Aristotle had the supreme merit of putting political theory on its proper basis: the teleological view of man and society. When treating natural rights, Green insisted that the concept could be maintained only on Aristotle's view:

> He regards the state (πολις) as a society of which the life is maintained by what its members do for the sake of maintaining it, by functions consciously fulfilled with reference to that end, and which in that sense imposes duties; and at the same time as a society from which its members derive the ability . . . to fulfil their several functions, and which in that sense confers rights.[43]

Here Green announced his decision to persevere in the track of Aristotle. When combined with his Idealist method of using concepts said to be true *a priori*, he so defined political theory as to exclude any empirical evidence which might call into question his faith of citizenship and reform. In his ethics he was responding to religious impulses that made it necessary for him to provide a definition of the human situation which made it meaningful to persons with an originally Evangelical outlook. Anyone thinking in the ethical terms provided by Green would ask whether a prospective course of action would help to produce that type of character and organisation of society which consist of a life of self-devoted activity on the part of all persons. To understand the ideal and to apply it to everyday practice is the effective source of both individual morality and political reform. Such a conception of the ideal expresses the quest for right conduct as carried on by the individual under the sense of personal responsibility for doing the best which alone can make him a reformer of his own practice or that of others. It accounts for the possibility of the question, 'Why should I trouble about making myself or my neighbours better than we are?' And it leads the man who asks the question to a real effort to improve human life.

CHAPTER EIGHT

THE PRINCIPLES OF POLITICAL OBLIGATION

I

IT IS NOT EASY to arrive at a just appreciation of Green as a political philosopher. His style verges on the impenetrable, and some of his problems were not political at all, but metaphysical and theological. Even when he made his meaning relatively clear, his form of statement created logical and linguistic difficulties. Yet in his political philosophy, the whole is somehow superior to the sum of its parts; the conclusions are still alive in a way that their metaphysical and ethical 'foundations' are not. Green was stating his vision of what a free and just society ought to be, and this has not dated as much as the philosophical form in which it was put. And he was against ideas which needed to be criticised, although not always for the reasons he stated. Thus he directed his polemic against social Darwinism, which had all the glamour and danger of pseudo-science; against chauvinism and imperialism; against the dogmatic individualism and insensitivity to human suffering of a Herbert Spencer; against Utilitarianism, which he put on another plane as a doctrine which had once performed commendable services, but could now no longer be seriously maintained. Another source of strength in Green's writing about politics, was the strong sense of personal responsibility which led him to relate his technical work to concrete problems and the intellectual puzzles which grew out of the attempt to apply political theory to their resolution. His faith in citizenship had led him to participate in actual politics, although never at the exalted level more usually associated with the Balliol of his period. From these activities he acquired practical judgment and a not inconsiderable knowledge of how politics appeared to the ordinary citizen. These qualities tempered the doctrinaire and abstract aspects of Idealism, which became in his hands the nearest equivalent to an empirical study of politics then available. Aware of the socially shared values that underlie law and political machinery, Green thought it important to understand how the individual is affected by membership in groups, a relationship which ought to be, but seldom is, considered by theorists of rights and duties. Thus the problems he posed were significant, as were the answers he suggested. These still merit serious consideration, when translated out of the technical terms of his system.

Green did what he could with the intellectual equipment at his disposal. His successors at Oxford have not thought it worth their while to apply newer techniques to political philosophy. Their reasons for abstaining have recently been considered and condemned by Sir Isaiah Berlin who has said: 'To neglect the field of political thought, because its unstable subject-matter, with its blurred edges, is not to be caught by the fixed concepts, abstract models and fine instruments suitable to logic or linguistic analysis—to demand a unity of method in philosophy and reject whatever the method cannot successfully manage—is merely to allow oneself to remain at the mercy of primitive and uncriticised political beliefs'.[1]

When applied to Green, this sentence is enlightening on two scores: it serves as a warning that much imprecision is to be expected in political thought (although Sir Isaiah seems to think that Green exceeded his allowance); and it suggests that not to criticise political beliefs at all is far worse than to have a discussion carried on in terms which may not meet the highest standards of philosophical rigour. To question a received idea or the unexamined premiss of some new view is to contribute to the awareness of statesmen and their public, perhaps to inaugurate dialogue on questions which badly need airing. Such an intervention may produce an effect disproportionate to its logical merit or intellectual originality. Thus Green's concept of positive freedom seems to have liberated many from the narrow individualism of the Manchester School and Nonconformity. In short, he challenged liberal orthodoxies and introduced some novel propositions for public consideration: the possibility that an increase in governmental activity (in education, for example) might add to the liberty of individuals rather than diminish it. To restore or create alternatives for political action, which have been obscured by existing definitions of the situation—this is one function which can be performed by a political philosopher whose method is deficient in important regards.

This is not to say that a political philosophy ought to be judged by its ascertainable consequences, rather than by the validity of its propositions. Put in this form, such an assertion would be rejected by almost all of those who have theorised about politics. Yet it is a peculiarity of the subject, that political philosophers have been willing, indeed eager, to discuss what practical effects are apt to follow from holding their ideas. Marx as well as Plato, Sorel as well as Hegel, thought that political action, if based on their respective views, would be transformed for the better. Not only did they recommend certain institutional arrangements and political strategies as likely to resolve problems of their time and place; but also they used models, concepts and perspectives consciously or unconsciously calculated to persuade their readers of the desirability or inevitability of such solutions. Nor have their critics disagreed about the propriety of judging ideas by their effects. Much modern political philosophy has taken the form of debating whether subscription to the ideas of Plato undermines belief in the open society; whether Rousseau or some more typical figure of the eighteenth century may be held responsible for the excesses of the French Revolution. Similarly, nineteenth century schools are judged in terms of their alleged contributions to the totalitarianisms of our century. Professors Popper, Talmon and Berlin accept the notion that political ideas should be known by their fruits as well as their validity. In their own criticism, they sometimes seem to assert the historical proposition that certain ideas such as holism, historical inevitability or moral futurism have prepared the way for Nazism or Communism. At other times, they seem to be criticising logical form: such a concept as positive freedom facilitates, or offers no safeguards against, totalitarian sophistries designed to rob men of their personal freedom and opportunity to participate in political decisions. Does the fact that a theory may be thus abused constitute an adequate refutation of it?

This question is being raised here, since many of Green's concepts belonged to the same logical family as those criticised by Professors Popper and Berlin. Yet as far as can be determined, Green's thought did not produce the undesirable consequences attributed to such ideas. Green himself seems to have assessed the potential effects of his ideas with a fair degree of accuracy. Every political philosopher must go through an analogous process of assessing, not only what he himself believes, but what needs to be said in order to prevail over competing ideas he finds inadequate or dangerous. A concept inherited from a situation which no longer exists should not be used to bar urgently needed reforms. In Green's day the negative definitions of freedom as well as methodological individualism of the kind advocated by Professor Popper were well known. Unfortunately, they had the effect of making it difficult to justify even moderate proposals for social and economic amelioration. The problem was how to incorporate within the same theory a criterion for state action which applied equally well to the protection of individual freedoms and the claim for a more equitable distribution of social opportunities. A balance was wanted; Green thought it could best be attained by the notion that freedom consisted of the right of every individual to make the most of those powers admitted to be worth realising by the moral consensus of the community. Certainly there were and are powerful objections to so redefining the term. But it is somewhat artificial to ignore what use was actually being made of the negative theory of freedom, while pointing with alarm to dangerous implications of the positive theory of freedom, dangers which never made themselves felt in England. The rest of Green's theories can be understood in similarly strategic terms. His emphasis upon the inevitable trend of historical development, as well as the moral obligations he wished to deduce from it, was directed against other theories which still had a hold on the minds of politicians and their constituents. His particular targets were those which purported to prove scientifically that efforts to improve society were futile because of persisting characteristics of human nature and politics: some few must necessarily dominate and always will do so by the government's power to coerce, a power which alone compels obedience and maintains order. Against these conservative theories of man's nature and history, Green set out a theory of progress, the speed of which would be determined by man's will.

Green once wrote of Locke and Hume that both had given to their ideas 'the stamp of that personal power which persuades men. . . . They wrote as citizens and men of the world, anxious (in no bad sense) for effect. . . .'[2] And he likewise praised Plato and Aristotle because they represented themselves, not as discoverers of previously unknown truths, but rather as spokesmen for those principles on which the good citizen had already been acting. Both of these purposes underlie his own work in political philosophy: he wrote as a citizen anxious for effect and he hoped to state the principles implied by the actual policies of his society. By formulating these principles, he hoped to make men fully conscious of what they valued, a kind of self-knowledge which could serve as a guide for action in the present and future.

In this definition of political philosophy there was much of value, although Green did not see how incompatible such an analysis was with the *a priori* and teleological aspects of his method. For it is one thing to scrutinise actual political decisions and laws in the search for operative principles, standards of evidence, workable distinctions and modes of compromise; it is quite another to insist that the nature of man and reality prescribe one and only one definition of what is good. Green's political philosophy suffered most from those aspects of his theory which were meant to provide a secure foundation for religious faith. Much of his analysis was, however, separable from his metaphysics and theology. This was most evident in his statement of the values which were in fact being acknowledged in personal conduct and political behaviour. For it is valuable to know what men share despite their overt disagreements, expressed through party slogans or public speeches. If the members of a given society share to a significant degree assumptions about the proper goals of politics or, at least, the rules by which disagreements ought to be settled, then a statement of these goals and rules can be advantageous. This is true in the purely technical sense that the society, once in possession of an acceptable statement, is less apt to breach rules just as it is less likely to adopt means inappropriate to the attainment of its agreed ends once it knows what they are. These ends, of course, are simply those of that one society, and the services of this kind which a political philosopher can render are to knowledge of itself and not of the eternally good or true. If judged from this more modest perspective, Green can be said to have shed much light on the moral and political consensus of his society. This was no small service, because his statement registered a shift in political power and in modes of thought and feeling. Like Benthamism and Manchester Liberalism, Green's Idealism was both an effect and a cause. It could not have been accepted at all were it not responsive to existing forces; but once formulated, it exerted a certain independent power by its definition of the situation and statement of the priorities which ought to be accepted by the principled citizen and statesman.*

2

The modern reader's difficulties with Green's lectures on political obligation begin with their author's use of language, and are compounded by his philosophical method. Almost every term he used to discuss politics here takes on a special meaning: 'natural law' and 'natural rights', both phrases with a long and respectable history, cannot be understood in any of their previous usages when encountered in Green's work. At the time when these lectures were delivered, his audience knew that what he had to say about political obligation was but the application in detail of principles elaborated in his ethics, a subject which itself was said to

* This aspect of Green's thought is considered at length in Chapter X.

rest upon metaphysical and epistemological foundations. Today Green's readers are not apt to know the origin or use of his terms. But even if they did, this would remove one source of objection without touching another. For confusion must always result when terms with long-established usages are made to serve purposes quite unlike anything previously associated with them. Whatever advantage is achieved by the new usage is apt to be offset by the problems raised because of a shift of meaning.

So far as his language was concerned, Green apparently felt that he had sufficiently alerted his audience to his way with words. In any case, he was scarcely disposed to apologise for what he considered to be one of his most constructive innovations. For he assumed that so to rephrase and transform terms is the essence of philosophy. What he had done in providing God, freedom and immortality with Idealist glosses, he now proposed to repeat in the realm of political philosophy. If the subject differed somewhat from his previous work, it also shared much with it; indeed he regarded his analysis as cumulative. With the conclusions he had already attained, he thought he could make substantial advances in political thought upon anything previously achieved in English thought. He did not think himself obliged to repeat his proofs from the beginning. His reader is apt to be misled. When Green criticises Hobbes or Locke, he appears to do so on the ground of their internal contradictions. Ostensibly the author is being proved to be inconsistent with his own premises, a type of critique to which there could be no legitimate objection. But Green never limits himself to this procedure. When his criticism is closely examined, it turns out that it rests upon the imputation of an alleged error in metaphysics or epistemology. Nor was Green in any sense concerned with the history of thought for its own sake. He cared little for the type of scholar who 'would love to rehearse the views of past thinkers, would feel their eternal plausibility and, in interpreting them, would think of himself as little as they think of him'.[3] Green tended to regard other philosophers as persons who did or did not prepare the way for his own thought. As Santayana has remarked, Idealists established what they regarded as a law of progress in philosophy, a subordination and development among philosophical systems, as though they all moved somehow in single file with the very last as their secret goal.[4] In this Green followed Hegel who 'gave out that he had understood every system much better than those who believed in it, and had been carried by its inner contradictions (which its adepts never saw) to the next convenient position in the development of human fancy and of his own lectures'.[5] Green stated his own views on the value of studying the history of philosophy quite without ambiguity. No doubt his words were aimed at Jowett and Pattison, his erstwhile allies:

'The revived interest which is noticeable in the history of philosophy may be an indication either of philosophical vigour or of philosophical decay. In those whom intellectual indolence, or a misunderstood and disavowed metaphysic, has landed in scepticism there often survives a curiosity about the literary history of philosophy, and the writings which this curiosity produces tend further to spread the notion that philosophy is a matter about which there has been much guessing by great intellects, but no definite truth is to be attained. It is otherwise with those who see in philosophy a progressive effort towards a fully-articulated conception of the world as rational. To them its past history is of interest as representing steps in this progress which have already been taken for us, and which, if we make them our own, carry us so far on our way towards the freedom of perfect understanding.'[6]

Much, then, he believed, had already been established by his predecessors and himself in other domains of philosophy, and these results could now be put to use in political theory. The philosophical method he had made his own he called 'critical'. Beginning with knowledge itself, he asked what are its conditions. Such an inquiry involves, not the facts of experience, but what must be presupposed to allow of any experience at all. Such *a priori* truths cannot be affected by any evidence itself derived from experience, whether this be historical, sociological, or any other kind. From this epistemological inquiry, Green derived the notion of a spiritual principle realising itself gradually both in the institutions and individual members of a political society. Progress is another such notion, which must be assumed to be true if we are to understand how it is that we have knowledge. And, still using the same procedure, Green argued in his ethics that every human society presupposes the reality of some shared and acknowledged conception of a good common to all of its members. This is said to be true *a priori*.

Almost imperceptibly Green had shifted from epistemology to a consideration of actual human behaviour, ethical and political. We know that there are moral men, we are acquainted with their political equivalent, citizens who are the intelligent, co-operating subject of law and custom. The same procedure must be used here as that used to state the preconditions of knowledge. Just as facts imply a consciousness holding them in relation, so does a society imply the mutual recognition of rights by its members and their sense that there is a good common to them all. Thus there are said to be two presuppositions which are implied by the existence of intelligent co-operating citizens: first, the presence in each of them of the idea of a possible well-being of himself which will not pass away with any particular pleasure; secondly, the idea of having a well-being in common with some group which he must consider when he considers his own interest.

As Mr A. C. Ewing has remarked, the Idealist argument 'is not inductive but *a priori*. It cannot be consistently admitted by anyone who will not admit informative *a priori* propositions.'[7] Kant had sharply limited the scope of inferences about the nature of reality; he believed in synthetic *a priori* propositions in ethics, but not in metaphysics. Philosophers today are still stricter, denying that anything but tautologies may be derived from *a priori* propositions. But Green, following the post-Kantian Idealists in Germany rather than Kant himself, used an extremely loose procedure for determining what it is that we know and what may be said to be implied by it. As he himself applied this method to social and political questions, he announced, in advance of any empirical investigation, just what are the characteristics of all human societies. For many of the issues he dealt with, such as the relation of family to political organisation, were, in principle, accessible to empirical treatment and now are studied by anthropologists, sociologists and political scientists. Both the *a priori* and teleological elements of his theory are vulnerable to the charge that Green drew very general and unsubstantiated conclusions without considering simpler alternative hypotheses, or having analysed with sufficient care the meanings of his principal terms. Do we know enough about those 'intelligent co-operating citizens' of whom Green made so much? Men may co-operate for reasons which have little to do with sharing an idea of the common good. Such a notion ought not to be introduced into the discussion even by an Idealist unless and until empirical explanations have been found wanting. And has Green examined his terms carefully enough? Men may share a number of common ends; this is far from implying a metaphysical entity called the common good. The political activities of citizens in a large and complex nation may be due to a number of motivations and purposes, rather than the single purpose asserted by Green to be true *a priori*.

On more than one occasion his reader is left uncertain about the relation between the real and the ideal, between propositions asserted to be true on the basis of induction from empirical data and those which rest on deduction from so-called *a priori* truths. Not infrequently Green seems to be making his case on the basis of common sense conceptions of evidence and causation; or he is to be found arguing with some power matters of social psychology, the

attitudes apt to be taken by individuals because of their membership in social groups. Yet whenever he felt his general theory
menaced by evidence not to his liking, Green returned immediately to his *a priori* and teleological method. Thus it is never clear
what is the relation between those of Green's statements about
human behaviour which should be understood as derived by
induction from observation or historical evidence, and those other
statements which are asserted to have been proved by procedures
independent of observation. Both his method and his way of using
language contributed to this aura of ambiguity which surrounds
his political philosophy. But most of all the trouble lay in his
theological concerns. The truth is that he viewed political philosophy, not only as a branch of ethics, which is a defensible
position, but also as a branch of theology, which is not. Long
before he delivered his professorial lectures, he had decided how to
demonstrate the harmony among the apparently discrepant aspects
of man. The clue was to be found in Rousseau's theory of the
general will (as understood in its Idealist statement): ' . . . in the
individual, but not of him, as beyond him in such a way as to be
an object of his reverence and love, yet constituting his moral and
rational self, it reconciles the three principles—love of self, love of
our neighbour and love of God'.[8] Prichard argued that there is a
gap between the concept of 'good' and the concept of 'what I
should attempt to bring about'. He thought that one may concede
that something is good, but then ask further why one should take
the initiative to bring it about. Green, however, was concerned so
to put the matter of obligation that the two concepts logically were
inseparable. His treatment of obligation in his political philosophy
was therefore bound to be merely an illustration of the teleological
argument of his ethics.

3

Green centred his discussion on the problem of 'political
obligation'. This term stood for a cluster of issues, which although
not new to the subject, had not previously been put in this central
position. Indeed so learned a historian of ideas as Professor
d'Entrèves, has attributed to Green the first use of this phrase.[9]
This occurred when Green began his lectures by asking the question, 'Why ought I to obey the law?' This arises in terms of the
obligation to obey or disobey on the part of a subject towards his
sovereign; on the part of the citizen towards the state; and the
obligation of individuals to each other as enforced by a political
superior.[10] The sort of answer Green was bound to give had been

indicated by his decision in his ethics to adopt a teleological theory in which such terms as 'obligation' are always referred to man's purpose, present in his consciousness as the form of his ideal self.[11] This subordination of obligation to purpose is inherent in teleological, as it is not in deontological, theories, which makes duty rather than purpose into the fundamental question of ethics. To later deontological theorists such as Prichard, it appeared that Green was saying that duty or obligation needs some other ground or foundation; no act is worth doing for its own sake.

The *Lectures on the Principles of Political Obligation* are divided into three parts: a definition of law and its essential function; a criticism of the principal alternative theories of political obligation then current in Europe; and a consideration of the chief rights and obligations actually enforced by law in civilised states and the grounds for justifying obedience to such law.[12] Green thus assumed that European society was equitable, and from its practice he could be guided to the proper ground of obedience to law. This in any case, he would go on to argue, would coincide with the general principles of morality. By this contention that the duties of the good citizen and the good man coincide, that, properly understood, there is no conflict between what is demanded by the state and the individual's conscience, Green once again underlined his notion that there exists a spiritual principle which acts upon both.[13] The *telos* or goal is the development of a good character in individuals (good having been defined in Green's lectures on ethics). By this criterion laws and institutions are to be judged. Their value is to be estimated by the extent to which they give reality to the capacities of will and reason by giving men scope for their exercise.[14]

Although Green was moving in the direction of a theory of community, a strong residual individualism derived both from his theology and his liberalism led him to deny that morality can be attributed to anything other than the character of individual men. This denial straightaway creates a presumption against action by law. Law can force men to perform certain actions. But these actions are external. No law can make men moral, for morality depends upon a freely-willed motive, upon performing an act for the right reasons. Hence there is a presumption against the use of law when voluntary action is possible. The business of law is to maintain the conditions under which will and reason may be exercised. Those acts only should be enjoined by law that are 'so necessary to the existence of a society in which the moral end stated can be realised that it is better for them to be done or omitted from that unworthy motive which consists

in fear or hope of legal consequences than not to be done at all'.[15]
Obviously, the fewer such laws, the better for moral development.

Yet Green's attitude towards the proper function of law and
institutions was not the pure negativism of the Spencerian
individualist. Rather he felt with Arnold Toynbee that, 'to a
reluctant admission of the necessity for State action, we join a
burning belief in duty and a deep spiritual ideal.'[16] In short,
this entailed the reconciliation of individuality with community.
The older individualism had based its theory of political obligation
on natural rights. It was supposed that political society had been
established to secure these rights. Thus was determined the
standard for defining the proper relation among men as well as
the conditions under which individuals ought to submit to the
state. Of this style of thought Green said with evident distaste:

> The popular effect of the notion that the individual brings with him
> into society certain rights which he does not derive from society . . . is
> seen in the inveterate irreverence of the individual towards the state,
> in the assumption that he has rights against society irrespectively of
> his fulfilment of any duties to society, that all 'powers that be' are
> restraints upon his natural freedom which he may rightly defy as
> far as he safely can.[17]

Such a theory provides 'a reason for resisting all positive reforms,
all reforms which involve an action of the state in the way of
promoting conditions favourable to moral life'.[18]

Thus Green had to erect a theory which did not base law upon
natural rights, in the older sense. What, then, is the proper ground
of law and obedience to it? Why should the subject obey his
sovereign and the citizen his state? What should be the obligations
of individuals to each other as enforced by law? These are the
essential questions that must be decided by a theory of political
obligation. To them the natural rights theorists had answered in
terms of rights secured by a covenant antecedent to society. The
Utilitarians had answered that men should have their civil rights
respected and they should respect the law because 'more pleasure
is attained or pain avoided by the general respect for them; the
ground of our consciousness that we ought to respect them, in
other words their ultimate sanction, is the fear of what the consequences would be if we did not'.[19]

Both these theories of political obligation Green declared
inadequate and returned to his ethics to find the proper principle.
Society is based, not on contract or utility, but upon the spontaneous recognition by persons of other persons as ends in themselves and the further recognition that the interests of those others

is involved with their own interest. Such recognition of a common good is the essence both of morality and political obligation.

Power cannot create right. Therefore any normative theory must be able to distinguish what is from what ought to be. The great defect of natural rights and Utilitarian theories of political obligation is that they cannot account for such a distinction. Their error, as Green diagnosed it in the *Prolegomena*, is their belief in the possibility of a natural science of ethics. But such theories cannot account for the use of 'ought' in cases where a moral obligation exists to resist the powers that be, or to take an action that leads to unpleasant consequences. Here again, Green is criticising the older theories of reform for two reasons: their failure as ethical principles and their obstructive effect upon the moral initiative of reformers under the conditions of his day.

His own theory began with a subject who has a conception of himself as in an ideal unattained condition. This he seeks to realise in moral action. His power to do so is recognised by other conscious moral agents who regard such powers as a means to that ideal good of themselves which they also conceive. 'No one therefore can have a right except as a member (1) of a society and (2) of a society in which some common good is recognised by the members of the society as their own ideal good.'[20] Some form of community founded on such unity of self-consciousness, on such capacity for a common duty or common good must be presupposed in any grouping of men from which the society we know could have developed. The idea or the common good underlies the conception both of moral duty and legal right. Both imply the twofold conception (a) 'I *must* though I do not like', (b) 'I must *because* it is for the common good'.

What, then, is the proper rationale for law? It is the moral function of law that alone can justify obedience to it. Function, not origin, is the criterion. 'A law is not good because it enforces "natural rights" but because it contributes to the realisation of a certain end.'[21] Here Green re-introduced his teleological definition of goodness as the proper ground for political obligation:

> The claim or right of the individual to have certain powers secured to him by society, and the counter-claim of society to exercise certain powers over the individual, alike rest on the fact that these powers are necessary to the fulfilment of man's vocation as a moral being, to an effectual self-devotion to the work of developing the perfect character in himself and others.[22]

And Green calls such powers, when recognised by society, 'natural rights' on the ground that they are essential to the realisation of man's true nature. This is a translation which utterly transforms. Green's appropriation of this term with its numerous and conflicting associations has caused many a reader to wonder what this Idealist version of 'natural right' can possibly mean. Green first suggested it as an equivalent for *jus* or *Recht*, 'a system of correlative rights or obligations actually enforced, or that should be enforced by law'.[23] But this formulation is ambiguous, for it leaves unanswered two questions: Are there rights and obligations which ought to be enforced, although not recognised by law? If so, what can be the standard by which such powers are to be considered as legitimate in the absence of such recognition? To the first query Green answered that no actual system of rights and obligations is all that it should be. The statute book may not incorporate all the claims acknowledged as legitimate by the society. To the second query Green answered, changing his ground, that there is a meaningful sense in which it may be said that rights and obligations ought to be maintained by law, although they are not. And that sense is teleological: such rights and obligations are 'natural' because necessary to the end which it is the vocation of human society to realise.

At this point Green creates the impression that the most important aspect of any power conceded to be a right is its relation to the 'moral end, as serving which alone law and the obligations imposed by law have their value'. A law is good not because it enforces natural right but because it contributes to the realisation of a certain end. We only discover what rights are natural by considering what powers must be secured to a man in order to attain this end. Green thought that any objection to calling such rights 'natural' would be removed if he avoided two errors made by earlier theorists: he would admit that rights are not the arbitrary creations of law or custom; and, on the other hand, deny that there are rights antecedent to society, rights which men brought with them into a society formed deliberately by contract among themselves. Thus rights are natural 'in the same sense in which according to Aristotle the state is natural; not in the sense that they actually exist when a man is born and that they have actually existed as long as the human race, but that they arise out of, and are necessary for the fulfilment of, a moral capacity without which a man would not be a man'.[24] Innate rights exist in the same sense as innate duties: both are equally necessary to the realisation of moral capacity.

Nothing could appear less equivocal than this teleological statement of rights. Unfortunately, later in his exposition Green changed his formulation of this concept when he gave the following definition: 'A right is a power of which the exercise by the individual or by some body of men is recognised by a society, either as itself directly essential to a common good, or as conferred by an authority of which the maintenance is recognised as so essential.'[25] Here the criterion was expanded to include three further considerations: whether a claimed right is or is not essential to a common good; whether it is conferred by a power, the maintenance of which is considered essential; and, finally, whether in both of the foregoing cases, the society has registered its recognition. Of course, it may be that Green meant to identify the 'common good' with 'the fulfilment of a moral capacity without which a man would not be a man'. But if this was the case, then he could not have meant what is ordinarily conveyed by the phrase 'common good': something benefiting the members, or most of them, of a given political community. Rather 'common good' must mean 'the realisation of a given type of character'. What 'recognition' may mean is at this point not yet clear. At first Green seems to have been saying that a claim to rights must be acknowledged by whatever procedure is used for making law in a society; but then he asserted that the existing social relations of a society may be said to embody moral principles not yet registered in its laws.

In his introductory remarks, he touched upon rights only so that he could clarify the proper rationale for law and this, in his view, was moral and teleological. Thus he had set out at the beginning both the ground for obedience to law and the appropriate field for state action. At this point, he was not so much developing new arguments as illustrating the political application of the principal conceptions of his metaphysics and ethics. This was meant to demonstrate to his audience the wholeness of his view of life. On essential points his statement maintained a continuity with the individualist tradition of Liberalism; yet it provided a new emphasis when it acknowledged that the state must maintain conditions favourable to moral life and even actively promote the development of character by removing all possible hindrances. This is a negative standard justifying 'positive reform'. Does it really provide an unambiguous standard? Surely contradictory inferences are easily drawn from it. A person, applying this criterion to a proposed enactment, might not know whether to emphasise its negative or its positive aspects: whether to be on his guard lest he impair self-reliance and voluntary action; or whether to consider the added contribution to the common good by state action. If compulsory education is to be justified, should this not be done on the positive ground of contributing to the common good rather than the negative one of removing hindrances? Green was seeking a balanced position intermediate between two views of state action which he regarded as equally extreme and one-sided. But, in these lectures, his own views were more evident in his rejections and qualifications than in any positive alternative to competitive theories. Just as he had denounced the theory of natural rights because it stimulated individuals to make claims upon the state without assuming any corresponding duties, so he denounced paternalism because it lessened the scope for self-imposed duties:

> It is one thing to say that the state in promoting these conditions [favourable to moral life] must take care not to defeat its true end by narrowing the region within which the spontaneity and disinterestedness of true morality can have play; another thing to say that it has no moral end to serve at all, and that it goes beyond its province when it seeks to do more than secure the individual from violent interference by other individuals. The true ground of objection to 'paternal government' is not that it violates the 'laissez faire' principle and conceives that its office is to make people good, to promote morality, but that it rests on a misconception of morality. The real function of government being to maintain conditions of life in which morality shall be possible, and morality consisting in the disinterested performance of self-imposed duties, 'paternal government' does its best to make it impossible by narrowing the room for the self-imposition of duties and, for the play of disinterested motives.[26]

4

Having applied his ethical theory to the function of law, Green moved on to examine the chief doctrines of political obligation then current in Europe. Such polemics played an important part in the exposition of his own views, for in this way he could achieve three objectives at once: he could develop the substance of his own teaching, demonstrate his philosophical method in action, and discredit other political philosophers in the field. His analysis was never a point-by-point examination of the author within his original framework of assumptions. Rather Green took up the unresolved dilemmas of earlier thinkers or the basic assumptions which he thought had led them astray. Spinoza, Hobbes and Locke he represented as fully involved in a social contract theory. In Rousseau the concept of social contract was at war with another and more rewarding concept, that of the general will. Austin's theory of sovereignty was not wrong but incomplete, a defect which has provoked mischievous inferences.

The major criticism Green made of social contract and natural rights theories was that they assumed rights said to be inherent in the individual quite apart from his performance of any duties. On the basis of his own ethics, Green argued that political obligation cannot be validly derived from contract. Just as any contract presupposes the recognition by its parties of a good common to them both, so all other obligations involve a similar acknowledgment. Only the teleological view of man and society can provide an adequate theory of rights. It was because Plato and Aristotle conceived the *polis* as the *telos* of the individual that any true theory of rights must build on the foundation of their root concepts.

Green attacked Hobbes because he wished to derive from a contract of all with all the sovereign's right to power over his subjects. This argument will not do. For, in its notion of a contract, it presupposes just that state of affairs it claims to account for—a régime of recognised and enforced obligations. Locke's treatment of social contract had the same defect. And this consisted in its presuppositions, not in its truth or falsity as an account of a historical event. The concept of a 'state of nature' cannot validly be distinguished from that of a political society. It is inconceivable that men should suddenly contract themselves out of one into another unless the state of nature were virtually identical with a political society.

Only when men are conscious of the law of nature are they bound by it. But then it ceases to be a law of nature. 'It is not a law according to which the agents subject to it act necessarily but without consciousness of the law. It is a law of which the agent subject to it has a consciousness, but one according to which he may or may not act; ie, one according to which he *ought* to act.'[27] From this law all those theorists derive the obligation to submit to civil government.

At this point, Green springs his trap. If it is acknowledged that the law of nature is an ethical law based on consciousness, then two questions must be asked: How can the consciousness of obligation arise without recognition by the individual of claims on the part of others? Secondly, given such a society of man capable of the consciousness of obligation, how does it differ from a political society? The first question, aimed at Hobbes, involves Green's recognition theory of rights; the second, aimed at Locke and Rousseau, raises the issue contained in Green's theory that every society, however primitive, already presupposes the idea of a common good. Thus the social contract theory 'must needs be false to itself in one of two ways'.

To account for the possibility of a social contract based upon the compact of all with all, its theorists must assume a society subject to a law of nature, prescribing the freedom and equality of all. But such a society governed by such a law would have no reason to establish civil government. Hobbes attempted to supply a motive for change when he represented the state of nature as a state of war in which no reciprocal claims are recognised. When Hobbes denied that recognition of claims exists in the state of nature, he thereby destroyed the only basis for the obligation to honour the social contract. The absence of recognition means the absence of obligation.

On the other hand, if, as in Locke, it is denied that the state of nature is a state of war, then it becomes possible to have a theory of obligation. But in that case there is no motive to establish civil government. If in the state of nature men were free and equal and governed by a law of nature, from this 'political society would have been a decline, one in which there could have been no motive to the establishment of civil government'.[28] Thus Green claims to have destroyed the theory of social contract. However his argument is based upon his own definitions of terms rather than upon those of the authors he criticises.[29] For someone who accepted Green's position, its plausibility was increased by this sort of exercise. But it is of dubious value to someone who does not accept Green's philosophical method. Apparently Green was willing to concede the difficulties which remained unresolved in his own translation of the issue, for he added a startling remark, a paradox which involved him in a position even more unusual than before:

> Whether or no any particular government has on this ground lost its claim and may be rightly resisted, is a question, no doubt, difficult for the individual to answer with certainty. In the long run, however, it seems generally, if not always, to answer itself. A government no longer serving the function described . . . brings forces into play which are fatal to it.[30]

Suddenly Green introduced the notion of a self-regulating mechanism at work in history, in this case operating to remove any government no longer serving its true function. This was the theodicy of his political faith. It had previously made its appearance when he discussed the reasons for the decline of the Greek *polis*:

> 'There is no clearer ordinance of that supreme reason, often dark to us, which governs the course of man's affairs, than that no body of men should in the long run be able to strengthen itself at the cost of others' weakness. The civilisation and freedom of the ancient world were shortlived because they were partial and exceptional.'[31]

Except for this remark, Green's consideration of earlier political philosophers had been destructive. But when he came to Rousseau, his method and tone altered. For in the conception of the general will, Green had long ago found the clue to the problem of political obligation. All that remained was to bring out the essential truth by extricating it from the formula of the social contract. Or so he said. What he really did was to rephrase Rousseau so as to make him appear as a predecessor of Idealism in the form Green gave it.

It was Rousseau's merit to have seen what other members of the social contract school had missed. They had all approached the problem of political obligation in the same way. Their substantive errors followed from this defective method. They never paid sufficient attention to society and its effect upon the development, moral and political of its members. In short, all they saw was a number of individuals regulated by a supreme coercive power. They never apprehended what a true political community is, and thus failed to see how men are made moral by it: the process by which men have been clothed with rights and duties and have come to be conscious of their obligations. Consequently philosophers had defined the issue as though their problem was to reconcile the claims of formed, self-sufficient individuals with those of the political sovereign. When so put, this problem can be dealt with only by representing the individuals governed as consenting to the exercise of government over them. This consent no doubt exists so long as there is no conflict between the individual and government. But the principle of obligation must explain how an individual can feel compelled by his own principles to obey even in the event that his inclination or interest runs counter to that of the government. Such a case cannot be covered by the theories of political obligation just surveyed. So long as government is conducted according to the wishes of its subjects, they consent to it. But this is only to discuss those occasions when there is no interference by the government with the 'natural liberty' of its subjects to do as they like. The test of the theory comes when this liberty is interfered with.

When such conflict occurs, the political philosopher must square the sovereign's right with the natural right of the individual. It is just then that it becomes clear how inadequate is the theory that the right of the sovereign is founded on consent. For it cannot handle issues of conflict. The theory of consent is a fiction which is created to compensate for the original error in the framing of the issue: 'the power which regulates our conduct in political society is conceived in too abstract a way, on the one side, and on the other are set over against it, as the subjects which it controls, individuals invested with all the moral attributes and rights of humanity'. Here Green is repeating the *a priori* argument of the *Prolegomena* and these lectures. Only as members of a society, as recognising common interests and objects, do individuals come to have these moral attributes and rights of humanity. The power, which in a political society they have to obey, is derived from the development and systematisation of those institutions for the regulation of a common life without which they would have no rights at all. This, Green reminds us, is involved by the balance he had argued at such length: without society, no individuals; without individuals, no society.

5

It was in terms of Rousseau and Austin that Green set out his own theory of sovereignty. Rousseau had provided a theory which could do justice to the experience of the citizen: the state is founded on a general will, which is not to be confused with the mere majority, or the will of all. For the general will is always rational and always for the good, however imperfectly actual government may express it. From this will, both outside the individual and within him, he derives his capacity for right, freedom and duty. And Green declared, with his usual kind of pre-emptive claim, the general will provides the only principle by which we can make any sense of the relation between man's self-consciousness and social relations. When rephrased into Idealist concepts and purged of the elements Rousseau had retained from earlier discussions of right, his theory would serve as the cornerstone of Green's own statement of what he understood by sovereignty.

Locke had conceived of the sovereignty of the people as held in reserve after its first exercise in constituting a government. Sovereignty was to be exercised again only if the legislature were false to its trust. Rousseau, in contrast, supposed the sovereignty of the people to be constantly exercised. By its act of organisation the society becomes a sovereign and continues to be so. Rousseau put a new content into the theory of sovereignty. He was not aware that he had done so. He still confused it with the older notion of it as the supreme coercive authority with power to compel obedience. To this legal conception of sovereignty, Rousseau adds the notion of a common will that wills nothing but what is for the common good. But those readers of Rousseau who know only this legal theory will come away with the notion that the essential attribute of sovereignty is the supreme coercive power. And thus they will ignore that attribute of pure disinterestedness which, according to Rousseau, must characterise every act that can be attributed to the sovereign.

Thus Rousseau creates the impression of treating sovereignty in the sense of some power of which it could be reasonably asked how it was established in the part of government where it resides, when and by whom and in what way it is exercised. Yet Rousseau had in mind something essentially different. His idea was what Plato and Aristotle would have said 'is the source of the laws and discipline of the ideal policy, and what a follower of Kant might say of the "pure practical reason", which renders the individual obedient to a law of which he regards himself, in virtue of his reason, as the author, and causes him to treat humanity equally in the person of others and in his own always as an end, never merely as a means'.[32] Yet Rousseau himself thought that he was treating the sovereign just as had other philosophers of the social contract; he did not perceive how incompatible this treatment was with his real innovation—the notion of a supreme and disinterested reason. What he should have done was to have based his case on the conception of the sovereign as entitled to obedience because it represents the general will of the society.

At first glance, there seems to be a considerable gap between Rousseau's and Austin's theories of sovereignty. For Rousseau the essence of sovereignty is the general will; for Austin, the power of a determinate person or persons to put compulsion without limit on its subjects, to make them do exactly what it likes. But the general will cannot be identified with the will of any determinate person or persons. According to Rousseau, it can be expressed only by a vote of the whole body of subject citizens. And even when they have been assembled there is no certainty that their vote does express the general will. Nor does their vote necessarily command any power.

Although these two views seem mutually exclusive, Green treated them as complementary. His own theory of sovereignty rested neither upon consent alone nor upon coercion. The sovereign is habitually obeyed by its subjects because of their feeling that by doing so they secure certain ends. Austin was right both in pointing out the importance of habitual obedience and in asserting that a fully developed state implies a determinate supreme source of law. But the error of Austin was his subsequent assertion, that the essence of sovereignty lies in its power to compel obedience. For if by 'sovereign power' is meant the influences which really make the members of a state obey, then this power must be sought in the general will. The essence of sovereignty is, will not force'.

The source of Green's antagonism to Austin derived, not so much from what Austin said, as from the implications subsequently drawn from that author's work. The Austinians, having found their sovereign, exaggerated its importance and thought the sovereign, with its coercive force, to be the real determinant of the people's habitual obedience. But this is not the case. If we mean by 'sovereign power', the real determinant of the habitual obedience of the people,

> We must look for its sources much more widely and deeply than the 'analytical jurists' do. . . . It can no longer be said to reside in a determinate person or persons, but in that impalpable congeries of of the hopes and fears of a people, bound together by common interests and sympathy, which we call the general will.[33]

Thus Green gave a new definition of sovereignty by treating it in the Hegelian style, in a 'fuller, less abstract sense' as the real determinant of the habitual obedience of the people. This turn in Green's argument is puzzling. Up to this point, his method had been non-empirical, resting upon certain presuppositions or states of mind. But here he treated sovereignty purely phenomenally. Hobhouse quite accurately termed Green's statements on this score as 'propositions . . . rather in social psychology than in metaphysics'.[34]

How can this change in the level of the argument be explained? Possibly because Green thought that even on empirical grounds he could prove Austin wrong. And it was important to do this as convincingly and on as many levels as possible because Austin's work reinforced the popular theory of evolutionary ethics. In the *Prolegomena*, Green described this as professing 'to explain, on the method of a natural history conducted according to the principle of evolution, the process by which the human animal has come . . . to exhibit the phenomena of a moral life'.[35] Its adherents traced the language of moral injunction, of 'ought' and 'ought not', to

> the joint action of two factors—to the habit of submission to the commands of a physical or political superior, surviving the commands themselves and the memory of them, combined with that constant though ineffectual wish for a condition of life other than his own, which is natural to a being who looks before and after over perpetual alternations of pleasure and pain.[36]

On this basis moral and political philosophy is simply abolished.

No propositions involving obligation are worth discussing. 'Ought' must be replaced by 'forced'.[37]

Against this Green argued that the cause of men's obedience is their free recognition that custom, law and institutions embody, however roughly, a notion of right which they share. The legal sovereign does not exercise an unlimited power of compulsion. It is effective only to the extent that it is supported by the subjects' conviction that the government is contributing to the common good. Green quoted with approval a passage from Maine, 'the vast mass of influences which we may call for shortness moral, perpetually shapes, limits or forbids the actual direction of the forces of society by its sovereign'. Maine uses 'moral' for what Green has hitherto called 'the general will'. Thus quite apart from any right of revolution based on the ultimate sovereignty of the people,

> it may be fairly held that the ostensible sovereign . . . is only able to exercise this power in virtue of an assent on the part of the people, nor is this assent reducible to the fear of the sovereign felt by each individual. . . . Let this sense of desire—which may properly be called general will—cease to operate, or let it come into general conflict with the sovereign's commands, and the habitual obedience will cease also.[38]

This remark recalls the conception of a self-regulating principle introduced briefly into the discussion of Locke. This notion is now expanded. There is no doubt that Green took himself to be analysing actual states, for he discussed historical cases such as sovereignty in the Roman Empire, the British rule in India, the Russian Empire. In all of these situations, the sovereign authority was obeyed because it maintained a customary law recognised by the people as in their common interest. Empirically, then, the Austinian theory of sovereignty was inaccurate. The sovereign did not derive his power from coercion.

Green's purpose in this discussion can be understood as disposing of two alternative answers to the question of why men obey: one answer, identified with Austin, is that men obey because of their fear of a supreme power. This is met by Green's assertion that the aggregate influences which make men obey are moral. Another answer is that men obey because they in some sense have consented to laws. This Green denied by pointing out that such a theory cannot explain an obligation to act against personal inclination or interest. Yet this is what we mean when we talk of being obliged to do something.

Green, having eliminated, to his own satisfaction, all alternative explanations, is left with his own. He was sufficiently self-critical to acknowledge that it was not without difficulties, particularly on the question of when, if ever, the individual is justified in resisting his sovereign. This was for him a thorny issue because it raised the problem of how to reconcile what what was worth preserving in the individualist tradition of Liberalism and Protestantism with his Idealist emphasis upon the common good and social recognition of rights. Two questions confronted him: Must not the individual judge for himself whether a law is in the common good? And if he decides that it is not, does he then have the right to resist it? The first issue is the right of private judgment on the part of the citizen, always assuming that he exercises this right on the proper basis (in Green's terms, by judging the law in terms of its effect upon the common good). The answer comes back that certainly every citizen should decide for himself whether a given enactment meets that test. Otherwise he would not be an intelligent and committed citizen obeying laws because they embody rights acknowledged by himself as just.

Suppose that after such an exercise of individual judgment and conscience, the citizen decides that the law violates the common good. He has then to decide how to register his protest. Green thought that in a country such as England, with a popular government and settled methods of enacting and repealing laws, the answer of common sense is quite good enough. The citizen, by legal methods, should do all he can to have the law repealed, but he should not violate it. For the common good would suffer more from resistance to the legal authority than from the individual's conformity to a bad law.

This is, however, not a hard case. Genuine difficulties arise in other circumstances, among which Green discriminates four types: when a law is issued by a sovereign whose legal authority is questionable; when the government is of such a kind that no means short of resistance can be found for obtaining the repeal of the law; when the whole system of law and government is so dominated by private interests hostile to the public that there no longer is any common interest in maintaining it; and when the authority issuing the law is so easily separable from the forces which really maintain public order and rights that this authority may be resisted without danger to order and rights. This fourth instance raises no real issue and may be dismissed without further consideration. In discussing the remaining contingencies, Green, although doing so in an abstract fashion, clearly had in mind American examples dating from the conflict about slavery and the outbreak of the Civil War. If a man belonged to a seceding state, did he not have as much a right to fight for his state as for the Union? This illustrates the difficulty of deciding rights in cases where it is not easy to determine the legitimate sovereign. For all modern states have experienced similar occasions when men have deemed themselves entitled to resist an authority which on its side claimed the right to enforce obedience and turned out actually to be able to do so. Which side was, then, in the right? Somewhat surprisingly, Green decides that in such instances there was nothing amounting to a right on either side. There being no recognition sufficiently general to confer the right of compulsion or resistance, right was in suspense on the point at issue. But then, returning to the case of the citizen of a seceding state in the American Civil War, he makes the remark that although there may not be a right on either side, this does not mean that there is not a better and worse choice on the basis of the probable effects upon the common good. Since the seceding states had a special interest in maintaining slavery, the side of the Union was the one which ought to have been taken.

This lame conclusion derived from the fact that Green's definition of rights was based upon a combination of two criteria and that he has been honest enough to choose an embarrassing instance where only one condition could be met. A right is a power which will, if granted, contribute to the common good, and which is so recognised by the society. Since recognition was here lacking, there was no right, although there was a good and an evil choice. The reader does not know whether to applaud Green's candour in admitting difficulties or to wonder why he thought that he had so improved upon the older natural right philosophers. Probably no political philosophy can deal adequately with exceptional cases by the principles it applies to ordinary ones. But Green thought that he could, on the basis of his argument, make resistance into a right. Thus he actually raised the standard for such a theory and claims that it should provide, not only for a right to resist, but for the duty to do so. Despite the troubles he has himself encountered thus far in the exposition of his doctrine, he once more attacked the writings of the seventeenth and eighteenth centuries. There the question was never put on the right basis. It was not asked when, for the sake of the common good, the citizen ought to resist the sovereign, but what sort of injury to person or property gave him a natural right to resist. But on the ground Green now provided there can be no right to do anything unless it is for the common good, and in such a case there is a duty.

This seems to offer hope for new light on the case of resistance to a despotic government when no law, written or customary, can be appealed to against a command contrary to the public good, when no rival agent of sovereignty exists, and when in the absence of any participation by the people, there is no means of repealing the law by legal means. The duty of resistance, Green tells us, is equally possible for a majority or minority. To oppose a law may be a duty before a majority of citizens so conceives of it; and the fact that a majority does conceive of opposition as a duty does not necessarily make it such. That is, in the first instance there might be a law contrary to the common good; and in the second, there might not. But what of recognition, the other criterion? When this is taken into account, we are told, a presumption is created that 'resistance to a government is not for the public good when made on grounds which the mass of the people cannot appreciate; and it must be on the presence of a strong and intelligent popular sentiment in favour of resistance that the chance of avoiding anarchy . . . must chiefly depend'. Once again the two criteria may produce conflicting judgments. And the possibility of this is increased by still another admission by this author who here appears almost morbidly anxious to produce points damaging to his theory. For 'it is under the worst governments that the public spirit is most crushed; and thus in extreme cases there may be a duty of resistance in the public interest, though there is no hope of the resistance finding efficient public support. (An instance is the Mazzinian outbreaks in Italy.)'[39]

On his own showing, Green concludes that no precise rule can be laid down on just what conditions create the duty to resist a despotic government. He does offer some prudential guides but concedes that they are not likely to be considered in times when revolution is being considered. Indeed the effort to use such yardsticks, he admits, would paralyse the revolutionary's power of action. No critic could make out a better case against using Green's double criterion. Throughout he has been sober and realistic. But he did not demonstrate the superiority of his own principles. Perhaps he should have taken the line that a theory of obligation applicable to the ordinary situations which arise in a constitutional democracy cannot offer guidance in extreme instances. His theory of progress, here, as elsewhere, a barrier to realism, led him to believe that revolutionary situations were not likely to arise again.

Earlier, when writing on Cromwell and the Puritans, he had displayed some sympathy for a tragic or demonic view of history. He had asserted that Cromwell had been motivated by unselfish enthusiasm, but that this quality was perfectly consistent with 'the imputation to him of such unscrupulousness, violence, simulation and dissimulation, sins which no one has escaped who ever led or controlled a revolution'.[40] Green's philosophy of history is worth consideration at this point because he himself attempts to save his theory of rights and obligation by resorting to his theodicy: the assertion that in proportion to the amount of good citizenship in any political movement, whether in rebellion or in more peaceful times, there will be a good result of that movement. One way of putting the point is that there is no better way of proceeding in politics than by consulting the criterion of the common good; another, and the author's language indicates its theological quality, is the following: ' . . . we can only fall back on the generalisation that the best man—the man most disinterestedly devoted to the perfecting of humanity . . .—is more likely to act in a way that is good as measured by its results, those results again being estimated with reference to an ideal of character. . . .'[41]

This argument occurs at the end of the chapter called 'Sovereignty and the General will'. It is a vindication of good citizenship defined in terms of devotion to the common good and represents a reassertion at this critical place of the philosophy of history found in his theology and ethics. In the next chapter, perhaps the best known in his lectures, Green is arguing not only that 'Will, not Force, is the Basis of the State', but also that devotion to the common good, produces beneficient political results, while devotion to selfish interest can, despite appearances, produce only the contrary result. To this engagement to demonstrate that from good comes good and from evil evil, Green devotes most of a chapter which is ostensibly on another point. And the argument changes from the empirical level, at which it had been pursued for a time, back to that of *a priori* assertions about the nature of the state. For what is involved in claiming that will is the basis of the state is Green's secular religion of citizenship, with its teaching of altruism and its prescription of self-sacrifice to duty. His view of the world depends on the idea of God, as a spiritual principle, realising himself in the establishment of obligations by law and authoritative custom and the gradual recognition of moral duties by individuals. In this scheme the idea of the common good plays a crucial rôle. Green makes it into the criterion of political obligation. He contends that this idea progressively realises itself in history. Hence he is committed to a theodicy indicating the general implications of his conception of the common good. How all these notions are related to political obligation, as Green defined it, may be seen from the passage with which he closed his lectures on that subject:

I am properly *obliged* to those actions and forbearances which are necessary to the general freedom, necessary if each is not to interfere with the realisation of another's will. My *duty* is to be interested positively in my neighbour's well-being. And it is important to understand that, while the enforcement of obligations is possible, that of moral duties is impossible. But the establishment of obligation by law or authoritative custom, and the gradual recognition of moral duties have not been separate processes. They have gone on together in the history of man. The growth of the institutions by which more complete equality of rights is gradually secured to a wider range of persons, and of those interests in various forms of social well-being by which the will is moralised, have been related to each other as the outer and inner side of the same spiritual development. . . . The result of the twofold process has been the creation of the actual content of morality.[42]

Thus Green argues that to promote the common good is the essential characteristic of a state. He asserts further that such an idea has been a determining element in the consciousness of even the most selfish men who have been instrumental in the formation or maintenance of states. Napoleon did good to the extent that in seeking his own ends he had to further those of the French Revolution. 'His selfishness gave a particular character to his pursuit of these ends, and (so far as it did so) did so for evil.' 'Caesar again we have learnt to regard as a benefactor of mankind, but it was not Caesar that made the Roman law, through which chiefly or solely the Roman Empire became a blessing.'[43] The assertion, then, that an idea of social good is realised in the formation of states is not to be met by the selfishness and bad passions of men who have been instrumental in forming them.

In this way, Green established to his own satisfaction that the idea of the common good provides the basis of the state. The fact that the state implies a supreme coercive power has produced the erroneous view that coercion is its essence. Actually just the reverse is true. There can be a supreme coercive power only because it is recognised by citizens as serving a proper function. A state is not to be defined as an aggregate of individuals under a sovereign but as a society in which the rights of man are defined and harmonised. Thus the state does not create rights but gives fuller reality to rights already existing. A state presupposes other forms of community with the rights that arise out of them, and exists only in sustaining, securing and completing them. Once the state has come into existence, new rights arise in it. It leads to a further moral development of man. The citizen can claim rights but only those which are contributory to some social good which the public conscience is capable of appreciating.

The terminology used here is worth some attention. For one thing, Green was the first to use the notion of the 'state' in its German sense; for another, he gave 'society' an interpretation which persisted for a long time as the tool of analysis used by English philosophers when they speculated about matters which today would fall within the domain of anthropology or sociology. Both terms were laden with values and used in a technical sense unknown to ordinary discourse or even international law: 'It is not, however, supreme coercive power simply as such, but supreme coercive power exercised in a certain way and for certain ends, that makes a state; namely, exercised according to law, written or customary, and for the maintenance of rights'.[44]

If a sovereign's power is exercised neither according to a formal constitution nor to customs which are the equivalent of a constitution it no longer maintains rights and thus ceases to be a state. Czarist Russia Green considered to be a state only by courtesy on the supposition that the Czar's power, although not subject to a constitution, was exercised in accordance with what the society recognised as the common good.

This attempt by Green to incorporate the concept of constitutionalism into his philosophical theory of the state is somewhat curious. For although he was here dealing with a most significant aspect of English politics, one which he himself valued highly, the fit between actual constitutional practice and his philosophical notion of recognition was not too good. Presumably, whatever a society recognises as consonant with the common good is legitimate from Green's viewpoint. But such sanctioned usages might include the exercise of power by the sovereign without any limitation by law, written or unwritten. Recognition cannot, therefore, be used as an equivalent for constitutionalism. Green's attempt to attach his own value preferences to the concept of 'state' appears to have been an unhappy innovation. From more than one point of view, it was inferior even to the notoriously unsatisfactory schemes of classification found in classical political philosophers, for they at least recognised that there exist different types of government, each with a distinctive constitution and type of laws. Not all governments are constitutional in the sense that their rulers are actually limited by known and operative rules. Indeed, as Montesquieu remarked, some governments could not survive the introduction of constitutional procedures. Perhaps Green attempted to re-introduce the distinction between legitimate and vitiated governments by reserving the term 'state' for legitimate governments alone. But this seems to have been somewhat indiscriminately combined with the notion that modern governments are qualitatively different from those which have existed in the past. When such modern governments are also constitutional and maintain the rights of their citizens, they may be called 'states'. It is perhaps worth noting here that subsequent theorists who attempted to use something like Green's categories found they had to modify his terminology. Thus Lord Lindsay was to speak of the theory of the 'Modern Democratic State', rather than of states as such, and to imply that there is another theory of the medieval state, and still another of the Greek city-state.[45] But Green himself seems to have thought that there was but one ideal type of state for which all previous human political development was a preparation. No doubt this mode of thought, although not the form Green gave to it, was Hegelian in origin.

The notion of the 'concrete universal' found in Hegel cannot be paraphrased in mere prose, for it involves both an abstract idea of the state and the growing approximations to that idea allegedly found in actual historical development. Thus there is a systematic ambiguity about all Idealist uses of the concept of the state which Green did not escape. Most often he reserved this name for those governments which fulfil the full range of purposes which are said to characterise this form of human organisation. This was an application to politics of the teleology he had declared to be a necessary part of any moral theory and combined with his position that the common good is the goal of the state. 'A state is made a state by the functions which it fulfils of maintaining the rights of its members as a whole or a system, in such a way that none gains at the expense of another.'[46] Professor Sabine has remarked that this definition was a great source of confusion: 'before the Idealists no English thinker had used the word in any special sense or indeed had made any common use of it at all'.[47] Even at the time Green apparently felt a twinge of doubt about the special meaning he gave to this term, and announced that he would consider the claims of any other word which would carry the same weight. But, he insisted, what was needed was a word to differentiate that modern type of organisation having a systematic law to harmonise whatever rights are recognised, in addition to possessing a power strong enough to protect the society from disturbance within and aggression from outside. Before the state came into being, there existed societies of men already possessing rights, whose dealings with each other had been recognised by custom.

What Green understands by society may be inferred from his statement that a state presupposes other forms of community with the rights which arise out of them. The state sustains, secures, completes and harmonises these rights. And in time it leads to a moral development of men to a point beyond what they could have attained outside it. This process should not obscure the fact that, in order to make the state, there must have been families the members of which recognised in each other powers necessary for the fulfilment of the common good. These families must have been joined together in some larger unit, such as a tribe which acknowledged the rights of its members, and then proceeded, since the recognition of a right is not yet a definition of it, to formulate a general law specifying and reconciling claims. When such a law has been voluntarily recognised by a community of families or tribes and is maintained by a power strong enough to enforce it within the community and to protect it from external agression, then the elementary state has been formed. This is hypothetical history, conjectures alleged to be true *a priori*.

Thus far Green seems to define society in terms not very different from those used in Aristotle's politics.[48] But Green's theory of rights adds the notion of mutual recognition to Aristotle's teleological view of the *polis* as embodying the common good of its members. The state for Green is the form which society takes in order to maintain rights. Such a definition raises problems when applied to actual states. How, for example, could it be applied to the United States before the Civil War? Was not slavery legal? Did not the power of the state punish anyone attempting to free slaves from the restrictions which denied them rights otherwise universally conceded to citizens? Did not deprivations of this kind constitute a violation of the slave's rights against the state?

To these questions which he put to himself, Green answered that it is meaningless to speak of rights except in a society where men consciously recognise reciprocal claims. Yet it must not be forgotten that actual states at best fulfil but partially their ideal function. Thus it is possible that rights derived from social relationships are violated by the laws of the state. These rights ' . . . arise out of the fact that there is a consciousness of objects common to the slave with those among whom he lives—whether other slaves or the family of his owner—and that this consciousness constitutes at once a claim on the part of each of those who share it to exercise a free activity conditionally upon his allowing a like activity in the others, and a recognition of this claim by the others through which it is realised'.[49] Already the slave, within limits, acts and is treated as a member of a society. In principle this is the same capability as that required to live with any other human beings, provided that there is supplied whatever training may be needed. If the state denies the slave not only the right to citizenship but the means of training his capability for citizenship, it violates his right founded on actual social relations between him and others.

Here, we are told, there may be a conflict between existing social relations and the state. Yet Green maintains that for the member of a state to say that his rights derive from his social relations and to say that they derive from his position as a member of the state is one and the same thing. The state regulates and harmonises rights. The other forms of community which precede the state neither continue to exist outside it, nor are they superseded by it. They continue within it, but attain a new fullness as they come into the harmony produced by its action. Thus the citizen cannot properly claim a right against the state as natural rights theorists would do. No one can make such a claim except as a member of a society, and the state is for its members 'the society of societies, the society in which all their claims upon each other are mutually adjusted'.[50]

Where does this leave the citizen who regards the laws of his state as unjust because violating the rights of some who live within it? Does this mean that he, under no conditions, has the right to disobey? To these questions Green replies as he had earlier in considering the justifiability of resistance to an ostensible sovereign. Again there is no clear-cut answer. The state may be disobeyed only for the purpose of making its actual laws correspond more closely with its inherent tendency and idea—the reconciler and sustainer of the rights arising out of men's social relations. Green is in the curious position of defining the state in terms of its idea, while admitting that this idea is never in fact completely realised. Thus he explicitly denies the Hegelian version of the Idealist theory. If the state fulfils its ideal function, the individual would be obliged to regard its laws as having absolute authority. But since this is never the case, the unconditional obedience to the state demanded by Hegel is inappropriate. The principle that a citizen should never act otherwise than as a citizen does not carry with it the obligation to obey the law of his state in any and all conditions. Disobedience must be based on an acknowledged social good. Whether a citizen chooses to claim a right by obeying or disobeying the law is a matter of circumstances. A citizen may properly attempt to repeal laws which prohibit the instruction of slaves or assisting runaways; but although there is always a presumption in favour of obedience even to bad laws, the public interest may be best served by violating an existent law. Such was the case when the public conscience recognised that slaves had a capacity for right which was being denied them because a powerful class in its own interest resisted any alteration of the law. And because of such recognition, there was no danger that disobedience will create a breach in popular obedience to law.

But what if no recognition of the implicit rights of the slave can be elicited from the public conscience? Has the citizen still a right to disregard these legal prohibitions? Green, who has been wavering throughout this discussion, once again takes an unexpected position. In the absence of recognition, the right of helping the slave may be cancelled by the duty of obeying the prohibitory law. This, he is prepared to say, would be the case if the violation of the law in the interest of the slave were liable to produce general anarchy. 'Such a destruction of the state would mean a general loss of freedom, a general substitution of force for mutual good-will in men's dealings with each other, that would outweigh the evil of any slavery under such limitations and regulations as an organised state imposes on it.'[51]

How should this treatment of rights be assessed? Does it really repay the inconvenience involved in dropping ordinary language in favour of Green's way of phrasing these issues? These are the questions raised by Green himself, both in criticising other theorists and in applying his own concepts.

6

Few philosophers in England and the United States now feel it necessary to base moral and political philosophy upon 'metaphysical foundations' which imply the use of synthetic propositions *a priori*, teleological assumptions about the nature of man and insight into the direction of history. But even if Green's method were not generally judged to be discredited on technical grounds, it would be suspect. For when applied to political philosophy, it led to the conclusion that the principles at work in society and the state, the assumptions upon which civil institutions have been founded and maintained, were simply identical with his own preferences. It is impossible to accept at face value any intellectual procedure which claims to demonstrate that every one of its author's values is derived from the nature of reality. Indeed the generalisations Green claimed to have drawn from meticulous analysis of knowledge and its conditions seem in part fanciful. What to him were indubitable postulates of reason now appear to be the result of wishful thinking. Such were the assertions that moral progress is a law of human history and that force is a mere survival destined to play an increasingly negligible part in domestic and international politics. Surely it was an act of faith, even in his time, to believe that the outcome of political conflict is always determined by the moral quality of those involved, and that destruction awaits any government attempting to alter by violence the basic law of its people or to exploit a part of its population. Green's method made it easy for him to confuse value with fact, ideal with reality. The ideals themselves were worth defending, but Green was distracted by the pressure to find an unassailable basis for belief away from the rigour which he himself thought the first requirement of the philosopher. Had he been content to analyse the ideas and procedures actually operative in society and politics, more of his conclusions would be taken seriously. In short, had he been willing to settle for less, he might have achieved more. His philosophical style only made his work less accessible to the sort of reader he cared most to reach; it did not make his ideas invulnerable to the technical criticism of other philosophers.

Perhaps the most striking change Green proposed for the consideration of Liberals was the central place and supreme value he assigned to the theory of the common good. This notion had long been associated in the minds of middle-class Englishmen with mercantilism as described and condemned by Adam Smith. That it might have moral value, that it need not be the rationale of *raison d'état* and aristocratic privilege, that it might be achieved by conscious thought and state action rather than by the invisible hand and voluntary agency—these were not familiar ideas to the followers of Gladstone and Bright. If forced to state what they believed to constitute the crucial difference between those orders of a government which were legitimate from those which were not, Liberals were still most apt to answer by some version of Locke's theory of consent: Citizens ought to obey those laws, and only those laws, to which they or their representatives have consented. Green argued that the proper Liberal view is that governments ought to be obeyed to the extent that they do or do not promote a good common to all those subject to their commands. This they cannot do directly, but only by removing obstacles to self-realisation.

It was in the *Prolegomena to Ethics* that Green presented his reasons for believing in the reality of the common good and its progressive realisation in history. The substance of that argument need not be rehearsed here. It forms part of Green's continuing effort to prove we must postulate the real existence of a good common to all the members of any given society. Otherwise we cannot account for the willing sacrifice by individuals of a personal interest to something conceived of by them as a superior good for other members of their group, whether small and immediate, as in the case of their family, or large and more remote, as in the case of their nation-state. Two types of criticism may be made of Green's position: the first, linguistic, dealing with the terms of his analysis and their use; the second, in his conception of obligation, his definition of the fundamental concepts of moral and political philosophy.

If we examine Green's central notion apart from his *a priori* statement of it, he turns out to have confused the use of the word 'common' in the two phrases 'common end' and 'common good'. Men may co-operate on occasions when they happen to share particular ends, but this proves nothing about the existence of a single good common to them all. An end is not common to different persons in the sense of being a state of each of their minds, but only in the sense of being related to similar states of each of their minds. And the end which they share coincidentally may be the result of the working in them of any one of a number of desires. Thus Green 'failed to distinguish a common end which is a private good from a common good, and he failed to do so because he did not properly analyse the meaning of his words'.[52] Moore was right in his criticism of the carelessness with which Idealists used language. If Green's writings are examined in detail for clues to what he meant by the 'common good', some bewildering synonyms emerge. It appears to have been Green's disciple, D. G. Ritchie, who first pointed out that while Green in his ethics used 'self-satisfaction' or 'self-realisation' as the equivalent of the highest good, in his writings on politics the term 'common good' is most frequently employed in that same sense.[53] Even as a criterion for moral goodness, 'self-realisation' is a concept which leaves much to be desired; as a criterion for the goodness of political arrangements and as a synonym for the 'common good', it will not do. At one point in his ethics, Green wrote :'To anyone actuated by it the idea of a perfection, of a state in which he shall be satisfied, for himself will involve the idea of a perfection of all other beings, so far as he finds the thought of their being perfect necessary to his own satisfaction'.[54] Such language does not appear to describe accurately all moral action, or even what is regarded as its most commendable type of manifestation. 'A mother pursues the good of her children neither as a means to her own self-satisfaction, nor just "so far as" she finds the thought of their well-being essential to it.' Her own well-being has little to do with her action. The actual well-being of the children is what she aims at, not the idea of her own self-satisfaction.[55]

All such difficulties with 'self-realisation' or 'self-satisfaction' as a theory of the form taken by moral action are compounded when these notions are applied to politics and identified with the 'common good'. For here Green's strong inclination to deny the possibility of conflict among duties is particularly unfortunate. Nothing is more common in politics than cases when 'self-realisation' is incompatible with the 'common good', when these terms are interpreted by the actors themselves rather than by philosophers who suppress the conflict by using *a priori* definitions. By the use of a technical definition of freedom as mastery over impulse or passion, Green tends to gloss over the degree of repression which may be called for in the name of the common good. As one who took his notion of the good as much from the Evangelicals and Puritans as from his philosophical sources, Green found it easy to applaud curbs placed upon instinct and passion. He ignored the possibility that psychological damage may be caused to the individual by the imposition of his community's standards. Green's moral ideal contained an uncritically high evaluation of ascetic altruism. But to equate self-sacrifice with self-realisation is a dubious use of language. No doubt some degree of discipline and sacrifice is always demanded, and properly so, from a mature adult who acknowledges any moral obligation other than self-indulgence. Yet can it be said that there is any presumption in favour of abnegation as such? Freud, who did not disregard the need for discipline, saw the issue rather more clearly than did Green. For Freud speculated that there will always be an irresolvable conflict between man's instinctual desires and the controls imposed by his society, the values of which are accepted by him and made part of himself. This conflict, by its repressions and frustrations, demands a heavy toll from even those who apparently are unscathed. An example drawn from politics is to be found in the telling evocation by R. H. S. Crossman of the dinner tendered Mr Krushchev in 1957 by the National Executive of the Labour Party. On that occasion the Soviet leader harangued his hosts in a display of his great personal power:

> 'What impressed me most about Khrushchev was his uncomplicated energy. He behaved like a bull in the full flood of its virility, surrounded by a herd of castrated oxen. And in a sense that is just what he is. For one of the main achievements of Western democracy is to castrate the brutal ambitions of the natural leader, to inhibit his natural readiness to rely on violence, and teach him to fulfil the frustrating task of a public servant instead of becoming by violence the public's master.'[56]

There is a significant point being made here. For it does not matter whether one's sympathies are on the side of an authority requiring a sacrifice regarded as legitimate (as in the case of Crossman) or on the side of the exceptional leaders' will to power (as in the case of

Nietzsche). What must not be forgotten is that in every instance of repression a price has to be paid, a loss suffered, a disharmony created which cannot be regarded as a good *per se*. In all such cases, it must be asked whether the repression called for is justified by the good which is alleged to follow from it. More repression may be demanded than can be justified. Neither sacrifice nor satisfaction are goods in themselves, and the defect in Green's theory is that he makes it impossible to confront the issues involved in such conflict because he has postulated an identity between self-realisation (defined as the invariable victory of will over impulse) and the common good.

Green's secularised asceticism is equally evident in his insistence that self-sacrificing citizenship was the obligation placed upon all conscientious men. Latent in this view was the assumption that human activity may be considered good only when it produces some improvement of character commensurate with the common good. In short, there are no purely personal and non-social goods. Intellectual and artistic work is of value only when it aids other men. Green was so much influenced by his indigenous Evangelical tradition and German philosophical emphasis upon duty, that he here committed one of his great deviations from liberal individualism. That school had maintained that men should be allowed to do what they wish with their lives provided that they do not interfere with a like freedom for others. But for this philosopher, the investigation of truth for its own sake, the creative activity of the composer, painter and performer, could not be placed among the unequivocal goods of human life. In a well-known passage in his *Prolegomena to Ethics*, he spoke of his time as being one in which there was no excuse for enjoying the pleasures of eye or ear or those of abstract and not immediately productive thought, so long as the mass of men were denied the opportunity of realising their potentialities.[57] The nature of the claim of other men upon an individual seemed clear to Green: 'It is a claim for service in the direction of making more generally possible those recognised virtues and excellences which rest upon the will to be perfect. Neither a man's inclination nor his talent is as important as the common good. 'In some Italian principality of the last century, for instance, with its civil life crushed out and its moral energies debased, excellence in music could hardly be accounted of actual and present value at all. . . . Under such conditions much occupation with music might imply indifference to claims of the human soul which must be satisfied. . . .' In less extreme circumstances, the question of interest to the moral man is: 'Has he talent to serve mankind—to contribute to the perfection

257

of the human soul—more as a musician than in any other way? Only if he has will he be justified in making music his main pursuit.' Music is to be justified as a human activity only if there are no prior claims. In that case, it may be pursued because of 'that intrinsically valuable lifting up of the soul' which music affords.[58]

Quite apart from the question of whether Green can at the same time call music 'intrinsically valuable' and yet suggest that it is properly pursued only after more important matters are taken care of, the modern reader may wonder about this aspect of Green's moral and political ideal. For it is by no means self-evident that the autonomy of the individual should always be subordinated to the welfare of the larger community. Although Green saw the necessity of safeguarding the individual in his sphere of political freedom, his morality was of the sort well described by Matthew Arnold as the Hebraism and Philistinism of English dissent. Although it is understandable how such ascetic altruism may appear to be morally superior to hedonism, yet it may be questioned whether Green rated private pleasures sufficiently highly. His Evangelical sensibility sometimes blinded him to the possibility of purely innocent and individual pursuits which need no social justification.

Green thought that he had hit upon an unassailable definition of the common good when he identified it with the realisation of a certain type of character. He did not appreciate the danger of allowing a government to aim consciously at the creation of a particular kind of human being. In part, his lack of perception was due to a very different historical experience than that of the twentieth century; in part, to the technical difficulties of the notion of 'self-realisation'. This, when used as a political ideal, can be dangerous either when it is defined vaguely or precisely. When conceived in Green's terms, as a moral least common denominator of what decent people really think when they measure their claims against those of others in relation to the common good, then surely what emerges is too loose a notion to be of any practical use. If, on the other hand, if the real self is defined in quite precise and exclusive terms, it may become the vehicle of a monistic and coercive view, determined either by an élite or by a dominating majority. This possibility appeared in Green's treatment of the propriety of restricting, by state action, the sale of intoxicating liquors. For in his view, such sale does manifestly interfere with the development of that type of character which it is the goal of society to create. It is true that he ultimately conceded that the actual enactment of legislation should not occur until this point of view is generally recognised. But 'recognition' is a vague concept in Green's work, and it has already been seen how he was unable to reconcile it with the notion that there are rights which ought to be granted, even though in fact the state in its laws does not recognise them. Green never satisfactorily justified his teleological approach to politics. His exposure to Aristotle as teacher and student led him to think that he could isolate and utilise that ideal of human character he thought to be immanent in Western society. But is there indeed any one ideal upon which a free and secular society may agree? Should we not, within limits, treasure diversities of human type rather than attempt to place premiums upon one variety of character? Certainly every society must, in the final analysis, decide certain questions which might be regarded as involving the deliberate reward or punishment for certain dispositions—such as the definitions of what constitute crime, pathological behaviour, obscene expression and the like. But all such matters are more safely decided piecemeal and in the light of particular circumstances rather than by some prior philosophical determination of an ideal type of character.

This discussion has been concerned with the question of whether Green was justified in urging that the concept of the common good may safely be equated with that of 'self-realisation'. The conclusion is that he was not. But even if he had been able to escape from vagueness and ambiguity in his treatment of the 'common good', strong doubts would remain about the utility of this concept, particularly as the keystone of a political theory. In the history of political thought in the West, no position is more orthodox than that the just ruler ought to seek the good. And in this effort his authority ought to be exercised, not in the interest of himself or his class, but in that of the entire community. Although this ideal has been widely accepted, it has proved to be almost impossible to apply in practice. The notion has become part of political rhetoric: antagonists claim that their party is seeking the common good while another is not. But what are the elements of that good which is common to all the members of a modern nation-state? There is no meaningful consensus, except perhaps that defence of its territory against alien invasion, preservation of internal order and the maintenance of a reasonably impartial system of justice are generally, if not universally, recognised as benefits enjoyed by all members of a political society. As for Green's own use of the concept of the common good, it is relatively unambiguous only when he uses it in the way made familiar in English politics by Bentham, Cobden and Bright. A state is not being properly ruled while 'it is not fulfilling its primary function of maintaining law equally in the interest of all but is being administered in the interests of classes. . . .'[59] No doubt moral disapproval is an appropriate judgment against the members of a régime which rules in such a way that they alone benefit. But such flagrant cases of self-serving present no problem. It is rather more usual for the citizen to be confronted with mixed cases in which the good of a ruling group is also a good of one or more other groups, or is claimed to be. In all disagreements among groups about the relation of the government to their separate interests, any specific determination of the common good is almost impossible to come by. Thus, both as an abstract ideal and as a criterion of actual governments, the notion of the common good is of dubious value. It is a poor starting point for a complex political theory, for it cannot sustain the weight Green placed upon it.

The terms Green chose to use in his analysis of politics and society served neither his own investigations nor those who followed him, for he introduced into English political philosophy words which were as vague as they were unprecedented. When he spoke of the 'state', he meant to convey both the conception of an ideal, unattained condition of a political order, and the organisation of actual governments which aim at that ideal. But he should not have attempted to naturalise this technical term in the sense which had made its fortune in German, and to relate it to 'society', without specifying how and why his usage differed from Hegel's. For in some passages he implies that his own view resembles Hegel's in considering the state as harmonising the interests and ideals of society, a work which society itself would be incapable of performing; in others, he implies that the relationships already existing in society are the standard for the laws of the state. Indeed, as in his case of slaves denied their rights, it would seem that resistance to the state is justified if it violates claims recognised in society. Which of these two concepts is meant to carry the higher authority in case of conflict between them we are not told.

Nor was this usage any more fortunate in its application to relations among nations. Every state *qua* state, we are told, enforces rights and obligations as defined in relation to its underlying purpose. And the moral purpose of states are not qualitatively different. They vary only in the extent to which they apply the same standard and realise the same moral ideal. All men have the same moral purpose and so too have their political associations when they fulfil their proper function. Thus Green could argue in his treatment of international politics that there is nothing in the nature of the state which makes war inevitable in a system of nation-states.[60] It is only deviations from that nature which create war and, since no existing state truly realises all the ideal attributes of its idea, international conflict may be explained by certain survivals from forms of political organisation which preceded the state. All this creates the curious necessity of applying, in the event of hostilities, the term of 'non-state' to what in peace are considered as 'states'. There is also a possibility, which Green does not touch upon, that in a war between a state and a non-state, all the right, from his point of view, could be said to fall on the side of the state.

Green's way of thinking contains some implications of which he was not aware and rests upon assumptions he never explored. His conception of states was founded on the belief that since they harmonise goods within their respective societies, they cannot conflict among themselves. For they all have the same aim. But it is evident now, and it was evident in Green's time, if all human societies have some hierarchy of goods, that the good regarded as of supreme value has varied enormously from place to place and from period to period. Green's way of accounting for such variations was his philosophy of history. Following Hegel, he eliminated from consideration societies outside the essentially European and Christian tradition on the ground that they were not truly progressive and thus 'historical'. Secondly, he attempted to prove a progressive evolution within western societies which would account for all variations in the conception of the good acknowledged as common as well as for the number of persons to whom consequent rights and duties were regarded as applying. From the beginning, there had been agreement on what constituted the common good and, essentially, its content has never regressed. Such apparent differences as exist among societies and periods may all be subsumed under two forms of historical progress: the addition of new virtues to those already included in the common good, and the gradual extension of the numbers of persons to whom this improved version of the good is applied. Human societies are thus divided into the progressive and non-progressive; and the progressive societies vary according to phase or stage. The ideal of the common good is increasingly embodied in their actual institutions and all apparent exceptions to progress, such as war, may be attributed to survivals from an earlier phase. Thus Green made a full-scale attempt to prove not just that states aim at some common good (which may be anything at all), but that they aim at the same good, in one or another of its progressive manifestations. Implicit in this theory of history is the distinction between Western and Christian societies which are progressive, and all the others which are not. It is an irony that Green, so strong a Little

Englander and anti-imperialist, should have made such a distinction.

Another aspect of his philosophy of history was his theory of progress. He would not have been willing to admit that a society could ever regress, that it might recall rights once granted or restrict the number of those treated as full members of the society. For he not only accepted the Christian ethic in a generalised and secularised version but he thought it to constitute the goal towards which human history has been moving. His teleology is built into his philosophy of history, and progress too was declared to be true *a priori*. Thus it seemed simply impossible to him that in such states as Germany, Western Europe and the United States, that there could ever occur any substantial curtailment of rights. Like Emile Durkheim, he would have thought that if a state disregards the rights of individuals:

> Could we not correct it with authority by reminding it that the rights of the individual are so closely bound to the structure of the great European societies and our whole mentality that to deny them, under the pretext of social interest is to deny the essential interests of society itself.[61]

As in the case of his belief that force would play an increasingly smaller part in human affairs, Green's belief in progress makes melancholy reading after the two world wars and totalitarian experiences of the twentieth century. For it was Germany, whose thinkers he so much admired, which was to demonstrate how erroneous was his view of human history and how government may be organised on principles more dreadful than Green ever imagined possible.

How adequate was the theory of rights presented in his work? It is not unfair to say that all the unresolved difficulties in Green's theory of the common good recur in his treatment of rights. For he attempted to shift the basis for rights from the theory of consent used by natural rights theorists to his own version of the common good. And he introduced the Idealist notion of social and conscious recognition as an essential ingredient of rights. A right is a claimed power which should be granted if it promotes a good common to all those within a given political society. More: this power must be perceived as so doing by the members of the society, or be implied by existing practices and relationships themselves recognised as legitimate. Professor Sabine has rephrased this point in its most plausible form: 'A moral community . . . is one in which the individual responsibly limits his claims to freedom in the light of general social interests and in which the community itself supports its claims because the general well-being can be realised only through his initiative and freedom.'[62] Green neither wished to gain recognition for new rights, nor to discard those already in force, but rather to provide a more adequate account of the process actually operative in communities such as his own, and in citizens such as himself. It may be doubted whether, for all his criticism of J. S. Mill's work, a list of substantive rights Green himself believed in would have differed much from a similar one drawn up by Mill. But Green thought that his own system could provide a rationale of these rights which was consistent with itself in a way not open to Mill. Was this in fact the case?

When Green's own analysis of particular cases was examined earlier, it turned out that the two criteria he prescribed did not always yield the same result. A claimed power may in fact contribute to some good common to all the members of a society, but not be acknowledged; again, such a power may be implied by existing social relationships, but to resist existing laws which deny the claim, may demonstrably produce results inimical to the good of the society as a whole. Nor is Green's account of 'recognition' sufficiently clear. In ordinary instances, he tells us, regular legislative practice in a constitutional state is quite good enough as an indication of what is recognised. But, as we know, it is not an ordinary instance that provokes genuine bewilderment or conflict about the status of a right. Neither majority nor minority views are necessarily decisive in such a case, and so we must look at existing social relationships. Here Green's account of a slave in a society which otherwise grants full rights to all its members again seems unrevealing. The slave, by having a full, human relation to some persons such as his family, is said to have demonstrated his right to be a member of the larger community, which is thus obliged to recognise his claim. But has not 'recognition' been transformed here from the criterion of right into a process itself considered to be subject to a higher standard? This is to assert that some rights are tacitly, but not legally, recognised. And what constitutes tacit social recognition? The existence, we are told, among men of relationships which imply certain rights. Those individuals who do in fact enjoy them may not deny them to others without denying the basis of their own claim. But surely this is to introduce a question of logic into what previously has been defined as a matter of fact. What if slave-owners fail to recognise their slaves' claim to rights? In the presence of conflicting views about which rights ought to be recognised, who will decide what are the rights immanent in the existing social system?

Green, without realising it, was sliding from a formal to a substantive argument. What he considered as rights resembled those granted to English subjects in his own time. But he thought that the concept of recognition, in his Idealist form, could account for and justify those rights. Because every man wishes to be granted certain claims he acknowledges similar claims on the part of others. The number and quality of such acknowledgments are always to some extent registered in the legislation of the state, and ought to be even when they are not. But what ground is there for believing that the claims in fact recognised by individuals and society will in any way resemble those rights actually granted by governments Green regarded as legitimate? To the extent that he confronted the issue at all, he did so through his philosophy of history. Strictly speaking, a theory of rights, defined purely as socially acknowledged claims, says nothing about their content. If the members of a society recognised cannibalism as a practice, not only justified but mandatory in certain circumstances, no one using Green's criterion would have a right to object to being eaten under such specified conditions. Indeed, as in Hegel's illustration of his own theory of punishment, a person who was treated otherwise than by the recognised usage of the society might properly complain that he was being treated as something less than a full member of it.

Nothing could be more certain than that Green would have repudiated any practices substantially at variance with the values of his own society. Yet on the basis of recognition alone, he could not have excluded what he manifestly would have wished to exclude. Nor is this the worst which can be said about Green's theory. For it is simply inconsistent with itself. It is impossible to reconcile the assertion that rights are such only when socially recognised, with the contrary view that there exist rights which ought to be granted, whether or not they are in fact recognised. Green's effort to maintain his philosophical position helped to lead him astray here. As an Idealist, he felt compelled to maintain his well-known maxim that there is no right but thinking makes it so. This is, as Mr Plamenatz has pointed out, a version of the dictum '*esse est percipi*'.[63] There appears to be no reason to assume that something does not exist if it is not the subject of conscious attention. On Green's own showing, a slave ignorant of the doctrine of rights and denied them by his masters, nevertheless is capable of them. When he criticised theories already in the field, he did so on the assumption that his own method alone was valid, and by displaying how impossible it was to apply these other tests. Yet, after developing his own, he proceeds to qualify them until they lost both their original consistency with his system and whatever sharpness of definition they once had. Yet it was in these respects that Green's treatment of the subject was meant to improve it. While his reader may admit the evident candour and practicality displayed in the concessions, he may remain unconvinced that 'metaphysical foundations' are necessary or even useful in political philosophy. Certainly Green did not himself meet the standards by which he criticised his predecessors in the field.

Everything which has already been said about his theory of rights applies equally well to that of obligation. When ought a subject to obey his sovereign? When ought he to resist commands and on what basis? Here again Green's proposals for the sort of dialogue which a conscientious citizen might carry out with himself or others is excellent as a list of difficulties to be explored, but remains inconclusive as answers to them. He himself admits that his theory *qua* theory does not resolve the contradictions or remove the doubts confronting the actor in an extreme situation. Indeed, at one place, Green concedes that the very effort to perform the sort of analysis he recommended would probably paralyse the actor in his effort to reach a decision. Again, the reader may conclude that possibly there is no help which the philosopher can render beyond analysing the alternatives and assessing their likely consequences in relation to the actor's goals. To clarify possible courses of action, to discredit loose thinking and dubious argument —these are not small services in such situations. But it is no good pretending that any philosophical reasoning can eliminate the pull of conflicting loyalties, which characterise those occasions when men must choose between an established government and its revolutionary rival. Some modern 'crisis philosophers' have attempted to construct theories resting upon the assumption that extreme situations are the paradigm of human experience; Green's thought is predicated on the opposite view, which denies the significance of such situations. Surely this attitude stemmed from a religious need. For, in one part of his mind, he knew well enough that political life abounds in conflict of duties and in situations where neither right nor advantage to the common good are easily decided. From his own civic experience he was acquainted with the fact that decisions must often be made, not on the basis of some substantial and indubitable good, but rather as the result of calculating a merely marginal advantage, which is the best which can be made out of things as they are. But he had invested citizenship with a moral sanction and an urgency which brooked no qualification. In fact his political philosophy was less an analysis of English political life than a vision of what it might be.

Green's philosophical work thus may be regarded as an abstract and crabbed utopia. The fellowship, the altruism, the self-sacrifice it prescribed were not the essential features of political life in England or anywhere else. But where was the origin of this claim to participate and contribute in a genuinely moral community consciously directed towards a self-realisation fully compatible with the common good? In part it represented the hopes of those who felt that the extension of the franchise in the Second Reform Bill and after could be much more than a class victory. For this Liberal vision contemplated the creation of a new and positive spirit of unity which might animate a reconstruction of national life on the basis of spiritual equality. Much remained to be done in the way of reform, the question was whether it would be done in the name of pulling down aristocratic privilege or of raising the level of community among classes, and thus increasing the obligations felt by the advantaged classes to those which were not. This was the visionary aspect of Green's thought, in which he stated his aspiration for a new phase of citizenship and community with higher obligations than had been thus far acknowledged in England. But his ideal also reflected an aspect of English political and social life which already existed and indeed had played an important part in reform movements. Much of the confusion and ambivalence of Green's thought may be ascribed to the style of mid-Victorian politics in which he had his political experience. If he gave it a new life and intellectual power, he for his part based his view of the future on a projection of tendencies already long at work. This political milieu, and Green's relation to it, will receive full attention below. But it is well to have before us a more detailed account of the implications Green drew from the general principles which have been already discussed. In his lectures on political obligation, he included discussions of right in the sphere of international politics, the state's relation to private property and the regulation of economic life. Much in these sections resembles the work of Kant and Hegel in that the ostensible discussion of abstract principle is in fact dominated by actual political situations weighing on the mind of the philosopher. At the same time, it must not be forgotten that Green was committed to proving that his way of phrasing issues could include what was familiar and accepted; he thought he could eliminate ancient and unnecessary conflicts among men of political good will by the superior categories he introduced from his German models. It is precisely this claim of gaining new comprehensiveness without sacrificing the essentials of Liberal belief which has now to be examined.

CHAPTER NINE

FROM THE OLD LIBERALISM TO THE NEW: PRIVATE PROPERTY, CAPITALISM AND STATE INTERVENTION

I

GREEN'S POLITICAL THEORY IS often described as the principal link connecting the Old Liberalism of the Manchester School to the New Liberalism which inspired the social legislation enacted by the Asquith government before war came in 1914. Laski contrasted a negative and individualistic Liberalism with its positive and collectivist successor and identified Green with the latter: he 'gave to the idea of positive liberalism its letters of credit. . . . Under the philosophic auspices of Green . . . the main gains in the legislation of the last fifty years are to be recorded'.[1] Indeed the 'New Liberals' at the turn of the century, active politicians like Haldane, as well as theorists like Hobhouse, had themselves approved this interpretation: 'The teaching of Green and the enthusiasm of Toynbee were setting Liberalism free from the shackles of an individualist conception of liberty and paving the way for the legislation of our own time'.[2] Both of these judgments now need sharp qualification, for their authors accepted Dicey's famous distinction between individualism and collectivism, a view of nineteenth century history which has undergone severe criticism in the best recent work done by administrative and economic historians. And from the standpoint of this study, Laski and Hobhouse paid too little attention to the systematic ambiguity and mediating quality inherent in Green's style of thought. Their interpretation exaggerates the rôle he assigned to the state; it plays down his allegiance to the ideas of the Manchester School and minimises his distinctively mid-Victorian assumptions about the nature of English political life. This chapter and the next will present a detailed analysis of Green's political ideas in terms of their intellectual origins and institutional context. By these means it may be possible to understand both his own doctrine and the strikingly different uses later made of it by men who considered him their teacher and guide.

Any consideration of Green's position must begin with the fact that he found Liberalism in the throes of a doctrinal crisis. Earlier there had been something like a coherent programme. Politics had appeared to Liberals 'as a whole in which the parts were very closely united. Free trade, non-interference, a policy of peace, re-entrenchment of expenditure, popular government at home, self-government for the colonies—these were not isolated views. . . .'[3] By 1880 many of the issues associated with the party of Cobden, Bright and Gladstone had lost their urgency and popular appeal. The Corn Laws had long since been repealed, and free trade established, while discrimination by law against Nonconformists was for the most part a thing of the past. In a series of memorable budgets Gladstone had reduced taxes, and the Second Reform Bill had pointed the way to universal suffrage. True, Disraeli's Imperialist policy had to be fought, Ireland continued to be troublesome, and secondary education was far from what it should have been. But what most perplexed Liberals was the new type of social and economic legislation which increasingly became the focus of domestic politics.

To these difficulties, Green reacted in the style of his theology. Almost without realising it, he attempted to reconstruct Liberalism on a Broad Church basis through the use of Idealist concepts. Denying that there was any truth in the sharp distinctions which would have forced Liberals to choose between individualism and collectivism, he presented a larger synthesis which, if accepted, would preserve the unity of the party. Devotion to the true spirit of Liberalism was said to be the only article of faith. The old doctrine was still correct, but it had to be adapted to new conditions. The removal of obstacles, the encouragement of individual and group initiative—these were still the proper goals of Liberalism. There was a presumption against state action when other means were available, but this was not to be interpreted as an absolute interdiction against measures demanded by the common good of the community. Above all, every proposed state action ought to be considered in terms of its effects upon individual human character. Much of this was vague but ambiguity was not necessarily a disadvantage. An age likely to be attracted by a religion without dogma was apt to prefer a socialism without doctrines.

The doctrine of John Bright, phrased in the purest style of the Manchester School, stood in the same relation to Green's political philosophy as did Evangelicalism to his theology.[4] In both cases, the original orthodoxy when recast into the language of philosophical Idealism, took on some traits altogether foreign to its original formulation, which nevertheless remained ineffaceable in other characteristics. On occasion Green's borrowings from Bright and Cobden were little altered by translation: this is true of his theories of international politics and capitalism. But when it came to stating his views of private property and the right of the state to restrict freedom of contract, there was an obvious strain produced by the poor fit between ideas turned out in Manchester and Birmingham and those of Königsberg and Berlin. Even a Broad Church willingness to overlook differences and obliterate distinctions could falter in such circumstances. But Green nevertheless persisted in his effort to find a point of view comprehensive enough to include the various sources of his own creed and all those who considered themselves as radicals or socialists, liberals or conservatives. Professor Sabine has described this synthesising intent:

> Green's philosophy attempted to state a moral platform so broad that all men of social good-will could stand on it, and in a measure he succeeded. Its purpose was to transform liberalism from the social philosophy of a single set of interests seen from the point of view of a particular class into one which could claim to take account of all important interests seen from the point of view of the general good of the national community.[5]

For those accustomed to think of Green as the philosopher of 'collectivism', it may seem unaccountable that the English statesman he placed above all others was John Bright. And yet this was a devotion from which he never swerved. It had begun early. At a time when Bright's name could scarcely be mentioned in country houses, London clubs and the older universities, Green eulogised him in a phrase which said much about both of them. 'A sober man among drunkards;' this was Green's supreme praise for the man he thought to have kept alive the cause of reform during the Palmerstonian era. Much later, when the younger man made that statement of principle which is sometimes cited as a rationale for the positive state, he spoke in order to justify a programme long supported by Bright. In fact, Green's 'Lecture on Liberal Legislation and Freedom of Contract' was for the most part a plea to enact legislation proposed by the Gladstone government in which Bright was a Minister. Green saw himself as following in the succession of the 'radical' tradition of the Manchester School, but correcting its class bias and adding to the groups loyal to it those persons from other classes who acknowledged the obligation to improve their countrymen's lot. He led a reaction against that aspect of radicalism which made no demand for a personal contribution to the social good. This image of himself and his public had an effect upon Green's redefinition of liberalism or radicalism (like Arnold Toynbee, he used the terms interchangeably). He had long thought that what was best about Bright's principles could be better stated in the terms of Idealism. This assertion had perplexed the acute analytical intelligence of Bryce and Dicey, his undergraduate friends of the Old Mortality. However great this personal admiration for Bright, Green could not accept the arguments by which Bright sought to prove his case.

No one had more difficulty in understanding Green on this point than the future author of *Law and Public Opinion in England during the Nineteenth Century*. Dicey wrote:

> 'He [Green] is a philosophic radical, but of a very peculiar kind. Almost all his definite opinions might be endorsed by Bright or Cobden, but neither ... could understand the process by which Green's opinions are obtained, nor the arguments by which they are defended. An idealist in philosophy, he argues for the most utilitarian of political schools on idealist principles; and attaching the greatest importance to national life, constantly expresses a contempt for so-called "national honour" and imperial greatness which might perhaps offend the nationalism of even Mr Cobden.'[6]

This judgment admits the bafflement felt by a thinker who seldom experienced trouble in formulating and applying abstract categories. Yet Dicey could scarcely be blamed. It is not easy to find a common ground between Bright's notion of how nations ought to behave to one another and Hegel's more bellicose and irresponsible views. Nor is the conception of private property as a natural right derived from applying labour to a thing, an idea taken more or less directly by the Manchester School from Locke, altogether compatible with one aspect of the Idealist theory. For although neither Kant nor Hegel were consistent on this point, they may be interpreted as making private property contingent upon society's recognition that this form of ownership is an indispensable means to the development of personality. And the individualism of the free traders, their overriding concern with economic life which Matthew Arnold never tired of deriding, seemed to be at the opposite pole from the solemn German insistence on spiritual principle and disdain for mere material enrichment.

To wed these two schools was no easy task. In part the instability and ambivalence of Green's theories of property and state intervention may be attributed to the discrepant nature of his sources. Yet, as will soon appear, the German philosophers by

no means agreed among themselves. Nor were they altogether
immune to the individualistic and materialist values of that
'society of shopkeepers' which was becoming a European rather
than a purely English phenomenon. Even on the purely intellectual level, Kant in his political writings was not unaffected by
Locke. Hegel, for his part, had studied carefully the work of the
English classical economists, whose insight he praised and
incorporated into his notion of 'civil society' which prepares for
and is completed by the 'state'. Thus when Green defined the
proper function of the state as regulating external actions only,
and 'hindering hindrances to the good life', he at once was echoing
Kant and generalising from the principles used by the Manchester
School to destroy monopolies said to be blocking the natural
development of individual initiative. Kant, although making no
reference to economics, had stated:

> 'Now, everything that is wrong is a hindrance of freedom, according
> to universal Laws; and Compulsion or Constraint of any kind is a
> hindrance or resistance made to Freedom. Consequently, if a certain
> exercise of Freedom is itself a hindrance of the Freedom that is
> according to universal Laws, it is wrong; and the compulsion or
> constraint which is opposed to it is right, as being a *hindering of a
> hindrance of Freedom*, and as being in accord with the Freedom which
> exists in accordance with universal Laws.'[7]

If German philosophers were affected by English individualism
and its teaching that a man's freedom may be limited only when its
exercise interferes with the like right of others, English and
Scottish economists had not altogether denied positive functions
to government. When Green posited the need for the state to do
what cannot be left undone without damaging the interests of all,
he could have been rephrasing Adam Smith's views on education.[8]
The most important convergence between the British economists
on the one side and the German philosophers on the other, was
in the conception they shared of a natural self-regulating principle
converting individual self-seeking into some general good, whether
of a particular economy, or of the human species, seen in the
perspective of its history. Green was always seeking to synthesise
what was best in the two traditions.

Why did Green admire Bright as much as he did? Some aspects
of the man Marx called 'Father Bright' were unattractive. Indeed
his political style could have served as a model for the late John
Foster Dulles, with his unhesitating claim that human morality
and divine justice were always on the side of himself, his class and
his nation (whenever it followed his policy). Bright had no doubts

whatever about the intrinsic justice of capitalism and the right of the middle class to rule. All that was wrong with Great Britain as it was could be ascribed to the past when the aristocracy had ruled by force. At the time that Bright led the fight to enfranchise working men, he did so because he believed that their interests coincided with their masters' and that the middle class, working through the Liberal Party, could serve the joint interest of both. He supposed that the extended franchise would destroy the political power of the aristocracy and by itself satisfy all the claims of the working class. But Bright's pronouncements on acts meant to protect workers against employers were full of self-righteousness. Factory Acts he opposed as intolerable invasions both of the employer's freedom of contract and that of his employee. For trade unions he had no more sympathy than had his closest friend, Cobden, who announced roundly that they were all 'founded upon principles of brutal tyranny and monopoly. I would rather live under a Dey of Algiers than a trades committee.'[9] The same angry moralism appears in Bright's utterances whenever there was any question of the state protecting industrial workers against their employers. Only in the stony world of the United States Supreme Court's decisions before 1937 can there be found a more principled rejection of human obligation to the powerless.

Were this the only side to Bright, Green's admiration for him would remain mysterious. In fact Bright had some unusual merits. He was never afraid to oppose public opinion: he made himself unpopular by his criticism of the Crimean war; he threw his weight to the Union at the time of the American Civil War. Professor Asa Briggs in a perceptive essay has remarked that 'In English politics the importance of Bright was that he turned Liberalism into a creed, that he made men seek reform because reform was "right", that he refused to separate the spheres of morality and politics.'[10] With his essentially religious claim for liberal government based on the principles of responsibility, self-respect and justice, he provided a model for the style of politics that Green taught in his gospel of citizenship. Although called a radical and demagogue by the upper classes, Bright himself claimed to be a conservative in the true sense of the word, that is of advocating those changes that were required to attain a lasting stability. Green, who from the first thought conservatism contained much of value, emphasised this aspect of Bright:

'They say he is a revolutionist, when they themselves advocate a system which empties the country of its yeomen, the natural support of true conservatism, and, by treating five-sixths of the people as political aliens, leads, by inexorable necessity, to revolution.'[11]

Behind Bright's extraordinary efforts on behalf of the second Reform Bill lay his faith in the identity of interest between employer and employee, and the moral superiority of both to the landed class. Although he regarded this group as doomed by modern industrial society, which he regarded as altogether benevolent, he had learned from experience how difficult it was to dislodge the traditional rulers of the country from their commanding positions in the state and Established Church. Indeed, by the skilful use of its social prestige, the landed aristocracy had succeeded in seducing the upper part of the middle class into aping its mores and political attitudes. And so Bright advocated the extension of the franchise to classes that he thought could not be so corrupted. The proper liberal programme is an appeal to the justice, the intelligence and the virtues of the entire people. But for the people to rule, there were certain prerequisites: the abolition of all privileges derived from birth alone, the creation of a genuine universal suffrage, a system of national education and the removal of disabilities imposed by law upon persons holding religious beliefs other than those taught by the Established Church. As for international relations, Bright took the line that all international disputes may be solved peacefully. Wars in the modern world are always due to imperfect democracy at home, and the unnecessary use of force abroad. Both derive from the same obsolete fallacy, long disproved by political economy: that the interests of a man or nation may be advanced only at the cost of others. Disguised as the theory of the balance of power, this notion has long served the purposes of aristocracies, which alone profit from war. But Bright thought it 'pretty near dead and buried'. In 1864 he told his Birmingham constituents that this mistaken theory 'has loaded the nation with debt and with taxes, has sacrificed the lives of hundreds of thousands of families, and has left us . . . a doubled peerage at one end of the social scale, and far more than a doubled pauperism at the other.'[12] And all of this Green accepted and repeated with little variation.

2

What men reject in thinkers otherwise congenial to them is usually significant. Green explicitly denied Hegel's view that states have no moral responsibility to one another. He did not deign to take note of Hegel's comment that the 'inner dialectic of civil society . . . drives it . . . to push beyond its own limits and seek markets, and so its necessary means of subsistence, in other lands which are either deficient in the goods it has overproduced, or else generally backward in industry, etc.'[13] Such a link between capitalism and imperialism appeared absurd to a follower of Bright and Cobden. Green was remarkably uncritical of capitalism as a system. Here again he passed over everything in Hegel which pointed to the origin of the state in the conflicts which could not be resolved by the economic system. Green strayed no further from Manchester orthodoxy in his theory of capitalism than he did in his conceptions of war, empire and national interest. Although he did not deny that great evils existed in the capitalist order as he knew it, with its pauperism, bad housing and uneducated and drunken proletariat, he attempted to prove that these evils were no necessary part of capitalism, but rather ought to be attributed to the unliquidated legacy from the middle ages. The appropriation of land in most European nations had taken place by force, rather than by appropriation based on expenditure of labour. Because the original landowners were conquerors, and they and their titled descendants had controlled the structure of government, the evils of the past had been perpetuated.

So runs the argument of Green's chapter on 'The Right of the State in Regard to Property'. In all the major countries of Europe, the labour market is filled with men 'too badly reared and fed to be efficient labourers; who for this reason, and from the competition for employment with each other, have to sell their labour very cheap; who have thus seldom the means to save, and whose standard of living and social expectation is so low that, if they have the opportunity of saving, they do not use it, and keep bringing children into the world at a rate which perpetuates the evil'.[14] The cause of this 'impoverished and reckless proletariat' Green found in the past. Wherever a demand for labour has been created by the investment of capital in mining or manufacture, those who answered were men

> whose ancestors, if not themselves, were trained in habits of serfdom; men whose life has been one of virtually forced labour, relieved by church-charities or the poor law (which in part took the place of these charities); who were thus in no condition to contract freely for the sale of their labour, and had nothing of that sense of family-responsibility which might have made them insist on having the chance of saving. Landless countrymen, whose ancestors were serfs, are the parents of the proletariate of great towns.[15]

The other great historical influence came through the practical domination of the land-owning class which allowed itself rights, 'incompatible with the true principle on which rights of property rest, and tending to interfere with the development of the proprietorial capacity in others'. The only justification for the appropriation of land by individuals is that this arrangement contributes more to social well-being than if the land were held in common. But landlords have been allowed to do things clearly opposed to the well-being of the society as a whole: to turn fertile land into forest, to clear out a village by enclosure, leaving its people without a place to live, to build houses of unhealthy structure in unhealthy places, and to forbid the construction of dissenting chapels. And not only have these evils been tolerated but the law has positively prevented the creation of a land-owning peasantry that would develop its resources to the full and become self-reliant and industrious owners instead of cringing and indigent tenants.[16]

This situation is especially serious because wealth made by land is in a very different category from that made by trade and manufacture. Land is a 'commodity of a limited extent'. One man cannot acquire more land without others having less. And since from land must come raw materials and sites for industry, room for men to live and to communicate with one another, the land must be subjected to special control by the state in the interests of the community as a whole.[17]

The same degree of control is not necessary for other sources of wealth. In manufacture and trade, 'the increased wealth of one man does not naturally mean the diminished wealth of another'. The wealth of the world constantly increases as the production of new wealth by labour exceeds the constant consumption of what is already produced. Therefore in the accumulation of wealth, so far as it arises from the saving by anyone of his labour, there is nothing which lessens a similar chance for anyone else. While it is true that the accumulation of capital leads to the employment of large masses of hired labourers, there is nothing that keeps these labourers from being on a small scale capitalists themselves.[18] Their combination in work gives them every opportunity, 'if they have the needful education and self-discipline' to form societies for the investment of savings.

In fact, as we know, in the well-paid industries of England, the better sort of labourers do become capitalists, to the extent often of owning their houses and a good deal of furniture, of having an interest in stores, and of belonging to benefit-societies through which they make provision for the future. It is not then to the accumulation of capital, but to the condition, due to antecedent circumstances unconnected with that accumulation, of the men with whom the capitalist deals and whose labour he buys on the cheapest terms, that we must ascribe the multiplication in recent times of an impoverished and reckless proletariate.[19]

Thus Green took over from Bright and the Manchester School, not only their pacificism and free trade but the ideology they used to attack the land-owning aristocracy. When it came to the land, the 'radicals' favoured legislation, not to socialise it, but to introduce free trade and individual ownership. But legislation of this sort is to remove the past with its obsolete principles from control of a system which can be left to run itself once hindrances are removed. These middle class reformers admitted, as did Green, that all was not well with the workers. But this cast no doubt upon the intrinsic merits of capitalism. It was 'an unrestrained landlordism', and 'influences of feudalism ... which tend to throw a shiftless population upon the centres of industry'.[20] This population was left to be freely victimised by 'deleterious employments, foul air and consequent craving for deleterious drinks'. And their 'health, housing, and schooling were unprovided for'. Public health measures and supervision of private housing had to be introduced. Most important of all, the working class must be educated and encouraged to develop the middle class virtues of self-reliance and self-control. This could best be done by making them 'on a small scale capitalists themselves'. For Green assumed that private property was among the pre-requisites of developing character.

3

Private property may be regarded as either natural or conventional; as a right or as the worst form of wrong; as derived from the individual or from the community. Authors who defend property as natural have often based their argument upon an individual right alleged to be logically or chronologically prior to the state. 'Natural' means in this instance, 'not the perfection of a thing, as it does in Aristotle, but the primitive or original form of a thing; ... or more accurately perhaps, that the natural represents something essential, which may be modified for practical purposes by the conventional, but cannot be wholly set aside'.[21] Even among those who have considered private property to be natural, there has been no consensus about its basis. Locke gave an important lead to subsequent defenders of private property by his assertion that it is an institution of natural law, and has its origin in labour: a man may rightfully appropriate for his exclusive use, enjoyment, and testamentary disposition, everything with which he has mixed his labour. Locke's version of this theory and the numerous qualifications he appends to it, such as confining appropriation to what an individual can himself use, lack internal consistency and, in any case, cannot be applied without highly ambiguous results to any modern industrial system. Put in the form that every man has the right to the whole product of his labour, this theory was used by Marx to condemn those accumulations of capital which enable their owners to control the means of production. Even Locke is far from maintaining a pure natural law argument, for he contends that from the time money was introduced and accepted by men, the basis of property shifted from the natural to the conventional. But there is no point in exploring here the difficulties of Locke's position, for it could not possibly serve as the basis for Green's thought on the subject. The systematic assumptions of Green's own metaphysics and ethics made it impossible for him to accept any theory of natural rights as inherent in individuals considered without regard to their society and its common good.

Green found a more sympathetic theory in German philosophers beginning with Kant. Although some of them were drawn to the older notion that property is a natural right inherent in the individual, they nevertheless by the logic of their overall argument, had to conclude that private property is rightful only when recognised by the society, or its general will, as essential to the moral development of its members. Kant himself rejected both the view that property is a wrong (found in Rousseau's *Discourse on the Origin of Inequality*), and Locke's effort to derive the right of property from the isolated individual in the state of nature. Even in the state of nature, Kant states, man acquires his title to things, not mechanically by mixing his labour with them, but transcendentally by directing his will upon them.[22]

Property is derived from the right of the individual to will and therefore to appropriate any object so long as he does not injure anyone else. Some commentators have seen this doctrine as a reassertion of the older natural right theory in a sublimated or attenuated form.[23] But it seems more accurate to say that Kant confines property to the status of a contingent right in the state of nature. Only in civil society can there be a right of property so-called:

> The *rational Title of Acquisition* can therefore only lie originally in the Idea of the Will of all united implicitly. . . . For by a single Will there cannot be imposed upon others an obligation by which they would not have been otherwise bound.—But the fact formed by Wills actually and universally united in a Legislation, constitutes the Civil state of Society. Hence, it is only in conformity with the idea of a Civil state of Society, or in reference to it and its realisation, that anything External can be acquired. Before such a state is realised . . .

Acquisition . . . is consequently only *provisory*. The Acquisition, which is peremptory, finds place only in the Civil state.[24]

Since the only rights are those which are recognised by each as being valid for all, Kant thus attributes to the community organised in the civil state the power to determine property rights.[25] He himself assumed that this moral consensus will recognise appropriations by individuals, but nothing in his theory guarantees this. Indeed, he justified the expropriation of Church properties during the Reformation on the ground that this general consensus (*Volksmeinung*) no longer supported such institutions. And he added that the same might justly be done with estates granted the aristocracy in return for its military services, if and when this was generally felt to be desirable. He advocated that the state should use as little constraint as possible, and that it regard its duty as seeing to it that the maximum liberty of each be compatible with the maximum liberty of every other.

Hegel's treatment of private property was striking. He attributed to it a far higher value and autonomy than was to be expected from his general theory of the state. His attempt to give property an ontological basis was most 'undialectical', a fact which has been commented upon, not only by his Marxist interpreters, but by Hegelians such as Reyburn.[26] Hegel took up Kant's justification of private property and developed it further. Out of the notion that individuals realise their external freedom by directing their wills upon inanimate objects, Hegel constructed a more ponderous argument. Private property is the purest and most valuable means of developing individual character. It is far superior to any of the clan or communal arrangements of the past. This should be recognised by the state: justice prescribes that the division of goods should be unequal since men are unequal in their abilities.[27] Property is the paradigm of ethical life, which is realised in the state. Or as Hegel himself put it, 'The rationale of property is to be found not in the satisfaction of needs but in the supersession of the pure objectivity of personality. In his property a person exists for the first time as reason.'[28] This is to identify free will with private ownership. Hegel's language is such as to suggest that he would hold that 'I have, therefore, I am'. H. S. Holland commented that 'personalty' here 'nearly spells personality'.[29]

The implications of this part of Hegel's thought have been most carefully considered by Professor Marcuse. Although he seems to play down those limitations upon private property which Hegel conceded, however reluctantly, Professor Marcuse's analysis reveals much about the distortions in Hegel's thought produced by his position in society.* Hegel repeatedly identified philosophical truths with situations found only in a competitive economy. In his *Logic* he had described freedom as 'perfect and perennial ownership', thus identifying the principles of Idealism with those of private property. Hegel, when he argued that recognition is necessary to confirm a right, identified recognition with contract in an acquisitive society.[30] His English disciples did not escape this same error.

Green's treatment of private property follows without deviation the method developed in the *Prolegomena* and applied in his lectures on *Political Obligation*. First, he dismisses the historical question of what forms property has taken in the past; although important it cannot take the place of a metaphysical enquiry into more significant issues: what is it in the nature of man that makes it possible and moves him to appropriate; why is it that he conceives of himself and others as having a right in their appropriations; and on what ground is this conception treated as a moral authority? The argument flows along well-defined channels. Appropriation is an expression of human will, it is the individual's effort to realise a conception of his own good. Private property is a right in the technical sense of Green's system, that is, the recognition by everyone who concedes the same right to others because it is an interest common to all. Thus private property has its basis in social recognition, because only within society can there be such a thing as a right, and all rights rest on the common will. 'Each member of the society within which the right subsists contributes to satisfy the others in seeking to satisfy himself, and . . . each is aware that the other does so; whence their results a common interest in the free play of the powers of all.'

All this is highly abstract, and if Green had stopped at this point, it would be difficult to know just what importance to attribute to these maxims. But he attempts to measure the actual property relations of his time against his moral criterion of property. As was his habit, the modulation from theory to practice is made by the notion that all spiritual principles must be realised through the imperfect medium of human beings and their institutions.[31] Therefore, because of the historical accidents that are connected with the origin of any actual government, there result many characteristics of this institution of property as it

* Hegel wrote: 'The middle class, to which civil servants belong, is . . . the pillar of the state so far as honesty and intelligence are concerned. A state without a middle class must therefore remain on a low level.' (Hegel, *Philosophy of Right*, p. 291.)

actually exists, which cannot be derived from the spiritual principle which is its foundation. 'Still, without that principle it could not have come into existence, nor would it have any moral justification at all.'[32] Once this has been said, and Green has repeated the Hegelian judgment that individual private property within the framework of the state is morally superior to the communal property of the clan, the stage is set for his judgment of property relations.

He found much to condemn in the actual state of affairs:

'in which all indeed *may* have property, but great numbers in fact cannot have it in that sense in which alone it is of value, namely, as a permanent apparatus for carrying out a plan of life, for expressing ideas of what is beautiful or giving effect to benevolent wishes. In the eye of the law they have rights of appropriation, but in fact they have not the chance of providing means for a free moral life. . . . A man who possesses nothing but his powers of labour and who has to sell these to a capitalist for bare daily maintenance, might as well, in respect of the ethical purposes which the possession of property should serve, be denied rights of property altogether.[33]

This is a stunning admission on Green's part, and the repeated contrast between 'in fact' and the moral justification of property, would seem to indicate that he is about to come down on the side of a drastic curtailment of the property rights thus far granted capitalists. When he considered education or temperance, the same chain of reasoning produced a kind of empirical thump on the Idealist table: 'But we must take men as we find them'. Quite significantly, Green does not extract the same conclusion in reference to property rights. Instead he argues that the presence of so many men in a position of not effectively enjoying any of the benefits of private property is due, not to the unchecked powers of capitalists, but to the historical setting of the societies in which capitalism grew up. Using the Manchester version of original sin, he goes on to defend freedom of bequest and freedom of trade against the charge that they contribute to the growth of a 'proletariate'. It was not the accumulation of capital, but unconnected antecedent conditions of landowning that produced an impoverished and reckless proletariat. The benefits inherent in capitalism may yet overcome the disabilities imposed by the antecedent system. If it is to do so, the freedom of bequest must be preserved because, as a general rule, the father of a family, if left to himself and not biased by any special institutions of his country, 'is most likely to make that distribution among his children which is most for the common good'. On this general point, he immediately makes a qualification that supported Bright and the Liberal

Party in making an exception of freedom of bequest in regard to the ownership of landed estates. But Green proposed no such limits on capital. As for freedom of trade, this merely describes transactions in which commodities are bought where they are of least use and sold where they are of most use. 'The trader who profits by the transaction is profiting by what is at the same time a contribution to social well-being.'[34] No limitations on freedom of trade are proposed here although, elsewhere, Green does apply them to the sale of intoxicating liquors.

This treatment of property rights, with its bias against landed wealth and relative whitewashing of industrial and mercantile capital, indicates the degree to which Green followed the Manchester School. Although his own application of Idealist formulae gave little reason for alarm to the followers of Bright, there was always the notion of social recognition as registered by the state to menace the rights of bequest and freedom of trade for the capitalists. Green's empirical conclusion that under capitalism many, perhaps most, of the workers are denied property rights could be easily turned to the conclusion that the existing distribution of wealth should no longer be tolerated. This suggestion was made in a volume published in 1912 by a group of thinkers who, for the most part, acknowledged their debt to Green. This book, the work of the Christian Social Union, was edited by Green's former student, Bishop Gore, under the title of *Property: Its Rights and Duties*. In it L. T. Hobhouse pointed out the genuine difference between the property that builds character and the property which gives power to a few over the many. The judgment applied by Bright and Green against landowners was here equally logically applied to capitalists. Hastings Rashdall in his contribution indicated the dual possibilities of Green's theory of property and cited the fact that from it Green's followers had gone on to either socialist or individualist conclusions. Criticising Bernard Bosanquet's insistence on private property as a means of developing character, Rashdall made three effective points: that socialism condemns not private property but private capitalism, that there is no reason to assume that the definition of private property should be identified with the existing system of inheritance and capitalisation; and finally that an uncritical acceptance of the benefits of property ignores the moral disadvantages produced by a society based on unlimited competition. Rashdall concluded that it is futile to attempt to settle the question of property rights by any *a priori* theory. In every case, the issue must be resolved by a calculation of the effects, social and moral, that would be produced by a particular piece of legislation limiting property rights. Rashdall's suggestion seems closer to Green's characteristic method in actual politics than the highly abstract treatment of the subject found in *Political Obligation*. For, in practice, Green tended to give more weight to the practical effects of an enactment than to the philosophical criterion which was to be used to appraise the act. Why, then, was his position on private property so much an apologetic for middle-class forms of wealth? L. T. Hobhouse, defending Green against the onslaughts of a graduate class at the London School of Economics in the 1920's, suggested that Green, for tactical reasons, had to be cautious about what he said about property. In short, he feared that he might alienate men, who might otherwise be disposed to adopt his mode of thought, were he to make clear its implications for this explosive subject.[66]

Another spokesman for the New Liberalism of the period just preceding the war of 1914 was rather less kind. J. A. Hobson thought that any defence of private property on the ground of self-moralisation was founded upon two false assumptions: the first, that free competition as a general practice actually exists; second, that the value of anything actually depends upon the individual conduct of its owner. And as used by Bosanquet and his fellow members of the Charity Organisation Society, the criterion of self-moralisation was not being applied in the same way to the rich and poor. The COS condemned the careless use of charity because goods which come miraculously debauch the character of the recipient.[36] But it did not go on to denounce the bequests, rents and stock-market gains of the rich. To the rich, it applied the criterion of stewardship, that is, how well they used what they had (no question being raised about how it came into their hands); to the poor, the criterion of whether income bears a close relation to the effort expended. All this suggested to Hobson that there was some distorting element in the situation which kept Green's followers from perceiving that the theory actually implies a double condemnation of economic rents and other unearned sources of income: 'Firstly, by enabling a man to reap where he has not sown, by divorcing satisfaction from previous effort, they crush the sense of independence in the recipient and derationalise his life. Secondly, since all "unearned" elements of income are truly the earnings of the work of some one else or of society, such individual or such society, by losing the natural reward of its effort, is disabled from realising itself. The ground landlord who "realises himself" in the rents he draws from his slum property is preventing the docker and the seamstress from realising themselves, and is destroying for them the possibility of rationally organising life.'[37]

Was Green's theory of property and of state interference merely a justification of most features of the existing system? Or was the theory itself profoundly ambiguous or even potentially radical? These questions may be best resolved by an analysis of Green's most famous application of his political philosophy, his lecture on 'Liberal Legislation and Freedom of Contract', delivered at Leicester in 1880. His sections on private property in *Political Obligation* date from the same period, and hence any discrepancies will merit attention.

4

Freedom of contract, freedom to do what one wills with what belongs to one—these are no absolute rights good in themselves; but are valuable only as means to the end by which all rights are to be measured.

> 'That end is what I call freedom in the positive sense: in other words, the liberation of the powers of all men equally for contributions to a common good. No one has a right to do what he will with his own in such a way as to contravene this end. It is only through the guarantee which society gives him that he has property at all, or, strictly speaking, any right to his possessions. This guarantee is founded on a sense of common interest.'[38]

The meaning of this statement, and indeed this whole essay, has often been misinterpreted as a general sanction for state interference. This was not Green's meaning. The lecture was delivered to a Liberal party organisation; it naturally stated Green's positive opinions summarily and without the qualification that appears in *Political Obligation*. And what is usually overlooked is that his arguments were meant to support measures, present and potential, of the Liberal party. What were these measures? Land laws for Ireland and Britain and temperance legislation. What other measures did he analyse or contemplate? National education, factory acts, public health measures. Land laws and temperance legislation had long been agreeable to Bright, who in 1880 was a member of the Liberal government. The other measures, while constituting distinct violations of the laissez-faire principle in economics and the voluntary principle in politics had been enacted in the past and were not based on socialist principles. To Green capitalism did not menace the social good. As he summarised his justification for state legislation, it was limited to a strictly defined category of cases. 'It is the business of the state, not indeed directly to promote moral goodness for that, from the very nature of moral goodness, it cannot do, but to maintain the conditions without which a free exercise of the human faculties is impossible'.[39]

Certainly this constitutes a breach with strict individualism: it asserts a positive, if limited, function for the state. But it maintains a presumption in favour of voluntary action because it only, and not acts prescribed by law, can genuinely express morality. The purpose of state action is to free its citizens from hindrances or disabilities so that they may develop their moral potentialities. Private property is an indispensable means to that moral development. Yet it too is founded on a sense of common interest. 'Every one has an interest in securing to every one else the free use and enjoyment and disposal of his possessions, so long as that freedom on the part of one does not interfere with a like freedom on the part of others, because such freedom contributes to that equal development of the faculties of all which is the highest good for all.'[40] What this means in effect is that Green denies that any genuine conflict of interests can exist between individuals and the state, provided that the basis of their rights are fully understood. The development of character, the realisation of the moral potentialities of all citizens, can and should proceed smoothly once all obstacles are removed. Green has changed the meaning of Liberalism while keeping its formula of removing obstacles to that smooth functioning of the self-regulatory mechanism it believed to exist in the market and in foreign trade. Fifty years before, Liberals had fought the fight of reform in the name of individual liberty against privilege. In 1880 Liberals, Green claimed, were fighting the same old cause of social good against class interests. 'The nature of the genuine political reformer is perhaps always the same. The passion for improving mankind, in its ultimate object, does not vary. But the immediate object of reformers, and the forms of persuasion by which they seek to advance them, varies much in different generations.'[11]

British political history since the first Reform Bill seemed to him to fall into three divisions. The first, beginning with the reform of parliament and extending to Peel's administration, is marked by the struggle of free society against privileged corporations. With Peel began the struggle of society against monopolies; in other words, the liberation of trade. The realisation of complete freedom of contract was the special object of this reforming work. The free-trader 'only interfered to prevent interference'. The third phase began with the more democratic parliament of 1868. Factory acts were extended to every factory and workshop; a beginning in compulsory education was made in the education act of 1870. Green sought to classify these measures under the same Kantian formula of removing hindrances. These measures embodied the principle of equality; they also took into account the positive theory of freedom, the theory of progress as the increasing development and exercise on the whole of those powers of contributing to social good with which citizens are endowed, in short, their capacity to make the most and best of themselves.

Thus in the new phase of citizenship opened up by the Reform Bill of 1867, the liberation to be done consisted of removing obstacles to personal development. A contract to work under conditions fatal to health is such a hindrance, the purchase or hire of unhealthy buildings is another. But what about compulsory education? 'Without a command of certain elementary arts and knowledge, the individual in modern society is as effectually crippled as by the loss of a limb.' Does not state action diminish the independence and self-reliance of the people? To this question Green answered that a society where public health was protected and necessary education provided for spontaneously no doubt would be preferable to one in which the compulsion of law is needed to secure these ends. 'But we must take men as we find them.' Until such a condition of society is reached, it is the business of the state to insist that these things be done. The man who, of his own right feeling, sends his child to school suffers no moral degradation from a law which, if he did not do this for himself, would seek to make him do it. To such a man the law is felt, not as constraint but as a powerful friend. Other men, less benevolent or more ignorant, cannot be left to do as they like. 'Left to itself, or to the operation of casual benevolence, a degraded population perpetuates and increases itself.' Either workers must be well enough off to reject working conditions incompatible with health or decent housing or education, or the law must remove such conditions.

The alternatives considered here are crucial to Green's argument. 'Given a certain standard of moral and material well-being, people may be trusted not to sell their labour or the labour of their children, on terms which would not allow that standard to be maintained.' Failing that, the law must prevent their selling their labour. Here, in other words, Green chooses between changing economic conditions or establishing minimum standards. His choice was minimum standards. How far he was from socialism can be seen from his conclusion, 'With a population such as ours was forty years ago, and still largely is, the law must prevent it [the sale of labour] and continue the prevention for some generations, before the sellers will be in a state to prevent it for themselves.'[42]

The full meaning and potential difficulties of Green's re-definition of freedom are difficult to grasp when applied to such matters as education and public health. They appear more clearly when he applies his theory to restricting the sale of intoxicating drinks. He here discusses no one measure such as 'local option' but the principle of such restriction generally. This is the same as that of other legislation which restricts individual liberty when it becomes an impediment to social good. 'There can be no doubt that the present habits of drinking in England do lay a heavy burden on the free development of man's powers for social good, a heavier burden probably than arises from all other preventible causes put together.'[43] Hence it follows from Green's criticism that it is as right to restrict the liquor traffic as to have factory acts, education acts, public health acts. The arguments used against such acts form the only objection to temperance legislation: that the people must become temperate through spontaneous individual action, that as they become better housed and educated, they will shake off the habit. To this Green answered that a drunken population naturally perpetuates and increases itself. Every year that the evil is left to itself, it becomes greater. Those affected by it feel no desire to be rescued from it.

This mode of argument recalls the difficulties of Green's theory. It again raises the question of how the common good is to be defined, and whether this theory of positive freedom to make the most and best of oneself may not authorise very sweeping invasions of personal freedom in the name of developing character. The argument that Green uses suggests Rousseau's notion of forcing men to be free. Consider what was said about the father who is obliged by law to send his child to school: Green claims that if the parent would have sent the child in any case he does not feel the law to be a constraint. Somewhat disingenuous, this. Of course, as a matter of fact we do not feel robbed of our freedom by the requirement that children must attend school until a certain age. But Green's rationale of the compulsion, that those things should be enjoined by law which are essential to the development of character, glosses over potential coercion in other and more important cases. As a criterion for state interference, it is open to objection. First, it may be too arbitrary in deciding what items, such as temperance or prohibition, are essential to character; or it may be too vague to provide any very precise criterion for draw-ing the line. How Green himself drew the line is quite clear from his writings. He did not favour extensive state interference and indeed his theory contains a presumption against it. But in other hands, the theory could be used for almost any purpose, particularly when combined with the notion that once universal manhood franchise was attained there no longer was any danger of legislation designed to serve the special interest of one class, rather than the common good:

> The danger of legislation, either in the interests of a privileged class or for the promotion of particular religious opinions, we may fairly assume to be over. The popular jealousy of law, once justifiable enough, is therefore out of date. The citizens of England now make its law. We ask them by law to put a restraint on themselves in the matter of strong drink. We ask them further to limit, or even altogether to give up, the not very precious liberty of buying and selling alcohol, in order that they may become more free to exercise the faculties and improve the talents which God has given them.[44]

What this religion of citizenship entailed for Green and his circle is greatly clarified, if to 'Liberal Legislation' are added Arnold Toynbee's popular addresses to audiences of working men and employers in the North of England, from 1880 to 1882, and his two lectures on 'Progress and Poverty' given in London in 1883. One of these addresses, called suggestively 'Are Radicals Socialists?', covers somewhat the same ground as Green but in greater detail. Toynbee was no revolutionary, and he warned against potential evils of 'collectivism' in a way anticipated by Green but not so clearly articulated by him in his own lecture on the subject. Yet Toynbee was opposed to the earlier English economists. He took up the study of economic history and theory which he infused with Green's spirit. He believed in the power of co-operative and friendly societies and trade unions to raise the standard of life for the working classes. The state's duty was to assist such effort by free compulsory education, by regulation of the hours of labour, and to supplement contributions made by the workman through his own voluntary societies for providing insurance in sickness and old age.

Toynbee's essay began with a statement of the original radicals' principles, those of Joseph Hume, Molesworth, Cobden, Bright, Fox and Villiers. The old radical creed may be summed up in three words—justice, liberty, and self-help. Their programme was carried by the repeal of the Corn Laws and the passage of the Second Reform Bill. Thereupon bread was cheaper and steadier. In time almost all of the Chartists' grievances were met as well. When the workmen obtained the suffrage, they repealed the law which made trade-unions illegal and the law of conspiracy which had so hindered their organisation. Still to be attained were the legislation of free-trade in land, the reform or abolition of the House of Lords, and universal suffrage.

Yet, remarked Toynbee, while free-trade and the extension of the franchise and the greater prosperity of the community all seemed to be great and solid gains, fundamental criticism was not lacking. Men like Karl Marx, Toynbee noted, were taking the line that it was impossible for working men under the conditions of private property and competition to raise themselves above the level of bare subsistence. Such critics described vividly the gradual rolling together of huge masses of capital, while at its feet were masses of workmen living in penury, though in nominal independence. In the end, they say, the people will arise, and the present social system with its slavery will be swept away. Was Marx correct?

> We in England smile at all this as a mere dream, so remote does revolution seem from our slow course of even progress. But if it is remote, it is because we in England have taken steps to modify the conditions which make revolutions imminent. If we can rightly smile at such pictures it is because we have developed among artisans and labourers vast voluntary societies wielding masses of capital, and have partially realised the Socialist programme. There are two great agencies which have been at work in England to produce that result: First, those voluntary agencies, the result of the self-help in which Radicals believe; and, secondly, the action of the State in which Socialists believe.[45]

Yet there was no doubt that serious material inequalities and injustices existed. While voluntary and state action had done much to mitigate the conditions of the working class, more remained to be done. And Toynbee here proposed a new radical programme. The Liberals, he said, had in their Irish Land Act of 1881 recognised the fundamental principle of Socialism, that between men unequal in material wealth, as were Irish tenants and their English landlords, there can be no freedom of contract. Therefore the Liberals stood committed to a programme which combined voluntary action with state action, a kind of radical socialism. Its maxims were these:

> First, that where individual rights conflict with the interests of the community, there the State ought to interfere; and, second, that where the people are unable to provide a thing for themselves, and that thing is of *primary social importance*, then again the State should interfere and provide it for them.[46]

Toynbee's formula, like Green's, is profoundly ambiguous. By his use of 'socialism' he did not mean the destruction of private property or communism, but the protection of the state for all citizens when the good of the whole community is involved. And yet state action should be taken only when voluntary action is impossible,

> ... without undermining that old independence, that habit of voluntary association, of which we are justly proud, for if we undermine that—that pride which has made the English workman sacrifice everything to keep himself out of the workhouse, which has made workmen bind themselves together in Friendly Societies and Trades Unions and in Co-operative Societies—if we undermine that, then, it would be better to leave our works undone.[47]

But, he thought, it was possible to work out a programme that combined the best features of voluntary association with that of state intervention. As an example, he proposed that municipalities or the state in some form should have power to buy up land and rent it below market value for the erection of decent dwellings for the working class.

But would this not be class legislation which radicals have always opposed? No, because it would be in the interest of the whole community. No one is safe until all citizens have the chance of living decent lives. The poorest class needs to be raised in the interest of all classes. But would this not diminish self-reliance? No, because it does for the people what they cannot do for themselves, and gains for them a position in which they shall not need assistance. Radicals still are keenly alive to the necessity for self-reliance. Outdoor relief under the Poor Law should be abolished because outdoor relief lowered wages, degraded the recipient and diminished self-reliance. And when the Poor Law was abolished it should be done by workmen themselves sitting as Guardians. As citizens, they would then have recognised their duties.

This was radical socialism and, Toynbee argued, it differed significantly from both Tory Socialism and Marxist Socialism.

> The radical creed ... is this: We have not abandoned our old belief in liberty, justice, and self-help but we say that under certain conditions the people cannot help themselves, and that then they should be helped by the State representing directly the whole people. In giving this State help, we make three conditions: first, the matter must be one of primary social importance; next, it must be proved to be practicable; thirdly, the State interference must not diminish self-reliance. Even if the chance should arise or removing a great social evil, nothing must be done to weaken those habits of individual self-reliance and voluntary association which have built up the greatness of the English people.[48]

Clearly this would not be an easy position to maintain, for it was a middle way between the old radicalism and the new. Nor was it

easy to judge exactly what were the implications of such a programme. But for a time this was no disadvantage, since both
parties competed in social welfare legislation. What gave Green
and Toynbee their great force was not the precision of their
formula for state action but the fact that they offered in social
reform an outlet to the religious aspirations of their generation
through self-sacrifice and philanthropy.

When Toynbee compared his 'radical socialism' to Tory and
Marxist socialism, he proclaimed this religious element, denounced
class struggle and affirmed the gospel of duty, the proper creed of
citizenship.

> We differ from Tory Socialism in so far as we are in favour, not of
> paternal but of fraternal government, and we differ from Continental
> Socialism because we accept the principle of private property and
> repudiate confiscation and violence. . . . It is this indeed which
> utterly separates English Radical Socialists from Continental
> Socialists—our abhorrence and detestation of their materialistic ideal.
> To a reluctant admission of the necessity for state action, we join a
> burning belief in duty and a deep spiritual ideal of life. And we
> have more than an abstract belief in duty, we do not hesitate to unite
> the advocacy of social reform with an appeal to the various classes
> who compose society to perform those duties without which all social
> reform must be illusive.
>
> To the capitalists we appeal to use their wealth, as many of their
> order already do, as a great national trust, and not for selfish purposes
> alone. . . .
>
> To the workman we appeal by the memory and traditions of his
> own sufferings and wrongs . . . to avoid the great guilt of inflicting
> upon his fellow-citizens the injustice from which he has himself
> escaped. We call upon him to reform his own social and domestic life,
> —to put down drunkenness and brutal violence. Decent habitations
> and high wages are not ends to be sought for their own sake. High
> wages—now at least—are often a cause of crime. . . .
>
> I repeat, we demand increased material welfare for those who
> labour with their hands, not that they may seize upon a few more
> coarse enjoyments but that they may enter upon a purer and a higher
> life.[49]

These words of Toynbee admirably sum up Green's political
programme. It differed from Bright's programme both in its
Idealist mode of thought, and in the admission that there was an
intolerable degree of inequality in English society. Green and
Toynbee sought to moralise the competitive society of capitalism.
Although Green was too close to Bright to engage in a fundamental
critique of capitalism, he never objected to trade unions and factory
acts. He taught a theory of community drastically different from

the atomistic individualism of the Manchester School. And in the name of community, he called upon all those who had privileges to sacrifice them to their duty as citizens. In Oxford Green and Toynbee put to rout the Old Liberalism.[50]

Nevertheless, both Green and Toynbee displayed considerable vagueness about the proper goals for social policy. In part, this was due to the fact that both emphasised abstract moral criteria rather than inquiry into what specific measures were needed to produce the results they desired. And perhaps because of their uncritical retention of many middle-class sentiments and assumptions acquired from the Manchester School, they never resolved certain issues of social reform. One unexamined premiss was their view of private property; another was the paternalistic moralism which dominated their thought. They would support the aspirations of the lower middle class and the working class if, and only if, such gains were used to live according to the middle-class standards of their sponsors. This persistent moralism applied to the disadvantaged classes led to the expectation that every act of justice or equality would produce a transformation which was not required from those holding wealth and advantage by birth or achievement in other classes. But perhaps this is but an inevitable attitude of the middle-class intellectual in politics. Most was expected from those who had been given the least in the way of education or opportunity. The motives of reformers who side with those born beneath them requires at least the prospect that they, once saved from poverty, should not simply fall into the same materialism and taste for luxury as the upper classes. This is perhaps one of the disabilities of the type of social reformer canonised by Green and Toynbee, along with the fuzziness produced by the aim of improving individual character. The origins of these characteristics was in the political style Green knew and practised.

CHAPTER TEN

A MID-VICTORIAN STYLE OF POLITICS: THE REFORMER, MUTUAL AID AND THE VOLUNTARY SOCIETY

I

IN HIS FORD LECTURES, Mr Kitson Clark has pointed to two forces as being especially important in shaping Victorian England: the political movement to extend the franchise and abolish aristocratic privilege, and the religious movement to make England thoroughly Christian in fact as well as name.[1] We have seen how Green's thought was a response to these two themes, indeed, that it is best understood as an effort to combine them in a philosophical form which gave a quasi-religious sanction to citizenship and reform. But to leave the matter there on the level of *Geistesgeschichte* would tell us nothing about Green's own practical objectives or the political uses to which his ideas were later put. Only by relating his political philosophy to his environment can we discern its contemporary meaning and the limits imposed upon him by existing patterns of action; only by charting the discrepant interpretations made by men claiming to be his spiritual executors can we disentangle the ambiguities of his thought and those of the political and religious traditions from which it derived. The Liberalism of Bright stressed political equality but opposed extensive state action in social and economic matters, a position better fitted to its clients of the middle and lower-middle classes than to most industrial and agricultural workers. More than is usually realised, Green's theory of state interference incorporated these views, although he phrased them in philosophical terms which blurred distinctions once held in a more rigid form. As for the revival of Protestantism, this had produced two incompatible attitudes towards charity and the obligation of man to his fellows. On the one hand, there was a reinforcement of belief in the economic virtues and the identity of poverty and sin, views more likely to proscribe charity than to encourage it; on the other hand, as the result of the impulse originating in Methodism, a sense of obligation to aid those in need.

On balance, Green's moral and political ideas were humanitarian rather than punitive in relation to poverty and suffering; they stressed human interdependence and the duties imposed by solidarity. But Green also accepted the values of self-help, thrift and sobriety, all characteristically assumed to be good by mid-Victorian politicians, all prominent in the milieu of local Liberal organisations and temperance agitation within which Green chose to live as a resident of Oxford city. How incompatible these principles of self-reliance and self-interest were with charity and altruism Green failed to realise, perhaps because of the profound ambivalence he concealed from himself and others by the vague terms in which he thought. These qualities account for the conflicting interpretations made of his work by men considering him their model. Green is too often described as the first English political philosopher to justify collectivism or even the Welfare State. In fact his Idealism pointed in different directions, and its practical effects were determined, not by the qualities now regarded as essential to distinction in philosophy, but by the absence of them. As Professor Gellner has pointed out, the use of a concept 'may depend on its lack of meaning, its ambiguity, its possession of wholly different and incompatible meanings in different contexts, *and* on the fact that, at the same time, it . . . emits the impression of possessing a consistent meaning throughout—on retaining . . . the aura of a justification valid only in one context when used in quite another'.[2]

Some of the errors in interpreting Green's ideas have resulted from a neglect of their origin and application. Although formed in what Mr Kitson Clark has called the 'high noon of Victorianism' (between 1850 and 1875), his thought was most influential between 1890 and 1914. His interest in politics, which began when a schoolboy in the 1850's, continued unabated until his death in 1882. As a University teacher with a following not confined to Balliol, he first made himself felt in the late 1860's. Thereafter no one at Oxford, with the possible exception of Ruskin, rivalled him in his power to stir men from their inherited allegiances and make them aware of how much remained to be done by way of reform. But none of his work relevant to politics was available in print until A. C. Bradley edited the *Prolegomena to Ethics* in 1883. Five years later, Nettleship completed his own memoir and the publication of Green's collected works. That same year saw the appearance of *Robert Elsmere* and Mrs Ward's controversy with Mr Gladstone, then Prime Minister. Both events brought Green's name and a version of his theory to the general public. By 1911 six impressions of the *Works* had been printed, five editions of the *Prolegomena*, a separate edition of Nettleship's memoir and, most popular of all, an edition of *Political Obligation* by Bosanquet to which A. D. Lindsay (later Lord Lindsay of Birker) added a preface.*

To Green's personal effect as a writer and Oxford teacher may be added his indirect influence upon men whose university teachers were his disciples or colleagues. With the exception of Cambridge, the universities of England, Scotland and Wales were on the whole Idealist in their teaching of philosophy. At Oxford Green's ideas and attitudes for a long time continued to attract students who encountered them in their study of Greats, or through the teaching of men like Edward Caird who succeeded Jowett as Master of Balliol. Until 1914 there was a steady stream of volunteers for Toynbee Hall and the other settlement houses. Lord Beveridge has told how deeply he was impressed by Caird's Lay Sermon urging his listeners to discover why so much poverty existed, despite the presence of great wealth.[3] He personally resolved to take steps to remove this anomaly; so too did his contemporary, R. H. Tawney, who acknowledged his own debt to Caird.[4]

From the posthumous publication of his lectures to about the outbreak of the First World War, Green's reputation was at its zenith. Some members of both parties; Civil Servants, particularly in education; clergymen in the Church of England and the Non-conformist churches; journalists and publicists with university training in philosophy—were apt to know Green's ideas in one or another form. A man who was twenty at Green's death, would have been forty in 1910; Asquith himself, who came up to Balliol in 1870 and was tutored by Green, was fifty-eight in the year of his struggle with the House of Lords.† Laski, on the basis of

* The *Prolegomena to Ethics* was published in May, 1883 (first edition), 1,000 copies; it was reset (second edition) in 1885, 2,000 copies; again reset in 1891 (third edition), 2,500 copies; reset in 1899 (fourth edition), 3,000 copies; reset in 1906 (fifth edition), 2,000 copies. Thereafter, only new impressions of the fifth edition were issued: 1911, 2,000; 1919, 1,500; 1925, 1,500; 1931, 1,500. The Clarendon Press, Oxford, which was kind enough to furnish these figures, reported that the book went out of print in 1949. 17,000 copies were sold in all.

The sales figures of Longmans, Green & Co. Ltd. were destroyed in 1940, but they have furnished the following printing figures: *Philosophical Works*, Vol. I, 2,130; Vol. II, 2,000; Vol. III, 2,000. These would seem to be the first printing order. The separate edition of the *Principles of Political Obligation* has been printed in 15,602 copies.

† In the General Election of 1906, 31 old Balliol men were elected: 22 Liberals; there were 4 Balliol men in the Cabinet. In the first General Election of 1910, were 29 Balliol men, with 15 Liberals; in the second, 30, with 15 Liberals. (*Oxford Magazine*, XXIV [14 February, 1906], XXVIII [17 February, 1910], XXIX [6 February, 1911].)

conversation with Asquith, thought that the mind of the Prime Minister had been prepared, while at Balliol, for social legislation inconceivable to Gladstone. Asquith in his own writing sometimes implied this was so, although on other occasions he took a different line. But even in his case it is impossible to claim any direct effect of Green's abstract ideas upon the making of history. Certainly no other political philosopher was more important during this period, but the number of his readers indicates that the technical quality of Idealist language and concepts put a limit on his influence, which in any case was only one of the forces operative at that time. Although Green's formulae were in some form adopted by many who did not know him directly, there is no accurate way of determining their contribution to legislation. It is more profitable to regard Green as a significant example of attitudes held by a man both sensitive to the main currents of ideas of his day and familiar with arrangements and procedures which, although not formally part of the Constitution, played an important part in its operation.

What Green thought possible during his lifetime and worth aiming at in the future, were determined by his image of English politics and society. Middle-class reformers, both religious and secular, had long practised, and not without success, a variety of techniques for getting social legislation into the statute book. These achievements seemed for a time to eclipse both the explicit programmes of the political parties and the feeble means of direct pressure available to those most in need of help. Green seems to have accepted the view, then much in vogue, that Parliament was less significant as a power for good or evil in social welfare than private philanthropy and those forms of mutual aid developed by the more prosperous working-men. His conception of the proper scope for state action could not but be affected by such assumptions, which made him unwilling to use the coercive power of the state except for a strictly delimited set of purposes. These Bosanquet summarised without deviating from Green's own statement, when he insisted that there is a presumption against welfare legislation: before the state undertakes any such action, Parliament ought to ask whether there is an indubitable case for believing that there is 'a definite tendency to growth, or a definite reserve of capacity, which is frustrated by a known impediment.'[5] And Green's definition of the state presupposed other forms of community, the claims of which it reconciled and completed. In addition to those which are natural, such as the family, there existed voluntary associations spontaneously formed by working-men to do by collective action what was beyond their individual resources:

friendly, building and co-operative societies, as well as trade unions, then relatively unbelligerent and limited to skilled workers. Because so little was known about the proportion of workers thus covered or the adequacy of benefits, many men of good will believed that a large range of services were being provided by efficient organisations which deserved every encouragement. Such a belief in voluntary action combined easily with other articles of Green's mid-Victorian Liberal faith: the value of free participation in an enterprise dedicated to self-help; the notion that private property is an indispensable means to developing individual character; and the refusal to assign any responsibility to the capitalist system for existing poverty and unemployment. Placing much store in political solutions and educational schemes, Green thought that the industrious workman, once he added the franchise to his membership in co-operative, friendly society and trade union, would hold his fate in his own two hands. He need only labour hard, remain sober, practise thrift, and work through extramural instruction to improve his own education, and through the Liberal Party to better that of his children. Not everything could be done by voluntary action: the state would have to provide proper schools and remove such anomalies as religious discrimination and class-biassed land laws. It ought to aid those who could not aid themselves to become temperate. For all these exceptions to his general presumption against state action, Green's rationale was the removal of hindrances to the improvement of individual character. This criterion was moralistic, involving the determination by upper-class persons of those moral traits to be encouraged; it excluded from consideration the economic arrangements of the society, as well as the possibility that the interests and tastes of middle-class reformers might not be those of the working classes.

Much can be told about political ideas by determining the perspective of the theorist. Does he look at politics from above, the point of view characteristic to rulers manipulating subjects, or from below, that of the subjects themselves? Does he conceive of government as the imposition of a will, or as subject to the constitution, the consent of the governed or the natural law? A clear-cut model is presupposed by any thinker who fancies himself as cast in the *persona* of the legislator. Reminding himself of Solon, he recalls actual situations when a single man had the power to establish the basic law; the legislator ought to be the man who can determine what is best for those subject to the arrangements he will impose (presumably in the light of some knowledge or insight which he possesses and they do not). To know that Plato, Rousseau and Bentham conceived of themselves as legislators is to know much about their respective conceptions of democracy. A recurrent image in Green's thought was the social reformer, a type he esteemed as of higher value than the saint. We shall see how this was a generalisation from specimens found in his milieu. No other mode of life seemed to him more worthy. It is not at all difficult to understand his admiration for Wilberforce and Shaftesbury, Chadwick and Florence Nightingale. But the social reformer as idealised by Green and Toynbee was apt to expect that those whose lot was being improved by his efforts would adopt his values. Those who would not were excluded forthwith from benefit. Professor Titmuss has remarked on the extent to which this outlook was incorporated into the provisions and administration of the Old Age Pensions Act of 1908:

> 'If poverty was a mark of waywardness then the poor needed moral condemnation or rewarding; as the . . . Act . . . set out to apply in separating the worthy from the unworthy poor by withholding pensions from those "who had habitually failed to work according to ability and need and those who had failed to save money regularly". If poverty was a matter of ignorance then it was the moral duty of one class in society to teach another class how to live, and to lead them through sanitation, soap and thrift to a better station in life. . . .'[6]

If there were traces of such an attitude in those of Green's students who supported the social legislation of the Liberal Parliaments before 1914, it dominated the thinking of the Charity Organisation Society, which was perennially in opposition. Bernard Bosanquet and C. S. Loch, on the basis of principles they attributed to Green, led the battle against breaking up the Poor Law, against state-provided old-age pensions, and even free lunches for poor schoolchildren. J. A. Hobson decided that the London Ethical Society, which included a large number of Idealist philosophers at the movement's height, 'was committed so strongly to the stress upon individual progress as to make it the enemy of that political-economic democracy which I was coming to regard as the chief instrument of social progress and justice'.[7] Hobson's opinion, although fair comment on Bosanquet, was by no means equally applicable to all Idealists identifying themselves with Green. Many of them laid less stress on his moralistic individualism than on the humanitarian and egalitarian attitudes stated with such intensity in his ethics. This was the case with the early Idealist Fabians such as Ball and D. G. Ritchie, Gore and Holland, the founders of the Christian Social Union, and many of the New Liberals. Yet it is probably true that none of them altogether resolved the ambivalence of Green's values or the ambiguity of his intellectual formulae. These were responses, neither merely passive nor uncreative, to patterns of reform in his time. Not the least of his achievements was to give a weighty philosophical underpinning to activities hitherto purely practical in nature, and making their appeal to the generosity, compassion and self-sacrifice of a small number of individuals largely middle-class in origin. Green, by his transposition of their ideals into a system commanding the respect of many intelligent persons at Oxford and elsewhere, accelerated the flow of university-trained men into settlement houses, university extension and philanthropy. What happened to them after he had rallied them to such causes depended on the individuals, the organisations they entered and the general forces shaping social policy. These they affected, but in the nature of the case, it would be absurd to assert that their influence in any meaningful sense determined the course of events.

Yet Green and those whose lives were altered because of his work and that of his disciples, were symptomatic of what was happening to the most articulate and thoughtful members of the Liberal Party in the transition between the politics of Gladstone and Bright to those of Asquith and Lloyd George. To unravel the complexities of Green's own thought and of his influence may shed some light on matters of greater importance. Among those which have not yet been analysed and explained to the satisfaction of historians are the origins and subsequent development of social services into what is often, if too loosely, considered as the guarantee by the government of all the minimum needs of its subjects. Professor Asa Briggs, in a penetrating paper, has revealed what is wrong with the tendency to substitute for the Whig theory of English history as the progressive unfolding of liberty and representative government another vision of the past as 'leading inevitably and inexorably along a broad highway with the "welfare state" as its destination'.[8] The term 'welfare state' like its predecessor 'collectivism' needs explanation before it can be decided what any one person or factor contributed to it. But it may be well to begin at the beginning of a complex process which took a course that is only now being charted. What appears beyond dispute is the significance, for good or evil, of that heterogeneous group immortalised by their description in the 'Communist Manifesto' as: 'economists, philanthropists, humanitarians, improvers of the condition of the working class, organisers of charity, members of societies for the prevention of cruelty to animals, temperance fanatics, hole-and-corner reformers'.[9] Within this world of social reformers, Green lived and found the ideals he taught in his ethics and politics.

2

To the European political exiles interned within the neglect of London after 1848, what the English called politics seemed little more than a particularly irritating variety of the cant so dear to their hosts. For what else could be said about parties so dominated by aristocrats, so closely tied to churches, whether Established or Nonconformist? This was a country whose statesmen justified, by semi-theological discourses, an unprecedented exploitation of workers. At the same time that they paid lip-service at home to the throttling code of Evangelical respectability, they engaged in *Realpolitik* abroad. As for the issues debated in Parliament, these held little interest to the radical Continentals. Respecting only those parties which derived from an ideology and engaged in direct action, they found it galling that English public life came to nothing more than empty agitation by all kinds and sizes of associations. Even the rich and well-born would meet with their social inferiors in the interest of improving the drainage system, or sending more missionaries to China which the Royal Navy had recently opened to the opium trade and other advantages of Christian civilisation. Ultimately reformers and philanthropists were surely either hypocrites or fools. While their works might mitigate ever so slightly the inherent evils of the capitalist system upon which their own position depended, such activity only obscured class conflict. Karl Marx, with a note of perplexity unusual in a man who ordinarily found the truth plain enough, recorded how the treasurer of the First International, Fred Stepney-Cowell, was 'a very rich and distinguished man, but wholly, if in a somewhat foolish fashion, devoted to the worker's cause'.[10] Very similar remarks were made by one of the most perceptive and sympathetic men of his century, who also found himself, against his will, a respectable inhabitant of London. Alexander Herzen wrote of the years after 1848:

> One cannot recollect those days without acute pain.... Even the most serious persons are sometimes overcome by the fascination of mere forms, and manage to convince themselves that they are in fact doing something if they hold meetings with a mass of documents and protocols, conferences at which facts are recorded, decisions are taken, proclamations are printed, and so forth. . . . England teems with hundreds of associations of this kind: solemn meetings take place which dukes and peers of the realm, clergymen and secretaries, ceremoniously attend: treasurers collect funds, journalists write articles, all are busily engaged in doing nothing at all. These philanthropic or religious gatherings fulfil the double function of

serving as a form of amusement and acting as a sop to the troubled consciences of these somewhat wordly Christians. . . . The whole thing was a contradiction in terms: an open conspiracy, a plot concocted behind open doors.[11]

What gave the game away to the exiles was the presence of clergymen at ostensibly political meetings. Their experience in Europe had taught them what might be expected from churches and priests. But in England not even the workers knew enough to be anti-clerical. This country, so advanced in trade and industry, seemed centuries behind in its attitudes to religion.* Engels wrote:

About the middle of this century, what struck every cultivated foreigner who set up his residence in England was what he was then bound to consider the religious bigotry and stupidity of the English respectable middle class. We, at that time, were all materialists, or, at least, very advanced freethinkers, and to us it appeared inconceivable that almost all educated people in England should believe in all sorts of impossible miracles.[12]

As the nineteenth century drew to a close, Engels, as the survivor of the collaboration which produced 'scientific socialism', was asked to write prefaces to the new editions of works written almost fifty years before by Marx and himself. Among the judgments he revised was his earlier estimation of the mid-Victorian 'respectable middle class'.

It had turned out not to have been so stupid after all. Frightened by the atheistic revolutionaries of 1789 and 1848, the British bourgeois had felt that he must keep the common people in order. The foremost means of acting upon the masses is religion. Hence the bourgeois

regardless of the sneers of his Continental compeers, . . . continued to spend thousands and tens of thousands, year after year, upon the evangelisation of the lower orders; not content with his own native religious machinery, he appealed to Brother Jonathan, the greatest organiser in existence of religion as a trade, and imported from America revivalism, Moody and Sankey, and the like.[13]

* Engels, a frequent visitor in the north, knew his Nonconformist England. He liked to tell of the time that he had been invited to Sunday dinner by one of his Manchester business associates. Inevitably the conversation came around to the sermons preached that morning, and Engels found himself being interrogated about which church he had attended. His reply was that on Sunday mornings nothing appealed to him more than a long walk. Upon hearing this, his host remarked, 'You seem to hold peculiar religious views, Mr Engels— somewhat Socinian, I think!' (Ernest Belfort Bax, *Reminiscences and Reflections of a Mid and Late Victorian* [London, 1918], pp. 50-51.)

As for the philanthropic reformers and their voluntary societies which had so annoyed Herzen, they were dismissed by Marx and Engels as that part of the bourgeoisie which wishes to reduce social grievances in the hope that insignificant concessions will guarantee the dominance of their class. What they wished was a bourgeoisie safe from the dangers of proletarian antagonism. Nor did the Christian Socialists come off any better in the 'Communist Manifesto'. That Maurice and Kingsley were 'parsons', that their movement appealed to Christian values—this was enough to betray their real significance. The parson, always the agent of the landlord, continued in the same rôle under Christian Socialism. In fact, this was but another form of 'feudal socialism', that extraordinary rear-guard action fought by the aristocracy in its losing struggle against the bourgeoisie. To arouse sympathy and to rally the support of the proletariat, the landed aristocracy had to formulate its case in terms which put it on the side of social justice. 'Young England' and Christian Socialism had the same sources and came to the same thing.

In this way arose feudal socialism: half lamentation, half lampoon; half echo of the past, half menace of the future; at times, by its bitter, witty and incisive criticism, striking the bourgeoisie to the very heart's core, but always ludicrous in its effect, through total incapacity to comprehend the march of modern history. . . .

Nothing is easier than to give Christian asceticism a specialist tinge. Has not Christianity declaimed against private property, against marriage, against the state? Has it not preached in the place of these, charity and poverty, celibacy and mortification of the flesh, monastic life and Mother Church? Christian Socialism is but the holy water with which the priest consecrates the heart-burnings of the aristocrat.[14]

Thus Marx and Engels wrote off those minority movements within the aristocracy and middle classes which protested against the injustices of capitalism. All consciously deceive, or are themselves deceived, about their actual motives. Appeal to the Christian social ethic is sham, as is any talk of a common good not to be identified with the good of any one class. Subjectively, perhaps, those who use such terms may have good intentions; objectively they had quite another effect. They contributed to the ideology of the ruling class. And ideology is a weapon no less than the police.

Writing in 1892, Engels saw no reason to change the analysis he had made with Marx in the Manifesto:

And to-day, the very people who, from the 'impartiality' of their superior standpoint, preach to the workers a Socialism soaring high

THE POLITICS OF CONSCIENCE

above their class interests and class struggles, and tending to
reconcile in a higher humanity the interests of both the contending
classes—these people are either neophytes, who have still to learn a
great deal, or they are the worst enemies of the workers—wolves in
sheep's clothing.[15]

Workers should be deceived neither by such talk about a common
good, nor by the campaign of Christian evangelising promoted by
the bourgeoisie. In 1892 it seemed to Engels that both lines of
deception had failed. Religion can be no lasting safeguard to
capitalist society. However great a retarding force it may be, in
the long run, it is doomed to be broken down. While the sons of
the Chartists had been led astray by religious dodges, their grand-
sons would be worthy of their forefathers.[16] Socialism must come
to Britain and it would have nothing to do with Christianity.

It is worth comparing this prediction, made in 1892, with
Engels' original conclusion to the *Condition of the Working Class in
England*:

> It is particularly easy to forecast future events in England because in
> that country every aspect of social development is so plain and clear-
> cut. The revolution *must* come. It is now too late for a peaceful
> outcome of the affair [—the antagonism between the workers and
> the bourgeoisie—] to be possible.[17]

Writing fifty years later, Engels explained that the revolution
had not occurred for two reasons: when the British had become
prosperous through their temporary monopoly as a manufacturing
centre, their bourgeoisie could bribe certain sections of the working class; as for the rest of the working class, it had been taken in
by the successful campaign of evangelism paid for by the
bourgeoisie. What, then, did he predict for the future? That
Britain, now no longer alone as a manufacturing centre, would
cease to be able to buy off its skilled workmen, that the new trade
unionism, which had begun to organise unskilled workers, would
lead to a class-conscious and irreligious socialism.

This second prophecy of 1892 was no more accurate than that of
1844. It may be said that both errors had a common root in the
failure of Marx and Engels to understand the true significance of
religious and voluntary movements. But let us consider Engels'
remarks not so much as a prediction of the future as a concession
of mistakes made in analysing the past. He was admitting that
religion played a critical rôle in preventing the development of a
militant and revolutionary working-class movement in the first
country to attain a completely capitalist economy. True, he
insisted that religion is an anti-revolutionary force serving

302

capitalist interests. But he assigned almost as much importance to religion as did any of those, like Elie Halévy, who explicitly denied the value of the Marxist analysis. The twentieth century Marxist who would deny Halévy's explanation is therefore in the position of refuting Engels as well.

The essential question of Halévy's *History of the English People in the Nineteenth Century* is much the same as that Engels put to himself in 1892: 'Why was it that of all the countries of Europe England has been the most free from revolutions, violent crises and sudden changes'?[18] But Halévy specifically rejected the theory of history which Engels attempted to maintain. 'If the materialistic interpretation of history is to be trusted . . .,' Halévy remarks, ' . . . the England of the nineteenth century was surely, above all other nations, destined to revolution, both political and religious. But it was not to be so.' What, then, can account for such a degree of continuity and stability at the same time as profound social change? Neither economic organisation nor political institutions offered sufficient explanations, Halévy argued. These must be sought in another type of social phenomena: 'beliefs, emotions, and opinions, as well as . . . the institutions and sects in which these . . . take a form suitable for scientific inquiry'.[19] It is worth noting that Engels and Halévy did not disagree about the crucial part played by religious phenomena in preventing revolution. But whereas Engels attempted to rescue his theory by asserting that religion in an industrial society can be only a temporary brake on inevitable developments, Halévy was concerned to discover in detail how religious forces could have had such an effect.

Halévy's enterprise was in many ways comparable to that of his German contemporary, Max Weber. Both took Marxism seriously enough to devote much of their work to demonstrating its inadequacies when used as a monistic theory reducing all historical phenomena to the question of which class controls the means of production. Neither Weber nor Halévy were concerned to replace Marxism by a rival theory designed to prove that religions are always and everywhere the essential cause of events. But both thought that a rigorous use of the comparative method could demonstrate that in certain historical instances religion has exerted a force independent of the forces of production. When Weber offered his hypothesis about the critical effect of Calvinism upon the development of capitalism, he did so within the much broader framework of his *Religionssoziologie*. There he dealt with a number of actual cases where religious belief, by creating varying attitudes towards economic activity, have significantly affected human behaviour. Why had capitalism occurred only in western

Europe although purely economic conditions were equally propitious in China and India? His answer was that Calvinism had oriented men towards the world in ways that made success in one's calling meaningful, and yet did not condone enjoyment of the pleasures to which wealth would otherwise have been directed. The major world religions have produced a great variety of attitudes towards economic activity. By no means did all of them simply mirror productive relations. Weber distinguished between certain instances in which religious forces were partially determining and certain others in which they were decisive. It was his judgment that even here the driving force seldom derived from theological ideas. Rather it was religious interests, such as the concern for salvation, which furnished the emotional dynamic. But ideas nevertheless perform an important function. By defining the meaning of potential courses of action, ideas influence their choice and direction. In Weber's metaphor, religious concepts, like switchmen, have determined the tracks along which the dynamic of interest has moved. Thus it was not the creeds, catechisms and official ethical manuals that produced the attitudes he studied but the psychological sanctions which, originating in religious commitments, gave direction to practical conduct by their 'definition of the situation'.

Halévy, like Weber, believed that the indirect and unanticipated consequences of religious movements were often more significant than the specific theological intentions of their founders. But whereas Weber studied the effects of religion upon economic activity, Halévy centred his attention upon politics, especially those of Great Britain in the nineteenth century. His history was conceived and executed in the spirit of a style of political analysis which originated in Montesquieu and was deepened by Tocqueville. Montesquieu suggested that when a state's religion is stable, it may survive political difficulties that otherwise would cause it to fall. Tocqueville, in a rather more sophisticated analysis, argued that if there is to be that minimum of order requisite to the maintenance of a political society, individual wills must be held in check by one or more means. The force of the state may be employed to achieve that objective, which also may be attained by the action of society or that of religion. Presumably to the extent that men's wills are so restrained, there becomes possible a corresponding diminution in the extent and strictness of state action. The relation between Tocqueville's hypothesis and Halévy's is evident. In his own analysis of the French Revolution, Tocqueville attempted to isolate its unique quality. This he found in the fact that at one and the same time religion, civil society and the state had all been reversed.

The violence and uncontrollability of events stemmed from the fact that the revolutionaries were proceeding on the basis of new principles in every aspect of life. When religion ceases to dominate men's wills, the most crucial political effect is neither apathy nor a mere absence of conviction. Rather the way is opened to a whole host of new secular ideals. These are not necessarily evil in themselves. Indeed, Tocqueville singled out for especial praise the disinterested idealism that characterised the first phase of the Revolution. But in a period of profound change it is dangerous to scrap all previous sources of order. When such an attempt is in fact made, men lose all their norms; they become *déréglés*, a term that anticipates Durkheim's concept of *anomie*.

Elie Halévy taught most of his life at the *Ecole libre des sciences politiques*, founded after the defeat of 1871 and the Commune to discover where France had gone astray in its political development. Halévy's great history of modern Britain was meant to be both a work of scholarship and a contribution to the French search for political wisdom. Certainly, Halévy's major hypotheses all depend upon a sustained if implicit comparison between the series of revolutions since 1789 in his own country, and the British peaceful evolution from an aristocratic to a democratic constitution. His method, like that of Montesquieu and Tocqueville, was comparative and sociological. That is to say, he considered British phenomena as constituting, not a natural and inevitable political pattern, but rather one that at every decisive turn calls for an explanation in terms of special conditions prevailing there, as they did not elsewhere. This method also focuses upon the reciprocal effects of politics, society and religion. No other major historian has been so sociological in practice.

On the continent, religion was identified with an established church controlled by the same social classes that ruled the state. Opposition to the government meant opposition to the church. Hence the almost universal connection between radicalism and atheism on the continent. But in Britain, because of the existence of so many sects and free churches, workers could not and did not identify religion with the Church of England. Nonconformity, as revivified by Methodism, reached into the working class, organised it in the class and chapel and thus played a part in creating a corporate sense and structure. Thus the free churches created an atmosphere in which the two continental watchwords of 'revolution' and 'reaction' had no meaning. When members of the lower classes protested against injustices, they did not feel compelled to

THE POLITICS OF CONSCIENCE

attack the system as a whole, nor did their revolt extend to every aspect of spiritual discipline. Rather they could appeal to values that were founded on a religious claim, and which were shared by at least a few members of every social class. And throughout much of the period of struggle, working-class leaders were subject to the discipline of their sects.

The contrast between France and Britain was no less marked when it came to the nature of working-class leadership. On the continent it was the middle class which had provided the revolutionary élite; whatever the origins of their British counterparts, they, for the most part, had been imbued by Evangelicalism with a spirit from which the established order had little to fear. Indeed, the long-range effect of the Methodist movement had been to blur the lines dividing social classes. Because religion ranked high among the indices of status, the ambivalent and pervasive consequences of Methodism produced a sort of religious spectrum with barely perceptible transitions starting from the older Nonconformist sects, and continuing from the various types of Methodists to the Evangelicals within the Church of England and finally the other parties within the Established Church. It was not at all unusual for a family whose fortunes were on the rise to move along the path from Nonconformity to the Anglican Church. British life thus had a unique quality: instead of drastic differences separating classes, there existed imperceptible gradations.

That the Revival touched some members of every class turned out to be of capital importance. This meant that a channel existed for communicating grievances, that some voices in the Commons and the Lords could be found to speak on behalf of classes formally excluded from political participation. And noble names and middle-class funds were occasionally available for the benefit of agitations carried out to improve the lot of disadvantaged groups further down in the scale. Often this type of virtual representation was not good enough. It was not for nothing that the franchise was sought and won, first by the middle, then by the working classes. Yet the fact remains that there were no continental analogues for the small but significant number of upper- and middle-class reformers who served the cause of those otherwise disenfranchised. All this presupposed the existence of an Evangelical social ethic, to which appeal could be made against class interest and the teachings of the political economists. Social conscience operated fitfully, and in the long run it was no substitute for the representation of the working classes by their own party. But at the very height of the manufacturer's victory in the 1840's, factory acts protecting certain restricted groups of their own employees were enacted despite the opposition of this powerful group. True, these acts were in themselves inadequate, but the principle contained in such state regulation of private enterprises was to be extended steadily until state guarantee of a minimum standard of life became an unchallenged principle of politics a century later. The Hammonds, scarcely apologists for the 'Bleak Age', wrote:

> 'We may say of all the industrial legislation of this period that it was legislation forced on the governing class, in spite of their intellectual misgivings, by the public conscience.'[20]

This public conscience in part was Evangelical in origin. Run down the list of those who led the agitation for the Ten Hours Act: Sadler, Bull, Wood, Oastler, Stephens, Brotherton, Grant—all were Evangelicals. John Fielden had been a Sunday School teacher; Lord Shaftesbury was, of course, an Evangelical of the strictest sort.[21]

It was one of the peculiarities of the Wesleyan Revival that the spirit it produced was at once philanthropic and conservative, combining social reform with individual piety. Not all Evangelicals were of this type, but those who were played a significant part in seeking particular reforms and getting them into the statute book. In this process it was often upper-class Evangelicals who provided the link between the governing class and those below who would benefit from state action. As for working-class movements, not infrequently their leadership derived from the lay-preachers of Nonconformist sects, such as Joseph Arch, founder of the National Agricultural Labourers' Union, and Thomas Burt and Charles Fenwick, the first trade unionists to sit in Parliament. The Labour Party led by Keir Hardie, Snowden, Henderson and Lansbury had the same quality and the same origins. It based its arraignment of the existing system on the fact that it violated the spirit of Christian morality. And so it appealed to a moral consensus rather than to a denunciation of that morality as a mere class ideology. By prejudging the political significance of Christianity, the Marxists forfeited what in Great Britain turned out to be one of the working classes' greatest source of strength, both for the moral energy of its leadership and for its success in swaying the larger public it sought to convince.

In 1914 Dicey, surveying some sixty years of social legislation, remarked that one of the major puzzles of the period was why wealthy Englishmen had resisted it so much more feebly than would have been anticipated by statesmen or economists in 1850. How account for such a flagrant disregard of class interest? The answer, Dicey suggested, lay in the combination of an intellectual error with a moral virtue. The mistake of the rich and well-born was their failure to realise the significance in the long run of any single humanitarian measure or the cumulative effect of a series of such measures; the moral virtue was an increasing sympathy with the sufferings of the poor. The net result of agitation by novelists, journalists, philanthropists, clergymen and trade-unionists, had been to make the condition of the poor into a matter of conscience for the rich.

> 'The desire to ease the sufferings, to increase the pleasures and to satisfy the best aspirations of the mass of wage-earners has become a marked characteristic of the wealthy classes of Englishmen. . . . No criticism, in any case, of public opinion in England is worth anything which fails to take into account the goodwill of the richer classes of Englishmen towards their less prosperous neighbours.'[22]

Dicey, for reasons of his own, spoke only of the groups above, not of the pressure from below applied by many who had acquired their capacity for organisation from their Evangelical origins. On those matters where public opinion had to be created rather than found, they had inherited an enormously successful instrument of agitation. This was the method used by the Methodists in their proselytising: the emotional appeal of the great mass meeting followed by the tightly-knit small local group connecting in turn to a central organisation. Perhaps the first political use of such machinery was in the campaign for the abolition of slavery. Through 'information, agitation, the parent society, the local branch, the picture and the handbill', public opinion was created to make itself felt in Parliament. It has been remarked that 'every Englishman since Wesley who had organised a campaign of propaganda, had copied intentionally or unintentionally the Wesleyan model'.[24] Skilfully employed, it won the day for the Anti-Corn Law League while it could not stave off the defeat of the Chartists. The Methodists were consciously imitated in their system of classes and class leaders by the Great Northern Political Union and the Chartists.[25] Later trade unions made use of the same scheme. Thus Wesleyan modes of organisation and agitation, as well as its social ethic, became part of British political life.

When Herzen condemned the public meetings, the hundreds of associations bringing together individuals of various classes and stations, he missed the secret of British reform movements, just as did Marx and Engels. Freedom to carry on propaganda, a governing class that included some few spokesmen for needed piecemeal changes, a philanthropic ethic which increasingly condemned suffering and injustice—all these contributed to what to Herzen seemed 'a contradiction in terms, an open conspiracy, a plot concocted behind open doors'.

This is neither to say, as did contemporary apologists, that all was well in nineteenth-century Britain, nor even that social progress was adequate. No reader of Marx and Engels or the Hammonds or Charles Booth will easily forget the conditions of life and work to which labourers, industrial and agricultural, were subjected. But the fact remains that, in comparison to the situation elsewhere, there was a miscellaneous group of reformers who did much to mitigate suffering and to shake the complacency of those who regarded themselves as the natural rulers of society. And this was done by a good deal of hard work on the part of these individuals. It could not have been done at all had there not existed some common ethic by which appeal to a given evil or condition could in the long run be demonstrated to require action. Much of what was achieved came as the result of shame at the discrepancy between the official moral standards of society and what in fact existed. Of course religious feelings were not the only force at work. Secular reformers did fully as much.

Any such schematic attempt to trace through a complex and rapidly changing society the effects of a single phenomenon will inevitably distort and exaggerate. There can be no doubt that the total picture was a good deal more complex than has been thus far indicated. For one thing, by the end of the century, working-class movements had assumed a position which enabled them, not only to call attention to abuses or genuine needs, but to mount and maintain a growing pressure upon all parties. From this time on, social legislation came increasingly, although not exclusively, as strategic concessions from the governing classes. And, as the administrative historians have begun to insist, the bureaucratic apparatus that was earlier installed to administer the new tasks assigned by Parliament became to some extent an independent force for working for further and more effective legislation along the lines suggested by the initial enactments. It was not only the civil servants, but secular reformers in general, who from the very beginning played a part in reform agitation at least as important as that of the Evangelicals. The relations between the Clapham Sect and the circle around Bentham, for example, were more often those of co-operation and admiration than antagonism. And in the curious world of social reformers and agitating groups, the alignments among the believing, the unbelieving and the sceptical were not easy to characterise. On some questions such as improving sanitary conditions they found it easy and natural to work together;

on others, such as education, no such concerted effort could succeed. This point did not escape Halévy's attention. Indeed it seemed to him that the fundamental paradox of English society was the partial junction and combination of Utilitarianism and Evangelicalism, two forces based on very different and apparently hostile principles. How could this be explained? His answer was that not only did the practical objectives of the two groups often coincide, but that in significant ways, they shared assumptions about the nature of man and society. Although Benthamism identified the good with happiness, it did so with the qualification that present and short-run pleasures must be sacrificed to achieve those in the future that promise to be more durable or worthwhile. The rational calculation, the exaltation of work, the asceticism of Evangelical morality—all had their counterparts in Utilitarianism. Economic asceticism, as Weber had noticed, was closely akin to that of Protestantism.* And if the Benthamites taught that society was a fiction and that only individuals ought to be counted in determining the greatest good of the greatest number, some of them assumed that the state might, by its sanctions, intervene to establish a harmony of interests in society. Even those Utilitarians who rejected this form of the doctrine nevertheless welcomed the formation of associations in which common ends might be pursued at the cost of its adherents freely surrendering some part of their individual rights. The Christian Socialists also threw their weight behind co-operative and friendly societies, although opposing militant trade unions. For the Christian Socialists wished to reconcile the classes, and engage in projects of amelioration, based not on class warfare, but on the notion of common obligations. These notions Green took over from them; although respecting the purely secular and Utilitarian reformers, he clearly preferred those with a religious or quasi-religious outlook.

3

What attracted Green most in the Evangelical tradition was its philanthropic humanitarianism. He identified himself with the saving remnant of his age, those few who could not abide the sight of the suffering otherwise ignored or considered inevitable by members of their class. Sometimes little could be done by individuals and groups to relieve distress deeply rooted in the new society, which was as yet so little understood; sometimes, the

* Halévy read the first version of Weber's essay in 1905. His footnote both acknowledges and qualifies his debt: 'For the kinship between economic asceticism and Protestant asceticism, see the subtle, often indeed the excessively subtle, observations of Max Weber . . .' (*England in 1815*, p. 586 n.)

associations, formed to eliminate a particular evil or satisfy some need, appeared merely fatuous.* Yet both by direct action and by legislative means, the social reformer played a creative part in devising and executing the social services that added some measure of humanity and justice to industrial society. Such humanitarianism was often emotional, but it spurred action when reason, in the form of political economy, denied that anything could be done. Remedies were specific, seldom calling into question the structure of capitalist society, although frequently violating the precepts of laissez-faire. Evangelicalism conceived of religion as regeneration, and emphasised the obligation of an individual who has himself seen the light to pass on his benefit to others, to act when confronted with suffering or injustice. Green shared these attitudes, which went along with contempt for the individual ascetic or the Churchman preoccupied with dogma or ceremonial. In his lay sermons he assigned charity a prominent place in the religious life. The denial of the self so as to serve others is the true meaning of faith and witness to God's presence:

'This work, which is at once God's and our own, and in which therefore his presence is witnessed not with signs from without but

* G. K. Chesterton's well-known lines hit off this aspect of the Christian Social Union: (Maisie Ward, *Gilbert Keith Chesterton* [N.Y.: Sheed & Ward, 1943], pp. 163-4):

'The Christian Social Union here
  Was very much annoyed;
It seems there is some duty
  Which we never should avoid,
And so they sang a lot of hymns
  To help the Unemployed.

Upon a platform at the end
  The speakers were displayed
And Bishop Hoskins stood in front
  And hit a bell and said
That Mr Carter was to pray,
  And Mr Carter prayed.

Then Bishop Gore of Birmingham
  He stood upon one leg
And said he would be happier
  If beggars didn't beg,
And that if they pinched his palace
  It would take him down a peg.

He said that Unemployment
  Was a horror and a blight,
He said that charities produce
  Servility and spite,
And stood upon the other leg
  And said it wasn't right.

And then a man named Chesterton
  Got up and played with water,
He seemed to say that principles
  Were nice and led to slaughter
And how we always compromised
  And how we didn't orter.

Then Canon Holland fired ahead
  Like fifty canons firing,
We tried to find out what he meant
  With infinite enquiring,
But the way he made the windows jump
  We couldn't help admiring.

I understood him to remark
  (It seemed a little odd.)
That half-a-dozen of his friends
  Had never been in quod.
He said he was a Socialist himself
  And so was God.

He said the human soul should be
  Ashamed of every sham,
He said a man should constantly
  Ejaculate "I am"
When he had done, I went outside
  And got into a tram.'

with demonstration from within, is summed up in the one word, charity, or Christian love. Mere knowledge puffeth up, as St Paul says, but charity edifieth. Charity, that is to say, is constructive. In the temple of Christian fellowship, where no man seeks his own but every one another's good . . . charity is building a presence-chamber of God.'[26]

Thus Green celebrated charity as constructive, as regenerating both its agent and recipient, and by its demands, making it impossible for the moral man to enjoy comfort so long as his fellow has none. There is no mistaking the fact that Green was taking as his model the Evangelical philanthropist. Yet at the same time neither the theology of Evangelicalism nor its Tory politics were acceptable to him. Wilberforce and his allies had helped secure the abolition of slavery but supported the Government's actions at Peterloo and the repressive Six Acts of 1819 which followed; Lord Shaftesbury led a multitude of reforming campaigns including that for Factory Acts, but nevertheless opposed the Reform Bills of 1832 and 1867. Such an outlook 'took for granted the social divisions which its benevolence softened'. The world was divided into those who did good and those to whom good was done.[27] Later in the century, social reformers were to question on Christian principles the structure of society itself, asserting that 'wherever society is divided into a minority of "Haves" and a multitude of "Have Nots", charity is twice cursed, it curseth him that gives and him that takes'.[28] This comment indicates the reservations held by the Webbs about the social value of philanthropy; these were in part shared by Green and Arnold Toynbee, but were altogether foreign to Lord Shaftesbury. Each of these attitudes revealed much about the persons holding them. Lord Shaftesbury, who introduced the upper classes to the idea of personal work among the poor, did so in the spirit of paternal benevolence. But the settlement house movement, connected with Toynbee's name and supported by many of Green's disciples, emphasised comradeship. As the Hammonds remarked, 'It was the aim of these reformers to bring together rich and poor in a common interest in the better government of the squalid and neglected districts of London rather than to try merely to soften the worst inequalities of life by a Christian kindness that was apt to degenerate into patronage.'[29] The Webbs tended to think that individual action availed little unless the system as a whole was changed; Green and Toynbee still were most concerned about the effects of action upon character.

Lord Shaftesbury would scarcely have understood the Webbs' outlook. He himself on religious grounds had simply reacted against inhumanity wherever he saw it: in the factories and in the mines, in the employment of chimney sweeps, the treatment of the insane, the absence of drains and public health measures, the lack of adequate housing, the failure to provide for homeless children. His energy was enormous. At his funeral there marched representatives of more than two hundred voluntary societies with which he had been associated. More than any other man of his age, Shaftesbury aroused the Christian conscience of his well-to-do countrymen. Despite his public life, he was a lonely and dedicated man who, like his model, John Wesley, showed how much can be done by an unquestioning faith and a methodical asceticism. Disregarding his political career, declining cabinet posts and the Order of the Garter, Shaftesbury represented the Evangelical social conscience acting through legislative and voluntary action to humanise an impersonal economic order and the society it had thrown up. Yet his faith was narrow. Converted as a child by his nurse, he never moved from his early beliefs in the literal inspiration of the scriptures. Nor did he ever question the system of land tenure or the principle of aristocracy: no theorist, he never conceived any alternative to the industrial order that produced the conditions he found intolerable; no democrat, he never favoured extending the franchise so that the under-privileged might claim justice for themselves. Shaftesbury's greatness lay in his acknowledgment of the obligation of the powerful and well-placed to their miserable fellows. But, in his mind, society was divided into those who gave and those who received. Equality was no part of his ideal.

Men like Shaftesbury were never numerous, especially in his class. Born into a great family, he was educated at Harrow and Christ Church. More often reformers came from the middle class. In his analysis of voluntary action, Lord Beveridge attempted to isolate the elements common to the most prominent and effective persons of this kind, ranging from Shaftesbury to the Webbs. On his list manual workers were as sparsely represented as aristocrats. He concluded:

'It is common, of course, to all of these men and women that they set out to do things without asking what they would get thereby for themselves. Three other points stand out from this review. One is the significance of the middle class, that is to say, people who have to work for a living but do not as a rule work under the direction of another or to fixed hours. A second point is the significance of the religious motive. The third point is the need for material resources to put new ideas into practice; some of the pioneers had fortunes of their own; others had the fortunes of friends at call.'[30]

Such persons, despite their differences, tended to co-operate and to use the same pattern in their campaigns. Without any conscious collaboration or plan, they evolved a distinctive method of proceeding. Thus many British social services have followed this course of evolution: a middle-class person was shocked into action by the conditions of work in a given industry or by the failure to provide a much needed service, say the education of crippled children. This individual became virtually obsessed with the cause: he created an organisation, the directing committee of which used funds raised from anyone who could be convinced to contribute. Next came public meetings, chaired preferably by someone with a noble name. This was only the first act in a campaign of propaganda. Perhaps the founder is interested in direct voluntary action, perhaps in enlisting the support of the state. If the first, then the private agency may remain the primary means; if the second, Ministers are interviewed, legislation suggested, questions asked by friends in Parliament, articles planted in a friendly newspaper or review, pamphlets issued, significant facts collected and publicised. At last the time was judged ripe for introducing the bill into Parliament, and this was most often done by a Private Member's Bill. But it was by no means usual for such a proposed act to be enacted at the first attempt. Rather, it more likely was rejected out of hand, and only after repeated efforts would its proponents succeed in getting its merits investigated by a committee. Long years would pass, evidence piled up on what had been found out before, and finally the proposal might be favourably reported. Even then, if it lacked Government support its chances were slim. After more time and effort had eroded resistance, the House of Commons might pass the measure, only to have it defeated in the Lords. But that bastion against change could also be taken if only patience and funds could outlast it. And so the statute at last becoming law, its proponents could take a breath and congratulate themselves. Yet their task was not finished, nor the history of their reform over and done with. For the form of the enactment may have been inadequate from the point of view of effective administration. In such an eventuality, it may turn out to be the civil servants charged with putting the law into effect who press for considerable revisions and extension of its scope.[31]

Or the reform association, once armed with a statute as a precedent, may by subsequent agitation succeed in securing an enlargement of the general principle implicit in the initial enactment. Later, after much subsequent experience, there might be an act putting together related legislation. And perhaps during the Asquith government's years of reform the principle of financing the measure was altered and aid made more systematic and complete. Finally after 1945 all such schemes are incorporated into the 'national minimum' recommended by the Beveridge Report of 1942, and to a great extent enacted into law by the Labour Government after 1945. Whether the 'Welfare State' has been attained or, if attained, is worth keeping—are questions now in the realm of political disagreement as well as sociological investigation.

Increasingly, historians of English social services have agreed that there was nothing in their development which resembled a conscious plan or historical inevitability. Rather, they emerged in piecemeal fashion, and this haphazard and unco-ordinated attention to various categories of need carried with it inherent disadvantages of administration which have never been altogether overcome. Professor Titmuss has argued that this phase of creating a body of services 'untidily human and perversely shaped' continued until 1945:

> The benefits and stimulus of combination—of mutual aid—among the workers joined with the passionate effort of social reformers drawn from all classes in society to achieve first an advance here and then there. The advances that were made represented an accumulation of political and social compromise; each perhaps constituting, in the circumstances of the day, the limit of reform which could be put into effect without upsetting the existing order.[32]

This description applies almost equally well to the period before the Liberal legislation of this century as to that which followed it. No one who has studied this history as a whole has doubted that reformers brought to their work a remarkable quality of social invention and organisational skill, as well as humanitarian zeal and personal stubborness. To take an example from the career of those influenced by Green, Mrs Humphry Ward personally discovered the situation of crippled children unable to attend school, and carried through a campaign to provide for them. As the result of her allegiance to his teaching, she had established a settlement house (then called Passmore Edwards, now known as the Mary Ward Settlement). Its rooms were filled at night, but empty during the day. Mrs Ward had heard of a class for crippled children held at another Settlement. Through friends on the London School Board, she began a similar school. Then investigation proved that many more such children existed than anyone had expected, 'helpless children left at home all day, perhaps with a little food within reach, while mother and father were out at work, with *nothing on earth to do*, and only the irregular and occasional visits of some kind-hearted neighbour to look forward to'.[33] Ten years after she began her campaign there were thirty such schools

THE POLITICS OF CONSCIENCE

with 2,452 children. In 1918, Mrs Ward succeeded in persuading the House of Commons to add to Mr H. A. L. Fisher's Education Bill a provision making it compulsory for Education Authorities throughout the country to make similar arrangements for the education of their physically defective children. She carried on a campaign from her own house, sending out circular letters to ninety-five Education Authorities, sifting and printing their replies, and forwarding these to every member of Parliament. As a result the 30,000 uneducated and uncared for invalid children who remained throughout the country came under the protection of the state.

4

From this pattern of social improvement carried on in his time largely by a small minority of middle-class persons, Green drew the inspiration for the type of character he celebrated in the *Prolegomena to Ethics*. For there he assigned an extraordinary value to all such activity. The very essence of ethical behaviour is said to be the unremitting struggle to 'reform' the practice of oneself and one's society to conform more closely to the moral ideal. And the 'reformer' is that exceptional individual who accepts as an urgent personal vocation the need to improve life for others, while sacrificing his own personal pleasures. In the final book of the *Prolegomena*, so much is made of these terms that it becomes clear that they form the link between Green's abstract theory and his recommendations to those among his hearers who wished to know how they might live up to their obligations as defined by their mentor. Of course Green did not invent this symbol, but he made it less political and more social, and connected it to a consciousness of guilt.

For the mid-Victorians 'reform' was a word which stood for a complex of thought and feeling. There was an early, literal sense of the word, which meant the restoration of an original excellence by the elimination of those abuses that had come to mar an institution.[34] F. D. Maurice used the word in this way, and somehow made a teleological and organic theory into a profoundly effective critique of capitalism in the year of the Great Exhibition.*

* 'To reform signifies literally to form again, or form anew. Instead of being equivalent with the putting one thing away and putting another thing in its place, it implies what is almost opposite to this, the putting into its proper and original shape that which has got out of shape. A person who undertakes a reform says this: "Here is a thing you are all complaining of, which you say is out of order. . . . Now that must be because it has lost its *form*. It has become more or less *deformed*, and we must try to find out what its true form is . . . that we may enable it to fulfil its office healthily and free. You ask a surgeon or

316

Green, who at Rugby had read Maurice, an associate and correspondent of his uncle, D. J. Vaughan, felt it necessary to rephrase the concept of reform to accommodate something quite different in meaning: the notion of improvement, not by return to any previous state of affairs, but rather by progress to some new and higher form of the original ideal. The connection between 'reform' and 'progress' was not fortuitous. Both concepts were at the same time ethical attitudes and philosophies of history. Green's ethics had made improvement into one of the essential qualities of morality. The ethical achievement of a person or society cannot rest at any given point without the gravest danger of decadence. Since the spirit of morality must constantly be adapted to changing conditions, the political and social institutions which are its concrete expression must accordingly be 're-formed'. Green sought to identify the ethics of Philosophical Idealism with one particular pattern of politics:

> No one doubts that a man who improves the current morality of his time must be something of an Idealist. He must have an idea, which moves him to seek its realisation, of a better order of life than he finds about him. . . . It is an idea to which nothing real as yet corresponds, but which, as actuating the reformer, tends to bring into being a reality corresponding to itself.[35]

It is the reformer who resolves the confusion about obligation which has its origin in 'popular philosophy'. Without inventing a new revolutionary morality, he clarifies, corrects and advances the old. Because the reformer is concerned with the reality of the spiritual principle rather than with its temporary manifestation in conventional morality or existing arrangements, he has the courage to propose what appear to be innovations. 'Rival parties adopt him as their own or cast him from them, as may suit their purpose; but he is fulfilling a work which they know not of, a work which has many points of contact with the political and social movements of the day, but which is yet distinct from them both in origin and end.'[36] What the reformer has, and others lack, is moral initiative, and a vivid sense of personal responsibility for making the society live up to the duties imposed by the morality immanent in its structure. 'The reformer cannot bear to think of himself except as giving effect . . . to his project of reform; and thus, instead of merely contemplating a possible work, he does it.'[37]

---

physician . . . to come in as a reformer. . . . You do not ask him to give you some new functions. . . . But you fancy that he can find out . . . what the proper form of these functions is and that he may know some way of removing that . . . which has deranged the function." ' [John Frederick Denison Maurice, 'On the Reformation of Society,' (Southampton and London, 1851), pp. 4-5.]

There can be little doubt that the reformer, as portrayed by Green, was a middle-class type, and that the teaching of the *Prolegomena* was directed towards an audience of the same social origin. For he was not addressing men who had to worry about subsisting from one day to another. Yet the conditions of their ancestry were neither so opulent as to debauch them, nor so exigent as to destroy their generosity. This composite portrait of Green's public emerges clearly from the final book of his lectures on ethics. There, at the climax of his polemic against Utilitarianism, he attempted to compare its probable effects with those likely to be attained by his own Idealism. Just as Beatrice Webb later was to speak of the 'average sensual man' as the material with which the social planner must work, so Green constructed the type of the average thinking man, *l'homme moyen intellectuel*.[38]

What would be the probable effects upon such a person if he characteristically acted upon the Utilitarian maxim to maximise pleasure and minimise pain? Upon Green's maxim to do that which tends to realise his better self? When taken literally, Green argued, the Utilitarian theory must produce a 'hedonistic fatalism' which paralyses moral initiative, and so supports whatever it is that exists. A consistent Utilitarian, once his own needs are satisfied, has no reason to trouble himself about those of other people. And this was precisely the situation of middle-class persons, now that their own political and religious disabilities had been removed. There was a grave possibility that henceforth they would acquiesce in any set of arrangements from which they themselves profited. The one way of reaching their social conscience was through philosophy, to which an increasing number was turning in order to find a guide for personal action. Neither Christianity, in its Evangelical form, nor the social code of the aristocracy was a possible option. Yet more and more persons felt the need for a theoretical justification of their conduct and had the material means to live as they saw fit.

> Good people, of the sort who fifty years ago would have found in the law of their neighbour's opinion, or in the requirements of their church or sect, or in the precepts of Scripture as interpreted by church or sect, sufficient direction for so much of their work and conduct as it would have occurred to them to think in need of any direction . . . now . . . to an extent unknown in previous generations . . . are seeking a theoretical direction for individual conduct . . . and . . . seem to themselves to be largely influenced in conduct by this theoretical direction. . . .
>
> In the European nations a constantly increasing number of persons find themselves in circumstances in which a large option is allowed

them as to the plan on which they will conduct their lives. . . . They can 'please themselves' in regard to a large part of their action; and they are naturally interested in finding a theory which . . . will always give them a basis for arguing with themselves and others, whether that conduct is justifiable or otherwise.

Philosophy was, therefore, the special concern of a small but significant number of persons, for the most part of middle-class origin but now with some unearned income that made them free within certain limits to do what they wished with their lives. Certainly such people did exist and not a few of them were in fact preoccupied with the question of duty and right conduct. Beatrice Webb, for example, inherited £1,000 per year from her capitalist father. On this sum she and her husband were able to do their research and promote with conspicuous success the Fabian cause. And although Mrs Webb did not know Green's work, she very nearly reproduced his language when she attempted to set down what had been the persistent interest of her life. The distinction between the higher and lower self, the notion of a calling to which the conscientious person otherwise free ought to dedicate himself, and a contempt for the mere pleasure-seeker or opportunist—these are the dominating ideas of her autobiography:

> Beneath the surface of our daily life . . . there runs a continuous controversy between an Ego that affirms and an Ego that denies. . . . With some individuals this half-submerged but often continuous controversy changes in subject-matter as years go on; with others all controversy dies down and the individual becomes purely practical and opportunist and scoffs at those who trouble over ultimate questions of right and wrong. But where the individual has had the exceptional luck of being able to choose his work, . . . there may be set up a close correspondence between the underlying controversy and all his external activities. . . . The internal controversy . . . in my own consciousness, from girlhood to old age, led me in early life to choose a particular vocation. . . . The upshot of this controversy has largely determined my day-to-day activities, domestic, social and professional.[40]

To the type of person here described, Green recommended his philosophical justification of 'simple, religious citizenship'. This phrase conveys in brief his conception of the good man in good society. By 'simple' he meant the austerity of Evangelical asceticism, secularised and put into the service of social renovation; by 'religious' a selfless passion for making Christian values prevail in his society; by 'citizenship' that moral development which comes from active participation in the life of a community where all men are treated as ends and never as means.

The culmination of the *Prolegomena* came in Green's appeal to all those with advantages to renounce them, and to sacrifice their personal pleasures so that all their fellow men might have the opportunity to realise their potentialities as human beings. Society was denying the possibility of self-development to its weaker members, who were being left 'to sink or swim in the stream of unrelenting competition. . . . So far as negative rights go—rights to be let alone—they are admitted to membership of civil society, but the good things to which the pursuits of society are in fact directed turn out to be no good things for them.'[41]

This outburst of emotion was almost unique in Green's professorial lectures, for he counted as self-indulgence any public display of emotion. Yet many in his audience at Oxford and his readers, after their publication, seem to have been touched by this revelation of their author's faith. This elaborate intellectual system turned out, after all, to be a philosophy of life with a personal implication for any conscientious person seeking guidance.

When Green spoke of the ' "Christian worker", who devotes himself, unnoticed and unrewarded, at the risk of life and at the sacrifice of every pleasure but that of his work, to the service of the sick, the ignorant and the debased,' he simply called the attention of his audience to the Evangelical philanthropist, a type that Green found rather than created. But when he made his audience uneasy about 'the pleasures of eye and ear, of search for knowledge, of friendly intercourse,' he began to transform the image of philanthropy.[42] For up to this time, middle-class philanthropists seldom questioned the organisation of society which made it possible for them to give and for the poor to receive. Their religion taught them charity, but charity, thus defined, involves the act of giving, the subjective virtue, rather than the objective effect of the gift. That the arrangements of society might be completely reorganised they did not consider, but instead accepted the world they found and practised charity within it. A Christian has the duty to relieve his suffering fellow. If God has seen fit to make a man rich, then the beneficiary must treat his riches as a steward administering a trust to the less fortunate. No guilt, however, attached to the possession of wealth. But beginning in the 1870's, some middle-class philanthropists began to suspect that they were profiting from a distribution of wealth and advantage that they could not justify morally. The difference between the older philanthropy and the new cannot be better illustrated than by comparing the words and life of a father, Dr Joseph Toynbee, and Arnold Toynbee his son.

The Toynbee family came of Lincolnshire yeomen stock and is

said to have been Evangelical in the early nineteenth century when Joseph Toynbee came to London.[43] In time he became a Fellow of the Royal Society and perhaps the outstanding aural surgeon of his day. He lost his life in experimenting on anaesthesia. An ardent philanthropist, he was the promoter with Lord Morpeth of the earliest Health of Towns Bill. In this cause, he helped found the Health of Towns Association, an agency to disseminate facts, to organise lectures and public meetings to petition Parliament. 'It is only by "pressure from without",' cried a speaker at its inaugural meeting, ' "that anything useful can be accomplished, and petitions must be poured in in order to awaken the Legislature from the torpor to which it is habitually addicted".'[44] This association with its goals, its methods and its membership illustrates how much matters were managed. Edwin Chadwick inspired it and wrote its resolutions. He was supported by Lord Shaftesbury, then Lord Ashley:

> The most striking feature of the Association was its comprehensive social and political basis. On its Committee of 1844 the aristocracy (represented by Normanby, its chairman, and the Earl Lovelace) and the Bishops (represented by London, St Davids, and Norwich) sat cheek by jowl with W. E. Hickson, the tradesmen's son, and John Leslie, the tailor of Conduit St. The doctors were represented by John Simon, Joseph Toynbee, and R. D. Grainger. . . . Prominent Whigs were there, like Normanby and Morpeth, side by side with Young England in the person of Disraeli and Lord John Manners; radicals like Hawes and Sheil spoke on the same platform as Sir Robert Inglis and Lord Ashley.[45]

But Dr Toynbee worked directly at philanthropy as well as by agitation for legislative action. As a young man he would visit the most depressed sections of London to do what he could. Thus he began a 'Samaritan Fund' to provide nourishment for the sick, put up his own money for ventilators in rooms with no such facilities and attempted to cure men of alcoholism by using coffee and other substitutes. He never discussed religious questions, either with the persons he aided or with his own family. Like so many others he was sustained by a faith of his own making. Its deities were honoured in the names of his children who were called after Wordsworth, Dr Arnold and Coleridge. Dr Toynbee's social attitudes were uncomplicated, indeed naïve, as can be seen from his description of Rochdale, where the Bright family had their factory and the Rochdale Pioneers founded the first Co-operative store:

> Ah! one of our manufacturing towns is a wonderful sight. . . . We passed Rochdale when coming and saw it well from the railway.

Fancy a valley full of great red-brick buildings with enormous chimneys pouring out for ever the blackest smoke. . . . It rained at R. [ochdale] yesterday and the place looked as gloomy and dark as Tartarus, and still to me it was a pleasant sight, for I could but think of the thousands upon thousands working manfully there and while living by honest labour, they were preparing comfort for thousands upon thousands elsewhere. We saw the heather-clad hills again, but for some reason they did not appear so beautiful as before.[46]

Only a vague shadow passed over the world at the sight of industrialism at work; the official optimism was only slightly marred. And how far from guilt was the philanthropy the good doctor described in his letters as he apologised to his children for his absence.

My only excuse is that I have been taken up with duties, and when I tell you, my dears, that they have not been quite selfish, but, on the contrary, tending to confer a good deal of happiness, present and future on the labouring classes, you will not be less ready than usual to excuse me.

Or, most innocent of all:

It seems strange that the working people cannot afford to educate their children, provide themselves with proper homes, or pay for medical attendance without assistance from the rich. But, doubtless, the kindly feeling this induces is a boon for both rich and poor.[47]

Dr Toynbee's philanthropy bore the marks of his age: he was infinitely kind but a great distance separated him from the objects of his benevolence; he regretted suffering, but never questioned the system that produced it. There was no trace in him of that sense of guilt which, twenty years later, was to draw from his son one of the most extraordinary public confessions of his day:

We—the middle classes, I mean, not merely the very rich—we have neglected you; instead of justice we have offered you charity, and instead of sympathy, we have offered you hard and unreal advice; but I think we are changing. If you would only believe it and trust us, I think that many of us would spend our lives in your service. You have—I say it clearly and advisedly—you have to forgive us, for we have wronged you; we have sinned against you grievously—not knowingly always, but still we have sinned, and let us confess it; but if you will forgive us—nay, whether you forgive us or not—we will serve you, we will devote our lives to your service, and we cannot do more. We will do this and only ask you to remember one thing in return . . . if you get a better life, you will really lead a better life.[48]

The differences between father and son derived in large part from the effect of Green's teaching upon the younger Toynbee. Yet when the Balliol reformers spoke of replacing charity by justice, they did so from a point of view which, although far less condescending than that taken by the previous generation of philanthropists, nevertheless was not that of working-class persons. It would be exaggerating to assert that Green and Toynbee made their services to the classes beneath them conditional on the acceptance of the values esteemed by the reformers. Toynbee did say that whether or not the working class regarded social service by middle-class persons as a gesture of repentance, that service would be forthcoming as an act of conscience by those who had profited from an unjust set of arrangements. But it is surely important that Green and Toynbee, like the Christian Socialists before them, thought that their activities would produce solidarity among classes, that co-operation between middle-class reformers and what they considered the better part of the working class would create a moral community in the sense that the virtues of the preceptors as well as their intellectual training would become more generally diffused. The relationship was thus to be tutelary; it was no accident that the impulse transmitted by Green and Toynbee was at its best in the field of adult education. In their time there was no question of who was to lead and who to follow. Yet this position could produce in advanced Liberals a sense of disappointment when Labour began to press its claims as an independent party, with working-class leadership. This was not what they had hoped for.* Nor could they feel altogether pleased at the prospect of social services being performed by the professional bureaucracy of a central government rather than by the voluntary services of persons like themselves. For was not their objective the improvement of individual character? Green's emphasis upon this criterion has too often been understood as simply a protection of personal liberty against the organic theory of the state. But it also placed limits upon state action and defined its end. The common good was not to be identified with mere material improvement; the good society, with the affluent society. The reformer thus had

---

* This appears very clearly from the Reverend Samuel Barnett's account of the impulse which created Toynbee Hall and the settlement movement: 'Men at the Universities, especially those who directly or indirectly felt the influence of T. H. Green, were asking for some other way than that of institutions by which to reach their neighbours. . . . Thus it came about that a group of men and women at the Universities distrusted machinery for doing good. . . . Their desire was, as human beings, to help human beings, and their human feeling protested against forms of help which put the interest of a class or of a party before that of individuals. . . .' [W. Reason (ed.), *University and Social Settlements* (London, 1898), pp. 12-15.]

purposes of his own. While these were disinterested in one sense, they subjected the freedom of workers to do what they liked with their money to restrictions not imposed upon their employers. Toynbee, in a passage which ought to be read together with his admission of collective guilt said:

> If working men are to expect their employers to act with larger notions of equity in their dealings in the labour market, it is at least rational that . . . workmen shall set about reforming their own domestic life. It is at least reasonable that . . . working men shall combine to put down drunkenness and brutal sports. High wages are not an end in themselves. No one wants high wages in order that working men may indulge in more sensual gratification. We want higher wages in order that an improved material condition, with less of anxiety and less uncertainty as to the future, may enable the working man to enter on a purer and more worthy life.[49]

5

Toynbee's combination of guilt with moralism was not uncommon among middle-class reformers, who often opposed direct action by the government to improve the position of working men. Even in the area of the labour market, Green and Toynbee seem to have hoped that employers and those they hired would in time come to reconcile their claims by a spontaneous recognition of their mutual obligations to the whole of the community. But rather more vivid than such hopes for the future was the Idealist's image of what was already being done by individual and group initiative. For they believed that there existed already a voluntary system, which had developed spontaneously among the workers, guided by their middle-class friends, who had used their influence in Parliament to make legal the activities of co-operative, friendly and building societies as well as the trade unions of artisans and skilled workmen. Now that these constituted a powerful movement, they must be included in any definition of the ends and consideration of the means to be used by the legislator. Thus political and social policy should not be construed as the choice between a pure individualism or collectivism, as Dicey later suggested. For such organisations of working-men offered hope of a *via media*. Their members accepted obligations imposed by their collective purposes, and so transcended mere individualism; at the same time, having learned the lessons of self-help, they did not look to the government for support. What was being done was the work of free men, who were not the creatures of a centralised and omnipotent bureaucracy. Functions which might be most dangerous if executed by agents of the government could safely be entrusted to voluntary agency. So long as individual character was being developed among workmen along the lines approved by their preceptors, there could be no objection. This philosophy was summed up in a chapter called 'The state, self-government and self-help' which catches the atmosphere so enthusiastically reported by Baernreither, an Austrian who carefully interviewed both the leaders and middle-class supporters in the 1880's of workingmen's associations.[50] The viewpoint of the Co-operatives was stated in a work often reprinted,* one of whose authors was an intimate friend of Green and Toynbee, A. H. D. Acland, who succeeded Tom Hughes on the Central Board of the Co-operative Union.

> The advantages of Co-operation . . . are . . . (1) The prevention of waste, and of a position of disadvantage to those who can least afford such disadvantage. (2) The encouragement of sympathy with public aims, and a desire for the well-being of the community generally. (3) The development of intelligence, self-reliance and business knowledge in a manner that has had a real educational and political value.[51]

The moral overtones of such approval for self-help were not unimportant in the decision to give the friendly societies a prominent place in the administration of Lloyd George's pensions act in the next century.

It was true that, to the extent social services existed at all in Green's England, they were not the work of the state. But that the protection offered by such associations were adequate, or that even their benefits could be provided from the income of most

---

* Many of Green's leading themes appear in this influential statement of the Co-operatives' aims: 'The general purpose of the societies . . . is, that . . . the work done shall be done not in the interest of . . . one individual, or a few, but in the interest of the general body of those who are concerned. . . . The idea is, no doubt, but imperfectly realised as yet. But the principle of equitable association for the general good is . . . being carried out. . . .

If Co-operators act up to their principles . . .; if they try to get rid of self-seeking and laziness, they will retain the "respect and sympathy of the community" which are of such real importance to the working class.

For they can show that the streams of charitable gifts which have been poured out have often made things worse, but this has made things better; they know that while the gift of the franchise has not always appeared to educate men, this at least helps to educate men in a real sense. They believe in advancement neither by privilege, name, nor wealth, but only by merit; and yet they do not want to pull down or to set class against class, but rather to build up, and to promote that sympathy and friendship between class and class which is of such vital importance to the national welfare.' [Arthur H. Dyke Acland and Benjamin Jones, *Working Men Co-operators* (London, 1884), pp. 9-10, 20.]

industrial and agricultural workers—these were assertions which did not survive the first social surveys of Charles Booth and Seebohm Rowntree. Yet for some time the friendly societies were regarded as one of the oustanding successes of English social organisation. The first Parliamentary act to use the term, defined it as

> a society of good fellowship for the purpose of raising from time to time, by voluntary contributions, a stock or fund for the mutual relief and maintenance of all and every the members thereof, in old age, sickness, and infirmity, or for the relief of widows and children of deceased members.[52]

Men who knew one another paid money into a common fund which they or their families could then draw upon in time of need. Many abhorred any thought of contact with the agencies established by the New Poor Law of 1834. Thus Dickens describes old Betty Higden, 'Patiently to earn a spare, bare living and quietly to die, untouched by workhouse hands—this was her highest sublunary hope'.[53] Voluntary organisations helped to provide a sense of self-respect, and, at the same time, fellowship and conviviality. Meetings of trade-unions and friendly societies were often held in public-houses, the only social centre, apart from the chapel or church, available to those seeking relief from cramped and depressing living quarters. Often this connection to the public house was criticised: by clergymen for obvious reasons; by reformers like Bentham who thought that meeting in a public house to encourage thrift was 'like choosing a brothel for a school of continence'.[54] The same difficulty arose for trade unions and workmen's political organisations. One Unitarian minister, a close friend all his life of the working class, was much disturbed by the 'injurious impression Trade Unions gave to the class socially above them (whose help they needed politically and legally) by their custom of meeting in a "pot-house" for the transaction of their business'.[55] Green led a campaign in Oxford to build a Liberal Hall, so that the Party faithful might not be subjected to temptation.

Friendly societies were at first feared by the government and employers as potential sources of working-class combinations against the established order, and then at a later time patronised by upper-class persons who saw in them a way of lowering the poor rates.[56] But finally a stage was reached when the friendly societies came to be cited as evidence for the contention that the worker did not need the state to help him in providing for insurance against the contingencies of sickness, disability or old age.

Whenever such an estimate of friendly and other voluntary societies is encountered, it may be safely dated as mid-Victorian or later. This view found characteristic expression in the words of C. S. Roundell, Postmaster-General in the Government Green defended in his lecture on 'Liberal Legislation and Freedom of Contract':

'... Self-help and self-reliance are the only sure guarantees for social, national, and, may I add, moral progress. Legislation which encourages the people rather to rest upon State-help than to rely upon themselves, however well-intentioned, will prove incalculably mischievous in the end; and to every measure which is brought forward with the object of improving the condition of the people, this simple test should be applied—will it tend to encourage them to rely upon self-help?'[57]

By 1880 the Charity Organisation Society argued that the benefits of friendly societies were readily available to any respectable member of the working force. The bureaucracies of the friendly societies thereafter joined the COS in fighting any state scheme financed by the Treasury rather than by those who would profit from benefits. As Mr Gosden has written, the friendly societies, after a long struggle to win freedom from upper-class persons who wished to dictate their policies, ended by accepting the point of view held by those who regarded themselves as the moral preceptors of the classes below them. Despite the failure of all superannuation schemes attempted by the friendly societies in the nineteenth century, they nevertheless aligned themselves against any attempt to alter workers' protection against the disabilities brought by old age. Once legal recognition was given to them, the friendly societies underwent a development in which the original convivial function gave way to calculation of purely financial benefits, the national bureaucracies came to dominate local branches, and preservation of the status quo became their most urgent objective.[58]

The great defect of these friendly societies, trade unions and co-operatives was that they did not extend into the poorer sections of the working class. Above all, it was the artisans and the more highly paid workmen who could profit from them. But for the first time, a large body of the workers saw the possibility of saving.

Instead of spending his small surplus, the Victorian workman applied it, first to meeting the contingencies of life, in which the State, under the influence of *laissez-faire* doctrines, refused him its help, and secondly to saving up for old age or for a rainy day by buying his own house through a Building Society or investing in a Building Society or a Co-operative Store. The Victorian workman

THE POLITICS OF CONSCIENCE

learned readily the lesson which his masters were fain to teach him. He was as thrifty as they could desire; and in many respects his thrift both made him more tolerant than his fathers of the system under which he lived and led him to assimilate to it his ways of action and thought. The 'Lib-Lab' policy of the Victorian working-class leaders is readily understood, when it is related to the economic basis of Victorian society.[59]

Self-help, mutual aid, thrift: such were the virtues of these workmen and their organisations. By their acceptance of these values, they, after a vigorous campaign of agitation, were finally admitted to the franchise in 1867. Green's view of capitalism, his notion of what could be done within its framework, his theory of the proper limits of state action and the right of the state in regard to property were all shaped by the experience of this period. He wrote in his *Lectures on Political Obligations:*

It is true that the accumulation of capital naturally leads to the employment of large masses of hired labourers. But there is nothing in the nature of the case to keep these labourers in the condition of living from hand to mouth, to exclude them from that education of the sense of responsibility which depends on the possibility of permanent ownership . . . from being on a small scale capitalists themselves. . . . Their combination in work gives them every opportunity, if they have the needful education and self-discipline, for forming societies for the investment of savings. In fact, as we knew in the well-paid industries of England, the better sort of labourers do become capitalists to the extent often of owning their houses and a great deal of furniture, of having an interest in stores and of belonging to the benefit-societies through which they make provision for the future.[60]

Such working-men with such virtues could be safely admitted to the franchise. Green followed Bright in the agitation which brought the Reform Bill of 1867. Indeed his first political speech came at a meeting of the Oxford branch of Bright's National Reform League. Yet his support of the franchise had been in part based upon the judgment that the working classes had earned it by their moral progress and their restraint in using the power of their trade unions.

Looking back upon this period from the time after 1874, . . . he [Green] once said to me, 'We held our heads too high during Gladstone's Ministry. We thought the working-classes had made much more moral progress than they really had.' Explaining this, he dwelt with great disappointment on the use made by the workmen of their half-holidays and their shorter hours. He even said that it was better they should not have a half-holiday, but should be kept

328

constantly at their work, so that they should not have time to drink. With regard to the agricultural labourers, he said that they had behaved very wrongly, doing wanton injury to the farmer by suddenly striking in the midst of harvest in hay-time, with the very object of causing the farmers loss.[61]

There was a connection between Green's favourable estimate of voluntary societies and his dislike of violent action by workers, agricultural and industrial, between his exaltation of philanthropy and his moralistic concern about what use would be made of time that did not have to be spent at the employer's tasks. It would be unjust to identify him with that amalgam of middle-class, capitalist and nonconformist attitudes which Matthew Arnold called Philistinism: 'It is notorious that our middle-class Liberals have looked forward to this consummation, when the working-class shall join forces with them, aid them heartily to forward their great works, go in a body to their tea-meetings and, in short, enable them to bring about their millenium'.[62] But Green was not altogether unaffected by that emphasis upon the economic virtues which formed the unattractive part of the Protestant Ethic. His interpretation of the friendly and benefit societies was closely akin to that of other observers interested in the working class: he thought them to be engaged in forms of thrift or personal accumulation of wealth, just as middle-class persons were. Mr Brian Abel-Smith has pointed out the error involved in this judgment of activities undertaken out of the desire on the part of working people to help one another when in need. 'Thus all this working-class "self-help" was elevated to a position of singular moral stature in the eyes of influential opinion.'[63] And the belief that some workers could save served as a potent argument against the government entering the field as well as strengthening stiff-necked attitudes based on the poor law. Green's views were, therefore, ambivalent, oscillating between the humanitarian impulse of the Wesleyans and the economic ethic of the older Nonconformity. In time, his disciples were to split on the question of choosing among the Majority and Minority Reports of the Poor Law Commission of 1905.

Nor was his support of trade unions unqualified. It was not just that he condemned the use of strikes. Rather there were limits imposed upon his sympathy by his own position as a reformer and by the principles he used to judge working class organisations. Although Green himself wrote little about this question, it may be conjectured that his views did not differ much from those of his uncle, the Reverend D. J. Vaughan, who worked so closely with members of trade unions at Leicester.

Vaughan said in a sermon: 'I frankly confess to a deep sympathy with what I take to be the fundamental moral principle of Trade Unionism. It is, as I understand it, the assertion of the brother-hood of men; an earnest effort to realise the brotherhood in a practical form, by combining together so as to insure to all a fair and adequate reward of their labour.'

But, added his biographer, Vaughan felt that trade unions were increasingly to be censured. They displayed 'a growing tendency to think and speak rather of *"rights* than of *duties"*—a tendency to narrow the ideal of brotherhood to one section of workers, to one class of men, and to ignore the solidarity of society. . . .'[64]

6

To the limits imposed upon the humanitarian reformer by his insistence that society should be based upon principles of solidarity and morality must be added the conflict between the two discrepant attitudes towards charity which he was apt to hold simultaneously. The newer of these prescribed philanthropy while the older interdicted it. This last came naturally to a class which thought that its own success, such as it was, came from the superior character of its members just as the condition of the poor was due to their inferior character. Much of the support for the New Poor Law had come from this group. The guiding principle of the New Poor Law was that its administration should seek, not so much to relieve the poor, but to deter them from asking for relief by making unpalatable the conditions for its receipt. In this way, the rates would be lowered and a free labour market would be created. In the words of the Royal Commission 'the existing system of Poor Laws in England is destructive of the industry, forethought and honesty of the labourers; to the wealth and morality of the employers of labour and of the owners of property; and to the mutual goodwill and happiness of all. . . .'[65]

This emphasis upon developing 'industry, forethought and honesty' in public assistance to the poor was further extended to private activity by the Charity Organisation Society when it was founded in 1869. Its official titles from that time to the present reflect changing attitudes and social policy. Founded as the 'Society for Organising Charitable Relief and Repressing Mendicity', its strict individualism and upper-class condescension became so intolerable by 1910, that it had to change its name to the 'Society for Organising Charity and Improving the Condition of the Poor'. Further changes in the relation of private to public responsibilities in social work after the Second World War were reflected in the present title of the 'Family Welfare Association', adopted in 1946.[66] The COS for fifty years was the leading organisation in its field of activity and deserves attention here both as a typical mid-Victorian creation and as an expression of one side of Green's teaching.

Its importance derived not from any originality in doctrine but rather from the dogmatic and unqualified way in which it expressed one of the existing attitudes towards the poor and the economic system. The cause of pauperism was said to be indiscriminate charity. Because of emotional and unscientific aid, the poor never learned to work or save but lived on instead in a demoralised condition, with unhappy consequences for their own characters and the productive power of the economy. What should be done? The principles of the Poor Law ought to be applied. Only the deserving poor should be the recipients of philanthropy; all the rest should be left to the grim workhouses established by the Poor Law to deter applications for relief. A careful screening was to be performed by volunteer investigators from the upper-classes, whose duty would be to determine the merits of each case. Thus information would determine charity and a science could be developed to aid only the worthy and this at the least possible cost. Closely allied to these objectives was the ambitious project of co-ordinating the many unrelated private agencies and converting them to the philosophy of the COS. The organisation was based upon the well-to-do volunteers willing to do social case-work and their conviction that charity should be awarded in the light of its potential effects in each instance. Thus the criterion was to be that of the objective consequences for the recipient rather than subjective gratification on the part of the donor. All this marked an advance upon the unexamined assumptions of the past, and the beginnings of modern social work were contained within this movement which for the first time considered individual circumstances as relevant to relief. But the COS combined valuable technical innovations with an inflexible and patronising social philosophy.

It declared that individual independence and character were all important, and that the poor could attain everything of value without aid except in most unusual circumstances. Provision for the 'ordinary contingencies of life', such as sickness and old age, were indispensable means of developing character. To any objections the Society responded, as did Mrs Bosanquet:

'But what if the social conditions will not permit them to meet the responsibility? It is a vain and idle hypothesis. The social conditions *will* permit them; for their very effort to do so will make them steady and efficient workers, whose services will be valued by the community, and will be supplemented by the help of the young people who will grow up in such a family as theirs will be.'

The family was said to be the true nucleus of society. No obligations were more important than those imposed by family ties: caring for the young and old; mutual aid at times of illness or emergency.

For the state to assume any of these duties would be no kindness, but rather the destruction of precisely those moral qualities which it is the function of the state to maintain. By such arguments, the COS found a new form, as J. A. Hobson noted, to express 'the opposition of the propertied classes to schemes of old age pensions, feeding of school children at the public expense, public provision of work for the unemployed, and other 'proposals of public aid for the poor and needy'.[66] Such issues were simply not understood by those who thought that character was nine-tenths of life. Although it prided itself on knowledge of social facts, the COS officially took the line that only one-third of the population belonged to the working classes. Not long thereafter Charles Booth demonstrated that in London '30% of the population lived at or below the level of subsistence'.[69]

The man whose name was most associated with the COS, Charles Loch, wrote much to criticise the folly of 'those whose whole object in life seems to be . . . to withdraw labour from the higgle of the market. . . . The charter of the working man is freedom of exchange not only for commodities but for labour.'[70] Curiously enough, Loch, like Bernard Bosanquet, was a former student of Green. Both thought that his conception of the state and political obligation implied the objectives of the COS. How did they justify this claim?

Bosanquet had an intimate relation to the COS throughout his life. Not the least of the reasons which led him to give up an academic career in Oxford was his desire to take an active part in the Society's work, which he considered to be a practical expression of the philosophy of active social reform he had learned from Green. The COS was virtually a family enterprise: his brother, Charles B. P. Bosanquet, served as its first Secretary; his wife, Helen Dendy Bosanquet, was the District Secretary for Shoreditch when they married, served on the council of the COS with her husband and edited the *Charity Organisation Review.* C. S. Loch, the next Secretary, was a Balliol friend of Bosanquet, as was F. H. Peters, whose sister Loch married. The *Philosophical Theory of the State*, in which Bosanquet assigns absolute value to the state, is clearly inconsistent with itself whenever there is any question of private property or charity. These constitute areas in which individual character becomes the overriding consideration for Bosanquet. Although in an address to the Fabian Society he declared himself prepared for any amount of collectivism, he insisted that it 'be guided by sound doctrine'.[71] And this in his mind was identical with the teachings of the COS and indeed of Green himself. From his teacher he had learned that private property is essential to developing character because it provides the means for 'carrying out a plan of life' and 'giving reality to a good will'.[72] The COS seemed to be based upon the same principles:

> We, the advocates of thrift, have always insisted on the value of 'constructive' saving,—saving embodied in the health and well-being of the family, and in the niceness of the home. . . . Thrift is, for us, the germ of the capacity to look at life as a whole, and organise it. It involves a recognition both of the area of life, as including the family and others whose security from disaster depends on the individual's prudence, and also of its duration as a lapse of time for which, and not merely for a few days or weeks, he must lay his account. Life thus looked at implies a higher, not a lower, standard of comfort, a more generous and not a more grudging acceptance of obligation, than the life of those who have never learnt to look beyond the passing day and their most single self. . . .[73]

In this passage, self-realisation and obligation have taken on a special meaning which was developed even more systematically by Loch than by Bosanquet.

All his life Loch believed that the rôle of the state in charity should be confined to that assigned by the Poor Law of 1834. 'Poor Relief,' he said, 'is for those who, for some reason or other, are defaulters in the contract of social obligation. They do not maintain themselves. They throw the fulfilment of their obligation on others—on the State or on members of the community.'[74] Here then is an interpretation of social obligation in a sense rather different from that usually associated with Green.

Loch long held an unique position in English charitable life. After he assumed the office of Secretary of the COS in 1875, he remained there until 1914. His services were recognised by a knighthood and the honorary degree of DCL from Oxford. He served on Royal Commissions for the aged poor, on the feeble-minded and on the poor laws. Together with Mrs Bosanquet and her husband, he was largely responsible for the Majority Report of the Royal Commission on the Poor Law of 1909, while the Minority Report was done by Beatrice and Sidney

Webb (who, like Bernard Bosanquet, was not an official member of the Commission). Loch held the office of Vice-President of the International Institute of Sociology and was Tooke Professor of Economic Science and Statistics in King's College, London, from 1904 to 1908. For much of his life, he was regarded as the greatest English authority on charity.

Green had been Loch's tutor at Balliol. R. B. Mowat, his son-in-law, noted that 'Loch was profoundly influenced by Green's character and philosophy and the two men remained intimate for life. . . . While at Balliol, he had been attracted to ideals of social service, both through Green's teaching and through the influence of Arnold Toynbee.'[75] Loch constructed for himself a personal religion he called 'The Church of Charity', a type of social activity which stressed the individualistic strand of Green's thought. Loch had entered the COS in the first instance because his Balliol mentors had drawn his attention to the discrepancy between his own lot and that of the many who were less fortunate; because Green and Toynbee had insisted upon the moral obligation of individuals to take direct action. Certainly there was some initial sense of guilt on Loch's part, but even more important was his need to find some cause to which he could subordinate himself. And this must aim at the moral transformation of the individual, unlike socialism which in his view sought only to recast society on the basis of an economic plan. 'To charity this position seems to exclude the ethical element in life and to treat the people primarily or chiefly as human animals.' Somewhat curiously the COS thought that its programme could lessen tensions among classes, and this theme of building solidarity is among the *leitmotifs* of Loch's personal declaration of faith:

'If I were asked why I joined the Society, I should answer that through its work and growth I hoped that some day there would be formed a large association of persons drawn from all churches and all classes who, disagreeing in much, would find in charity a common purpose and a new unity. . . . Such an organisation, I thought, could do more than Parliament, or preaching, or books, or pamphleteering. . . . It could make legislation effective, could see that it was enforced. Apart from all legislative interference. . . it could renew and discipline the life of the people by a nobler, more devoted, more scientific religious charity. . . . It could eventually provide out of all classes and sects a great army of friendly and by degrees well-trained workers. . . . It would open to many a new path for the exercise of personal influence—influence with the churches, the Guardians, the Friendly Societies, the residents of a district, and 'the common people'.

This, the hope that there might be what I have sometimes called a church of charity, undeclared it might be and invisible, but in a very real sense actual—a peacemaking, unifying body—has been constantly in my mind.'[77]

Loch's book, *Charity Organisation*, reflected his curious relation to Green's ethics and lay sermons. Beginning with the assertion that democracy has altered the conception of the state's duties to its citizens, the citizens' duties to the state and the duty of the rich to the poor, Loch argues that pauperism is the social enemy of the modern state. The state wants citizens; it cannot afford to have any outcast or excluded classes. And so the state must prevent pauperism. This might be taken to be a socialist statement, and indeed, from the same premises, other students of Green went on to condemn the existing economic system. But Loch centres almost exclusively on the repression of mendicity. All that he draws from his acceptance of democracy is the duty of richer citizens to give their services to this end. 'The new charity requires of the rich that, for the common good, they submit to the common yoke of labour and that they help the poor to become self-dependent and competent fellow-citizens.'[77] Loch gave his own twist to Green's anti-Catholic feeling: he attacked the charitable work of religious orders. These he charged with ignoring the gospel of noble citizenship which prescribes the achievement of a 'continually completer ideal of duty'. Honour was due to them for their concern with the afflicted, the sick, the fallen, the distressed. Yet religious charity is feeble and unscientific, the 'hopeless push and protest of the saint against the evils of a hopeless world'. What is needed is the recognition that doles, and other debauching gifts must be prevented by the acceptance of the principle that only needs certified by investigation will be relieved. Such a charity is the outward sign of that sense of membership in one common life. Here and now will be found a life eternal. Pauperism will be eliminated by the disinterested service of the wealthy. Beatrice Webb did not exaggerate when she wrote:

'Octavia Hill, C. S. Loch and their immediate followers concentrated their activities on schooling the poor in industry, honesty, thrift and filial piety; whilst advocating, in occasional asides or by parenthetical phrases, the moralisation of the existing governing class and its spontaneous conversion to a benevolent use of its necessarily dominant wealth and power.'[79]

Although Loch conceded that there are cases where genuine needs exist due to no fault of the affected individuals, he and his organisation were primarily concerned to eliminate mistaken benevolence rather than to alter for the better the fundamental economic system of production and distribution. Despite Loch's attempted use of Green's Idealism, he wished to revive the notion of iron laws found in classical political economy. Both Green and Toynbee stated their opposition to any such theory. Nor did Loch share their sense of 'collective sin'. Rather he assumed the superiority in every way of his well-to-do volunteers over those they visited, investigated and judged. But that Loch shared some assumptions with Green and Toynbee cannot be denied. For the COS linked its support of the Poor Law to the argument that if out-door relief were eliminated, a great stimulus would be given towards creating the desired virtues by making men provide for their old age and potential unemployment and illness. And for this nothing more was necessary than the existing system of mutual aid. Loch cited with approval the dictum of the Royal Commission on Friendly Societies in 1874 that 'no more potent agent can be devised for inducing a man to join a Friendly Society than the dread of the Workhouse'. Thus, Loch concluded, the COS's administration of relief is 'in harmony with the main lines of social development', and could argue that it was 'working "with nature"'. The climax of his book came in its triumphant citation of the statistics showing the growth of provident associations, co-operative societies, savings accounts and trade unions. The COS assumed that such a private system enabled almost all workers to cope with the predictable and contingent needs of life. No positive action by the state was necessary, and the capitalist system constantly produced 'great progress in the condition of the people'.[80]

7

How did Green himself regard the COS and the use made by its leaders of his ideas? There is no direct evidence, although occasional remarks indicate his sympathy with at least some of its objectives and attitudes. When discussing 'conscientiousness' in the *Prolegomena*, he gives the example of a man asking himself, 'Was I right in relieving that beggar yesterday?'

> In relieving the beggar was he not merely compounding with his conscience for his self-indulgence in shirking the trouble which a more judicious exercise of benevolence would have cost him; or merely giving himself the pleasure of momentarily pleasing another, or of being applauded for generosity, at the cost of encouraging a mischievous practice.[81]

336

These are indeed the questions the COS would have had the would-be philanthropist put to himself. And Green began a lecture on education with a comparison showing how high he rated the organisation of charity:

> So far as I have observed, the two questions of our time which compete with each other in a reputation for dulness are about the most important we can discuss. One is the organisation of charity; the other the organisation of schools. It so happens that the subjects are closely connected, for if only the money wasted during the last half-century upon so-called charities, public and private, for which no one in the long run has been better off, had been wisely spent during the same period on a system of properly organised schools, ascending in due gradation from the elementary to the high school, we might by this time have had not only a thoroughly educated but a socially united people.[82]

In *Political Obligation,* Green classified those laws which are unjustifiable because they 'check the development of the moral disposition'. These are three in number: 'legal requirements of religious observance and profession of belief; . . . prohibitions and restraints . . . which interfere with the growth of self-reliance, with the formation of a manly conscience and sense of moral dignity; . . . legal institutions which take away the occasion for the exercise of certain moral virtues (eg, the Poor Law which takes away the occasion for the exercise of parental forethought, filial reverence and neighbourly kindness)'.[83] From this last remark, Green seems to have advocated the abolition of 'outdoor relief' under the Poor Law, that is, aid to some of the poor who were excepted from the workhouse. This was the position of the COS which considered outdoor relief as inconsistent with the basic principles of the New Poor Law because it interfered with the natural operation of the labour market and diminished self-reliance. Arnold Toynbee, himself a member of the COS, once said, 'Radicals are as keenly alive as ever to the necessity for self-reliance; I would say, abolish outdoor relief under the Poor Law, because outdoor relief lowers wages, degrades the recipient and diminishes self-reliance.'[84]

But what is proved by all this? That Green was an extreme individualist? Obviously not, if the passage in *Political Obligation* is read through to the end. For there Green asks wherein lies the harm of these three types of law he has just condemned. The supporters of one view of law would answer that its only business is to prevent interference with the liberty of the individual. Here is individualism pure. What does Green say to this? While he admits that this view has led to real reforms and

337

to the abolition of mischievous laws, he goes on, however, to say that these laws were mischievous for other reasons than those adduced by extreme individualism. Having done this useful work, the individualist theory now tends to become obstructive because:

> In fact advancing civilisation brings with it more and more interference with the liberty of the individual to do as he likes, and this theory affords a reason for resisting all positive reforms, all reforms which involve an action of the state in the way of promoting conditions favourable to moral life.[85]

Green, then, explicitly rejects individualism. In its place, he puts a theory of 'positive reform' based on 'promoting conditions favourable to moral life'. It was for this reason that he introduced his teleological criterion of rights and obligations.

But if this is not an individualist theory, what is it? Certainly Green denied that laissez-faire is a valid principle of legislation; certainly he defended the claims of the state to restrict the freedom of the individual to do as he likes. Yet by the criterion Green offered, it would be impossible to decide in advance of any particular case, whether state action would be justified. Actually there is a presumption against state interference. If investigation revealed the probability that a proposed enactment of law would 'defeat its true end by narrowing the region within which the spontaneity and disinterestedness of true morality can have play', then such intervention would be prohibited.[86] On the other hand there are occasions when the state can serve moral ends and should do so, even if individual liberty is curtailed thereby. But take the question of old age pensions provided by the state: would such a scheme endanger responsibility, thrift, self-reliance? Would it damage character? The leaders of the COS, following, as they thought, Green's principles, opposed state pensions. On the other hand, Arnold Toynbee could say while advocating pensions, 'The middle classes, who have talked to us most about this subject, have overlooked the fact that thrift may often brutalise a man as much as drink. . . . A man may make huge efforts to save and raise himself, and so become narrow and selfish and careless of his fellow-men.'[87] Toynbee went on to recommend a solution on the question of social insurance, which in many respects anticipated the compromise Lloyd George was to adopt—the use of the friendly societies by the state in such a way as to maintain them while making many more workers eligible for their benefits. 'By making grants-in-aid under carefully-considered conditions of State audit . . . it might be possible for the great Friendly Societies in time slowly to reduce their rates of payment, slowly to enable more men to insure, and so in time to diminish pauperism—without, mind, invoking State aid on a large and monstrous scale, without interfering with those great self-helping voluntary institutions which have built up this nation.' That both the leaders of the COS and Toynbee could have invoked Green's teaching in support of their stand is one more indication of how it could point in different directions, depending on the prepossessions of the person applying it.

But perhaps the clearest, although nevertheless indirect, evidence of Green's reservations about the Charity Organisation Society emerges from several passages in Bernard Bosanquet's *Philosophical Theory of the State*. There Bosanquet politely rebuked his old tutor's nineteenth-century caution about prematurely congratulating the state for its economic achievements. Bosanquet, as always, defending the COS, took the line that Green had slandered the poor when he suggested that they encountered greater obstacles to the good life than others more fortunately placed. In a famous passage, Green had written: 'To an Athenian slave, who might be used to gratify a master's lust, it would have been a mockery to speak of the State as a realisation of freedom; and perhaps it would not be much less so to speak of it as such to an untaught and under-fed denizen of a London yard with gin shops on the right hand and on the left.'[88] To this Bosanquet replied with a certain condescension that it had now been established that there is no larger proportion of bad homes among the poor than among the rich. Indeed, Bosanquet wrote, owing to the growth of a more intimate experience with the poor, a knowledge gained in some measure because of Green's own initiative, social investigators have established that character is more important than environment. The essentials of life are far more identical throughout the so-called classes of society than is admitted by Green's passage about the dweller in a London yard.[89] Bosanquet was attempting to correct Green's interpretation of Idealism and to make it support the ideal state of the Charity Organisation Society, 'a state which cannot actively promote the well-being of its members, but can only remove obstructions and leave to them a fair field in which to run the race'.[90]

At the same time that Bosanquet's treatise appeared, another interpretation of Green attracted attention. Its author was Herbert Samuel, a rising young Liberal who had been impressed by Green's books while taking his First in Greats at Balliol; the introduction was by Asquith, who had preceded him by twenty years at that College. Interpreting Green in a sense quite opposed to Bosanquet's, Samuel insisted that, if the aim of the state is to help men make the best of themselves, it had to remove those obstacles to the good life created by poverty, sickness and lack of education. 'In any attempt to state the aims of Liberalism the proposals of social reform must take the first place.' These he proceeded to specify by a set of suggestions for state action in the fields of education, temperance reform, the conditions of unemployment, taxation and land-holding. Only the state could deal adequately with the power of capital which had created a situation where there was no real freedom of contract. The state, which Bosanquet celebrated while restricting the scope of its action, could be trusted to perform functions essential to the good of all its members:

> 'The State is not incompetent for the work of social reform. Self-reliance is a powerful force, but not powerful enough to cure unaided the diseases that afflict society. Liberty is of supreme importance, but State assistance, rightly directed, may extend the bounds of liberty.'[92]

To such statements of the New Liberalism of this future Cabinet member in the Asquith government, as well as those of Hobhouse, Sir Henry Jones and J. H. Muirhead, *The Times* responded by asking: 'Does it leave any part of human sentiment safe from the State's intrusion? What measure does it not justify?'[93]

The most exact answer to these queries must be that Idealism, as a theory of state interference, was profoundly ambiguous. Considered purely logically, it gave as much support to Loch and Bosanquet as to the New Liberals. Green's ideas and attitudes were appealing just because they papered over internal differences among Liberals. Up to a point, disagreements could be reconciled by verbal or intellectual means. But with the advent of the new type of social legislation and the rise of the Labour Party it became increasingly difficult to avoid taking a stand. As Mr H. L. Beales has noted, the Liberals before the First World War 'were suffering the fate of a Centre party which is not rooted in working-class support'.[94] Even when interpreted in an interventionist sense, the political ideas of Green and Toynbee could not be severed completely from their mid-Victorian assumptions: the semi-tutelary relationship they assumed towards the working-class, their high estimate of voluntary action as an efficient way of meeting social contingencies, their abhorrence of class as a basis of politics, their emphasis upon the improvement of individual character.

It is not easy to surmise how Green himself, had he lived,

would have reacted to the establishment of an independent Labour Party. Although he might have been offended, as were so many Liberals by a party based on a single class, it is not inconceivable that he might have joined that minority of Idealists like Lord Haldane and Lord Lindsay who affiliated themselves with Labour. Both Green and Toynbee died young and before they could witness the results of their call to middle-class persons to go out and aid those less fortunate. One of those who heeded the appeal wrote much later:

> 'That task was what really pierced the hearts of all of us younger people. We set out to make things better, by starting innumerable societies for the welfare of the poor—the urban poor especially—and establishing quantities of institutions, hospitals and homes for this end. It made us miserable to go from the homes of the poor to our own happy surroundings, and we felt that we could do so little, even if we were to go to live amongst the poor. We seemed to want something much more radical than this, for we knew that even in living with them we were not of them, and that they knew this too.'[95]

Had Green lived thirty years longer until 1912, he would have been faced with the necessity of choosing between quite incompatible interpretations of Idealism. It is of no great importance to decide which of them he would have chosen. All that can be said with certainty is that the practical applications he himself made of the doctrine fell within a pattern of politics which bore little resemblance to the forces later responsible for the 'Welfare State'. Green and Toynbee did not argue for an extensive use of governmental action in the sphere of economic and social life. Rather they protested against the dogmatic and abstract statements of the older form of Liberalism, which seemed to imply that the government was bound to remain impotent in the face of flagrant evils.* When Green spoke of 'positive freedom' he did not commit himself to any use of state power beyond that in fact advocated by Gladstone and Bright. Unfortunately some historians of political theory have stumbled into the trap set by

---

* Lord Milner summed up their creed in the following judgment: 'Toynbee has often been called a socialist; but he was not a socialist of the revolutionary type, nor did he ever adopt the doctrines of collectivism. But he was opposed to the extreme individualism of some of the earlier English economists and believed earnestly in the power of free corporate effort, such as that of co-operative and friendly societies and of trade unions, to raise the standard of life among the mass of the people, and in the duty of the state to assist such effort by free education, by the regulation of the conditions of labour, and by contributing to voluntary insurance funds intended to provide for the labourer in sickness and old age.' [*Dictionary of National Biography*.] Although Milner unfortunately used Dicey's language, his meaning is clear because of his examples.

Dicey so long ago: they have called Green a 'collectivist', implying by that term, the advocacy of extensive governmental action, or a presumption in favour of action by the community as a whole to achieve goods regarded as essential to its members.[96]

Dicey defined 'collectivism' in a way which was neither historically accurate nor logically rigorous. He implied that there once existed a policy of 'individualism', which after being strictly stated by theorists, was accepted as the working rule of governments. Then came a phase of withdrawal from the strict principle (favoured by Dicey himself) that government is justified in restricting an individual's freedom of action only when he harms others. 'Collectivism' was the omnibus term Dicey used to designate this alleged historical development as well as the intellectual position that in some circumstances governmental action is justified if it produces substantial benefits to the community as a whole without any significant loss of political liberty on the part of its citizens.[97] Such a nomenclature obscured the differences between those who rejected laissez-faire and the others who espoused state socialism.* Increasingly, economic and administrative historians have come to agree that pure 'individualism' in Dicey's sense was never practised by any government, English or American; similarly students of economic and political theory have established that even the most consistent advocates of laissez-faire left far more scope for state action than Dicey stated.[98] It can be said in Dicey's defence, that he was rather recording contemporary usage than coining a scientific nomenclature or asserting propositions about history. Certainly persons of the most varied opinions used 'individualism', 'collectivism' and 'socialism' as tags to describe their own positions and those of others. Political discussion was carried out with a vagueness which now seems to have obscured the real choices to be made. This absence of clarity no doubt served several purposes; what is worth noting here is the fact that the use of the concept 'individualism' registered the limits to which even the most advanced Liberals were willing to go. This is evident from a sermon of the Reverend David Vaughan, who outlived his nephew and survived until 1905. As an indication of Green's own likely position, had he lived as long as his uncle, this passage is as good as anything else available.

* 'We cut ourselves free from the domination of *laissez-faire*, but we did not jump to the conclusion that, because that was wrong, the opposite must therefore be right: we rejected the Socialist formula of "Nationalisation of the Means of Production, Distribution and Exchange".' [Viscount Samuel, *Memoirs* (London, Cresset Press, 1945), p. 26.]

The hope of Socialism ... is that individualism, or the free competitive action of the individual in relation to the production and distribution of wealth, will be gradually stamped out; and that Collectivism, or the collective action of society operating through legislation or the executive, will take its place and become everywhere paramount. Whether this is possible or not, depends upon whether that which is represented by the term 'individualism' is not, or is, a fundamental principle of human nature and an essential factor of the well-being of society. If it is, as I believe it to be, both the one and the other, then the hopes of Socialism must necessarily be wrecked and shattered upon this rock. That in the near future individualism will be still further curbed and curtailed by the action of the state, I make no doubt. But there will come at last a point, beyond which this curtailment cannot go; and at which some adjustment or *modus vivendi* must be sought and found between the two principles. That point of equilibrium will be discovered, I also make no doubt, very much on this side of the Ideal of Socialism.[99]

CHAPTER ELEVEN

THE LIFE OF CITIZENSHIP

I

NO WORD RECURS MORE often in the work of Green and his followers than 'citizenship'; no word is more difficult to define with any degree of precision or concreteness.* Its importance derived in part from the attempt to give a political meaning to the theory of equality, to associate the extension of the suffrage with a spiritual advance imposing new duties as well as new rights. Thus Arnold Toynbee, addressing the meeting of the Co-operative Union in 1882, in a speech which had a consider-able effect upon the development of adult education, asked: 'What part of education then is left for co-operators to appropriate? The answer I would give, is the *education of the citizen*.' Professor John MacCunn wrote a book called *The Ethics of Citizenship;* Sir Henry Jones, one called *The Principles of Citizenship*. The term constantly turned up in the publications of the London Ethical Society, the Christian Social Union and the Charity Organisation Society; it figured in some attempts to introduce into the Education Act of 1902 non-denominational teaching of *la morale civique* analogous to what was going on in France under the leadership of Durkheim. It seemed mandatory for Liberal statesmen associated with education to write on the subject. A. H. D. Acland, Bryce and H. A. L. Fisher all did so.

If the notion of citizenship included teaching persons newly admitted to political rights what were their corresponding obligations, it also was addressed to upper-class persons with advantages of wealth and education. These, for their part, were

* Not untypical was the statement by Bryce in his Yale lectures, to which he gave a title reminiscent of Green: 'Each member of a free community must be capable of citizenship. Capacity involves three qualities—Intelligence, Self-Control, Conscience. The citizen must be able to understand the interests of the community, must be able to subordinate his will to the general will, must feel his responsibilities to the community and be prepared to serve it by voting, working or (if need be) fighting. . . . The last, Conscience, or a sense of civic duty, is the rarest.' [James Bryce, *The Hindrances to Citizenship* (New Haven, 1909), pp. 7-8.]

344

to be taught to participate in local politics, rather than the competition for power and glamour at Westminster.* The conscientious citizen would also seek to aid workers' voluntary organisations for self-help, which needed all the support they could get from well-connected persons of the class above them. Dons and students alike at Oxford and Cambridge should attempt to extend education in every way; by supporting movements to establish universities in provincial towns, by opening their own foundations to students previously excluded, by themselves participating in schemes for university extension, even by admitting women to attend lectures and take degrees. All these activities associated with citizenship shared that earnest atmosphere which we have learned to connect with Green and his school; an essentially individual dedication, a distrust of machinery, the impulsion to make direct contact with the disadvantaged and do so on terms which excluded patronising relationships. The movements that grew out of Green's form of Idealism reacted in turn upon the philosophers. They were at once more realistic and empirical than other representatives of their school; they were committed to the union of theory and practice. As Collingwood wrote, 'The school of Green sent out into public life a stream of ex-pupils who carried with them the conviction that philosophy and particularly the philosophy they had learned at Oxford was an important thing and that their vocation was to put it into practice'.[2] The theological overtone carried by the term 'vocation' was appropriate in this context. Citizenship had for Green a religious significance. For him, as a student commented, 'civic duty, rightly regarded, is nothing less than a spiritual function, . . . the life of citizenship is a mode of divine service.'[3]

Green's generation used religious language and analogies with as little self-consciousness as the present generation of Oxford philosophers refer to games and their rules. Not all statements about the religious functions of citizenship ought to be accepted at face value. But it would be a mistake to ignore the fact that

* After Green's death, the local newspaper wrote: 'Some . . . have half-regretted that his life was not lived on a wider stage and among a wider circle. But to us it seems one of the dearest proofs of his strength of character that he was content to dwell "among his own people" and to show that that gift which might have otherwise adorned a Senate and commanded the applause of the world may be devoted as completely and not less usefully to the public life of a single town and to the furtherances of a few good causes. The citizens of Oxford, at any rate, have reason to be thankful for the choice which was made by Professor Green.' [*Oxford Chronicle and Berks and Bucks Gazette*, 1 April, 1882.]

students looked to their teachers for models, not only of how to think, but how to live. Thus Edward Caird could say of Green, 'There are not a few among the Oxford men of the last fifteen years to whom, as was once said of another teacher, "his existence was one of the things that gave reality to the distinction between good and evil".'[4] Sir Michael Sadler was launched upon his notable educational career by an act of self-dedication which occurred when he heard Arnold Toynbee read a paper to an undergraduate society.[5] Shortly after the deaths of Green and Toynbee, *The Oxford Magazine* wrote:

> The question has been asked, 'Is the new Oxford movement to be a Socialistic one?' and if this is interpreted to mean 'Is the most living interest in Oxford now that in social questions?' the answer must be distinctly, Yes! Oxford has turned from playing at the Middle Ages in churches, or at a Re-Renaissance in cupboards; and a new faith, with Professor Green for its founder, Arnold Toynbee as its martyr, and various societies for its propaganda is alive among us.[6]

It is worth noting that Green's life, brief as it was, incorporated three innovations: he was the first layman to be elected a Fellow of Balliol; he was its first professional philosopher; and the first Oxford don to be elected to the town council, not as a representative of the University, but by standing in the same way as any ordinary resident, in his case, of the North Ward. No doubt because he taught that 'both faith and reason found their highest expression in good citizenship'[7] Green's brief career in local politics took on an especial significance. He did much to reduce the bad feeling between the University and the town of Oxford. To his students, already excited by his ideas, this political activity produced a sense of shock, as though by breaking through the barrier which separates thought from action and town from gown, Idealist philosophy had been proved capable of transforming an antagonistic relationship which dated back to the foundation of the University. Green's life seemed to demonstrate, although on a small scale, that it was possible for speculation to inform and unify practice. Thus it was more than happy versatility that came to mind when it became known that Green had gone straight from the poll when he had been elected a town councillor to lecture on the *Critique of Pure Reason*.[8] In fact Green's civic activity seemed novel for two reasons: it supported his contention that general principles might validly be applied to politics; and his stress on the necessity of establishing communication between classes and between Oxford and the nation.

Only Nonconformists such as Bright had shown any disposition to apply moral categories to politics. Ever since the French Revolution the governing classes had accepted the commonplace that in government the subtle calculation of political expediency is preferable to the use of general principles. On this point as on so many others, Green provided an elaborate intellectual rationale for modes of feeling and thinking originating in classes which hitherto had not much affected Oxford. That there should be dialogue among classes rather than preaching, fellowship rather than condescension—these were motifs which figured prominently in his writings on education. Characteristically, he used very different arguments from the cynical remark, made after the passage of the Second Reform Bill, that it was now necessary to educate the new masters of society. There was of course his basic principle of self-realisation: men could not realise their potentialities without education, and this constituted a legitimate field for governmental action. Ignorance was therefore a hindrance to be removed. But Green also believed that among the best justifications for a free régime is the superior quality of information and criticism available to its leaders who, because of the conditions of their election, are forced to maintain a close relation to their constituents. These, for their part, are much more alert and energetic as participating citizens than they would be as passive subjects. In any case, the opinions of ordinary persons were valuable; they would be even more so if all Englishmen received a better and longer education. And there was another reason as well: when men of ability are prevented from getting the sort of training from which they could profit because they lack economic or social status, they become dangerously alienated from their political society. If educational 'opportunities were more generally offered, we should no longer so often come across workmen of keen intellectual interests and ability, embittered by the feeling that they have been cut off from the means of turning their powers to account'.[9] Education in common is the great social leveller and ought to be used by every democracy which believes in its avowals of equality.

His own life helped illuminate the meaning of his formal philosophical work for many who otherwise might have missed its significance. What appeared in a lecture as a woolly point about positive freedom became rather more clear when applied to the practical question of providing educational opportunity for those capable of profiting from it. This is not to deny that intellectual curiosity played a large part in the adoption of Idealism, or to assert that Green derived no support from the philosophy of community he found in classical thought. But important changes from his sources, whether Greek or German, came about as the result of his own political activity, which convinced him that the teaching of Aristotle, Kant and Hegel had to be modified in the light of English conditions. Although he never ceased to believe that Idealism was a necessary antidote to the native traditions of hedonism, empiricism and common sense, Green had his share of Burkean reverence for the solid qualities developed by his own people in their institutions. Experience had taught him how much hard work, organisational skill, capacity to compromise and realism had gone into the voluntary associations he had learned to know at first hand. Of a Liberal colleague on the Town Council, Green remarked: 'He was one of those men more frequently found in England than anywhere else, men who combined very great practical ability with extraordinary devotion to the public service'.[10] For Green believed that such persons had made so much out of society that the state had only to harmonise and complete their work, rather than attempt to do everything by its own action. Nor was this belief purely theoretical, based on a vision separated from everyday realities. Practicality meant a good deal to him, for he was impatient with those who could only talk. To many criticisms he would counter, 'Yes, but after all he is one of those men who know what is the best thing to be done'.[11]

In the same spirit Green himself did not shirk the heavy demands made on his time by his participation in numerous University and local causes, in Liberal party organisation, in the leagues and societies that maintained branches in Oxford as part of their national agitation. By his own life he demonstrated what he meant by citizenship: the devotion to duty within his own orbit, painstaking attention to detail and a concern for his fellows. The offices he held, the meetings he addressed or attended were of little intrinsic interest. Yet they showed more clearly than could any exegesis what he meant by political obligation. Most often Green devoted his energies, not to devising projects for remaking society as a whole, not to attacking the faults of its economic structure, nor even in seeking state inter-vention. Rather he played his small part in creating public knowledge and involvement in national issues and in administering the petty but essential business of his town. Once he said of Hare's scheme for de-localising parliamentary constituencies: 'I rather despise all these schemes for detaching people from their localities'.[12]

Certainly he was himself altogether hostile to that aspect of Hegel's outlook which led him to subordinate such smaller groupings as family, region and voluntary association to the omnipotent and centralised state. Even when Green advocated certain types of state interference, such as stricter regulation of the liquor trade, he came out strongly in favour of local option rather than a national solution imposed by Parliament. When a choice actually existed, he preferred that legislation be administered by the local authorities than by a ministry in London. He liked to make the distinction between a government that has sufficient power to do what is called for by the general interest, and one that habitually puts everything into the hands of a centralised administration. For if it is participation in government which is the best political education, which makes men into responsible citizens, then they should administer their own affairs. But in some cases purely practical considerations make a centralised solution necessary. Apart from the facts of the matter and reference to the common good, there is no formula which can settle in advance what ought to be done.

This train of thought was characteristic of his utterances on the issues of his day. It illustrates the extent to which Green's public service introduced into his ideas an empirical element which often dominated the *a priori* philosophical method he himself regarded as the contribution he had to make to English thought. Again and again, when he took a position on some particular issue of state intervention, he used such phrases as 'we must take men as we find them', or 'this theory . . . does not square with the facts'. Their prominence indicates that if Green's theory of obligation led him to political action, what he learned from civic activity made his thought something else than what it would otherwise have been. As Tocqueville remarked of Burke, an impressive practical wisdom and power of judgment may be gained from participation in the affairs of a free society. This type of knowledge is one of the recessive, but nevertheless crucial, elements in political theory. To read the *Principles of Political Obligation* without acquaintance with Green's field of activity as reformer and citizen, will almost inevitably produce a mistaken impression of what he knew and taught. Nor should it be forgotten that by his activity he produced a new type of university teacher who to his obligations as a scholar added those as a citizen: Caird, first at Glasgow and then at Balliol, where A. L. Smith and A. D. Lindsay both later Masters of the College, continued the tradition. A. C. Bradley and MacCunn in Liverpool, Muirhead and Tout in Manchester, Tatton and Bosanquet in London, were but a few of those who followed the pattern originated by Green.

2

Educational reform ranked high in the programme of Green and his circle. It is sometimes said that liberal thinkers have consistently exaggerated the benefits which can be attained by this means, that it is part of their unduly high estimate of human rationality. Yet it is not altogether clear who ought to be counted as more realistic among mid-Victorian politicians: those like Robert Lowe, who opposed an extensive system of public education at the ratepayers' expense, or those who, like Green, argued both the expediency and morality of something approximating to Continental and American practice. G. M. Young thought that: 'We are, *in hoc interim seculo*, footing the bill for the great Victorian omission. . . . This was the line of weakness along which Victorian culture was fractured. The Middle Classes . . . were stratified along the seam where the public schools met the grammar schools. With the political and social consequences I am not concerned. For our culture it was a major disaster . . . in the late Victorian age, the educated classes . . . were dragging behind them a growing mass with no interests at all. It had thrown up the sponge and was becoming to all intents and purposes a proletariat, and it was Northcliffe, I think, who first apprehended its existence and diagnosed its quality.'[13] The failure to construct an adequate system of secondary education was indeed to have significant consequences. Not a few of the analysts of England's relative economic decline in the past century have pointed to the contrast between what was done there on the one side, and in Germany and the United States on the other. And it is a measure of English social development that, a century after the great mid-Victorian reports on secondary education, public opinion is still excited by discussions of the relation between social status and access to educational opportunity. Whereas all of Green's political programme is now of purely historical interest, his writing on education would not be out of place in the sharp discussion which has been going on of the place held by the 'Establishment', 'Oxbridge' and the public schools.

No one wrote more pointedly than Green about the barriers to 'putting the real scholar in place of the mere gentleman, and preventing the limit of class requirements from being the limit of the education open to young men who have special capacity'.[14] The extension of the suffrage would mean little unless unaccompanied by the reconstruction of secondary and university education, and 'if not to a reconstitution of society through that of education, yet at least to a considerable change in its tone and to the removal of many of its barriers'.[15] It is not too much to say with Professor Dockhorn that Green's ideal was the 'Educative State' (*Erziehungsstaat*).[16] What Green proposed was to expand and improve the secondary schools, to make the older universities truly national institutions and to create new civic universities throughout Great Britain. To do so was not only 'a matter of justice to the poorer classes and dissenters', but also the only viable means of establishing contact among social groups which were dangerously estranged from one another at a time when the political constitution was becoming increasingly democratic.[17] Education in common, he declared, looking at New England, is the great democratic force. Men and women who have been at school together, or who have been to schools of the same kind, will always be at their ease together, will be free from social jealousies and animosities whatever their circumstances in life may be. Although ready to concede that some degree of social differentiation is inevitable in any society, he argued that 'in England these separations have been fixed and deepened by the fact that there has been no fusion of class with class in school or at the universities'.[18] And this seemed to him to be both unjust and dangerous.

For Green, as for Matthew Arnold, first-hand experience with schools led first to dissatisfaction with the voluntary system, and then to a theory advocating certain positive functions for the state. Arnold was to argue again and again that no need was more urgent than that for a coherent and effective system of schools. Only the state could provide such a system, and this had been recognised and acted upon by all other progressive nations. Above all, it was the example of Germany and France in education that led Arnold to assert that, 'We have not the notion, so familiar on the Continent and to antiquity, of *the State*—the nation in its collective and corporate character, entrusted with stringent powers for the general advantage and controlling individual wills in the name of an interest wider than that of individuals.'[19] What was the state of affairs that pushed Arnold and Green to adopt a theory of the state as having a positive function? For Green difficulties existed that did not press upon Arnold. Green identified himself as a radical, (as the followers of John Bright were called), and radicals stood for the voluntary principle in politics, economics and religion. The state in their eyes was associated with the land-owning aristocracy, feudalism, protection and the Established Church. And while universal education would seem to follow from the principle of equality, as the men of the

French Revolution perceived, in Britain there were special complications for the radicals who preached the need for a state system.

Education was commonly regarded as a private affair, an enterprise carried on for profit by private persons for other private persons who could afford to pay, and chose to pay, for the education of their children. This had the double advantage, in the eyes of the middle-class, of both keeping down taxes and preventing the growth of a tyrannical state. The first state grant for education came almost absent-mindedly in 1833 when £20,000 was given by Parliament to provide for school-building through the National Society and the British and Foreign School Society. The first of these represented the strict Anglicans, the second, the more liberal members of the Established Church and other denominations. But many Nonconformist bodies including the Wesleyans refused to have anything to do with either society. Thus the religious division of England, from the beginning, prevented any state scheme of education. Not until the end of the century, when religious animosities had died away to some extent, could the great Act of 1902 be passed. The Church of England claimed, and was granted, the right to conduct its own schools where religious instruction was given. The dissenters would not consent to their children attending such schools and insisted on maintaining their own. Uneasy compromises were worked out, throughout the century, to accommodate these religious differences. Meanwhile education suffered. And this view of 'every man for himself in religion' coalesced with that of 'every man for himself in business', both working against any proposal to give the state a positive function in education.

Both Green and Arnold, as well as James Bryce, were named as assistant commissioners by the Royal Commission of 1864, headed by Lord Taunton. Its task was to study 'the schools attended by such of the gentry, clergy, professional and commercial men as are of limited means, and of farmers and tradesmen'. The enquiry, although excluding the most prominent public schools, which had been the subject of an earlier Commission, ranged far and received much attention. It has been called 'a landmark in the educational history of England'.[20] The questions it raised included the adequacy of secondary education, both for young men and girls; the quality of teaching in the various categories of public and private schools; the respective virtues of fee-paying as opposed to rate-supported schools; the geographical distribution of schools and their relation to demand for them. Each assistant commissioner was given a district in

England or Wales. To their reports, each of which was printed separately, the Taunton Commission added its own remarks and recommendations. These were notable, not so much because of any legislation enacted on the basis of them, but rather because of the authoritative indictment they presented of the existing situation: 'For the first time the country was apprised, upon official authority, and after enquiry into some eight hundred endowed schools, of its deficiencies in respect of secondary education. Now at last it learnt how scanty were the opportunities even in flourishing industrial centres open to boys and still more to girls for obtaining a decent education after the primary stage, how inefficient were many of the schools, how uneven their distribution, how archaic their methods, how wasteful the use of educational endowments.'[21]

Green's report was stinging, so much so that it was sharply criticised by Lowe. No one who has formed his impression of Green from his philosophical works alone would anticipate the marked capacity for social analysis and flair for determining facts displayed here. Whoever assumes that Idealist philosophers must be uninformed and uninterested in the real world will go as wrong in Green's case as in Haldane's, whose critics doubted his capacity to reorganise the Army. A Balliol associate of Green commented: 'His passion for abstract thought was combined with a remarkable exactness about matters of fact and in no way interfered with his discharge of everyday duty. On the contrary, his hard abstract studies seemed to prepare him for dealing with practical questions; they gave him patience, perseverance, perception of the point, delicacy of touch.'[22] In a curious way, Green belied his own objections to the attitudes underlying the Greats School: the belief that the most valuable training is that in logic rather than in substance, the suspicion that it is worse than useless to apply any general theory to concrete situations. Political and social data were regarded as something to be acquired by common sense and practical experience; specialised social research was unnecessary. For did there not exist the machinery of the Royal Commission? An enormous amount of data was collected, summarised and published by a method which called for nothing more than skill in choosing expert witnesses such as factory inspectors, as well as judgment on the part of upper-class Commissioners, no doubt trained at Oxford or Cambridge. This source and style of social research should not be too much denigrated. Karl Marx knew enough to profit from it and was generous enough to acknowledge the worth of at least this work of the bourgeois state. Green's report is an

353

interesting example of this species. It made small allowance for the sensibilities of the governing class; it resembled his treatment of capitalism in that its particular target was the aristocracy.

At the centre of the problem was the fact that the men who held political power in the country were perfectly satisfied with their own scheme of education. This enjoyed the highest prestige, and monopolised the very name of 'public schools', as Green pointed out, as well as access to the older universities. Because of this, all educational questions were complicated by class distinctions.

> 'The subtle distinction between those who claim to be gentlemen and those whose claim is conceded, those who claim to be so but whose claim is not yet conceded and those who do not claim to be gentlemen at all, is England's own.'[23] It embarrasses all schemes of school reform. A given course of study is adopted for boys being educated for a certain kind of career. It gets the name of being the education of gentlemen and immediately the schools which give it are crowded with boys not destined for such a career; while others with more real aspiration for the subjects taught are virtually excluded on social grounds. Another course is projected with a view to careers that have to be begun earlier than the other and requiring different qualifications. It gets the name of being less 'gentlemanlike', is ticketed as 'second grade' and a great part of the boys for whom it is best adopted will not use it.[24]

Green's experience with education led him to formulate a theory which had as its central premises social equality and justice. Its chief mechanism was a state system of education, meeting needs which could not be met by the voluntary principle, and which could not be left unmet without the whole society suffering. Yet education was put in a special category, for Green maintained a presumption against state action when voluntary action is possible. An essential promise of the Liberalism of his day was the identity of interests between employer and employee, between the middle and the working classes. Once the franchise was universal, it was thought, the working classes would have no fundamental grievance, and thereafter could be expected to adopt the attitudes and values of the middle class. Hence their interests would coincide. Green's educational writings, while involving the principle of equality, are most concerned with middle-class education, and especially that of the lower middle-class dissenters. But here again the principle he formulated could be applied at a later date to the disabilities of the working class. And such an application would have pleased Green. His faith of citizenship taught equality and justice. He conceived of a new development of morality applied to the development of a type of character and an organisation of society appropriate to true citizenship. While he saw nothing in capitalism to prevent such a development, he thought that the principle of self-sacrifice would supersede that of self-interest. Capitalists and workers alike would be citizens and subject to a higher standard than aggrandisement of self or class. As Arnold Toynbee said of industrial disputes, such a democracy makes it possible, without shame or reluctance, to preach the gospel of duty to the whole people. Those who once had been unenfranchised had felt no duty because they had no rights. But with democracy that day has passed.

> In spite of a fundamental identity of interests between employers and workmen . . . there always will be, there always must be, antagonisms of interest; and these can be met only by moral ideas appropriate not to the feudal, but to the citizen stage. Men's rights will clash, and the reconciliation must come through a higher gospel than the gospel of rights—the gospel of duty. . . .[25]

The state scheme of education Green advocated was one that would provide a 'ladder of learning' by which boys of intellectual promise might mount from the humble, well-disciplined home to the universities. The prerequisites of such a ladder were the arrangement of schools in certain grades, determined, not by the social position of the boys using them, but by the standard of education given in them; and a free transition by means of scholarships from schools of a lower to those of a higher grade. There should be three orders of schools distinguished according to the age to which education is continued in each. 'There are boys, and these the great majority, including all of the labouring class, whose parents cannot reasonably be expected to keep them at school after the age of thirteen.'[26] Others may be induced to stay till fifteen or sixteen, when they will be put into some business. Relatively few may stay at school till eighteen when they will pass on to the universities.

Obviously, if a boy's schooling is to be continued until eighteen, it should include different subjects and be conducted on a different method from what would be desirable if it was to stop at fifteen or thirteen. Thus three grades of school are wanted, each aiming at a different standard of learning, according to the ages to which their students continue in them. But there is no reason why the same boy should not successively pass through schools of all the three grades. As a rule the boy who will remain in school till he is eighteen will be the son of well-to-do parents, but such a boy might well receive his elementary education along with the children of poorer families in a primary school.

The only hindrance to such an arrangement, apart from social prejudice, is that at present the primary school, having to receive all comers, may often contain children, unclean in their habits and language, with whom parents of refinement might reasonably object to their children being associated. But as education begins to tell on the poorer classes, we may confidently hope that this difficulty will be removed and that most of our elementary schools will become, as many of them are already, places to which children might be sent without scruple from the most refined and carefully managed homes.[27]

And just as a boy intended for the university might without disadvantage begin his education in the elementary school, so, by a proper use of scholarships and endowments, a promising boy, who otherwise would have to be put to manual labour at the age of thirteen, might be lifted to a school which would prepare him for the university. And when he had displayed his capacity for the university, another scholarship would be waiting which, with economy, would cover his expenses till the time of graduation.

Such a scheme, Green foresaw, would be opposed by the upper classes and the Established Church for one set of reasons and by many middle class nonconformists for another. While Green remonstrated with the nonconformists, he had no patience with the Church and upper classes. The nonconformists took the line that the state should not interfere with education at all. It could not do so, they said, without weakening the sense of parental responsibility. All that was wanted was voluntary effort to awaken this sense, which then could be left to do its work through spontaneously-formed associations. To this Green replied, 'No one can help respecting the spirit of this theory. The worst of it was that it did not square with the facts.'[28] Had all England been under the discipline of the nonconformist churches, the voluntary principle might have been possible. But this was not the case. The voluntary principle is inapplicable to education, because it is precisely those who need education most that are least capable of demanding it, desiring it or even conceiving of it. This argument, undeniably true when applied to education, became one of Green's main arguments in his lecture on 'Liberal Legislation'.

As for the opposition of the upper classes, Green took Bright's line that justice should be sought, not from them, but from the whole nation.

> The English aristocracy, we are told, is not an exclusive aristocracy. In one sense that is true, and that is what makes it such an awkward customer to deal with. A great capitalist generally ends

by buying a great estate. When the recollections of the counter have sufficiently passed away, he or his son is made a baronet. Perhaps in the next generation the family mounts a step higher still. Thus the oligarchy has a constant means of bribing the capitalists to its support. This corruption is eating the heart out of the upper commercial class, and it is but the highest outcome of a flunkeyism which pervades English society from the top to the bottom and is incompatible with any healthy political life. The English gentleman, we are sometimes told, is the noblest work of God, but one gentleman makes many snobs.[29]

By the extension of the franchise, the political power of this combination would be broken. By the organisation of a state scheme of education, the time will come when every citizen

> will have open to him at least the precious companionship of his own language . . . when all who have a special taste for learning will have open to them what has hitherto been unpleasantly called the 'education of gentlemen'. I confess to hoping for a time when that phrase will have lost its meaning, because the sort of education which alone makes the gentleman in any true sense will be within the reach of all.[30]

Once Green had filed his report after a year's work, he did not consider that his responsibilities had come to an end. In Birmingham, where he had carried out an important part of his investigations, those who held convictions similar to his own had organised the National Education League. Based on the nonconformists, one of its leaders was Joseph Chamberlain. Its programme was a campaign for new legislation that would make school attendance compulsory, maintain schools at public expense in all places lacking proper facilities, while establishing in them a religious teaching separated from that of any one church, including the Anglican. Because the members of the League felt that public sentiment ran contrary to purely secular teaching, it proposed to allow the reading of the Bible in the classroom, but not interpretation or commentary by the teacher. Through its agitation the League helped form public opinion to the extent that Gladstone's cabinet in 1870 was able to undertake significant educational reforms, although the Church of England schools survived. Green was an active member of the National Education League's Oxford branch. One reason why he favoured the Bill was that he thought its provision for unsectarian teaching of religion could be done by his own theology and ethics. In this connection he took some care to explain that he favoured, not secularism, but rather a religion without the dogmatic theology taught by the conventional churches.

357

As finally passed, the Elementary Education Act of 1870 was a compromise. Parliament forced changes upon the Government, which, in any event, intended, as Forster explained, to complete the voluntary system and to fill up gaps rather than to replace it by an altogether new scheme. The Education Department was to determine whether districts needed state schools and to provide school-boards where they did not exist. The Bill further provided that alongside the new schools supported by local rates, there would continue to function those voluntary schools which, by meeting stipulated conditions, qualified for state aid. Religious instruction in the new board-schools was limited by the Cowper-Temple clause: 'No religious catechism or religious formulary of any particular denomination shall be taught in the schools'.

Although this provision satisfied Green, he did not otherwise much like what the bill had done and condemned what it had left undone. In two lectures on the English elementary school system, he detailed his objections. Attendance for all children had not been made compulsory; school-boards were not everywhere established, and thus rural districts were left in an inferior position. And when boards were set up in towns, they were given power over their own schools only, and not over voluntary ones. Thus the boards were left impotent to co-ordinate the work of all schools in their district. This produced anomalies when, for example, in Church schools, a teacher might have to cope with students at six different levels. Obviously the standard of teaching suffered from the existence side-by-side of different types of schools which the board could not bring together. Green did not hesitate to declare that the whole 'denominational system was unjust and, in a certain sense demoralising'. He supported the National Education League's protest against subsidising such schools, as well as its stand that schools supported by public money be under public management. 'Religious teaching, in regard to which the rate-payers may have the most conflicting opinions, should not be provided for out of the rate-payers pockets.'[31] The interests of religion and morals were not to be identified with the Church of England; unfortunately teaching colleges were left under its control.

Yet these comments were not uniformly unfriendly in their judgment of the Act: its errors were more those of omission than commission; and showed that ultimately education was a sphere of activity in which men of good will ought to be able to reconcile their differences. In his final paragraph, Green summed up the modalities of his position. Here is to be found his equation of reform with liberalism and morality, his pacificism and his concern to establish a close connection between his general principles and the actual issues before the public:

> The points at issue between churchmen and dissenters may seem to some of us of slight importance, but to everyone who cares about the future of his country, everyone whose patriotism is of an higher order than that which finds expression in hooting the Russian Czar, the question, with what sort of mental equipment the children of the next generation are to go into the world, must be of supreme interest. Under God, it is to good books and a knowledge of the laws of nature that we must chiefly trust to make them, when they become their own masters, healthy and wise and virtuous. Yet we are still turning them out from school in the greatest number of cases without such elementary knowledge as will enable them to read the best books of their own language freely or make them acquainted with the simplest truths of science. It should surely be the first business of a reforming politician to see whether our schools cannot be made to yield some better result in the future. . . . The amount of intelligent public spirit that has of late been directed to the question is very remarkable. The establishment of school-boards in towns has had a great effect in quickening it; and, no doubt, if we escape a war which will postpone all social improvement indefinitely, it will continue to gain strength. But it remains for parliament to remove hindrances to the action of this public spirit, and to give more thorough command of educational appliances. For this reason I trust that all liberal politicians will be urgent in their demand that in all towns of a certain size school-boards, if they do not exist, shall be established; that union school-boards shall be established for the country districts; and that all public elementary schools whatever . . . shall be brought under the management of these boards.[32]

When in 1871 such a school-board was established in Oxford, Green hoped to be chosen as one of its members, but in fact he had to wait until the second election in 1874. This immediately preceded his election in 1875 to the Oxford town council, an event which did much to reconcile the University and town. For, as the daughter of Hugh Price Hughes noted, 'hitherto the two had been at loggerheads, the university despising the town, so it was felt, and the town cordially detesting while fawning upon the university'.[33] Green helped lead the campaign to build a grammar school and himself contributed £200. In addition he founded a scholarship for boys from the elementary schools of Oxford. Because of his visit to Birmingham on behalf of the Taunton Commission, he had become known to the masters of the King Edward's School who chose him to represent them on the governing body of the foundation.

Nor was his active interest reserved exclusively for secondary and elementary education. He took just as vigorous a part in every attempt to open Oxford to poorer students, to establish universities elsewhere and to extend Oxford's services to working-men. Green believed that the University had not done enough to educate students from the town. As early as the 1860's he took an active part in the delegacy established for that purpose. With the support of Jowett, Green succeeded in having Balliol provide a house outside the College for students with financial problems, the notion being that it would be thus possible to lower their expenses. Green left his rooms to preside over Balliol Hall.

In the 1870's the University Extension Movement began to make itself felt at the older universities, and when Oxford entered the field, it was largely due to Green and Jowett. Sir Michael Sadler, himself a leading actor in the movement, paid tribute to the men who, at a critical time, gave a new impulse to the democratic ideal of teaching all those willing and capable of profiting from instruction, whatever their age or formal training. Characteristically Sadler described Green's contribution and his friends' as 'touching existing forms of adult education with a new spirit of citizenship'.[34] By this time Green was solidly established as one of the most active Oxford representatives of the community of middle-class social reformers. The beginnings of University extension are usually associated with the work of James Stuart, then a young Fellow of Trinity College, Cambridge. When Stuart sought to set up a circuit, he put himself in touch with Green's uncle, the Reverend David Vaughan, who had retained his contact with Trinity during the years when he made a success out of the Workingman's College he had himself established at Leicester. The result was that Leicester was one of the first centres for University Extension.[35] But even if Green had not had this family connection to the movement, his own creed and that of Jowett would have made him a promoter of the cause at Oxford. Jowett had proposed, in a memorandum prepared for the Royal Commission of 1874 on Oxford, that the University set aside £40,000 for establishing colleges and lectureships in small towns. He saw adult education as a bridge which might unite the different classes of society and as a way of lessening hostility to the older universities. Green stressed the duties of solidarity. When Oxford made its first provision for Extension lectures in 1878, he was named the first chairman of the committee established for that purpose. A recent historian of the movement wrote, 'As to T. H. Green, it is impossible to measure the profound effect of his teaching'.[36] The same commentator noted the prominence of Balliol both in university extension and in the later Workers Educational Association. A. L. Smith and Lord Lindsay, both later Masters of Balliol and chairmen of the Tutorial Classes Committee, carried on in Green's spirit. Albert Mansbridge, founder of the WEA, said of Bishop Gore, another Balliol man affected by Green, 'Gore was the real founder of the institutions attributed to me.'[37] The Christian Social Union took an active part in the WEA which received support within Oxford from Sidney Ball who, as a Fabian Greenite, also pushed the work of Toynbee Hall in London and helped set up Barnett House in Oxford.

Balliol and New College joined in 1872 to make grants of £300 per year for the maintenance of the college at Bristol which now is Bristol University. In the Balliol contribution there was contained the stipulation that facilities be provided for adult education. When Balliol later granted another five years of support at £250 a year, the money actually came from the personal funds of Jowett and Green, who was particularly attached to Bristol by the long connection of his wife's family to that city.[38] The former home of the Symonds family is now a part of the University's buildings.

As though all this activity were not enough, Green also played an important part in the establishment of Mansfield College at Oxford. He had established a close relationship with Hugh Price Hughes, the noted Methodist, who later in the 'Forward Movement' sought to revive Wesley's impulse among the working-class by setting up missions and settlements. But Green was also on friendly terms with one of the most distinguished of Congregational ministers, the Reverend R. W. Dale of Birmingham. Green, who had so welcomed the opening of Oxford to the Nonconformists, now wrote Dr Dale that he thought that event had been a disaster. Perhaps because he understood the long-range political implications for the Liberal Party of a development which cut off the wealthiest Nonconformists from their traditional affiliations and attached them to the values of the aristocracy, Green sounded an alarm.[39] The sons of Nonconformists coming to the older universities were drifting away either into the Church of England or losing their Christian faith altogether. It was the obligation of Nonconformists, 'now that they had secured the opening of the Universities for their sons, to follow them there, in order to defend and maintain their religious life and faith'.[40] This letter played an important part in the decision to establish a Congregational College at Oxford. It also illuminates

THE POLITICS OF CONSCIENCE

the pattern of politics to which Green was committed, for Non-conformity, the Liberal Party and the temperance movement were all intimately interconnected.

3

If the need for public funds and direction in education helped push Green towards a more positive conception of the state, so too did his interest in temperance reform. This subject, which tends to strike later readers of Green as an eccentric and dreary foible, nevertheless furnishes both the background for much of his activity and insight into just what he meant by his theory of state interference. Recently Mr Kitson Clark has speculated about why historians have thus far refused to rate 'the effect of strong drink as the significant factor in nineteenth-history that it undoubtedly was'. He refers to the fact that elections, when disputed, usually hinged on the large amounts expended for buying votes by liquor, and remarks that whereas now we should seek to remedy the causes of drunkenness by providing better housing, wages, education and amusements, this mode of thought was not usual during most of the nineteenth century. 'Indeed any wide experience of drunkards, and it must be remembered that men in the middle of the nineteenth century saw much more of them than any normal person does now, would excuse a man for thinking that sobriety must come first, if the results of any other reform were not to be thrown away.'[41] In Green's view, the state is meant to develop what is worth developing in human character. In principle, it can best do this by allowing individuals to develop their characters by assuming responsibility for their moral choices. But there is a class of instances in which the state ought to act to remove certain conditions that in fact make genuine decisions impossible for some persons. Certainly education ought to be counted as one such barrier to self-realisation, as are preventable illnesses due to inadequate sanitation, and so too, in Green's view, is alcoholism. Therefore legislation on all these matters is justified, even if this means that the state is given power to regulate what in the strict theory of orthodox political economy is regarded as purely private and individual in character.

As Green came to know his society better, he perceived grave evils with which the voluntary system could not cope. Hence Bright's outlook had to be adapted to deal with conditions as they really were. All the maxims of Green's political philosophy either arose from or were made applicable to his essentially moral concerns with public health, education, and temperance. Although his mode of thought led him to apply the same formulae to the more complex issues of state intervention in economic life, he had no particular interest in, or knowledge of, the problems peculiar to capitalism. Social and political matters occupied his attention, and it was in relation to them that he first developed the notion that the true programme of liberalism is the removal of all obstacles which the law can remove to the free development of his full potentialities by every individual in the society. 'The whole body of citizens ought to be called upon to do that as a body which under the conditions of modern life cannot be done if everyone is to be left to himself and cannot be left undone without the whole body suffering.'[42]

Such a programme depended upon Green's confidence that the majority of the nation hitherto excluded from the suffrage could be safely admitted to a full part in national life. In taking this line, he was following the lead given by Bright. But Green's civic activity in Oxford indicates the extent to which he was led to go beyond his political hero. On the one hand, he supported Bright in his demand for a more broadly based suffrage; on the other, he rejected the voluntary principle in its application to strong drink. As a follower of Manchester Liberalism, Green threw himself wholeheartedly into the work of the Oxford Reform League. This was the local branch of the national organisation, which so effectively rallied support behind Bright that the Reform Bill of 1867 had become inevitable in one or another form before Disraeli 'dished the Whigs'. The first political speech ever given outside university walls by Green was delivered to the sympathetic audience of the League. At Oxford as elsewhere, this was 'the most important organisation among radicals and working-men'.[43] Green's reception in this milieu was cordial in the extreme, 'very unlike my old experience at the Union, where I always used to be always groaned at and interrupted.' In 1868 when the new constituencies created by the Reform Bill were contested for the first time, Green spoke in behalf of several university friends standing as Liberals. One of his efforts was directed to agricultural labourers in a 'sort of cart-house', where some of his 'best sentences were greeted by the neighing of a horse'.[44] Of these candidates, only one was successful, C. S. Parker, Green's old coach. This experience for the first time brought him into direct contact with the corrupt electoral practices then in vogue. Both money and alcohol were used to buy votes, and so Green had his eyes opened to what he called 'the disgraceful traffic in votes'. He even went so far as to say that, 'as long as we have a Parliament which is in fact a sort of club of rich men, we shall not have a parliament which has the interest of the struggling and suffering classes of society at heart.'* But despite this statement with its radical implications, Green showed the limits of his outlook by his faith that the extension of the suffrage would in the long run transform the quality of political life. For the first time it had become possible to describe the nation as made up of one people. Responsibility alone can develop character. Only after men become citizens in the full sense of the term, can they develop the qualities which opponents of reform insisted that they did not possess. After the troubled passage of the bill, Green commented in a public speech:

'We who were reformers from the beginning always said that the enfranchisement of the people was an end in itself. We said, and were much derided for saying so, that citizenship makes the moral man; that citizenship only gives that self-respect which is the true basis of respect of others, and without which there is no lasting social order or real morality. If we were asked what result we looked for from the enfranchisement of the people, we said, that is not the present question. Untie the man's legs and it will be time to speculate how he will walk.'[45]

On this and allied subjects, Green was both ahead of and behind his time. When it came to extending the suffrage, he was admirably level-headed in avoiding the panicked visions of Lowe and Bagehot. But his moralism, which is not unattractive when applied to civic questions, begins to appear in his insistence that the way of life developed by the Nonconformists was so obviously good that everyone, and particularly members of the working-class, should be compelled by law to imitate it. Curiously enough Bright, perhaps because he never questioned the principle of laissez-faire, always refused to sponsor any

* In view of the later struggle about reforming the House of Lords, Green's views on this subject are not without interest: 'The House of Lords was a club of great landowners which unfortunately was invested with co-ordinate power with the people's representatives in Parliament. He had always been a strong advocate for the maintenance of an Upper Chamber, but he said confidently, that if they did not substitute for the present club of great landowners some assembly that should really be more consonant with the sober wisdom of the English people, that Upper Chamber must inevitably disappear, and with it, as he believed, one of the great safeguards of wise legislation, for he did not wholly trust to the sudden gusts of passion in a democratic assembly. He believed that there must be something else than such an assembly, but that something else must not be a club of landowners.' [Speech to North Ward Liberal Association, 11 March, 1882 (*Oxford Chronicle and Berks and Bucks Gazette*).]

legislation restricting the sale of intoxicating liquors. Although himself a teetotaler, he took the line that, because the sale of strong drink had always been permitted, stringent action by the state would constitute an invasion of the property rights of those engaged in the trade. 'Law must be founded,' Bright said, 'on broad and general principles such as are consistent with political economy, but individuals may use their own discretion as to what they abstain from, and men may persuade each other to do many things which it would not be proper for the law to compel them to do.'[45] From one point of view, this discrepancy between the attitudes of Green and Bright is surprising. For both of them stemmed from the same long-standing connection between radicalism in politics, nonconformity in religion and temperance reform. Bright himself had gained experience in how to carry on an agitation from the campaign for moderation in drinking he joined as a young man. This tradition was to continue into the formation of the Labour Party, for both Keir Hardy and Philip Snowden did their first organising work for the temperance leagues of their respective nonconformist churches. This heritage of radical asceticism, connected in the past to Puritanism and Evangelicalism, and in Green's lifetime to the alliance of the Liberals and Nonconformists, was far from being a mere historical accident. Green thought he knew the classes that would be enfranchised by the Second Reform Bill well enough to be able to predict that their exercise of the suffrage would be, in more than one sense, sober and moderate. But his initial confidence was shaken by the Tory victory in the election of 1874.

It is significant that the country had been passing through a period of prosperity. An affluent society raises problems that have a way of disconcerting liberal individualists accustomed to arguing that the ordinary man may be trusted to decide questions involving the general interest. Tocqueville, in his consideration of American democracy, was still willing to accept the view of those he studied: the interest of each individual, if properly understood, leads him to make sacrifices that serve the long-run purposes of the collectivity. But when Tocqueville experienced at first-hand under the July Monarchy what it means to live in a society ruled by the principle that Guizot expressed in the formula of 'Enrichissez-vous', he began to reconsider the question of individualism. A somewhat similar process is observable in Green. Speaking at the dedication of Oxford's Liberal Hall, he attempted to diagnose the defeat suffered by the party two years earlier:

'The country had been passing through a phase of sudden and un-exampled commercial prosperity and political enthusiasm had been lost in what I may call a general riot of luxury in which nearly all classes had their share. The money and the beer flowed freely. Money quickly made was quickly spent, and it seemed as if all classes were disposed, not exactly to rest and be thankful, but at least to take their ease, eat, drink and be merry. In this state of things, in the middle of this general political inertia, came the election of 1874. It found the liberal party everywhere disorganised. It found the constituencies politically asleep, but it found what are called the vested interests, which the late government had harassed, alive and vindictive.'[47]

What emerges from this analysis is the fact that Green had already begun to think that the right to vote cannot, by itself, transform character. True, it is the precondition of developing intelligent, active and self-regulating citizens, and along with education offers opportunities which cannot be renounced. But unless a basic change takes place in the moral quality of those classes that are being reclaimed and invited to participate in the real life of the nation, no external measures, whether political or economic, will be effective. Even land reform, designed to moralise agricultural workers by giving them land derived from breaking up large estates would fail in its purpose, unless some-thing were done about the problem of drink. For here was the true opium of the people. This was equally true both of industrial and agricultural workers. Thus Green's preoccupation with the temperance movement shows how strong was the individualism left by his religous formation. Although he never renounced his faith in the importance of changing the total environment, increasingly he applied to all of society the reflections first occasioned by the disastrous career of his own brother. To Sir William Harcourt, whom Green considered to have pooh-poohed the importance of temperance legislation, he wrote:

'I must say plainly that I do not think there is a greater mischief a public man of authority can do than to depreciate the magnitude of this particular problem. . . . I can scarcely think that, if you had seen much of the life of the working classes at close quarters, you could have had the heart to speak as you did. Even here in Oxford, . . . anyone who goes below the respectable classes finds the degradation and hopeless waste which this vice produces meet him at every turn. It is idle to say that education and comfortable habits will check the vice in time. The education of the families of the sober will have no effect on the families of the drunken. Unless the vice is first checked by a real lift of the national conscience, education and comfortable habits are impossible in those very families that are to be saved from drunkenness by them.'[48]

Here was precisely the same argument Green used in his educational theory. In certain cases, usually although not always involving the working classes, the state must intervene to produce changes in character that can be brought about in no other way. Such an outlook stresses the primacy of the inner checks essential to the good man and the good citizen, but at the same time insists that environment plays a part in determining character.

This emphasis came to be of increasing importance for Green as time went on. One of his students recalled that before the passage of the Reform Bill Green had never spoken much about temperance, but seemed much more preoccupied with land reform. In 1867 he had a better opinion of the agricultural workers than of the landlords. From the breaking up of large estates, which he believed would occur very soon, great things would come. 'My impression is that his growing acquaintance with the weakness and poor qualities of the working class and their ridiculous political action in 1874 led him to the belief that to rescue them from moral degradation by means of Temperance Propaganda was the first necessity; and that unless this were done, legislation on land would help them little.'[49] And so Green threw himself into this work. Before long he had become a member of every temperance society in Oxford and was made the vice-president of the United Kingdom Alliance and president of the Oxford Band of Hope Temperance Union. The Oxford Diocesan branch of the Church of England Temperance Society made him its treasurer despite his statement that he was a 'questionable churchman and little known to the clergy'. In 1875 he set up at his own expense a 'coffee tavern' for working-men, and helped with the building of a Liberal Hall to take political meetings away from the pubs which had hitherto served this purpose. He took an active interest in promoting savings banks for those whom he thought would profit from thrift and reading rooms for those who sought more rewarding diversion than that offered in public houses.

The address he delivered to the national conference of the United Kingdom Alliance tells a good deal about his conception of what could be done by legislative action, and what must in the nature of the case be left to the opinion and jurisdiction of the locality.[50] Although his personal involvement in the issue is still evident, the full text of his speech demonstrates far better than any other of his statements that even on this point, his abstract principles and practical experience continued to interact. The sale of intoxicating liquor is no ordinary business to which the law ought to leave the greatest possible freedom. Rather, as a 'unique source of waste, disease, and crime', it requires at least special regulation. The narrower the limits within which the traffic can be reduced by the free action of the community, the better it will be for the community. Here is the liberal distinction between state and society and Green's own feeling that the local unit of government has in such matters an inherent superiority to the national legislature.

Further, assuming the principle *salus populi suprema lex*, Green predicated that 'when any community by a legally ascertained majority determines to exclude the liquor traffic altogether, the exclusion is in the circumstances a necessity of general welfare to which the tastes of individuals, although harmless in themselves, must yield.' But the country was so varied that it would be unwise to subject the liquor trade everywhere within it to the same degree of control. 'No restraint or prohibition would be effectual unless backed by local feeling and opinion, and the circumstances of different neighbourhoods are so various that an identity of feeling and opinion between them on this matter can hardly be looked for.' As for working-class reaction, it was clear that any Parliamentary legislation for the nation as a whole would be stamped as class legislation imposed from above. But if a labourer were to see local facilities for drinking reduced by a majority vote of his neighbours, he could not complain that he was being deprived of his beer by the rich. Thus local option was the best means of dealing with the regulation of a matter that constituted a significant exception to the liberal orthodoxy of the time.

What is worth noting in this formulation is the fact that it emphasises, not Green's philosophical definition of freedom, but his sense of the value of local participation and his empirical knowledge of how laws are apt to be received. One potent tendency in his formal writings is the assertion that men ought to act in such a way as to realise the best type of character. This view is combined somewhat arbitrarily with the notion that will, not force, is the basis of the state. How to get men to do that which improves their character is a point never elucidated in the *Principles of Political Obligation*. By the position Green assumed on this matter so dear to him, he gave a clear-cut indication that he respected the principle of consent as registered in majority rule. Experience had taught him the limits of state interference. He never would have attained such realism had he not ventured outside the walls of the University into the city.

Somewhat surprisingly for someone who held his views on private property, Green did not believe that there should be any compensation to owners of public houses who lost their licences because of local action. And he would not distinguish between those that had always observed existing regulations and those that had not. The value of all such businesses, he asserted, was artificial, arising out of a particular state of the law liable at any time to alteration. There was no essential difference between them and the owner of a ribbon factory whose property may have acquired an artificial value from the imposition of a heavy duty on foreign ribbons. No one would ever think of recompensing such a person for losses suffered by the repeal of the tariff, on which depended the profits of his undertaking. The risk he had taken, the profits or loss resulting therefrom, were no part of the state's concern. It could be safely assumed that most owners of public houses had long since been compensated for whatever their original investments might have been. This position was in marked contrast to that of Bright who thought that any regulation leading to financial loss constituted an invasion of property rights. But Green had rejected theories of vested right, said to be absolute, even when affecting adversely the good of the whole community. Nor did he consider compensation necessary in the field of education any more than in that of temperance. For he looked forward to a time when 'it would be considered that the state, by long continuance of a subsidy to voluntary schools, far exceeding the voluntary contributions to them, had fairly bought out all private claims to their use, and was entitled to regulate them as it liked'.[51] Such statements stand in distinct contrast to the theory of property developed in his formal writings. The brusque impatience manifest in them tell a good deal about the effect upon Green of his practical experience.

In his treatment of education and temperance, Green developed a criterion for state interference which was purely empirical in character, although this was concealed from himself and others by the elaborate philosophical framework within which it functioned. That is to say, the abstract argument taken by itself contains potentially contradictory elements. That part of it which carried a presumption against the use of law except in the most urgent and exceptional instances could conflict with the vague qualification that the state is always justified in hindering hindrances to the development of character. What Green did in applying this ambiguous formula to education and temperance was in effect to make actual conditions decisive. No doubt a society in which men voluntarily send their children to school and restrain themselves from excessive drinking is superior to one in which such conduct is enforced by law. But the fact is that, left to themselves, certain individuals and groups will not do what is necessary for the good of themselves and their children. Therefore, Green concludes, the state must compel them to do so. The legislator must take men as they are if he is to make them into what they should be. Thus the way was opened to an application of Green's political philosophy which could not have been anticipated from the abstract statement of its leading principles. The not inconsiderable ambiguity due to the terms of Green's intellectual formulation was further increased by the way he himself applied them to the causes in which he was most concerned. Yet this mattered little during the tenure of his influence.

Men attracted to his ideas were most apt to be seeking a cause to which they might devote themselves. An integrated life rather than an unmistakably clear theory was their objective. Thus they were ready to tolerate, indeed they positively preferred, statements of a sort which employed terms which were vague but comprehensive. And the status of middle-class reformers further encouraged them not to enquire too carefully into what might be the long-run consequences of their individual or group enterprises. The need for an object of self-dedication, a sense of class guilt and an intellectual preference for what was all-encompassing over what was precise and logical—all these counted for more than an unambiguous criterion for state activity. In any case, no rule could be expected to provide specific indications in isolation from the facts of any particular case. Paradoxically, the less precise the formulation, the greater was the scope given to politicians' judgement of the circumstances and expediency of one or another course of action. Such matters became more significant as the products of Oxford Idealism rose to high places where they took decisions. But while Green was alive, and for a time after his death, it was his style of life and personal example that mattered most.

4

The home of the Greens was a place where their University friends and students met the reformers and philanthropists of the city. Their host had the reputation, among the latter, of being always willing to listen and, if asked, to give his advice. If he himself consented to take up a particular cause, he could be counted on to do his share of the work. More than once his own money was given in support of his principles. Students and colleagues who saw Green at home were struck by how naturally he met townsfolk on terms of equality. The atmosphere of the house was quiet and unstrenuous; the Greens practising a simple, almost austere, hospitality characterised by rather less seriousness than might have been expected. Not a little of this was due to Mrs Green, a remarkable person, who continued to impress successive generations of Oxford friends drawn from varying backgrounds until her death in 1929 at the age of eighty-seven.

Oxford was already familiar ground to her when she met her future husband. Her father and brother had a broad circle of acquaintances, which included Jowett. Even so her first visit to him fell short of being a triumph. For once his silence, inevitable and daunting when with undergraduates, did not give way to friendliness in the company of a young lady. Miss Symonds could not manage to say much, and after their departure her brother reproached her for having disgraced the family.[52] In time this unhappy beginning was recalled with some amusement, for Mrs Green became a good friend of Jowett's and the other Balliol dons of her husband's era. Most of them never married; Green belonged to the first generation of Fellows allowed to continue in their posts after forsaking celibacy. Their position was unprecedented, and many of them retained attitudes more consonant with their former than with their newer status.

One of her husband's causes—that of university education for women—called forth an especial enthusiasm on the part of his wife. Both of them contributed a good deal to the establishment of the women's colleges at Oxford. Green was the first secretary, and then served as a member of the council of the Association for the Higher Education of Women. Mrs Green, after the Oxford Committee for Lectures was organised in 1873, succeeded Mrs Humphry Ward and Mrs Creighton as its secretary. As also happened in the settlement house movement, a split took place between those who wished the proposed college for women to be under the auspices of the Church of England and those others who opposed this arrangement. The Greens, as might have been predicted, associated themselves with Somerville College, rather than with Lady Margaret which had an Anglican affiliation. Mrs Green continued to serve on the council of Somerville College until her death, and established the traditional link between Somerville and Balliol.[53] Her portrait is to be seen in Somerville: 'Her grey hair is smoothly parted in the centre beneath a white lace cap, and a double row of amber emphasises the lace-edged high neck of her black dress. The small, firm mouth and keen grey eyes in the beautiful serene face testify to the capacity for caustic utterance which occasionally varied her tranquil kindness.'[54]

Of her fifty-seven years in Oxford, only twelve were with her husband. Green's health had never been robust. In 1880, when he was forty-four, he had a serious illness. Before he was fully recovered, he threw himself into the campaign connected with the general election. His pattern of life was highly demanding. As his wife later recalled: 'All this excitement was very bad for him, as hot rooms & public speaking & above all endeavouring to keep the pace tried him greatly.'[55] Two years later, he again fell ill; this time, his doctors diagnosed his condition as blood-poisoning, and he was told that he had but a few hours to live. This news he received with quiet courage, and began at once to summon his forces so that he could take care of what had to be done. Principal among them was the publication of the *Prolegomena to Ethics*, which he had almost completed and, what seemed to be equally important in his eyes, the payment of pupil-teachers in a school of which he was the treasurer. To his wife he spoke of his belief in God and immortality although he added, with the honesty that he could not suspend even now, that he could form no very clear idea of what the life beyond might be like. After asking to have the eighth verse of the Epistle to the Romans read to him, he found the effort of listening too great. It was his wish that he be buried in a cemetery in the North Ward that he had represented. To Mrs Green, 'almost the only thing personal he said to me when he knew that he was dying was that I was to try to be happy and lead a useful life and do all that we meant to do together.'[56] That night his mind began to wander, and he talked about the Irish Land Bill and the situation in Bulgaria. He died quietly the next morning. A great preacher who had been his student wrote, 'For us all, he wore something of the prophetic air, and his too early death gave power to his prophecy'.[57]

His funeral called forth an unusual display of grief from the city and University alike. Despite heavy rain, some two thousand mourners were in attendance. The local newspaper reported, in words heavily drawn upon by Mrs Humphry Ward in *Robert Elsmere*:

A more impressive sight has never perhaps been witnessed in Oxford than at the funeral of Professor Green on Wednesday last. In the long procession, which reached from the cemetery to Beaumont Street there were persons of all ages and of every station in life. The Vice-Chancellor with other high officers of the University, and the Mayor and Corporation of the City; the older graduates, and children from the elementary schools; college servants, tradespeople, under-graduates, the masters and scholars of the new High School; all these joined with a large circle of Professor Green's to pay their last tribute of affectionate regard. . . . The fact that the rain fell in torrents proved that idle curiosity played no part in attracting so large and various a concourse; the mourners were gathered together by . . . the sorrow at the loss of a trusted friend and the passing of a noble spirit. . . .[57]

Mrs Green stayed on in Oxford. She made her own place there, and she did not lack friends among the young. 'Whenever there was enthusiasm that could give a rational account of itself and that was not without a sense of humour, Mrs Green's instinctive sympathy was never overweighted with the maturity of her wisdom.'[59] In addition to her Somerville connection, she was long a familiar figure at Balliol. It was her destiny to be the nurse and death-bed attendant of many survivors of her husband's day. Jowett, attended by her during a nearly-fatal illness, wrote that she was worth a 'whole College of Physicians'.[60] When he died, she was with him. Later she was to be cast in the same rôle for Jowett's biographer, Edwin Abbott and for Strachan-Davidson, who called her 'an angel of consolation'. The differences between Green and Jowett had long since been forgotten. The Master's last wish was to be buried near Green in St Sepulchre's Cemetery, and they were separated only by one grave. Increasingly they became identified in death as the two great spirits of Balliol's golden age. Even Asquith, who had sided with the Master in his opposition to Green's philosophy, merged the two in his mind. When he became Prime Minister, he regretted only one thing—that Jowett and Green had not lived to see their belief in him justified.[61] But by the time of Mrs Green's death she seemed the survivor of an age incredibly far removed from the Oxford of 1929, both in its ideas and its politics.

The success of Idealism in Green's form had been due to a situation which hardly existed after the First World War. Perhaps the greatest change was in religious temper: the children of those who had abandoned Evangelicalism or other orthodoxies were repelled rather than attracted by the system which had seemed so alluring to their parents. This new generation, raised under a looser discipline and attenuated belief, saw no reason why they should forego the pleasures of the mind and arts just because they were individual goods with no ameliorative effects for others. Already the attractions of G. E. Moore had made themselves felt at Cambridge before 1914. And no less damaging to the long-range prospects of Idealism were the powerful intellectual and logical criticisms which originated in the same place, first under Moore and Russell, and then Wittgenstein in his first phase. To these forces, which even unaided might have put an end to the period of Idealist dominance, were added several developments quite unforeseen, and possibly unfore-seeable by Green: the changes brought by the War of 1914, the creation of a Labour Party independent of the Liberals and the responsibility for social welfare increasingly assumed by the state.

The sense of sin Green felt and imparted presupposed a great distance between middle-class reformers and those they wished to aid. The social gospel of Idealism was meant to bridge, by strenuous individual effort, the gap between the more and less fortunate, who would thereafter be linked in fellowship. Self-sacrifice on the one side was meant to be matched by self-improvement on the other. A secularised asceticism thus would be put to work in the one task on which all could agree: the development of individual character of a kind worth developing. But the feelings which Green drew upon—the craving for solidarity and a higher cause to which one might devote oneself—these could not survive the entry of a well-organised and purpose-ful Labour movement into politics. The pattern of response to Labour by Liberals, even of the most open-minded variety, can be observed in L. T. Hobhouse. It was he who claimed Green for the New Liberals. Early in the twentieth century, this wing of the Liberal Party was ready to welcome Labour to its ranks and work together for a greater degree of state intervention so as to distribute more equitably income and other benefits of the productive system. Hobhouse believed that the working class could and should seek to improve its wages and conditions of employment; he favoured the extension of social services and even the nationalisation of key industries. Yet when Labour attempted to speed the pace of improvement by an increased militancy and a political organisation, well-financed, staffed by a permanent bureaucracy and orientated towards gains for its own members, Hobhouse reacted sharply:

> Labour is presumably suffering from the wrongs of unequal distri-bution, and in all of its efforts commands, therefore, a certain sympathy. It does not follow that every particular effort it makes to right that wrong is wise, or even fair; e.g. the coal-porters no doubt deserve their extra money, but were they justified . . . in catching London out in a cold snap. . . . ?

Well, you will say *vogue la galère*. It all brings us nearer to the great class war, nothing is to be gained except by fighting. The moment you convince me of this I shall shut up shop as a radical or socialist or anything reforming, because I shall be convinced that human nature is hopeless and that the effort to improve society had better be left alone.[61]

It is significant that Hobhouse in 1914 still identified himself as engaged in a 'reforming' activity. For if improvement were based merely on class interest, then it had no moral significance to him. The point was that reformers could not welcome developments which made their own rôle redundant. Paradoxically, the long-run consequence of their activities was to do just that. For what came out of their many agitations was a machinery for bureaucratic action. After a certain point had been reached, social welfare came to be seen as a matter to be taken care of by the professional agents of the state rather than as a set of moral obligations to be assumed by exceptionally conscientious middle-class persons. No one considering the question from the point of view of those aided could doubt the superiority of bureaucratic administration, furnished as a matter of citizens' rights, to the improvised network of agencies created by the efforts of reformers and self-help organisations. That such persons and groups deserved much credit for the new state of affairs could not be denied. But philanthropy and voluntary action could never again have the moral quality and practical urgency Green and his generation attached to them.

The First World War, which transformed the European scene in so many other ways, contributed not a little to the demolition of Green's spiritual universe.* For one thing, as Elie Halévy commented, it proved that centrally-planned economic and social policies were in fact possible. Much of the machinery created in the belligerent countries was never dismantled; and in the Soviet Union planning became a standard procedure in peacetime. Again, the moralistic assumptions about politics made

* Gilbert Murray described this outlook as a 'philosophy, or *Weltanschauung*, or faith, . . . of which our chaotic generation has largely lost hold; the spirit of Liberalism among forms of thought, of Great Britain among nations, of the nineteenth century among the ages. We call it "pre-war," . . . it belongs to the time when men's minds had not yet been disorganised by the constant presence or menace of that disastrous influence and the moral and material world might alike be called a Cosmos rather than a Chaos. It was a time when we were actuated by hope rather than by fear, when we believed that men were as a rule influenced by reason, that justice was the great healer of social troubles and the natural aim of wise statesmanship; a time whose normal standards of conduct, public and private, often seem to us like ideals no longer attainable.' [Gilbert Murray, 'Herbert Albert Laurens Fisher, 1865-1940,' *Proceedings of the British Academy* (XXVI), p. 13.]

by mid-Victorian Liberals seemed laughable to many of those who survived a war, ostensibly fought on the basis of the highest principles, but subsequently revealed to be the result of stupidity and bad faith. And the War probably destroyed for ever the possibility that even a minority of upper- or middle-class persons could thereafter feel guilty for their social privileges. Those who fought and survived found it difficult to believe that they owed anybody anything.

All the articles of the Idealist creed became irrelevant to the world of the twenties and thirties. The value of self-sacrifice, the importance of striving to attain the ideal, the belief in progress and in the duties owed by one class to another—all this the younger generation considered to be inflated and diffuse hypocrisy. Often they could make nothing whatever of it. Stephen Spender, a member of an eminent Oxford and Liberal family, thus described how his father appeared to him:

> If I had to play football, he impressed on me that this was to harden the tissues of my character. His own accomplishments were to him difficulties surmounted with unflinching resolution at the cost of infinite pains. He spoke often in parables which illustrated the point that life was a perpetual confronting of oneself with vague immensities. . . . My father's habit of mind created a kind of barrier between him and us which asserted itself even in the most genuine situations.[62]

To some extent Spender's statement but reflects the perennial conflict between generations. How ironical and yet inevitable that the 'New Theology of Modernism', proclaimed by Mrs Humphry Ward and accepted by the fathers as bold and progressive, should have appeared to their sons as a set of priggish *clichés*. But this is not the whole story. Technical developments within philosophy had discredited the intellectual case for Idealism. And its decline coincided with the downfall of the Liberal Party and stemmed from many of the same causes. Not the least of these was the gradual disappearance of Nonconformity as a political force. The Liberal epoch had come to an end, and with it the tenure of Green's influence.

REFERENCES

CHAPTER ONE

1. Born 1836, died 1882.
2. James Bryce, *Studies in Contemporary Biography* (London, 1903), p. 99. Earl of Oxford and Asquith, *Memories and Reflections 1852-1927* (London, 1928), pp. 21, 24. Cf. also L. T. Hobhouse, *Democracy and Reaction* (2nd ed.; London, 1909), p. 79.
3. *The Works of T. H. Green*, ed. R. L. Nettleship (3 vols.; London, 1885-8), II, 335-553. Cited hereafter as Green, *Works*. Only the *Lectures on the Principles of Political Obligation* will be identified, and this as *PO*. All references to *PO* will be to paragraph numbers.
4. Among those Green influenced directly were: Bernard Bosanquet, A. C. Bradley, Edward Caird, Bishop Gore, H. S. Holland, J. MacCunn, J. H. Muirhead, R. L. Nettleship, D. G. Ritchie, Arnold Toynbee, W. Wallace; and indirectly, or with significant qualifications, F. H. Bradley, Lord Haldane, Sir Ernest Barker and Lord Lindsay. For a memorial tribute to Green by men trained by him, or affected by his work, see Andrew Seth and R. B. Haldane (eds.), *Essays in Philosophical Criticism* (London, 1883). A good many references are to be found in Klaus Dockhorn, *Die Staatsphilosophie des Englischen Idealismus: Ihre Lehre und Wirkung* (Bochom-Langendreer, 1937).
5. G. K. Chesterton, *G. F. Watts* (London, [1914]), p. 3, cited by L. E. Elliott-Binns, *Religion in the Victorian Era* (2nd ed.; London: Lutterworth Press, 1946), p. 59.
6. Letter from Marshall to Henry Sidgwick, 23 December, 1884, as paraphrased by Sidgwick in Arthur and E. M. Sidgwick, *Henry Sidgwick, A Memoir*, (London, 1906), p. 394.
7. Lewis R. Farnell, *An Oxonian Looks Back* (London, 1934), pp. 44-45.

8. J. H. Muirhead, *Reflections by a Journeyman in Philosophy*, ed. John W. Harvey (London: Allen and Unwin, 1942), p. 60. Thomas Hill Green, *Prolegomena to Ethics*, ed. A. C. Bradley (Oxford, 1883). Hereafter cited as *PE*. All references will be to paragraph numbers.

9. This occurred in 1869. Cf. A. E. Taylor, 'Francis Herbert Bradley, 1846-1924,' *Proceedings of the British Academy* [1926], p. 1.

10. *Ibid.*, p. 2.

11. Elie Halévy, *England in 1815*, trans. E. I. Watkin and D. A. Barker (London: Ernest Benn, 1949), p. 387.

12. Ernst Troeltsch, *The Social Teaching of the Christian Churches*, trans. Olive Wyon (2 vols.; Glencoe, 11.: Free Press, 1949), I, 44-45.

13. Letter of 31 August, 1865, Evelyn Abbott and Lewis Campbell, *The Life and Letters of Benjamin Jowett* (2 vols.; London, 1897), I, 413.

14. P. L. Parker (ed.), *The Heart of John Wesley's Journal* (London, n.d.), pp. 87-88 (extract from 12 June, 1742).

15. E. Douglas Bebb, *Wesley: A Man with a Concern* (London: Epworth Press, 1950), p. 37.

16. *Ibid.*

17. Parker (ed.), *John Wesley's Journal*, p. 68 (extract from 27 November, 1739).

18. *Ibid.*, pp. 298-9, entry of 25 August, 1763).

19. Robert F. Wearmouth, *Methodism and the Working-Class Movements of England, 1800-50* (London, 1937), pp. 20-21.

20. Halévy, *England in 1815*, pp. 410-15.

21. Bebb, *Wesley*, p. 124.

22. W. Roberts, *Memoirs of the Life and Correspondence of Mrs Hannah More*, III, 196 (extract from her diary, 8 July, 1802), cited by Halévy, *England in 1815*, p. 437.

23. R. H. Tawney, *Religion and the Rise of Capitalism* (Harmondsworth: Penguin Books, 1947), pp. 210-26.

24. J. H. Rigg, *The Living Wesley*, (London, 1891), p. 154.

25. Bebb, *Wesley*, p. 101.

26. *Ibid.*, p. 107. See also Bebb, *Nonconformity and Social and Economic Life* (London, 1935), Appendix VIII.

27. Parker (ed.), *John Wesley's Journal*, p. 407 (extract from 1 May, 1776).

28. Edward H. Sugden, *Wesley's Standard Sermons* (2 vols.; London, 1921), II, 320.

29. Cited by Robert Southey, *The Life of Wesley* 3rd ed.; (2 vols.; London, 1846), II, 369.

30. Max Weber, *The Protestant Ethic and the Spirit of Capitalism*, trans. Talcott Parsons (London, 1930), p. 178.
31. Matthew Arnold, *Culture and Anarchy*, ed. J. Dover Wilson (Cambridge, England: Cambridge University Press, 1946), p. 58.
32. *Ibid.*, p. 157.
33. Sir James Stephen, 'The Clapham Sect,' *Essays in Ecclesiastical Biography*, cited in *Property: Its Rights and Duties*, ed. Charles Gore (London, 1913), p. 166. For the most recent treatment of Evangelicalism in the nineteenth century, and one which stresses the second Evangelical revival, see G. Kitson Clark, *The Making of Victorian England* (London: Methuen & Co., 1962), pp. 21-26, 147-205.
34. *The Letters of John Stuart Mill*, ed. Hugh S. R. Elliot (2 vols.; London, 1910), II, 359. This entry is dated 14 January, 1854.
35. Clement C. J. Webb, *A Study of Religious Thought in England from 1850* (Oxford, 1933), p. 9.
36. Letter from R. L. Nettleship to H. S. Holland, 13 December, 1869, *Henry Scott Holland, Memoir and Letters*, ed. Stephen Paget (London, 1921), pp. 44-45.
37. Green, *Works*, III, 222.
38. John Henry Cardinal Newman, *Apologia Pro Vita Sua* (London, 1913), p. 493.
39. *Ibid.*
40. *Ibid.*, p. 495.
41. Green, *Works*, III, 223.
42. Mrs Humphry Ward, *Robert Elsmere* (3 vols.; London, 1888).
43. Mrs Humphry Ward, *A Writer's Recollections* (London, 1918), p. 169.
44. *Ibid.*, p. 252. The author estimated that the total sales in all languages came to about a million copies. See *Robert Elsmere* (Boston and New York, 1909), I, xiii.
45. Mrs Humphry Ward, *A Writer's Recollections*, p. 248.
46. *Ibid.*, pp. 133-4.
47. Letter from Green to Holland, 29 December, 1868, Paget (ed.), *Holland, Memoir and Letters*, pp. 29-30. Apparently these letters were not made available to R. L. Nettleship for his memoir of Green (Green, *Works*, III, xi-clxi).
48. Letter from Green to Holland, 9 January, 1869, Paget (ed.), *Holland, Memoir and Letters*, pp. 31-33.
49. Green, *Works*, III, 230-76.

CHAPTER TWO

1. G. M. Young, *Last Essays* (London: Rupert Hart-Davis, 1950), p. 206.
2. J. L. Talmon, *Political Messianism* (London: Secker & Warburg, 1960), p. 81.
3. Ivan Turgenev, *On the Eve*, trans. Gilbert Gardiner (Harmondsworth: Penguin Books, 1950), pp. 29-30.
4. Percy Dearmer (ed.), *Lombard Street in Lent* (2nd ed. rev.; London, 1911), p. x.
5. G. W. F. Hegel, *The Phenomenology of Mind*, trans. J. B. Baillie (2nd ed.; London, 1931), p. 251.
6. *Ibid.*, pp. 752-3.
7. Green, *Works*, III, lxviii.
8. Sidney Hook, *From Hegel to Marx* (London, 1936), p. 49.
9. *Ibid.*, p. 41.
10. A number of letters written to Mrs Green or to Nettleship allude to the fact that the Reverend Valentine Green was an Evangelical: those of C. S. Parker, W. L. Newman and Henry Nettleship are the most interesting. All are in the Balliol College Library. Captain L. H. Green has confirmed these reports, and added from personal knowledge, that two of Green's sisters continued to be strict Evangelicals until their deaths. F. H. and A. C. Bradley were the sons of the Reverend Charles Bradley, a leading preacher of the Clapham Sect. In addition to the article by G. R. G. Mure, 'F. H. Bradley,' *Encounter*, XVI, No. 1 (January, 1961), see Noel Annan, *Leslie Stephen* (London: Macgibbon & Kee, 1951), p. 6. I have been told by a nephew of Bernard Bosanquet, that the Reverend William Bosanquet, the philosopher's father, was a devout Evangelical.
11. F. H. Bradley, *The Presuppositions of Critical History* (Oxford, 1874), p. ii.
12. Helen Bosanquet, *Bernard Bosanquet* (London, 1924), p. 24.
13. Letter from Green to Holland, 6 October, 1872, Paget (ed.), *Holland, Memoir and Letters*, p. 65.
14. MS note from A. V. Dicey to Mrs Green, undated, Balliol College Library.
15. H. Bosanquet, *Bosanquet*, p. 147.
16. MS note from Mrs Green to R. L. Nettleship, undated, Balliol College Library.
17. J. H. Muirhead, *Reflections*, pp. 101 n.-102 n.
18. *Ibid.*, p. 99 n.
19. Richard Wollheim, *F. H. Bradley* (Harmondsworth: Penguin Books, 1959), p. 18.

20. MS note by Mrs Green, undated, Balliol College Library. Some of the preceding information was derived from a memorandum in the same place by one of Green's sisters, undated and unsigned.
21. Green, *Works*, III.
22. Conversation with Captain L. H. Green, December, 1959. Captain Green has also compiled most of the material on his family reported below, and been kind enough to communicate it to me.
23. *Dictionary of National Biography.*
24. Sir Gavin de Beer, *Sir Hans Sloane and the British Museum* (London: Oxford University Press, 1953), p. 80.
25. The lectures are in Green, *Works*, III, 277-364; see also 'Mr Green's report on the Schools in the Counties of Stafford and Warwick and Special Report on King Edward VII Free School, Birmingham,' Royal Commission of 1864 on Education, Schools Inquiry Commission, vol. VIII (London, 1868).
26. Green, *Works*, III, 364.
27. MS letter from W. L. Newman to Mrs Green, 27 November, 1882, Balliol College Library.
28. This is in part based on information compiled by Captain Green. See also N. G. Annan, 'The Intellectual Aristocracy,' in J. H. Plumb (ed.), *Studies in Social History* (London: Longmans, Green and Co., 1955), pp. 280-1.
29. *The Republic of Plato*, trans. with introduction and notes Francis Macdonald Cornford (Oxford: Clarendon Press, 1941), pp. viii-ix.
30. Green, *Works*, III, xxxv. See also Rev Edward Atkins (ed.), *The Vaughan Working Men's College, 1862-1912* (London & Leicester, n. d.) and A. J. Allaway, 'David James Vaughan. Liberal Churchman and Educationalist,' *Transactions of the Leicestershire Archaeological and Historical Society*, XXXIII (1957), 45-58.
31. The genealogical information is in J. A. Symonds, *On the English Family of the Symonds* (Oxford, 1894); there are additions and a summary in Margaret Symonds, *Out of the Past* (London, 1925), pp. 3-20. The citation is from Horatio F. Brown, *John Addington Symonds* (2nd ed., London, 1903), p. 16.
32. *Ibid.*, p. 17.
33. *Ibid.*, p. 352.
34. *Ibid.*, pp. 15, 14.
35. Green, *Works*, III, cviii-cix.
36. *Ibid.*, p. cix.

37. Green, *Works*, III,

38. For the most part, what follows is taken from Nettleship's account in Green, *Works*, III, xii-xvi. This is supplemented. by MS sources which he did not include in his memoir.

39. Letter from A. L. Grenfell to Mrs Green, 18 October, 1882, in Mrs Green's copybook, Balliol College Library.

40. MS letter from Henry Sidgwick to Mrs Green, 1 August, 1882, Balliol College Library.

41. *Ibid.*

42. Green, *Works*, III, xxi.

43. Abbott and Campbell, *Jowett*, II, 192.

44. Green, *Works*, III, xv.

45. *Autobiography of John Stuart Mill* (New York, 1924), p. 104.

46. MS letter from Henry Sidgwick to Mrs Green.

47. Charles Kingsley in *Politics for the People* (London, 1848), cited by Gordon K. Lewis, 'The Ideas of the Christian Socialists of 1848,' *Western Political Quarterly*, IV (September, 1951), 401. Professor Lewis's excellent essay should be read along with C. E. Raven, *Christian Socialism, 1848-54* (London, 1920) and G. C. Binyon, *The Christian Socialist Movement in England* (London, 1931).

48. Klaus Dockhorn, *Der Deutsche Historismus in England* (Göttingen and Baltimore, 1950).

49. Norman Wymer, *Dr Arnold of Rugby* (London: Robert Hale, 1953), p. 136.

50. Arthur Penrhyn Stanley, *The Life and Correspondence of Thomas Arnold, DD* (2 vols.; 12th ed., London, 1881), II, 13.

51. Copy of a letter from Green to David Hanbury, c. March, 1854, and memorandum from one of Green's sisters, undated and unsigned, both in Balliol College Library.

52. Green, *Works*, III, xvi.

CHAPTER THREE

1. Sir Henry Jones and John Henry Muirhead, *The Life and Philosophy of Edward Caird* (Glasgow, 1921), p. 376.

2. Charles Edward Mallet, *A History of the University of Oxford* (3 vols.; London, 1924-7), III, 456.

3. *Ibid.*

4. Jones and Muirhead, *Edward Caird*, p. 372.

5. L. E. Jones, *An Edwardian Youth* (London: Macmillan & Co., 1956), p. 41.

6. *Ibid.*, p. 21.

7. In the most recent treatment of the subject, Sir Geoffrey

Faber has questioned Parsons' contribution. Sir Geoffrey
Faber, *Jowett* (2nd ed. rev.; London: Faber & Faber, 1958),
pp. 101-102.

8. Cf. Mallet, *Oxford*, III, 315.

9. Sir Geoffrey Faber, *Oxford Apostles* (2nd ed. rev.; London, 1936), p. 163.

10. The phrase is Ben Johnson's. Cf. Sir Ernest Barker, *Reflections on Government* (London: Oxford University Press, 1942), p. viii.

11. Sir Ernest Barker, *Age and Youth* (London: Oxford University Press, 1953), p. 190.

12. John Henry Newman, *The Idea of a University*, ed. C. F. Harrold (London: Longmans, Green & Co., 1947), p. 97.

13. Mallet, *Oxford*, I, 186.

14. *Ibid.*, p. 195.

15. George F. Kneller, *Higher Learning in Britain* (Berkeley: University of California Press, 1955), p. 9.

16. Michael Curtis, *Oxford and Cambridge, 1558-1642* (Oxford: Clarendon Press, 1959), pp. 137, 146-7.

17. *Ibid.*, p. 263, citing Walter E. Houghton, Jr., 'The English Virtuoso in the Seventeenth Century,' *Journal of the History of Ideas*, III (1943), 57.

18. Mallet, *Oxford*, III 66-67.

19. Barker, citing Dr Arnold, in *Age and Youth*, p. 191.

20. Young, *Victorian England*, p. 95.

21. *Ibid.*, p. 93.

22. Alfred North Whitehead, *Essays in Science and Philosophy* (London: Rider and Co., 1948), p. 26.

23. *Ibid.*, p. 31.

24. *Ibid.*

25. *Ibid.*, p. 29.

26. *Ibid.*, p. 33.

27. Faber, *Oxford Apostles*, p. 163.

28. Cited in Mallet, *Oxford*, III, 320.

29. Mark Pattison, *Suggestions on Academical Organisation* (Edinburgh, 1868), pp. 161, 164, 165.

30. Jowett, *Sermons, Biographical*, p. 127.

31. Abbott and Campbell, *Letters of Benjamin Jowett*, MA (London, 1899), p. 241.

32. Letter from Jowett to A. P. Stanley, December, 1845, Abbott and Campbell, *Jowett*, I, 120.

33. Sir Leslie Stephen, *Studies of a Biographer* (4 vols.; London, 1907), II, 129.

34. Faber, *Jowett*, pp. 145-6.

35. Faber, *Jowett*, p. 316.
36. Letter from Jowett to John Nichol, 18 January, 1864, W. A. Knight, *Memoir of John Nichol* (Glasgow, 1896), p. 190.
37. Stephen, *Studies*, II, 135-6.
38. Brown, *J. A. Symonds*, p. 73.
39. J. A. Spender and Cyril Asquith, *Life of Herbert Henry Asquith, Lord Oxford and Asquith* (2 vols.: London, 1932), I, 36.
40. Lord Newton, *Lord Lansdowne* (London, 1929), p. 8.
41. *Ibid.*, pp. 9-10.
42. Brown, *J. A. Symonds*, p. 118.
43. *Ibid.*, p. 193.
44. Faber, *Jowett*, p. 90.
45. M. Symonds, *Out of the Past*, p. 214.
46. *Ibid.*, p. 215.
47. Letter from J. A. Symonds to H. F. Brown, 15 March, 1887, Horatio F. Brown (ed.), *Letters and Papers of John Addington Symonds* (London, 1923), pp. 199-200.
48. Faber, *Jowett*, p. 359.
49. Letter from Jowett to Nichol, 25 July, 1864, Knight, *Nichol*, p. 190.
50. Letter from Jowett to J. A. Symonds, 1880, M. Symonds, *Out of the Past*, p. 216.
51. Dean R. W. Church, *The Oxford Movement* (London, 1891), p. 299. Cited by R. W. Hunt, 'Balliol College,' *The University of Oxford*, Vol. III of *The Victoria History of the County of Oxford*, ed. H. E. Salter and Mary D. Lobel (London: Oxford University Press, 1954), p. 85.
52. Hunt, 'Balliol College,' p. 86, 86 n.
53. M. Symonds, *Out of the Past*, p. 214.
54. *Ibid.*, p. 213.
55. *Ibid.*, p. 219.
56. Knight, *Nichol*, p. 125. Sir Henry Studdy Theobald, *Remembrance of Things Past* (Oxford, 1935), p. 41.
57. Arthur J. Ashton, *As I Went on my Way* (London, 1924), p. 63.
58. Knight, *Nichol*, p. 126.
59. *Ibid.*, p. 214.
60. A. V. Dicey in Green, *Works*, III, xx. Although the authors of these judgments are not identified by Nettleship, the original letters to him are in the Balliol College Library.
61. MS letter from J. A. Symonds to Mrs Green, undated but postmarked 10 October, 1882, Balliol College Library.
62. Green, *Works*, III, xxi.

63. Green, *Works*, III, xix.
64. MS letter from Symonds to Mrs Green, postmarked 10 October, 1882.
65. Letter from A. L. Grenfell to Mrs Green, 18 October, 1882, in her copybook.
66. Green, *Works*, III, xix.
67. Knight, *Nichol*, p. 125.
68. Jowett, *Sermons, Biographical*, p. 219.
69. Green, *Works*, III, xx.
70. Cecil Woodham-Smith, *Florence Nightingale, 1820-1910* (London: Constable, 1950), p. 306.
71. Green, *Works*, III, xvii.
72. MS letter from J. A. Symonds to Mrs T. H. Green, postmarked 10 October, 1882.
73. Green, *Works*, III, xvii.
74. *Ibid.*, p. xxiv.
75. Rev. W. Tuckwell, *Reminiscences of Oxford* (2nd ed.; London, 1907), p. 105.
76. Letter from Professor Henry Nettleship to Mrs Green, undated, in her copybook (entitled 'Professor Nettleship's Recollections').
77. *Ibid.*
78. Green, *Works*, III, 296.
79. Knight, *Nichol*, facing p. 144. The original print is in the Bryce Papers, Bodleian Library, Oxford University.
80. When Lord Melbourne appointed Dr Hampden to an Oxford Professorship, he was threatened with a prosecution for heresy. Nervously he offered to retire from the field. Melbourne was not the man to retreat. Gradually he soothed Dr Hampden's anxieties. ' "Be easy," he said, laying a hand on his arm. "I like an easy man." ' David Cecil, *Lord M.; or, the Later Life of Lord Melbourne* (London: Constable, 1954), p. 142.
81. This was W. L. Newman. Green, *Works*, III, lxii.
82. MS letter from J. A. Symonds to Mrs T. H. Green, postmarked 10 October, 1882.
83. The original minute book of the Old Mortality with several membership lists is in the Bryce Papers. The most extensive printed list is in H. A. L. Fisher, *James Bryce* (London, 1927), I, 48. Knight, *Nichol*, pp. 137-152 is a basic source.
84. Cited in a letter from G. B. Hill to Miss Scott, 14 May, 1855, Lucy Crump (ed.), *Letters of George Birkbeck Hill* (London, 1906), p. 40.

85. Sir Edmund Gosse, *The Life of Algernon Charles Swinburne* (London, 1927), p. 53.
86. *Undergraduate Papers*, ed. John Nichol (Oxford, 1858), p. 96. For a complete bibliographical description of the publication see Wise, *Swinburne*, pp. 3-13.
87. Gosse, *Swinburne*, pp. 195-6.
88. Letter from A. V. Dicey to Mrs Green, 17 September, 1882, Mrs Green's copybook.
89. MS Letter from Mrs Green to Bryce, 26 April, 1903, Bryce Papers.
90. Knight, *Nichol*, p. 151.
91. Crump (ed.), *Hill*, p. 65.
92. Knight, *Nichol*, p. 150.
93. Gosse, *Swinburne*, p. 40.
94. Sir Harold Nicolson, *Swinburne*, (London, 1926), p. 43.
95. Gosse, *Swinburne*, p. 37 n.
96. Letter from A. L. Grenfell to Mrs Green, 18 October, 1882, in her copybook.
97. Knight, *Nichol*, p. 163.
98. This pamphlet was: 'Statements of Christian Doctrine and Practice extracted from the Published Writings of Rev Benjamin Jowett' (Oxford: J. H. and Jas. Parker, 1861). The preface was written by Dean Stanley; the extracts were made by Green and Miss Smith. Mrs Green, in a MS note written in 1893, observed that her copy of her husband's volumes of Jowett led her to believe that Green did choose the passages. In support, she cited a letter from J. A. Symonds to herself in March, 1861.
99. Green, *Works*, III, xxxv.
100. Knight, *Nichol*, p. 141.
101. A. and E. M. Sidgwick, *Henry Sidgwick*, p. 105.
102. Green, *Works*, III, xxxv-xxxvi.
103. *Ibid.*, p. xxxvi.
104. Janet Penrose Trevelyan *The Life of Mrs Humphry Ward* (London, 1923), p. 63.
105. Letter from Professor Nettleship to Mrs Green, in her copybook.
106. Elie Halévy, *Imperialism and the Rise of Labour*, trans. E. I. Watkin, Vol. V of *A History of the English People in the Nineteenth Century* (London: Ernest Benn, 1951), p. 140.
107. John Morley, *Life of Richard Cobden* (2 vols.; London, 1881), I, 130.
108. Green, *Works*, III, xlii.
109. Brown, *J. A. Symonds*, p. 162; Green, *Works*, III, xxxvii.

110. MS letter from J. A. Symonds to Mrs Green, postmarked 10 October, 1882.
111. Letter from Jowett to Nichol, 29 October, 1864, Knight, *Nichol*, p. 191.
112. MS letter from Green to James Bryce, 23 March, 186?, Bryce Papers.
113. Green, *Works*, III, xlv.
114. *Ibid.*, pp. xliii-xliv.
115. MS note by R. L. Nettleship, Balliol College Library.
116. Letter from Professor Henry Nettleship to Mrs Green, in her copybook.
117. Bernard Bosanquet, *Some Suggestions in Ethics* (London, 1919), p. 70.
118. A. G. C. Liddell, *Notes from the Life of an Ordinary Mortal* (London, 1911), pp. 82-83.
119. MS letter from C. A. Fyffe to R. L. Nettleship, Balliol College Library.
120. Green, *Works*, III, xlv. Green's views on education will be examined in detail in Chapter XI.

CHAPTER FOUR

1. J. P. Mayer, *Max Weber and German Politics* (London: Faber and Faber, 1944), p. 44.
2. T. H. Green, *The Witness of God and Faith*, ed. Arnold Toynbee (London, 1884). Reprinted in Green, *Works*, III, 230-76.
3. J. Wells (ed.), *Oxford and Oxford Life* (London, 1892), p. 136.
4. R. W. Macan, 'Religious Changes in Oxford During the Last Fifty Years' (Oxford, 1917), p. 13.
5. This was the judgment of W. L. Newman. See Green, *Works*, III, lxii.
6. Abbott and Campbell, *Jowett*, II, 77.
7. Mrs Ward, *Robert Elsmere*, I, 112-115.
8. Green, *Works*, III, 236-7.
9. *Ibid.*, p. 273.
10. *Ibid.*, pp. 240-1.
11. *Ibid.*, p. 260.
12. *Ibid.*, pp. 161-85.
13. *Ibid.*, p. 184.
14. *Ibid.*, p. 185.
15. *Ibid.*, p. 223.
16. *Ibid.*, p. 224.
17. *Ibid.*, p. 227.

18. M. B. Foster, *The Political Philosophies of Plato and Hegel* (Oxford, 1935), p. 74.
19. Green, *Works*, III, 184.
20. *Ibid.*, p. 270.
21. *Ibid.*, p. 236.
22. *Ibid.*
23. *Ibid.*, p. 269.
24. *Ibid.*, pp. 269-70.
25. *Ibid.*, p. 270.
26. *Ibid.*, p. 239.
27. *Ibid.*
28. Letter from Green to Holland, 6 October, 1872, Paget (ed.), *Holland, Memoir and Letters*, pp. 66-67.
29. Green, *Works*, III, 265-6.
30. *Ibid.*, p. 264.
31. *Ibid.*, p. 265.
32. Green, *The Witness of God*, ed. Toynbee, p. 8.
33. Green, *Works*, III, 181.
34. *Ibid.*, p. 226.
35. *Ibid.*, p. 249.
36. Nettleship in *Ibid.*, p. cv.
37. *Ibid.*, p. xxxii.
38. MS Letter J. A. Symonds to Nettleship, Balliol College Library.
39. Arthur O. Lovejoy, *The Great Chain of Being* (Cambridge, Mass.; Harvard University Press, 1948), p. 25.
40. Cf. Max Weber, 'Religious Rejections of the World and their Directions,' in *From Max Weber: Essays in Sociology*, trans. and ed. Hans Gerth and C. Wright Mills (New York: Oxford University Press, 1946), pp. 323-59.
41. Green, *Works*, III, 239.
42. *Ibid.*, p. 221.
43. Max Weber, 'Politics as Vocation,' Gerth and Mills (eds.), *From Max Weber*, p. 122.
44. Max Weber, 'The Social Psychology of the World Religions,' *Ibid.*, p. 275.
45. G. W. F. Hegel, *Lectures on the Philosophy of History*, trans. J. Sibree (London, 1857), p. 16.
46. Green, *PO*, p. 129.
47. *Ibid.*
48. Green, *Works*, II, 329.
49. *Ibid.*, III, 73.
50. John B. Lancelot, *Francis James Chavasse* (Oxford, 1929), p. 26.

51. Dorothea Price, *The Life of Hugh Price Hughes* (London, 1905), p. 134.
52. *Ibid.*
53. Henry W. Nevinson, *Changes and Chances* (London, 1923), p. 39.
54. Nettleship in Green, *Works*, III, c.
55. *Ibid.*, p. 274.
56. *Ibid.*, pp. 274-5.
57. George Santayana, *Egotism in German Philosophy* (London, 1939), p. 12.
58. Letter from Holland to Green, September, 1872, Paget (ed.), *Holland, Memoir and Letters*, p. 63.
59. Letter from Green to Holland, 6 October, 1872, *ibid.*, pp. 65-66.
60. *Ibid.*, p. 66.
61. For the histories of these two settlements, see J. A. R. Pimlott, *Toynbee Hall* (London: J. M. Dent & Sons, 1935); and *The Oxford House in Bethnal Green 1884-1948* (London: T. Brakell Ltd., 1948).
62. J. H. Muirhead, *Reflections*, p. 74. See also G. Spiller, *The Ethical Movement in Great Britain* (London, 1934), pp. 1-23.
63. *Ibid.*, p. 75.
64. *Ibid.*, p. 78.
65. Bernard Bosanquet, 'The Kingdom of God on Earth,' in *Essays and Addresses* (London, 1889), pp. 116, 123, 124, 125.
66. F. H. Myers, *Essays: Modern* (London, 1883), p. 269.
67. A. and E. M. Sidgwick, *Henry Sidgwick*, p. 190 n.
68. Muirhead, *Reflections*, p. 76.
69. *Lux Mundi* went through fifteen editions, the last of which was printed in 1904.
70. Arthur Michael Ramsay, *From Gore to Temple* (London: Longmans, 1960), p. vii.
71. Gordon Crosse, *Charles Gore* (London, 1932), p. 36.
72. *Ibid.*, pp. 49-50.
73. Ruth Kenyon, 'The Social Aspect of the Catholic Revival,' in N. P. Williams and Charles Harris (eds.), *Northern Catholicism* (London, 1933), p. 394. Miss Kenyon began her interesting essay by denying that the theology of the Tractarian Movement was necessarily conservative in its attitude towards industrial society. But on her own evidence, what she establishes is that in its first two periods the movement was not concerned with such matters. After *Lux Mundi* it did become so. But surely this was because of Green's influence.

74. Cited in L. E. Elliott-Binns, *Religion in the Victorian Era*, p. 240.

75. Ramsay, *Gore to Temple*, pp. 10, 13.

76. Letter from Green to Holland, 6 October, 1872, Paget (ed.), *Holland, Memoir and Letters*, pp. 67-68.

77. Letter from Jowett to the Rev John La Touche, 4 May, 1890, Abbott and Campbell, *Jowett*, II, 376-7.

78. Letter from Illingworth to the Rev Wilfred Richmond, 14 December, 1888, *The Life and Work of John Richardson Illingworth* (ed. his wife), (London, 1917), p. 90.

79. Charles Gore (ed.), *Lux Mundi* (London, 1889), p. vii.

80. Ramsey, *Gore to Temple*, p. 3.

81. J. R. Illingworth, in *Lux Mundi*, p. 195.

82. *Ibid.*, p. 212.

83. Holland, *ibid.*, p. 11.

84. Bishop Gore, in Paget (ed.), *Holland, Memoir and Letters*, p. 241.

85. Gilbert Clive Binyon, *The Christian Socialist Movement in England* (London, 1931), p. 156.

86. Crosse, *Gore*, pp. 47-48.

87. Charles Gore (ed.), *Property: Its Rights and Duties* (London, 1913).

88. Maurice Reckitt, *Faith and Society* (London, 1932), p. 92.

89. Binyon, *Christian Socialist Movement*, p. 179.

90. Ruth Kenyon in Reckitt, *Faith and Society*, p. 91 n.

91. MS 'Copy of the fragment of Mr Toynbee's Introduction to the "two Sermons," ' 1882-3, p. 5, Balliol College Library.

92. Henry Scott Holland, *A Bundle of Memories* (London, 1915), p. 145.

93. Young, *Victorian England*, p. 14.

94. Rev P. A. Wright-Henderson, *Glasgow and Balliol* (London, 1926), p. 44.

95. George Eliot, Epilogue to *Romula*, cited in *PE*, p. 362 n.

96. *Ibid.*, p. 362.

97. Beatrice Webb, *My Apprenticeship*, (London, 1926), p. 143.

98. Letter from Green to Holland, 29 December, 1868, Paget (ed.), *Holland, Memoir and Letters*, p. 29.

99. Cf. John Dewey, *Reconstruction in Philosophy* (London, 1921), chaps. iv, v. H. J. Laski, *The State in Theory and Practice* (London, 1941), chap. i and 'The Decline of Liberalism' in *Hobhouse Memorial Lectures 1930-40* (London, 1948), p. 2. L. T. Hobhouse, *The Metaphysical Theory of the State* (London, 1918); and *Democracy and Reaction* (2nd ed.; London, 1909).

100. Hobhouse, *Metaphysical Theory*, p. 19.
101. Lionel Trilling, *Matthew Arnold* (New York: 1939), p. 79.
102. Matthew Arnold, *Poems* (2 vols.; London, 1877), II, 271.
103. Green, *Works*, III, 248.
104. Lord Lindsay, *Karl Marx's Capital* (London, 1925), p. 34.
105. Beatrice Webb, *My Apprenticeship*, pp. 179-80.

CHAPTER FIVE

1. T. D. Weldon, 'Political Principles' in Peter Laslett (ed.), *Philosophy, Politics and Society* (Oxford: Basil Blackwell, 1956), p. 25.
2. A. J. Ayer and others, *The Revolution in Philosophy* (London: Macmillan and Co., 1956), pp. 2-4.
3. Annan, *Leslie Stephen*, pp. 131-2.
4. C. D. Broad, *Five Types of Ethical Theory* (London, 1930), p. 144.
5. A. and E. M. Sidgwick, *Henry Sidgwick*, p. 395.
6. Faber, *Jowett*, p. 357.
7. R. C. K. Ensor, *England: 1870-1914* (Oxford, 1936), p. 162.
8. Green, *Works*, III, 141.
9. G. M. Young, *Daylight and Champaign*, (London: Rupert Hart-Davis, 1948), pp. 55-56.
10. Mallet, *Oxford*, III, 308 n.
11. Brown, *J. A. Symonds*, p. 127.
12. Letter from Jowett to Florence Nightingale, 31 August, 1865, Abbott and Campbell, *Jowett*, I, 412-13.
13. Brown, *J. A. Symonds*, p. 117.
14. R. G. Collingwood, *An Autobiography* (Harmondsworth: Pelican Books, 1944), p. 53.
15. Logan Pearsall Smith, *Unforgotten Years* (London, 1938), p. 159.
16. *Ibid.*, pp. 160-1.
17. Ernest Gellner, *Words and Things* (London: Victor Gollancz, 1959), p. 244.
18. Mark Pattison, 'Philosophy at Oxford,' *Mind*, I (1876), 88-89, 92-94.
19. J. H. Muirhead, 'The Oxford Chairs of Philosophy,' *Contemporary Review*, LXXIV (1898), 727-8.
20. University of Oxford Commission, 'Minutes of Evidence taken by the Commissioners,' in *Reports from Commissioners, Inspectors and Others*, Vol. LVI, Part I, Cmd. 2868 (London, 1881), pp. 200-205.

21. Letter from Green to Holland, October, 1869, Paget (ed.), *Holland, Memoir and Letters*, p. 41.
22. MS Letter from J. A. Symonds to Mrs Green, 17 September, 1881, University of Bristol Library. 'He [Jowett] talked a good deal about the College. What struck me was his kindliness of tone towards everybody . . . his sympathy with the men he does not quite believe in, Bradley and Nettleship.' A version of this letter omitting these names is in M. Symonds, *Out of the Past*, p. 220.
23. MS Letter from Green to A. C. Bradley, 23 June, 1881, Balliol College Library.
24. Abbott and Campbell, *Jowett*, II, 109.
25. *Ibid.*, p. 193.
26. Nevinson, *Changes and Chances*, p. 40.
27. Jowett, *Sermons, Biographical*, p. 216.
28. *Ibid.*, pp. 142-3.
29. Hugh Lloyd-Jones, 'Greek Studies in Modern Oxford' (Oxford: Clarendon Press, 1961), p. 7.
30. H. W. C. Davis, *Balliol College* (London, 1899), p. 219.
31. Asquith, *Memories*, I, 19, 16-17.
32. Holland in *Life of Illingworth*, p. 316.
33. Gellner, *Words and Things*, p. 242.
34. MS Paper, 5 June, 1872, Balliol College Library. Another version in A. C. Bradley's hand bears the note: 'This either was sent, or was to be sent, to T.H.G. by some of us who in 1872 or 1873, made a little essay club. We were Nettleship, Tatton, Heberden, Goodwin, Theobald, F. H. Bradley and myself—perhaps more.'
35. Pattison, 'Philosophy at Oxford,' p. 87.
36. Nettleship in Green, *Works*, III, lxvii.
37. MS Letter from C. E. Vaughan to Nettleship, Balliol College Library.
38. Green, *Works*, III, lxv.
39. Asquith, *Memories*, I, 18.
40. Green, *Works*, III, cxxvi.
41. Ashton, *As I Went on My Way*, p. 61.
42. Green, *PE*, p. 313.
43. *Ibid.*, p. 317.
44. *Ibid.*
45. *Oxford Chronicle & Berks & Bucks Gazette* (1 April, 1882).

CHAPTER SIX

1. Matthew Arnold, *Poems*, II, 66.

2. Matthew Arnold, *Essays in Criticism, Third Series* (Boston, 1910), pp. 38-9.
3. Matthew Arnold, *Culture and Anarchy*, p. 85.
4. Brown, *J. A. Symonds*, p. 246.
5. Green, *Works*, I, 371.
6. Green, *PE*, p. 1.
7. *Immanuel Kant's Critique of Pure Reason*, trans. Norman Kemp Smith (London, 1933), p. 9.
8. Andrew Seth, in Andrew Seth and R. B. Haldane (eds.), *Essays in Philosophical Criticism*, pp. 8-10.
9. A. and E. M. Sidgwick, *Henry Sidgwick*, pp. 557-8.
10. T. S. Eliot, 'Arnold and Pater,' *Selected Essays* (London: Faber and Faber, 1951), p. 434.
11. *J. S. Mill, Letters*, Elliot (ed.), II, 362 (extract from his diary, 23 January, 1854).
12. Green, *Works*, I, 133.
13. This summary draws upon the admirable analyses of Professor C. C. J. Webb, in *A Century of Anglican Theology* (Oxford, 1923), p. 47, and in *Religious Thought in England from 1850* (Oxford, 1933), pp. 102 ff.
14. C. C. J. Webb, *Religious Thought*, p. 102.
15. Green, *Works*, III, 111.
16. 'Popular Philosophy in its Relation to Life,' in Green, *Works*, III, 92-125.
17. *Ibid.*, p. 117.
18. *Ibid.*, p. 94.
19. *Ibid.*, p. 125.
20. Seth and Haldane (eds.), *Essays in Philosophical Criticism*, p. 5.
21. Nettleship, in Green, *Works*, III, lxxxv-vi.
22. Hermann Lotze, *Logic*, English trans. ed. Bernard Bosanquet (2 vols.; Oxford, 1884). 'Professor Green not only executed an important part of the translation, but intended to take upon himself the task of revising and editing the whole.' (Editor's Preface, Vol. I.)
23. Edward Caird, *Hegel* (Edinburgh, 1883), p. 125.
24. Brown, *J. A. Symonds*, p. 338.
25. Seth and Haldane (eds.), *Essays in Philosophical Criticism*, p. 6.
26. A. C. Ewing (ed.), *The Idealist Tradition* (Glencoe, Illinois: The Free Press, 1957), p. 16.
27. Green, *PE*, p. 2.
28. 'Liberal Legislation and Freedom of Contract,' in Green, *Works*, III, 365-68.
29. Green, *Works*, III, 116-117.
30. Lovejoy, *The Great Chain of Being*, p. 10.

31. Nettleship in Green, *Works*, III, cxxvii.
32. Green, *PE*, p. 7.
33. *Ibid.*, p. 8, and Book I, *passim*.
34. *Ibid.*, Book I, *passim;* also Green, *Works*, III, lxxv-lxxxix.
35. Green, *PE*, p. 68.
36. *Ibid.*, p. 69.
37. *Ibid.*, p. 70.
38. *Ibid.*, p. 83.
39. Letter from Green to Holland, 6 October, 1872, Paget (ed.), *Holland, Memoir and Letters*, p. 66.
40. Green, *PE*, p. 174.
41. *Ibid.*, p. 186.
42. A. J. Ayer, *Language, Truth and Logic* (London, 1936), pp. 19-20, 12.
43. Green, *PE*, p. 186.
44. W. D. Lamont, *Introduction to Green's Moral Philosophy* (London, 1934), p. 190.
45. 'Fragment on Immortality,' in Green, *Works*, III, 159-60.
46. MS 'Copy of Mr Toynbee's Introduction to the "two Sermons",' p. 5, 1882-3, Balliol College Library.
47. *Ibid.*
48. Alfred William Benn, *The History of English Rationalism in the Nineteenth Century* (2 vols.; London, 1906), II, 404-409.
49. Green, *PE*, p. 182.
50. Thomas Case, 'Metaphysics,' *Encyclopaedia Britannica* (11th ed.; Cambridge, 1911), Vol. XVIII, 232, 244-5.
51. This account of their doctrine is based upon C. C. J. Webb, *Religious Thought*, pp. 109-22. Webb cites: the relevant portions of Bradley's *Appearance and Reality* (2nd ed.; 1902), pp. 331 ff., and of his later *Essays on Truth and Reality*, pp. 432 ff., 448 ff.; and Bosanquet's two volumes of Gifford Lectures on *The Principle of Individuality and Value* and *The Value and Destiny of the Individual*. Webb also invites the reader to compare his own *God and Personality*, esp. pp. 100 ff., 105 ff., 124 ff., 138 ff., and *Divine Personality and Human Life*, esp. Lecture IX, as well as his article, 'Bosanquet's Philosophy of Religion,' *Hibbert Journal*, October, 1923.
52. J. H. Muirhead, 'Hegel,' *Encyclopaedia Britannica* (11th ed.; Cambridge, 1910), Vol. XIII, pp. 207.
53. Green, *PE*, pp. 324, 295.
54. *Ibid.*, p. 295.
55. Unpublished notes cited in Lamont, *Introduction*, p. 211.
56. Bertrand Russell, *The Problems of Philosophy* (London: Williams and Norgate, n.d.), pp. 222-3.

57. Bertrand Russell, *The Problems of Philosophy* (London: Williams and Norgate, n.d.), p. 231.
58. *Ibid.*, p. 249.
59. G. E. Moore, 'The Refutation of Idealism,' *Philosophical Studies* (London, 1922), pp. 1-2.
60. G. A. Paul, 'G. E. Moore,' in Ayer and others, *The Revolution in Philosophy*, p. 59.
61. Mary Warnock, *Ethics Since 1900* (London: Oxford University Press, 1960), p. 46.
62. *Ibid.*, p. 47.

CHAPTER SEVEN

1. Sir Ernest Barker, *Political Thought in England, 1848 to 1914* (London, 1928), p. 12.
2. Green, *Works*, III, cxlv.
3. Green, *PE*, p. 253.
4. H. A. Prichard, *Moral Obligation* (Oxford: Clarendon Press, 1949), p. 114.
5. Green, *PE*, p. 247.
6. *Ibid.*, p. 177.
7. *Ibid.*, p. 172.
8. *Ibid.*
9. *Ibid.*
10. Green, *Works*, III, 371.
11. J. J. Rousseau, *The Social Contract and Discourses*, trans. G. D. H. Cole (London: J. M. Dent, n.d.), p. 19.
12. Green, *Works*, II, 315.
13. *Ibid.*, III, 370.
14. Sir Isaiah Berlin, *Two Concepts of Liberty* (Oxford: Clarendon Press, 1958), p. 18.
15. See E. F. Carritt, *Ethical and Political Thinking* (Oxford: Clarendon Press, 1947), p. 160.
16. Green, *Works*, II, 324.
17. Green, *PE*, pp. 180, 183.
18. *Ibid.*, p. 184.
19. *Ibid.*
20. *Ibid.*, p. 190.
21. Green, *PO*, p. 21.
22. Berlin, *Two Concepts of Liberty*, p. 39.
23. Green, *PE*, p. 190.
24. *Ibid.*, p. 217.
25. *Ibid.*, p. 199.
26. *Ibid.*, p. 201.

27. Green, *PE*, p. 202.
28. *Ibid.*
29. *Ibid.*, p. 260.
30. Hegel, *Philosophy of History*, pp. 19-20.
31. Green, *PE*, pp. 206, 286.
32. *Ibid.*, p. 209.
33. *Ibid.*, p. 216.
34. *Ibid.*, p. 217.
35. Jackson, *Bywater*, p. 5 n.
36. Matthew Arnold, *Culture and Anarchy*, pp. 131-2.
37. *Ibid.*, p. 61.
38. Green, *PE*, p. 270.
39. *Ibid.*, p. 186.
40. *Ibid.*, p. 257.
41. *Ibid.*, p. 259.
42. *Ibid.*, p. 269.
43. Green, *PO*, p. 39.

CHAPTER EIGHT

1. Sir Isaiah Berlin, *Two Concepts of Liberty*, p. 4.
2. Green, *Works*, I, 4.
3. George Santayana, *Winds of Doctrine* (New York, 1927), p. 57.
4. *Ibid.*
5. George Santayana, *Soliloquies in England* (London, 1922), pp. 205-206.
6. Green, *Works*, I, 4.
7. A. C. Ewing, *The Idealist Tradition*, p. 8.
8. Green, *Works*, III, 123.
9. A. P. d'Entrèves, *The Medieval Contribution to Political Thought* (London: Oxford University Press, 1939), p. 3.
10. Green, *PO*, p. 1.
11. *Ibid.*, p. 25.
12. *Ibid.*, p. 1.
13. *Ibid.*, p. 6.
14. *Ibid.*, p. 7.
15. *Ibid.*, p. 15.
16. Arnold Toynbee, 'Are Radicals Socialists?' in *Lectures on the Industrial Revolution of the Eighteenth Century in England* (London, 1908), p. 237.
17. Green, *PO*, p. 50.
18. *Ibid.*, p. 18.
19. *Ibid.*, p. 23.
20. *Ibid.*, p. 25.

21. Green, *PO*, p. 20.
22. *Ibid.*, p. 21.
23. *Ibid.*, p. 8.
24. *Ibid.*, p. 30.
25. *Ibid.*, p. 103.
26. *Ibid.*, p. 18.
27. *Ibid.*, p. 54.
28. *Ibid.*, p. 55.
29. *Ibid.*, p. 62.
30. *Ibid.*
31. Green, *Works*, III, 372.
32. Green, *PO*, p. 68.
33. *Ibid.*, p. 86.
34. Hobhouse, *Metaphysical Theory*, p. 121.
35. Green, *PE*, p. 7.
36. *Ibid.*
37. *Ibid.*, p. 8.
38. Maine, *Early History of Institutions*, cited in Green, *PO*, p. 84.
39. Green, *PO*, p. 108.
40. Green, *Works*, III, 309.
41. Green, *PO*, p. 112.
42. *Ibid.*, p. 251.
43. *Ibid.*, p. 129-30.
44. *Ibid.*, p. 132.
45. A. D. Lindsay, *The Modern Democratic State* (London: Oxford University Press, 1943), pp. 27, 33.
46. Green, *PO*, p. 132.
47. Sabine, *History of Political Theory*, pp. 738-9.
48. Aristotle, *Politics*, Bk. I, chap. ii.
49. Green, *PO*, p. 140.
50. *Ibid.*, p. 141.
51. *Ibid.*, p. 147.
52. J. P. Plamenatz, *Consent, Freedom and Political Obligation* (London, 1938), p. 81.
53. Ritchie, *Principles of State Interference*, p. 141.
54. Green, *PE*, p. 370.
55. J. D. Mabbott, *The State and the Citizen* (London: Hutchinson, [1948]), p. 43.
56. R. H. S. Crossman, 'Reading Khrushchev's Mind,' *Commentary*, XXXII, No 6 (December, 1961), 506.
57. Green, *PE*, p. 270.
58. *Ibid.*, p. 381.
59. Green, *PO*, p. 121.

60. This is discussed in detail below. See Chapter IX.
61. Emile Durkheim, *Sociology and Philosophy*, p. 60.
62. Sabine, *History of Political Theory*, p. 732.
63. Green, *PO*, p. 136; Plamenatz, *Consent, Freedom and Political Obligation*, p. 91.

CHAPTER NINE

1. H. J. Laski, *The Decline of Liberalism* (London: Oxford University Press, 1940), pp. 11-12.
2. L. T. Hobhouse, *Liberalism* (London: Williams and Norgate, n.d.), p. 219.
3. L. T. Hobhouse, *Democracy and Reaction*, p. 5.
4. For a list of Bright's speeches especially praised by Green see Green, *Works*, III, xxiv.
5. George H. Sabine, *A History of Political Theory* (3d ed.; New York: Holt, Rinehart and Winston, 1961), p. 737.
6. Cited in Green, *Works*, III, xx.
7. Immanuel Kant, *The Philosophy of Law*, trans. W. Hastie (Edinburgh, 1887), p. 47.
8. For other exceptions to laissez-faire, see Jacob Viner, *Adam Smith, 1776-1825* (Chicago, 1928), chap. v.
9. A. V. Dicey, *Lectures on the Relation between Law and Public Opinion in England during the Nineteenth Century* (London, 1914), p. 199.
10. Asa Briggs, *Victorian People* (London: Odhams Press, 1954), p. 212.
11. Green, *Works*, III, cxii.
12. G. M. Trevelyan, *The Life of John Bright* (London, 1925), pp. 333-4.
13. *Hegel's Philosophy of Right*, trans. T. M. Knox (Oxford: Clarendon Press, 1942), p. 151.
14. Green, *PO*, p. 228.
15. *Ibid.*, p. 229.
16. *Ibid.*
17. *Ibid.*, p. 231.
18. *Ibid.*, p. 226-7.
19. *Ibid.*, p. 227.
20. *Ibid.*, p. 230.
21. A. J. Carlyle in *Property: Its Rights and Duties*, ed. Gore, pp. 120-1.
22. Richard Schlatter, *Private Property* (London: Allen & Unwin, 1951), p. 256. Schlatter is paraphrasing Kant, *Philosophy of Law*, p. 92.

23. Hastings Rashdall in *Property: Its Rights and Duties*, ed. Gore, p. 53.
24. Kant, *Philosophy of Law*, p. 91.
25. *Ibid.*, pp. 186, 184.
26. Herbert Marcuse, *Reason and Revolution* (Boston: Beacon Press, 1955), pp. 193-5, 218; Hugh A. Reyburn, *The Ethical Theory of Hegel* (Oxford, 1921), pp. 130-1.
27. Hegel, *Philosophy of Right*, pp. 236-7.
28. *Ibid.*, pp. 235-6.
29. H. S. Holland in *Property: Its Rights and Duties*, ed. Gore, p. 182.
30. Cf. Hegel, *Philosophy of Right*, p. 156.
31. Cf. *Ibid.*, p. 279.
32. Green, *PO*, p. 217.
33. *Ibid.*, p. 220.
34. *Ibid.*, p. 224.
35. J. A. Hobson and Morris Ginsberg, *L. T. Hobhouse: His Life and Work* (London, 1931), pp. 78-79.
36. Cf. Hegel, *Philosophy of Right*, pp. 150, 277.
37. J. A. Hobson, *The Crisis of Liberalism: New Issues of Democracy* (London, 1909), pp. 195-6.
38. Green, *Works*, III, 372.
39. *Ibid.*, p. 374.
40. *Ibid.*, p. 372.
41. *Ibid.*, p. 367.
42. *Ibid.*, pp. 376-7.
43. *Ibid.*, p. 383.
44. *Ibid.*, p. 386.
45. Arnold Toynbee, 'Are Radicals Socialists?' p. 230.
46. *Ibid.*, pp. 233-4.
47. Arnold Toynbee, *Progress and Poverty* (London, 1883), p. 24.
48. Arnold Toynbee, 'Are Radicals Socialists?' pp. 236-7.
49. *Ibid.*, pp. 237-8.
50. *Ibid.*, p. xxv.

CHAPTER TEN

1. G. Kitson Clark, *The Making of Victorian England* (London: Methuen, 1962), p. 282.
2. Ernest Gellner, 'Concepts and Society,' Reprint of *Transactions of the Fifth World Congress of Sociology* (Washington, D.C., 2-8 September, 1962), p. 20.
3. Lord Beveridge, 'Welfare and Liberty: An Address to the Fleet Street Parliament on 11th November, 1957.'

4. Letter from R. H. Tawney to Melvin Richter [August, 1958].
5. Bernard Bosanquet, *The Philosophical Theory of the State* (London, 1920), p. 178.
6. R. M. Titmuss, *Essays on 'The Welfare State'* (London: George Allen and Unwin, 1958), pp. 18-19.
7. J. A. Hobson, *Confessions of an Economic Heretic* (London, 1938), p. 55.
8. Asa Briggs, 'The Welfare State in Historical Perspective,' *European Journal of Sociology*, Vol. II, No. 2 (1961), p. 222.
9. Friedrich Engels in *Karl Marx: Selected Works*, ed. V. Adoratsky (2 vols.; London: Lawrence and Wishart, 1942), I, 236.
10. Karl Marx, *Letters to Dr Kugelmann* (London, 1936), p. 85.
11. Alexander Herzen, cited in Isaiah Berlin, *Karl Marx* (London: Oxford University Press, 1948), pp. 176-7.
12. Engels, 'Introduction to the English Edition of 1892,' of *Socialism: Utopian and Scientific*, in Marx, *Selected Works*, p. 398.
13. *Ibid.*, pp. 410-11.
14. Marx, 'Manifesto of the Communist Party,' *Selected Works*, pp. 235-6.
15. Engels, 'Preface to the English Edition of 1892,' of *The Condition of the Working Class in England*, trans. and ed. W. O. Henderson and W. H. Chaloner (Oxford: Basil Blackwell, 1958), p. 364.
16. Engels, 'Introduction to the English Edition of 1892,' *Socialism: Utopian and Scientific*, pp. 414-15.
17. Engels, *Condition of the Working Class in England*, p. 335.
18. Halévy, *England in 1815*, p. 424.
19. *Ibid.*, p. 383.
20. J. L. and Barbara Hammond, *Lord Shaftesbury* (Harmondsworth, 1939), p. 69.
21. J. Wesley Bready, *Lord Shaftesbury and Social Industrial Progress* (London, 1926), p. 395.
22. Dicey, *Law and Public Opinion in England*, p. lxiii.
23. Young, *Victorian England*, p. 11.
24. Halévy, *The Triumph of Reform: 1830-41* (London: Ernest Benn, 1950), p. 340.
25. Wearmouth, *Methodism and the Working-Class Movements of England*, Part II, *passim*.
26. Green, *Works*, III, 245.
27. A. D. Lindsay in A. F. C. Bourdillon (ed.), *Voluntary Social Service* (London: Methuen, 1945), p. 302.
28. Beatrice Webb, *My Apprenticeship*, p. 203.

29. J. L. and B. Hammond, *Lord Shaftesbury*, p. 274.
30. Beveridge, *Voluntary Action* (London: Allen and Unwin, 1948), pp. 154-5.
31. This model is based in part on Edward Cheyney, *Modern English Reform* (London, 1931), p. 60; for another model, see O. MacDonagh, 'The Nineteenth-Century Revolution in Government: A Re-appraisal,' *The Historical Journal*, I (1958), 58-61. MacDonagh has been criticised by Henry Parris in 'The Nineteenth-century revolution in Government: A Re-appraisal Re-appraised,' *The Historical Journal*, III (1960), 17-37.
32. Titmuss, *'The Welfare State,'* p. 22.
33. Janet Trevelyan, *Mrs Humphry Ward*, p. 133.
34. Cf. *The Oxford English Dictionary*.
35. Green, *PE*, p. 299.
36. Green, *Works*, III, 10.
37. Green, *PE*, p. 299.
38. A phrase coined by V. S. Pritchett, *The New York Times Book Review Section*, 12 February, 1951.
39. Green, *PE*, p. 335.
40. B. Webb, *My Apprenticeship*, pp. xiii-xiv.
41. Green, *PE*, p. 245.
42. *Ibid.*, p. 258, p. 270.
43. I owe this information to Dr Arnold J. Toynbee, who is the nephew of Arnold Toynbee.
44. S. E. Finer, *The Life and Times of Edwin Chadwick* (London: 1952), p. 238.
45. *Ibid.*, pp. 238-9.
46. Letter from Joseph Toynbee to Gertrude Toynbee, 5 September, 1861, in Gertrude Toynbee (ed.), *Reminiscences and Letters of Joseph and Arnold Toynbee* (London, n.d.), p. 45. For a description of Rochdale, cf. G. D. H. Cole, *A Century of Co-operation* (London: George Allen and Unwin, 1945), chap. iii.
47. G. Toynbee, (ed.), *Reminiscences*, pp. 16, 39.
48. Arnold Toynbee, 'Progress and Poverty,' p. 53.
49. Arnold Toynbee, 'Wages and Natural Law,' in *The Industrial Revolution*, pp. 190-1.
50. J. M. Baernreither, *English Associations of Working Men*, trans. Alice Taylor (London, 1889), chap. iv.
51. Acland and Jones, *Working Men Co-operators*, p. 131.
52. Beveridge, *Voluntary Action*, p. 21.
53. Charles Dickens, *Our Mutual Friend*, chap. viii, cited by Beveridge, *Voluntary Action*, p. 54.

54. Cited by Beveridge, *Voluntary Action*, p. 27.
55. Rev Henry Solly, *These Eighty Years* (2 vols.; London, 1893), II, 287-8.
56. The most recent treatment of the subject is in P. H. J. H. Gosden, *The Friendly Societies in England* (Manchester: Manchester University Press, 1961).
57. Cited by Gosden, *Ibid.*, p. 164.
58. *Ibid.*, pp. 211-20.
59. G. D. H. Cole, *A Short History of the British Working-Class Movement* (London: George Allen and Unwin, 1948), p. 168.
60. Green, *PO*, p. 227.
61. MS Letter from C. A. Fyffe to R. L. Nettleship, Balliol College Library.
62. Matthew Arnold, *Culture and Anarchy*, p. 104.
63. Morris Ginsberg (ed.), *Law and Opinion in England in the 20th Century* (London: Stevens, 1959), p. 350.
64. Atkins (ed.), *The Vaughan Working Men's College, 1862-1912*, p. 21.
65. Extracts of Evidence, pub. H. M. Government, 1833, p. 338. Cited by Finer, *Edwin Chadwick*, p. 47.
66. C. L. Mowat, *The Charity Organisation Society* (London: Methuen & Co., 1961), pp. 168, 175, 177.
67. Helen Bosanquet, *The Strength of the People: A Study in Social Economics* (2nd ed.; London, 1903), p. 208. Cited by Kathleen Woodroofe, 'C. S. Loch,' *Social Service Review*, XXXII, (December, 1958), p. 406.
68. Hobson, *The Crisis of Liberalism*, p. 195.
69. Woodroofe, 'C. S. Loch,' 406.
70. Cited by U. M. Cormack, 'Developments in Casework,' in A. F. C. Bourdillon (ed.), *Voluntary Social Services*, p. 95.
71. J. H. Muirhead (ed.), *Bernard Bosanquet and his Friends* (London, 1935), p. 48.
72. Green, *PO*, p. 220.
73. Bernard Bosanquet, *The Civilisation of Christendom* (London, 1893), pp. vi-vii.
74. Cited by Woodroofe, 'C. S. Loch,' p. 407.
75. R. B. Mowat, 'C. S. Loch,' *Dictionary of National Biography, 1922-30*.
76. Cited by C. L. Mowat, *Charity Organisation Society*, p. 70.
77. *Ibid.*, pp. 80-81.
78. C. S. Loch, *Charity Organisation*, p. 6.
79. B. Webb, *My Apprenticeship*, p. 205.
80. Loch, *Charity Organisation*, pp. 31, 103, 104, 101.
81. Green, *PE*, p. 305.

82. Green, *Works*, III, 456.
83. Green, *PO*, p. 17.
84. A. Toynbee, *Industrial Revolution*, p. 236.
85. Green, *PO*, p. 18.
86. *Ibid.*
87. A. Toynbee, 'Progress and Poverty,' p. 52.
88. Green, *Works*, II, 314.
89. B. Bosanquet, *Philosophical Theory of the State*, pp. 266-70.
90. Hobhouse, *Metaphysical Theory*, p. 78.
91. Herbert L. Samuel (Viscount Samuel), *Liberalism* (London, 1902), p. 11. See also John Bowle, *Viscount Samuel* (London: Gollancz, 1957), pp. 37-38.
92. (Viscount) Samuel, *Liberalism*, p. 29.
93. Cited by C. L. Driver, in F. J. C. Hearnshaw (ed.), *Edwardian England* (London, 1933), p. 259.
94. H. L. Beales, 'Has Labour Come to Stay?', *Political Quarterly*, XVII (January-March, 1947), p. 53.
95. E. S. Haldane, *From One Century to Another*, p. 313.
96. Among many others, Crane Brinton, *English Political Thought in the Nineteenth Century* (London: Ernest Benn, 1949), p. 212. Also by Prof Brinton, 'T. H. Green,' *Encyclopedia of the Social Sciences*. See also Adam B. Ulam, *Philosophical Foundations of English Socialism* (Cambridge, Mass.: Harvard University Press, 1951), and R. C. K. Ensor, *England, 1870-1914*, pp. 162-3.
97. Dicey, *Law and Opinion*, pp. 64, 64 n.
98. J. B. Brebner, '*Laissez faire* and State Intervention in Nineteenth-century Britain,' in *Tasks of Economic History*, Supplement VIII (1948) to the *Journal of Economic History;* O. MacDonagh, 'The Nineteenth-century Revolution in Government,' *Historical Journal* (1958); Briggs, 'The Welfare State in Historical Perspective,' *European Journal of Sociology;* L. Robbins, *The Theory of Economic Policy in English Classical Political Economy* (London: Macmillan, 1952).
99. Atkins (ed.), *The Vaughan Working Men's College, 1862-1912*, p. 20.

CHAPTER ELEVEN

1. Arnold Toynbee, *Industrial Revolution*, p. 245. John MacCunn, *The Ethics of Citizenship* (Glasgow, 1894). Sir Henry Jones, *The Principles of Citizenship* (London, 1919). Arthur H. Dyke Acland, *The Education of Citizens*, (Manchester, 1883). James Bryce, *The Hindrances to Citizenship*

(New Haven, 1909). H. A. L. Fisher, *The Common Weal* (Oxford, 1924).
2. R. G. Collingwood, *An Autobiography* (Harmondsworth, Middlesex: Pelican Books, 1944), p. 17.
3. John MacCunn, *Six Radical Thinkers* (London, 1907), p. 220.
4. Edward Caird in Seth and Haldane, *Essays in Philosophical Criticism*, p. 7.
5. Michael Sadleir, *Michael Ernest Sadler* (London: Constable, 1949), p. 31.
6. *The Oxford Magazine*, I (21 November, 1883), p. 384.
7. Nettleship in Green, *Works*, III, xi.
8. D. G. Ritchie, *Principles of State Interference*, p. 131.
9. Green, *Works*, III, 475.
10. Green, Address to North Ward Liberal Association, 11 March, 1882, *Oxford Chronicle & Berks & Bucks Gazette*.
11. Green, *Works*, III, lxiii.
12. Bernard Bosanquet (ed.), *Aspects of the Social Problem* (London, 1895), p. 330.
13. G. M. Young, *Daylight and Champaign*, pp. 144-55.
14. Green, *Works*, III, 390.
15. *Ibid.*, p. 387.
16. Dockhorn, *Staatsphilosophie*, p. 7.
17. Green, *Works*, III, xlvii.
18. *Ibid.*, p. 458.
19. Arnold, *Culture and Anarchy*, p. 75.
20. H. A. L. Fisher, *James Bryce*, I, p. 109.
21. *Ibid.*, p. 109-10.
22. Green, *Works*, III, lxiii.
23. *Ibid.*, p. 403.
24. *Ibid.*
25. A. Toynbee, *Industrial Revolution*, p. 216.
26. Green, *Works*, III, 461.
27. *Ibid.*, p. 462.
28. *Ibid.*, p. 427.
29. *Ibid.*, pp. cx-cxi.
30. *Ibid.*, pp. 475-6.
31. *Ibid.*, p. 440.
32. *Ibid.*, pp. 454-5.
33. Dorothea Price Hughes, *Hugh Price Hughes*, p. 136.
34. Michael E. Sadler, 'Sadler, Owen, Lovett, Maurice, Toynbee,' *University Review* (April-December, 1907), 263. See also by the same author, 'The Development of University Extension' (Philadelphia, 1892), p. 5.
35. A. J. Allaway, 'David James Vaughan,' p. 54.

36. H. P. Smith, *Labour and Learning* (Oxford: Basil Blackwell, 1956), p. 34. For the significance of the university extension movement, see Thomas Kelly, *A History of Adult Education* (Liverpool: Liverpool University Press, 1962), p. 237. Also of interest is J. F. C. Harrison, *Learning and Living, 1790-1960* (London: Routledge and Kegan Paul, 1961).
37. Smith, *Labour and Learning*, p. 16.
38. Basil Cottle and J. W. Sherborne, *The Life of a University* (Bristol: J. W. Arrowsmith, 1951), p. 17.
39. For a sophisticated analysis of this trend, cf. G. Kitson Clark, *Making of Victorian England*, p. 272 *et seq.*
40. *Mansfield College, Oxford: Its Origin and Opening* (London, 1890), pp. 32-33.
41. G. Kitson Clark, *Making of Victorian England*, pp. 127-8.
42. Green, *Works*, III, 432.
43. G. Kitson Clark, *Making of Victorian England*, p. 201.
44. Green, *Works*, III, cx, cxiii.
45. *Ibid.*, p. cxii.
46. Cited by Asa Briggs, *Victorian People*, p. 222.
47. Green, *Works*, III, cxviii.
48. *Ibid.*, p. cxvii.
49. Letter from C. A. Fyffe to R. L. Nettleship, Balliol College Library.
50. Green's speech to the Conference of the United Kingdom Alliance is to be found in the *Oxford Chronicle & Berks & Bucks Gazette* (4 February, 1882).
51. Green, *Works*, III, 449.
52. *The Oxford Magazine*, XLVIII (7 November, 1929), p. 148.
53. Elizabeth Wordsworth, *Glimpses of the Past* (London, 1913), p. 152. Muriel St Clare Bryne and Catherine Hope Mansfield, *Somerville College, 1879-1921* (Oxford, 1921).
54. Vera Brittain, *The Women at Oxford* (London: Harrap, 1960), p. 42.
55. MS note from Mrs Green to R. L. Nettleship, Balliol College Library.
56. MS letter from Mrs Green to Nettleship, 24 December, 1887, Balliol College Library.
57. Henry Scott Holland, *A Bundle of Memories* (London, 1915), p. 146.
58. *Oxford Chronicle & Berks & Bucks Gazette* (1 April, 1882).
59. Leonard H. Green, Letter to the Editor, *Spectator* (14 September, 1929).
60. Letter from Jowett to Miss C. M. Symonds, 20 March, 1892,

Abbott and Campbell, *Jowett*, II, 448. Jowett was citing Roger North.

61. Spender and Asquith, *Life of Asquith*, I, 198.
62. L. T. Hobhouse, letter to Miss Margaret Llewelyn Davies, February, 1914. Hobson and Ginsberg, *L. T. Hobhouse*, p. 65.
63. Stephen Spender, *World Within World* (London: Hamish Hamilton, 1951), p. 5.

INDEX

REFERENCES TO NOTES. The letters fn. following a page reference (e.g. 160fn.) indicate a note at the foot of that page. The letter n. followed by a figure after the page number (e.g. 329n. 63) refers to the References to Chapters (pp. 377–406).

Abel-Smith, Brian, 329n. 63
Acland, A. H. D., 325
adult education, 13, 42, 323, 344–5
altruism, 131–2, 247, 256 *see also* asceticism; citizenship, concept of; reform
American Civil War, the, 93, 94, 171, 244–5, 251
Annan, N., 137, 138
Anti-Corn Law League, the, 46, 308
Aristotle, 55–9 *passim*, 84, 85, 92, 141, 148–9, 161, 200, 218–21 *passim*, 225, 234
Arnold, Matthew, 13, 23, 79, 83, 96, 133, 165, 172, 218–9, 258, 270, 329, 351–2
Arnold, Thomas, 41, 42, 46, 47, 49–50, 74, 75, 86, 96, 136
asceticism, 131, 208, 220, 257–8 *see also* individualism; reform
Asquith, H. H., 13, 65, 158n. 32, 162, 267, 294, 295, 373
Augustine, St., of Hippo, 20
Austin, J., sovereignty, theory of, 240–3
Ayer, A. J., 182

Barker, Sir Ernest, 13, 56n. 11, 191
Baur, F. C., 87, 91, 102
Benn, A. W., on Green's theory of personality, 184–5, 187
Bentham, Jeremy, 57, 204, 208, 259, 326
Berkeley, Bishop, 169, 172
Berlin, Sir Isaiah, 202–4, 223n. 1, 224
Beveridge, Lord, 294, 313n. 30
Booth, Charles, 309, 326, 332
Bosanquet, Bernard, 36, 37, 94, 119n. 65, 121, 124, 188, 202, 281,282,297,332,333,339–40
on Green's theory of personality, 186, 187, 211
Bradley, A. C., 13, 14, 83n. 95, 149, 152, 153, 156, 192
Bradley, F. H., 14, 36–8, 120, 124, 138, 155fn. 160fn. 188, 191, 194
on Green's theory of personality, 186, 187, 211
Briggs, Asa, 272n. 10, 298
Bright, John, 79, 80, 89, 94, 218, 254, 259, 267, 269–76 *passim*, 280–1, 328, 364–5

Broad, C. D.,
on Green, 137, 138
Broad Church Party, *see* Church of England, Broad Church Party;
Browning, R., 176
Rabbi Ben Ezra, 130, 167
Bryce, James, 13, 73, 80, 82, 93, 96, 270, 344fn. 352
Burke, Edmund, 173

Caird, Edward, 80, 82, 92, 93, 172, 173, 294, 346n. 4
Carlyle, Thomas, 47, 48, 75, 80, 82, 87, 89, 165
capitalism, theory of, 274–6, 280–1, 290
Case, Professor,
on Green's theory of personality, 186, 187
Chamberlain, Joseph, 357
charity, 13, 292–3, 295, 310–12, 330–7
as a religious obligation, 103, 345
Charity Organisation Society, 121, 282, 297, 327, 330–9
Chartism, 48–9, 308
Chesterton, G. K., 14n. 5, 311fn.
Christian Social Union, 13, 42, 118, 122, 126–8, 281, 297, 361 *see also* Church of England, High Church Party;
Christian Socialism, 41, 48–50, 310
Church of England, the
Broad Church Party, 26–7, 29, 49, 54
Christian Social Union and, 128
Evangelicalism and, 15
High Church Party, 26, 27, 118
Green's influence on, 122–6

Lux Mundi Movement and, 122–6, 127
citizenship, concept of, 19, 29–31, 77, 91, 110, 114, 124, 126, 128–9, 132, 212, 215–8, 265, 287, 344–6, 348–9, 354–5, 364
see also "common good", theory of
and "common good", 247
and "crisis of belief", 134
as a religious vocation, 30, 319
Clapham Sect, the, 24, 309
Clark, Kitson, 292, 293, 362n. 41
Cobden, Richard, 89, 259, 268–9
Coleridge, S. T., 47, 49, 87, 165
collectivism *see* social services; state, interference by;
Collingwood, R. G., 144
"common good", theory of, 13, 180, 197, 200–1, 208, 211–7, 229, 234–6, 244–9, 254–6, 261, 266, 286 *see also* metaphysics; political obligation; reason;
obligation and, 216–7, 247
reality of, 254–5
"spiritual principle" and, 213, 215
Comte, Auguste, 184, 208, 211
Conington, J.,
and Green, 75–7
conscience, crisis of, 12, 15, 29, 166
consciousness, concept of, 175–86, 195–7, 199, 210, 213–4, 216, 219, 237
contract, freedom of, 173, 269, 283–6
Cromwell, Oliver, 40, 41, 45, 47, 246–7
Crossman, R. H. S., 256n. 56

Darwin, Charles, 25, 126
Dicey, A. V., 73, 74, 80, 82, 307–8

Dicey, A. V.—*continued*
  collectivism and, 342
  on Green, 47, 81–2n. 86, 88,
    270n. 6
Disraeli, Benjamin, 268
Durkheim, Emile, 33, 262

education,
  equality, principle of, and, 354
  "voluntary principle" and, 356
educational reform *see* reform,
  educational;
Eliot, George, 120, 130
Eliot, T. S., 133, 139, 168
Engels, F., 300–3, 308
epistemology, 167, 173–81, 196,
  200, 207, 213, 228 *see also*
  Idealism, method of; progress, theory of;
Evangelicalism, 18 *see also* Green,
  T. H., Evangelicalism and;
  agnosticism and, 24fn.
  emotional impetus of, 21
  intellectual challenge and, 24–5
  social origins of, 15–16
  theology of, 16, 19, 25
Ewing, A. C., *The Idealist Tradition*, 191, 229

Faber, Sir Geoffrey, 146
  on Green, 137, 138
  on Jowett, 63, 68–9
Fabian Society, the, 121
faith,
  concept of, 126, 129, 130
  justification by reason, of, 183
freedom, theory of, 201–7
  negative and positive concepts
    of, 223–5
  "positive" freedom, 285, 341
Freud, S., 256
friendly societies *see* voluntary
  associations

Gellner, Ernest, 146n. 17, 293n. 2
Gladstone, W. E., 28, 60, 88, 97,
  140, 141, 143, 254, 268, 293
Goethe, J. W. von, 89, 90, 109,
  132fn. 169
Gore, Bishop Charles, 122, 123,
  126–8 *passim*, 168, 281, 361
Green, T. H.,
  and the Broad Church Party,
    54, 86, 194
  and the condition of the work-
    ing class in England, 81
  and F. H. Bradley, 37–8
  and naturalistic theory, 175, 176
  and religious dilemma, 86–8
  and the Thirty-nine Articles, 86
  and University reform, 150–1,
    353
  as a philosopher, 139–41
  as a political philosopher, 207,
    222–4
  ambiguities in work, 340–3
  as a teacher, 138–9, 149, 151–2,
    154, 156–8, 161, 163–4,
    294, 349
  Christian Socialism, influence
    on, 49
  criticisms of, 136–9, 148fn.
    184–6
  education and, 95–6, 337, 347,
    351–3 *see also* reform, edu-
    cational;
  Evangelicalism and, 15, 19,
    37–9, 41, 45, 116, 129–30,
    192, 194, 197, 310–12
  Faith, sermon on, 116, 117, 133,
    172
  family background of, 38–46,
    50, 91
  general character of, 46–7, 78–9
  German thought, influence of,
    on, 36, 87, 89, 90, 260–1,
    266
  humanism of, 30, 31

Green, T. H.—*continued*
  influence of, 13, 118–29, 281–2,
    293–5, 330–6, 344–6, 349
  intellectual background of,
    48–50
  *Lectures on the Principles of
    Political Obligation*, 13, 32,
    176, 177, 190, 192, 215,
    221, 279, 283, 293, 328,
    337, 349
    theological basis of, 105, 113,
      187, 231
  monasticism, attack on, 31, 110
  pacificism of, 94
  philosopher, role of, 103–4,
    162–3
  philosophy, 115, 117
    ambiguities in, 291, 292–3
    and history, 228
    and religion, 102, 117, 129,
      143
    as an autonomous subject,
      136, 140, 142, 143, 157
    instruction in, 145–8, 157–8,
      200–1
    "popular", attack on, 169–73
    *Popular Philosophy in its
      Relation to Life*, 175
  political activities of, 82, 94,
    222, 346, 348–9, 363
  political views, 93–5
  Prolegomena to Ethics, 14, 105,
    107, 114, 120, 130, 131,
    175, 176, 180, 183, 187,
    190–4 *passim*, 240, 242,
    254, 279, 294, 316, 318, 320
  puritan heritage of, 40, 41, 87
  religious beliefs of, 49, 115–16
    revolution and, 300–10
  republicanism of, 87, 93
  Roman Catholicism, dislike for,
    30–1, 129, 335
  state interference, ambivalence
    towards, 128

  theology of, 97, 134, 165
    ambiguities in, 118
    immanent concept of God,
      102, 105
    relationship of man to God,
      101–2, 108, 110
    rationalism of, 99, 165
    religious duty, 110
    religious experience, indi-
      vidual nature of, 115
    theodicy of, 112–14, 130, 183,
      187, 247

Haldane, E. S., 341n. 95, 353
Helévy, Elie, 12, 15n. 11, 303n.
    18, 304–5, 310
  on Green, 89
Hammond, J. L. and B., 312n. 29
Hardie, James Keir, 307, 365
Hegel, G. F., 14, 33, 35, 132, 171,
    172, 184, 199, 202, 203,
    208, 211, 216, 227, 270,
    271, 273–4, 278
  metaphysics of, 186
  philosophy, its purpose defined
    by, 36
  theodicy of, 112–14
"higher self", concept of, 104, 108
Hobbes, T., 172, 173, 196, 227,
    237
Hobhouse, L. T., 267, 281, 282,
    374–5
Hobhouse, L. T.,
  on Idealism, 132, 242
Hobson, J. A., 121, 282, 297n.
    7, 332n. 66
Holland, Henry Scott, 30, 35n.
    4, 117, 118, 122, 123, 127,
    129, 152, 180, 278
  Faith, essay on, 126
Hopkins, Gerard Manley, 30, 132
Hughes, Thomas, *Tom Brown's
    Schooldays*, 49

humanism, 183 *see also* the London Ethical Society;
Hume, David, 138, 148fn. 164, 167, 171, 225
Huxley, T. H., 19, 79, 161

Idealism,
criticisms of, 136-9 *see also under* individual names
German, 13, 33, 91, 201 *see also under* Hegel
language of, 116, 121, 152, 191, 193, 211, 226-7, 255-6, 260, 295 *see also below* method
Method of, 91, 102-3, 180, 193, 264-5
a priori propositions in, 114, 136, 179-80, 182, 189, 199, 206, 214-15, 219, 221, 225, 228-30, 240, 247, 251, 349
"critical", 173, 228
criticism, value of, 167-8
criticisms of, 189-90
political theory and, 54, 226-8, 253
synthesis and, 172
teleological, 55, 230, 255
verification principle and, 182
Illingworth, J. R., 124-6
Individualism, 130, 193, 194, 201, 207-8, 257-9, 337-8, 342-3
Methodist organisation and, 19
puritanism and, 23
see also Liberalism

Jowett, B., 9, 44, 51, 86, 92, 123, 137
and Balliol College, 52, 53fn., 54, 62, 64
and the Broad Church Party, 27, 29
and German philosophy, 71
and philosophy, 142, 143

and University reform, 62-3, 144-5, 300
antagonism to Green, 148-57, 200
Essays and Reviews, 71, 79
"gospel of work", 69
on *Lux Mundi* Movement, 124
politics, techniques in, 66-7
power and "self-realisation", 68, 69
religious beliefs of, 63-4, 71-2
success, emphasis on, by, 65-70

Kant, I., 14, 87, 172, 202, 203, 270, 271n. 7, 277-8n. 24
a priori propositions and, 229
"critical" method of, 36, 140, 167, 171, 173
deontological theory of ethics, 199
epistemology, 173, 186
Keble, John, 27, 86, 122, 123, 137
Keynes, J. M., 39fn., 138fn.
Kingsley, Charles, 47, 48, 128, 301
Krushchev, N., 256

Labour Party, the 340, 341, 365, 374
Laissez-faire, 49, 50, 132, 342, 324fn.
Lamont, W. D.,
on Green's theory of personality, 183, 186
land reform, *see* reform, land
Lansdowne, Marquess of, 65, 66, 75
Laski, H. J., 267, 294
law, 231-32
function as criterion for, 233
ethical theory applied to, 236
"common good" and, 244-6
"natural", 226
Liberal Party, the, 13, 29, 281, 296, 298, 340-1, 361-2, 376
House of Lords and, 66

Liberal Party—*continued*
Puritanism and, 41
Liberalism, 29–30, 62, 192, 201,
206, 267–91 *passim*, 340–2
Idealism and, 207–8, 211, 244,
268, 363
Individualism and, 203, 244,
268, 291
Manchester School of, 89, 194,
223, 267–71, *passim*, 274,
276, 281, 291 and original
sin, 280
Lincoln, Abraham, 94
Lindsay, Lord, 13, 53, 133, 250,
341
Lloyd George, David, 298, 338
Loch, C. S., 121, 297, 333–5
Locke, John, 148fn. 172, 173,
201, 206, 225, 227, 237, 240,
254, 270, 276–7
London Ethical Society, the, 13,
118–21, 128, 138, 297
general principles of, 121,
121fn
Lux Mundi Movement, the, 13,
118, 122–7 *see also* Church of
England, High Church
Party

Machiavelli, N., 57
Mannheim, Karl, 10
Marshall, Alfred, 14n. 6, 155
Marx, Karl, 133, 134, 224, 277,
288, 299, 301, 308
Maurice, F. D., 42, 44, 47–50,
126, 128, 301, 316–17 *see also*
Christian Socialism
Melbourne, Lord, 78
metaphysics, 165–90
ethics and, 177, 199, 200–1
politics and, 201
see also epistemology; Idealism,
method of; personality,
theory of; progress, theory of;

Methodism, 15
organisation in, 18–19
political importance of, 308
philanthropy, doctrine of, 19–22
social class composition in, 20,
22
Methodist Revival, the, 16, 17, 20,
21, 305–7
charity, two attitudes to, 23,
292–3, 310–16, 330–40
social consequences of, 17, 306
Mill, J. S., 24–5n. 34, 80, 131,
165–9 *passim*, 172, 201,
203–4, 263
Logic, 14, 141
Moore, G. E., 182
Idealism, criticisms of, 188–90,
194, 374
moral obligation, theory of, 187,
197–98, 207
teleological definition of, 198,
200
More, Hannah, 20n. 22
Muirhead, J. H., 14, 119, 120
Murray, Gilbert, 375n.

National Education League *see*
reform, educational;
natural rights, 221, 226, 277
Green's criticism of, 236–7
Idealist use of term, 233–4
Nettleship, R. L. 11, 14, 30, 39,
145, 149, 152, 160–1, 176, 192
on Green, 87, 88, 116
Newman, J. H., 19, 25–30 *passim*,
54, 122
The Idea of a University, 56, 61
Newton, Isaac, 56
Nichol, John, 80–3, 92, 93
and the Thirty-nine Articles, 86
Nightingale, Florence, 74, 143

obligation, moral *see* moral obligation, theory of

obligation, political, *see* political
    obligation
Old Mortality Society, the, 80–3,
    86, 89, 92, 96
Oxford Movement, the, 26, 53fn.
    61, 123
Oxford University, 54–62
    Anglican tradition of, 58, 61
    "Greats", importance of, 59–62
    intellectual tradition of, 54–7
see also Jowett

Peel, Sir Robert, 60, 284
personality, theory of,
    Green's defence of, 212
    individual, 208–9
    of God, 184–7
    relationship theory and, 187
see also consciousness, concept of
philanthropy, 200, 320–2, 329,
    375 *see also* charity; reform;
Philosophical Idealism *see* Ideal-
    ism
philosophy of history, 10, 105–6,
    132–3, 175, 203, 210, 247,
    261–2, 264
Plamenatz, J. P., 264
Plato, 224, 225
political obligation, 176–7, 187,
    226, 230, 236, 238, 246, 247,
    265
    contract and, 237
    "general will" and, 239–40
    sovereignty, theory of, and,
    240–3
    teleological theory of, 231
Popper, K., 224
progress, theory of, 114, 133,
    181–2, 193, 198–200, 206, 210,
    215–6, 225, 227, 228, 246,
    253, 285
    and "absolute good", 219–20
see also Idealism, method of;
    philosophy of history;

property, theory of, 269, 270,
    276–83
    moral development and, 284, 296
    property rights, 280–1
Puritanism, 40–1, 48
    poverty, attitude to, in, 22–3
    social class and, 20, 22–3
see also Individualism
Pusey, Dr., 26, 29, 61, 122, 123,
    143

Radicalism *see* Toynbee, Arnold
Rashdall, Hastings, 281–2
Rationalism, 33, 115, 118–20,
    168–9
reality, notion of, 172, 253
    "common good" and, 228
    criteria of, 187
    ethical rules and, 190
    theory of personality and, 186
    theory of relationship and, 187
see also Idealism: method, a *priori*
    propositions
reason, 77, 103, 160, 167–8, 183,
    196, 198, 210, 213, 214
    authority and, 27
    duty and, 208, 215, 217
see also Idealism, method of;
    personality, theory of;
reform, 13, 126, 266
    and the London Ethical Society,
    121
    and the "crisis of belief", 134
    concept of, 316–18, 338, *see also*
    citizenship, concept of
    educational, 350–61 *see also*
    Jowett, and University
    reform
    land, 366, 367
    social, 19, 31, 53, 131, 291,
    295–9, 306–24, 340, 375
    guilt and, 135
    religious fulfilment and, 134
    temperance, 205, 362–9

relationship, theory of, 174, 177–8,
180, 184, 188–9, 195, 206–7
see also personality, theory of
religious belief, 194
"crisis" of, 134, 160, 168
reason and, 193
revolution and, 300–10
teleological basis of, 193
rights, theory of, 234–53, 262, 265
definition of, 245
social recognition of, 244, 262–4
teleological basis of, 234–5, 237
see also "common good", theory
of
Rousseau, J. J., 224, 237
general will, theory of the, 230,
239
sovereignty, theory of, 240–1
Rowntree, Seebohm, 326
Russell, Bertrand, 138, 182
criticisms of Idealism, 188–8
374
Russell, Lord John, 66, 77
Ruskin, John, 137, 293
Ryle, G,
on Green, 136, 138, 140

Sabine, G. H., 250, 262–3n. 62,
269n. 5
Samuel, Viscount, 339, 342fn.
Santayana, George, 116, 227
"self-realisation", concept of, 13,
34, 104, 110, 204
a priori propositions and, 221
"common good", confused
with, 254–9
education and, 347
individualism of, 208–11
see also freedom, theory of;
personality, theory of;
Shaftesbury, Lord, 21, 297,
312–13, 321
Sidgewick, H., 90, 121, 131, 138,
165, 166, 168

and the Thirty-nine Articles, 86
My Station and its Duties, 120
on Green, 46, 48, 86, 187
sin, 108–10, 112, 114, 195, 217,
336
citizenship and, 134
reform and, 135, 374
Smith, Adam, 57, 93, 254, 271
Smith, A. L., 53
Snowden, Philip (1st Viscount),
365
social contract, theory of,
Green's criticism of, 236–7
Social Darwinism see Social Evolutionism
Social Evolutionism,
Green's refutation of, 176, 122
social services,
origins of, 297–8, 314, 315, 323,
325
Socialism, Radical see Toynbee,
Arnold
Socialism, Tory, 289–90
Sorel, Georges, 224
Spencer, Herbert, 23, 165, 222
evolutionary theory, 169
Spender, Stephen, 376n. 62
"spiritual principle", the, 177–89,
213, 215, 247
political theory and, 228, 231
see also relationship, theory of
state, the,
"common good" as the basis
for, 248, 250, 261
definition of, 249–51, 260–1,
295, 351
interference by, 212, 270–1,
283–91, 295, 323, 329, 335,
337–41, 349, 362, 367–9
see also contract, freedom of;
Individualism; property,
theory of; reform
Stephen, Sir Leslie, 121, 137, 138,
165

Stephen, Sir Leslie—*continued*
and the Thirty-nine Articles, 86
on Jowett, 63–4
Social Rights, 120
Strachey, Lytton, *Eminent Victorians*, 139, 168
"struggle", notion of, 113, 130
Swinburne, A. C., 35, 78, 80–3
Symonds, J. A., 35, 43–4, 67–8, 72fn. 77, 80, 8ofn. 90, 109, 142, 166, 172
on Green, 73, 163fn.

Talmon, J. L., 33, 224
Tawney, R. H., 20, 294
teleology, 193, 195, 206, 207, 210, 215, 217, 221, 225
see also Idealism, method of
temperance reform *see* reform, temperance
Temple, F., 96
Tennyson, Lord, 176
In Memoriam, 167
theology and politics, relationship of, 30–2
Titmuss, R., 297n. 6, 315n. 32
Tocqueville, A. de (Comte), 304–5, 365
Toynbee, Arnold, 13, 29, 95, 108n. 32, 118, 127, 129, 137, 184, 185, 232, 270, 287–91, 312, 320, 323–4, 338–9n. 87,340,341,344,346, 355n.25
Toynbee, Joseph, 320–2
Tractarianism, *see* Church of England, High Church Party
trade unions, 329–30 *see also* voluntary associations
Troeltsch, Ernst, 9, 16

universal suffrage, 212, 354, 357, 366
University Extension Movement, the, 360
Urwick, E. J., 121

Utilitarianism, 13, 62, 87, 91, 232–3, 310
Green's criticisms of, 131, 169–71,175,203–4,222,318
voluntary associations, 295–6, 309–11, 324–9, 338–9, 348–9

Wallas, Graham, 121
Ward, Mrs. Humphry, 37, 88, 97, 376
Robert Elsmere, 27–8, 79, 99–100, 106, 118, 140fn. 293, 372
Passmore Edwards Settlement, 37, 118, 315–16
Warnock, M., 190
Webb, Beatrice, 131, 318, 319n. 40, 335n. 79
Webb, Beatrice and Sidney, 312, 333
Weber, Max, 9, 69, 97, 111, 303–4, 310
Welfare State *see* social services
Wesley, John, 16–20
charity, doctrine of, 22
economic virtues and, 22
philanthropy as a religious duty, 20, 22
political opinions of, 21
Weslyan Revival *see* Methodist Revival
Wescott, Bishop, 42, 122, 123, 126, 127
Whitefield, George, 17
Whitehead, A. N., 60–1n. 22–6, 165
Wilberforce, W., 21, 79, 297, 312
Wittgenstein, L., 374
Wordsworth, W., 47, 48, 133
Workers Education Association, 361

Young, G. M., 11, 12, 33n. 1, 141, 350n. 13
Victorian England, 47fn. 98fn.

DATE DUE

MAY 9 '66			
MAY 25 '66			
APR 23 '68			
May 28			
MAR 18 '69			
MAY 30 '86			
GAYLORD			PRINTED IN U.S.A.